HISTÓRIA DE EMPRESAS E DESENVOLVIMENTO ECONÔMICO

TAMÁS SZMRECSÁNYI
&
RICARDO MARANHÃO
(organizadores)

HISTÓRIA DE EMPRESAS E DESENVOLVIMENTO ECONÔMICO

Segunda Edição Revista

Coletânea de textos apresentada na
II Conferência Internacional de História de Empresas
(Campus da USP, setembro de 1993)

ASSOCIAÇÃO BRASILEIRA DE PESQUISADORES EM HISTÓRIA ECONÔMICA

edusp

IMPRENSA OFICIAL SP

Dados Internacionais de Catalogação na Publicação (CIP)
(Sandra Regina Vitzel Domingues)

H 58s História de Empresas e Desenvolvimento Econômico / Tamás Szmrecsányi & Ricardo Maranhão (organizadores). – 2. ed. revista. – São Paulo: Hucitec/ Associação Brasileira de Pesquisadores em História Econômica/Editora da Universidade de São Paulo/Imprensa Oficial, 2002.

Inclui referências bibliográficas

ISBN	Obra completa	85-271-0354-0 (Hucitec)
	Volume V	85-271-0539-1 (Hucitec)
	Volume V	85-314-0687-0 (Edusp)

Coletânea de textos apresentada na II Conferência Internacional de História de Empresas (Campus da USP, setembro de 1993)

1. Empresas Multinacionais 2. Empresas multinacionais - Brasil 3. Capitalismo I. Szmrecsányi, Tamás (org.) II. Maranhão, Ricardo (org)

CDD - 338.88
338.880981
330.122

Índices para catálogo sistemático:

1. Empresas multinacionais: Produção: Economia	338.88
2. Multinacionais: Produção: Economia	330.981
3. Brasil: Multinacionais: Produção: Economia	338.880981
4. Capitalismo	330.122

Editora Hucitec Ltda.
Rua Gil Eanes, 713 – 04601-042 – São Paulo – SP – Brasil
Telefones: (0xx11) 5044-9318 geral; (0xx11) 5543-5810 vendas; (0xx11) 5093-5938 fac-símile
Home page: www.hucitec.com.br – E-mail: hucitec@terra.com.br

Co-edição:

Associação Brasileira de Pesquisadores em História Econômica
Caixa Postal 174 – 14800-901 – Araraquara – SP – Brasil
Telefone: (0xx16) 232-0444 Ramal 114
Home page: www.abphe.org.br – E-mail: abphe@fclar.org.br

Edusp – Editora da Universidade de São Paulo
Av. Prof. Luciano Gualberto, Travessa J, 374
6° andar – Ed. da Antiga Reitoria – Cidade Universitária
05508-900 – São Paulo – SP – Brasil – Fax (0xx11) 3091-4151 Tel. (0xx11) 3091-4008/3091-4150
Home page: www.usp.br/edusp – E-mail: edusp@edu.usp.br

Imprensa Oficial do Estado
Rua da Mooca, 1921 – Mooca – 03103-902 – São Paulo – SP – Brasil
Pabx: (0xx11) 6099-9800 – SAC 0800-123401
Home page: www.imprensaoficial.com.br – E-mail: editorial@imprensaoficial.com.br

Printed in Brazil 2002
Foi feito o depósito legal

SUMÁRIO

APRESENTAÇÃO

Este volume, que traz 18 dos 22 trabalhos apresentados na 2.ª *Conferência Internacional de História de Empresas* — realizada juntamente com o *I Congresso Brasileiro de História Econômica*, em setembro de 1993, no campus da USP em São Paulo — é dedicado à memória de Maria Bárbara Levy.

Deve-se a ela a iniciativa da organização, nas circunstâncias particularmente difíceis do governo Collor, da 1.ª Conferência, levada a efeito cinco anos atrás em Niterói (RJ), e cujos Anais foram publicados há algum tempo pela Universidade Federal do Rio de Janeiro. Aquele encontro deveria ter servido de forum e de marco para o estabelecimento de uma Associação Nacional de História Econômica, algo que só acabou se tornando possível mais recentemente, com a fundação e o início do funcionamento da ABPHE (Associação Brasileira de Pesquisadores em História Econômica), criada na esteira das reuniões de 1993. De qualquer forma, embora, infelizmente, Maria Bárbara já não esteja entre nós, a proposta dela foi inegavelmente vencedora, mantida e levada avante por seus amigos, colegas e ex-alunos, que, no mês de outubro deste ano, realizaram, novamente em Niterói, a 3.ª Conferência, conjugada ao *II Congresso Brasileiro de História Econômica.*

Os ensaios do presente volume acham-se agrupados em torno de seis eixos temáticos: (1) A História de Empresas como Área de Pesquisas; (2) Trajetórias das Empresas Multinacionais; (3) Empresários e Trabalhadores num Mundo em Transformação; (4) Investimentos Italianos na América Latina; (5) Estudos de Caso de Empresas Brasileiras e Estrangeiras; e (6) O Estado e as Empresas de Serviços Públicos. Todos os trabalhos aqui reunidos estão sendo publicados na língua original de apresentação dos mesmos. Além disso, a maioria é de autores estrangeiros, um fato que não deve causar estranheza, tendo em vista que se trata de um campo de estudos ainda recente e pouco sedimentado entre nós — apesar de já dispormos, inclusive há bastante tempo, de alguns estudos de excelente qualidade, como a monografia de José de Souza Martins sobre o Grupo Matarazzo, elaborada em 1966 e reeditada em 1973.

No primeiro bloco figuram dois ensaios de grande relevância e atualidade, da autoria de Steven Tolliday e de Pier Angelo Toninelli, fazendo o balanço, dentro das perspectivas norte-americana e européia, das contribuições teóricas e metodológicas da influente obra de Alfred Chandler, apontando-lhe tanto os méritos como as insuficiências. Não menos importante é a terceira contribuição do mesmo bloco, de Carlos Marichal, com a sua discussão da historiografia dos bancos latino-americanos — uma área muito pouco explorada, apesar de seu grande interesse.

Mais três ensaios, todos sobre empresas multinacionais, constam do segundo bloco. O mais abrangente é o de Mira Wilkins, que, tomando por base as suas próprias pesquisas sobre o tema, examina a evolução destas entidades básicas e decisivas do capitalismo contemporâneo. Entidades cujas estruturas dinâmicas continuam insuficientemente conhecidas, apesar da maioria das mais importantes já estarem atuando no mundo há mais de um século, como atestam os estudos de Peter Hertner, sobre o ramo eletrotécnico antes da I Guerra Mundial, e de Hubert Kiesewetter a respeito da penetração das máquinas agrícolas norte-americanas na Europa no mesmo período. Aos três trabalhos que acabam de ser citados, podemos agregar os dois do quarto bloco, sobre investimentos italianos na América Latina: o de Bruno Bezza examina o ingresso da Pirelli na Argentina e no Brasil durante as primeiras décadas do século XX, e Giandoménico Piluso faz o mesmo em relação aos bancos italianos que estenderam suas operações a nosso continente naqueles anos.

O terceiro bloco representa uma exceção no volume, ao ser integrado exclusivamente por ensaios de autores brasileiros. Pelo menos dois deles tratam de assuntos bastante polêmicos: Luiz Carlos Bresser Pereira discorre sobre as origens sociais e a orientação política da burguesia industrial paulista, enquanto Ary Minella disseca a atuação recente e o neoliberalismo dos banqueiros deste país na década de 1980. Os outros três, apesar de mais restritos e localizados, tampouco deixam de abordar assuntos de grande interesse. O de Elisabeth von der Weid discute a formação do operariado do Rio de Janeiro nas décadas iniciais de sua industrialização. Por sua vez, José Antonio Segatto reavalia as relações de trabalho vigentes na Light de São Paulo, a empresa que monopolizava os serviços de eletricidade e de transportes públicos do mais importante centro industrial da América do Sul. Finalmente, Newton Cardoso de Oliveira examina a institucionalização dos seguros de acidentes do trabalho na indústria têxtil do Rio de Janeiro durante o Estado Novo.

Igualmente específicos são os trabalhos do quinto e do sexto blocos. Este último versa sobre as relações entre o Estado e as empresas de serviços públicos; ambos os seus ensaios, na verdade, analisam a trajetória de empresas de eletricidade. Albert Broder faz um retrospecto histórico do setor na França antes de sua nacionalização em 1946; Ricardo Maranhão analisa a atuação da Light no Brasil em meados da década de 1950. Os três trabalhos restantes, do penúltimo bloco, são todos estudos de caso. Dois deles tratam de grupos bancários e financeiros — o de Carlos Gabriel Guimarães, sobre o Banco Mauá & Cia. (1854-1878), e o de Raúl Jacob, a respeito do Banco Francés Supervielle, do Uruguai (1887-1941). Finalmente, o estudo de Delia Beatriz Espina examina as etapas da inserção da IBM no Brasil.

Por motivos técnicos, deixamos de incluir neste volume os trabalhos de Almir Pita Freitas Filho, sobre "A Abordagem Empresarial na História Econômica no Brasil"; de Elizabeth Bortolaia Silva, "Modelo e Mito: Variações do Fordismo e da Japonização no Brasil"; de Luzia Monteiro Araujo Soares, sobre "A Light e a Semana de Energia de 1952"; e de Joan Carles Alayo i Manubens, sobre "La Participación de las Grandes Empresas en la Electrificación de Barcelona". Não queremos, porém, deixar de registrar e de agradecer a participação de todos eles na 2.ª Conferência, assim como a dos autores cujos trabalhos estão sendo aqui publicados.

Agradecimentos são também devidos às entidades que apoiaram e patrocinaram a realização daquele evento, notadamente: o Centro de Memória da UNICAMP; os Institutos de Estudos Brasileiros e de Estudos Avançados da USP; a Faculdade de Economia e Administração da mesma Universidade, assim como suas Coordenações de Cooperação Internacional (CCINT) e de Comunicação Social (CCS); o Instituto Herbert Levy, do jornal *Gazeta Mercantil*; o Banco Nacional do Desenvolvimento Econômico e Social

(BNDES); a Comissão de História Econômica do CLACSO (Consejo Latinoamericano de Ciencias Sociales) de Buenos Aires; a Fondazione ASSI (Associazione di Storia sull'Impresa) de Milão; a Fundação Banco do Brasil; e a Fundação de Amparo à Pesquisa do Estado de São Paulo (FAPESP), que também contribuiu financeiramente para a edição deste livro. A todas elas, bem como às inúmeras pessoas dos mais diversos níveis hierárquicos que nos ajudaram a promovê-lo com sucesso, dando origem a esta Associação Brasileira de Pesquisadores em História Econômica, aqui vai o nosso muito obrigado.

Todos os ensaios da primeira edição foram revistos pelos organizadores deste volume, com a eventual ajuda de seus respectivos autores.

São Paulo, agosto de 2001.

I
HISTÓRIA DE EMPRESAS COMO ÁREA DE PESQUISAS

Steven Tolliday
University of Leeds, England

BEYOND THE "ORGANIZATIONAL SYNTHESIS": PARADIGM AND THEORY IN RECENT AMERICAN BUSINESS HISTORY

Over twenty years ago, Louis Galambos drew on the theoretical approach of Alfred D. Chandler's *Strategy and Structure* (1962) to propose a broader framework for the analysis of economic institutions which he termed an "organizational synthesis"[1]. Ten years ago, in the light of the publication of Chandler's *The Visible Hand* (1977), he returned to the theme and amended and enlarged the original framework[2]. The approach of the "organizational synthesis" has remained extremely influential throughout American business history, and particularly in the area of doctoral research, where both Galambos and Chandler have shaped a generation of students.

The publication of *Scale and Scope* in 1990 provided a further monumental stage in the development of Chandler's empirical and theoretical work. In particular, it developed newer central concepts such as 'organizational capabilities' and 'economies of scope', and arguably retreated from some earlier ones such as 'economies of speed'. It also extended the analysis from a focus on US big business to a focus on international comparisons.

The empirical and theoretical work of *Scale and Scope* has been widely applauded, and other authors, like Bill Lazonick, have extended and developed the underlying theoretical framework and

---

1 Louis Galambos, 'The emerging organizational synthesis in Modern American History'. *Business History Review* 44, 3, Autumn 1970.

2 Louis Galambos, 'Technology, Political Economy and Professionalization: Central Themes of the Organizational Synthesis'. *Business History Review* 57, Winter 1983.

applied it to new areas such as the management of labour[3]. But Chandler's approach has not gone unchallenged. For some time, critics have pointed to the underlying functionalism and determinism of his approach[4]. But alternative frameworks had been rare. Recent work, however — sometimes tacitly, sometimes explicitly — is developing a more critical approach to the concepts of the Chandler synthesis.

This paper examines one key area in which these critical lines of approach are developing and evaluates their implications for the Chandler paradigm and the "organizational synthesis". They derive from attempts to understand the dynamics of technological innovation. Technology has often appeared as an external and independent determinant in the Chandler approach. Recent work by David Hounshell and John Smith, Nathan Rosenberg, Richard Langlois and others on the one hand and Thomas Hughes and "social constructionists" on the other, have posed multiple challenges to this approach and pose important difficulties for the paradigm. This is clearly not the only area where Chandler's interpretation is being widely questioned by American business historians. A second notable area is the issue of "historical alternatives", notably as developed by Charles Sabel and Jonathan Zeitlin, and extended by authors such as Philip Scranton, which challenges the exclusive focus on big business, the determinism of Chandler's approach, and aspects of his periodization[5]. A further contentious area is Chandler's use of international comparisons, where, for example, his interpretations of British and German experience in the light of

---

[3] William Lazonick, *Competitive Advantage on the Shop Floor* (Harvard UP, 1990); *Business Organization and the Myth of the Market Economy* (Cambridge UP, 1992).

[4] Steven Tolliday and Jonathan Zeitlin, 'Employers and industrial relations between theory and history', in Steven Tolliday and Jonathan Zeitlin (eds.), *The Power to Manage? Employers and Industrial Relations in Comparative-Historical Perspective* (Routledge, 1992), p. 4-5.

[5] See, Charles Sabel and Jonathan Zeitlin, 'Historical Alternatives to Mass Production: Politics, Markets and Technology in Nineteenth Century Industrialization' *Past & Present* 108, 1985; Philip Scranton, *Figured Tapestry. Production, Markets and Power in Philadelphia Textiles, 1885-1941* (Cambridge UP, 1989) esp. Ch. 1; and 'Diversity in Diversity: Flexible Production and American Industrialization, 1880-1930'. *Business History Review* 65, 1, Spring 1991.

the American model have been widely questioned[6]. But reasons of space prevent a wider survey, and it is in the area of business and tecnological change that the diversity of approaches is greatest and where the problems for Chandler's underlying paradigm have been most sharply posed. The difficulties that arise suggest that ideas of an 'organizational synthesis' are no longer adequate to deal with the plurality and complexity of approaches to the writing of business history that are becoming apparent.

The Organizational Synthesis

Galambos's surveys of the state of the debate in 1970 and 1983 were not meant to be definitive. Nor were they exclusively concerned with business history. In fact, a crucial part of their agenda was an attempt to suggest how a set of ideas derived from current methodological innovations in business history might be applied more broadly to illuminate issues in American political economy. Chandler's work signified a sharp break from a 'progressive' historiography of big business with a pronounced moralistic slant, and from the cultural/entrepreneurial school of Cochran, Gras, Cole and others. Instead his work placed the importance of organizational structures and business strategies at the centre of the stage and thus placed institutions and entrepreneurs in a very different context. Galambos's purpose was to develop and link these themes in an interdisciplinary fashion into a wider reinterpretation of business, politics and society in the United States. In both spheres, 'the primary processes of change involved organization building, both public and private, and the creation of new and elaborate networks of formal, hierarchical structures of authority that gradually came to dominate our economy, polity and culture"[7].

---

[6] For a representative sample of views see the comments of Roy Church, Jurgen Kocka and Hidemasa Morikawa in Steven Tolliday (ed.), '*Scale and Scope:* A Review Colloquium'. *Business History Review* 64, 4, Winter 1990, p. 690-736; Sanford Jacoby (ed.), *Masters to Managers, Historical and Comparative Perspectives on American Employers* (New York, Columbia UP, 1991).

[7] Galambos, 'Technology, Political and Professionalization' esp. p. 471; 'Emerging Organizational Synthesis'.

Nevertheless, in 1970 (and still to a considerable extent in 1983), it was possible to think in terms of such a central corpus of emergent methodology, model or paradigm that was 'emergent' in busines history and which was capable of being 'applied' more widely. A decade later it would be a rash scholar who would venture to try to define a core theoretical approach or paradigm in American business history. True, Chandler's work has been considerably extended and continues to tower over the field. But, even at the core the implications and theoretical consequences of Chandler's ideas are now much disputed. Bill Lazonick and Oliver Williamson, for example, both use Chandler's ideas as central building blocks in their own work: yet they sharply disagree over the meaning and application of Chandler's key concepts[8].

The sections that follow look at controversies surrounding approaches to the history of business and technology in three main areas: the relationship between the corporation and technical development; 'internal' versus 'external' dynamics of technical change; and issues raised by 'path-dependency' theories. No single model emerges from these debates, yet all gravitate towards conclusions that fit uncomfortably with an 'organizational synthesis'. In particular, they repeatedly stress much more contingent and malleable paths for technology, a wider range of possible technical and organizational forms, and the role of power and chance rather than technical or organizational logic in determining outcomes.

Firms and Technological Development

Technological change plays a central role in Chandler's overall interpretation of the dynamics of managerial capitalism. In his work, the emergence and diffusion of the modern corporation was a functional response to the organizational demands of wider markets and larger-scale technologies, manifest first in the United States and then on a global scale. Technological innovation in transport and communication created the broader markets that made mass production possible and simultaneously provided the techniques

[8] The most concise exposition of these divergent views is to be found in Ch. 6 of Lazonick, *Business Organization and the Myth of the Market Economy.*

of production which could fully utilize economies of scale and scope. This approach, which treats technology essentially as an exogeneous variable or 'underlying cause' has generated considerable dissatisfaction.

Many writers, and particularly those associated with the 'social construction of technology' school have emphasized that new technologies, including Chandler's telegraphs and railroads, were not simply technical artifacts, but rather complex systems involving artifacts, skills, needs and wants, and political regulation. The 'autonomy' of technology is limited. Technologies can only develop within complementary legal, managerial and social and economic structures[9].

The conventional neo-classical approach to technology has been that individual inventions and innovations might be exogeneous and at times fortuitous, but, taken as a large class, they could still be linked as dependent variables to conventional factors such as demand and investment, and thus be linked back into conventional analytic frameworks of supply and demand. Chandler's attitude to this position is ambiguous, asserting the importance of the firm as an actor on the one hand, but insisting on the need for successful firms to conform to the pressure of markets on the other. Critics such as Nathan Rosenberg and David Mowery have more radically stressed the dangers of accepting that demand side forces alone can explain technical change[10].

They and others have emphasized the role of firms in generating and shaping technical change itself. In this context, Rosenberg has particularly stressed the largely incremental nature of technical change (even of some apparently radical technical changes)[11]. This

---

9 Wiebe E. Bijker, Thomas Hughes and Trevor Pitch (eds.), *The Social Construction of Technological Systems. New Directions in the Sociology and History of Technology* (Cambridge MA, MIT Press, 1987); Wiebe E. Bijker and John Law (eds.), *Shaping Technology/Building Society. Studies in Sociotechnical Change* (Cambridge MA, MIT Press, 1992).

10 David C. Mowery and Nathan Rosenberg, 'The influence of market demand upon innovation: a critical review of some recent empirical studies'. *Research Policy* 8, April 1979; reprinted in Rosenberg, *Inside the Black Box.*

11 Nathan Rosenberg, *Inside the Black Box: Technology and Economics* (Cambridge UP, 1982).

is close to the more theoretical position of Nelson and Winter who portray firms as persistently groping in the dark for solutions to local problems as distinct from pursuing rationalist courses to solve logical or fundamental problems[12]. They and Giovanni Dosi[13] therefore emphasize that technologists tend to focus on a rather narrow range of issues. If raw material prices are rising they may focus on inventions that economize on raw materials etc. And they stress that the interrelatedness of systems may itself induce technical change: improvements in one part of a system may outpace slower or older methods in another part and force the need for upstream or downstream innovations to realize overall productive potential.

The historical work of Thomas Hughes, Edward Constant and others fits closely with this schema. Hughes in *Networks of Power* argued, against the background of the emergent electrical power industry, that much technical innovation takes place along advancing salients of progress which contain various redoubts or reverses. The task of the innovator is to remove reverse salients[14]. Constant, in the context of the development of turbojet technology, made a related argument (not dissimilar to Kuhn's scientific paradigms) that invention clusters around accumulated dissatisfactions with existing paradigms[15]. But these 'reverse salients' and accumulated dissatisfactions are not simply products of cogitation: they exist again in relation to the goals and choices of firms, and different firm strategies will result in a focus on different types of innovation.

These lines of thought have resulted in an intensified focus on how research is conducted in the modern firm. One area that historians have paid particular attention to is the role of science

---

[12] Richard Nelson and Sidney Winter, *An Evolutionary Theory of Economic Change* (Cambridge MA, 1982).

[13] Giovanni Dosi, 'Sources, procedures and microeconomic effects of innovation'. *Journal of Economic Literature* 26, September 1988.

[14] Thomas P. Hughes. *Networks of Power: Electrification in Western Society* (Baltimore, 1983).

[15] Edward W. Constant, *The Origins of the Turbojet Revolution* (Baltimore, Johns Hopkins UP, 1980); and 'Cause or Consequence: Science, Technology and Regulatory Change in the Oil Business in Texas, 1930-1975'. *Technology and Culture* April, 1989.

and research in the emergence of the modern corporation. In the United States in the 19th century individual entrepreneurs like Edison, Thomson or Sperry could be the focus of invention. But, how did the function of innovation come to be institutionalized in successful large corporations?

Important work by Bernard Carlson has illuminated how firms brought together previously distinct workshop and scientific cultures to develop ways to transform scientific breakthroughs into profitmaking innovations. Carlson stresses that Elihu Thomson, arguably the most prolific inventor of the early era of electricity, did not simply 'apply' science, but rather used it as one element only to inform his approach to the development of unique mechanical and electrical devices. "The electrical industry of the late 19th century", he argues, "was based as much on craft knowledge as on scientific theory"[16].

This work, together with that of Susan Douglas, Reese V. Jenkins and Bryan Pfaffenberger among others, emphasizes that technical knowledge has to be embedded in organizations to become effective. To understand the innovation, it is necessary not only to understand the knowledge base, but also the institutions within which that knowledge was developed and used. In the distant past, for example, medieval clock technology was stimulated and distinctively shaped by monastic culture[17]. In the more recent past, as Douglas has shown the inventors of radio not only invented a new technology but also designed new business arrangements and formed consumption patterns to make it into a marketable commodity[18], and Jenkins has argued that George Eastman's effective invention of a new mass market was as important as his scientific innovations in the creation of the simple roll-film camera[19].

One of the key theoretical difficulties in these approaches is to

---

16 W. Bernard Carlson. *Innovation as a Social Process. Elihu Thomson and the Rise of General Electric, 1870-1900* (Cambridge UP, 1991), p. 7.

17 David S. Landes. *Revolution in Time. Clocks and the Making of the Modern World* (Harvard UP, 1983).

18 Susan J. Douglas, *Inventing American Broadcasting, 1899-1922* (Baltimore, Johns Hopkins UP, 1987).

19 Reese V. Jenkins, 'Technology and the Market: George Eastman and the Origins of Mass Amateur Photography'. *Technology and Culture*, January 1975.

balance effectively the determining impact of social and cultural forces against the constraints of the world of physical artifacts. The elaboration of electrical technology in the late 19th century required specific developments in the knowledge base. But it also required the provision of capital and the shaping of markets. In a sense, therefore, it developed symbiotically with the creation of a new type of business organization (symbolized by the partnership between Elihu Thomson and Charles A. Coffin) and with the development of new concepts of potential markets and new strategies and structures to meet them. Rather than sell generators, lights and the necessary accessories outright to consumers, Thomson and his partners found that it was more profitable to persuade businessmen in towns and cities to organize utility companies that would purchase their inventions and in turn sell the service of lighting. As Hughes has argued, only by achieving this complex organizational task were they able to establish electric lighting as an industry[20].

In a sense, much of this could be read as complementary to Chandler's approach. Thomson and Coffin succeeded because they deliberately designed their business organizations and products in response to their strategies (i.e, structure follows strategy). But it is unlike Chandler in two critical respects[21]. Firstly it stresses the interactive development of technology and market demand: in linking electrical technology to business organization, Thomson and Coffin had to modify *both*. And secondly it stresses that technological development is not an 'internal' process but responds to a wide range of social, economic and cultural values[22]. Invention itself may therefore be an interactive process. In the classic case of the personal computer, for example, as the invention was taken up and used, consumers demanded changes and even used devices in ways

[20] Cf. Carlson. *Innovation as a Social Process* passim; Hughes, *Networks of Power.*

[21] For a vigorous critique of Chandler from this perspective see the contribution of Thomas Hughes in Tolliday (ed.), *'Scale and Scope:* A Review Colloquium'.

[22] This aspect has been forcefully developed by social constructionists such as John Law in the concept of 'heterogeneous engineering'. See John Law, 'Technology and Heterogeneous Engineering: The Case of Portuguese Expansion', in Bijker et. al. (eds.), *Social Construction of Technological Systems.*

significantly different from those anticipated by their 'inventors' or producers[23].

If studies of the creation and development of new technologies, markets and business institutions are pushing beyond the Chandler paradigm, so too are studies of the evolving conduct of research within established large corporations. Chandler's *Scale and Scope* stresses the competitive power of the 'organizational capabilities' of large firms in technological development. His work leaves us in no doubt that large firms can be effective innovators. But it is less clear on why this should be the case, and why large firms should handle this better than alternatives such as clusters, joint ventures or networks, or under what conditions managerial hierarchies may begin to inhibit or distort innovations. Lazonick's development of Chandler addresses this in part through his distinction betwen adaptive and innovative firms. But this tends to classify rather than explain firm behaviour.

One of the most impressive findings of Chandler's work is the frequency with which first-movers in three-pronged investments have remained leaders in their industry in the long-run and have proved capable of innovating and moving into new lines of business. But, why did their oligopolistic advantages not result in cautious, adaptive behaviour and decay? Chandler argues that in practice oligopoly did not lead to predatory and exploitative behaviour. Where it did, the firms concerned did not prosper for long. Rather, it enabled firms to overcome problems of risk and uncertainty and to use their large market share and vertical integration to achieve lower costs and higher productivity through administrative co-ordination. As an observation on the process of the rise of big business in America this has withstood scrutiny highly effectively[24]. Yet the last chapter of *Scale and Scope*, which contains a powerful critique of the withering away of many of these leading firms organizational capabilities by the 1970s and 1980s, poses awkward

---

23 Bryan Pfaffenberger, 'The Social Meaning of the Personal Computer, Or Why the Personal Computer Revolution was No Revolution'. *Anthropological Quarterly*, 61, 1988.

24 A few dents were made in it by Naomi Lamoreaux, *The Great Merger Movement in American Business, 1895-1904* (Cambridge, 1985) who found rather greater scope for oligopolistic exploitation in some sectors, though her overall conclusions broadly endorsed Chandler's views.

questions about the adequacy of the Chandler paradigm as an explanatory mechanism for how and why 'organizational capabilities' should be effectively deployed at times but become corrupted and decayed at others. If firms are, in fact, bundles of organizational capabilities (or in Nelson and Winter's terms of practices and routines) they are always liable to become inert or inflexible.

For all that Chandler's explanation is couched in terms of 'organizational capabilities' and focuses on the internal structural and strategic histories of firms, it remains unclear how far Chandler has finally distanced himself from neoclassical or transaction cost analysis. Essentially, firms that fail to conform to the requirements of their environments either by adapting their structures to the needs of strategy or by minimizing transaction costs will decline and disappear, while choices between markets and hierarchies are themselves ultimately determined by the natural selection of the market. It may be that it is only with hindsight that it is possible to define what is adaptive and what innovative behaviour.

Important recent studies have focused on these relations between large corporations and systematic innovation. David Hounshell and John Smith in their study of R&D at DuPont and Margaret Graham in her study of RCA, have shown how since the Second World War, corporate R&D has frequently experienced difficulties in transforming laboratory inventions into successful commercial innovations[25]. At times this has been the result of the influence of government funding or of their relations with scientific universities: at other times, as in the case of DuPont, it has been a result of the constraints of corporate culture and structure. In the 1930s, basic scientific research at DuPont created nylon and the basis for enormous new fields of profit and product development. But the organizational structures and the relationship between R&D and the rest of the corporation that were established at the time became entrenched and shaped the future process of innovation at the firm. After the Second World War, DuPont often pursued visions of 'another nylon' and oriented itself, at huge expense, towards the

[25] David Hounshell and John K. Smith, *Science and Corporate Strategy: DuPont R&D, 1902-80* (Cambridge UP, 1988); Margaret Graham, *RCA and the Videodisc* (Cambridge UP, 1987).

discovery of breakthrough technologies arguably at the expense of better balanced and more commercially oriented technical development. Rayon and Kevlar were notable products of this work — though neither was so profitable or fruitful in new products as nylon — but others such as Corfam became veritable sinks for corporate funds[26].

Studies such as these begin to unbundle the notion of 'organizational capabilities', illuminating both their powers for efficient and effective action and their simultaneous potential for dysfunctional behaviour and to stress the need for specific historical analysis at every stage to understand why capabilities were deployed in the particular direction in which they were turned.

Internal and External Capabilities

Chandler and Lazonick, following in a broadly Schumpeterian tradition, have stressed the centrality of large firms in the development of efficient forms and organizational capabilities. These views have often been counterposed to a tradition of Marshallian economics that has highlighted the role of 'external economies' operating through competition and the interaction of firms in markets and networks. Both views stress "organizational capabilities", but there is vigorous debate about where they are best created.

Some of the most important issues in this debate can be illuminated by looking at some important recent research on the role of technological change in the emergence of three new but major industries: microcomputers, videocassette recorders, and biotechnology. The first example draws on a number of studies of the microcomputer industry by Richard Langlois[27]. Langlois has argued

---

[26] Hounshell and Smith, *Science and Corporate Strategy*; David Hounshell, 'The Making of a New Industrial Fiber: The case of DuPont's Kevlar' unpublished paper April 1989; John K. Smith, 'The Ten-Year Invention: Neoprene and DuPont Research, 1930-1939'. *Technology and Culture* 26, 1, January, 1985.

[27] Richard N. Langlois, 'External Economies and Economic Progress: the Case of the Microcomputer Industry'. *Business History Review* 66, 1, Spring 1992; Richard N. Langlois and Paul L. Robertson, 'Networks and Innovation in a Modular System: Lessons from the Microcomputer and Stereo Component Industries'. *Research Policy* 21, 1992.

that the Marshallian and Schumpeterian models should not be rigidly counterposed. He concludes that, in the microcomputer industry, capabilities have developed primarily in a decentralized external market rather than in vertically integrated firms, "a case quite exactly the opposite to the picture of progress that Chandler paints in *Scale and Scope*[28]. Neither IBM nor Apple, nor Microsoft has been able to become a dominant, oligopolistic "first mover". But Langlois also stresses that it is often the dynamic interaction of internal and external capabilities that has proved most productive.

Thus, the powerful mainframe computer companies like IBM and Hewlett-Packard did not use their powerful internal organizational capabilities to pioneer in microcomputers. Instead, they stood to one side in the 1970s as a diverse collection, first of hobbyists and software pirates, and then of start-up companies like Apple, Osborne and Kaypro, shaped the industry and its technology around a pattern of design networks, open systems, and outsourcing. When IBM addressed itself seriously to entering this market in the early 1980s, it had to bypass its own organizational structures, break its own rules, and in effect sponsor its own start-up company to compete against itself, in order to find the innovative flexibility to break into the market.

Having entered the market in this way, IBM initially embraced open standards for its PC, declining to fight an uphill battle to defend patent and proprietary rights against fast-moving cloners. Instead, it actively accepted the growth of outsourcing and independent external innovation on the basis of IBM-compatibility. Subsequent attempts by IBM (with the PS/2), DEC, and Compaq to 'close' standards through the introduction of proprietary or incompatible machines resulted in corporate near-disasters, as clone-makers launched their own alternative standards and forced larger companies to re-externalize to remain competitive. Proprietary standards, notably those of IBM and Apple, have tended to converge, and open standards and modularity have come to be regarded as almost inevitable.

In part, Langlois argues, this pattern is linked to the characteristics of product and technology in the industry. Unlike mass consumer products in sectors like automobiles and consumer electronics, the

---

[28] Langlois, 'External Economies', p. 2-4.

product grew before the extent of its uses was defined, creating a high degree of uncertainty and change. Consequently, whereas traditional mass producers had often found that they could innovate faster at the centre than their suppliers, the reverse was true in microcomputers. Moreover, the distinctive role of modularity in computer design also enhanced the scope for external innovation, since one part of a system could change without all other parts having to change with it.

The second case, drawn from work on the origins of the videocassette recorder industry by Michael Cusumano, Yiorgos Mylonadis and Richard Rosembloom, illustrates another dimension of the interaction of internal and external capabilities[29]. In contrast to the persistence of open standards and external networks in microcomputers, the VCR industry passed through a decisive struggle over standards at an early stage of its development. Large firms fought a battle to determine a dominant product design and then competed on the basis of developing superior capabilities in mass production and incremental product improvements.

Sony, with its Betamax system, was the first mover in the industry, but it was surpassed by the joint operations of JVC and Matsushita, which entered as second-movers with an alternative and improved product (VHS) and captured a position of dominance in the industry. In part, this was a battle between two organizations or groups with highly developed internal organizational capabilities. Sony established an early lead through its design and production skills but was unable to sustain it in the face of comparable technical skills allied to the greater mass production capabilities of its rivals. The key element of Matsushita's success was not superior internal capabilities. Indeed Mark Fruin has recently shown that Matsushita represents the network firm, focused on design and distribution rather than production, *par excellence*[30]. Cusumano, Mylonadis and

---

29 Michael A. Cusumano, Yiorgos Mylonadis and Richard S. Rosenbloom, 'Strategic maneuvring and mass-market dynamics: the triumph of VHS over Beta'. *Business History Review* 66, 1, Spring 1992; Richard S. Rosenbloom and Michael A. Cusumano, 'Technological Pioneering and Competitive Advantage: The Birth of the VCR industry'. *California Management Review* 29, 4, Summer 1987.

30 W. Mark Fruin, *The Japanese Enterprise System. Competitive Strategies and Co-operative structures* (Clarendon Press, Oxford, 1992).

Rosenbloom stress that, in an industry in which demand was so enormous and growing so exponentially, it was rather its ability to outpace Sony in global commercialization, by creating a network of allied mass producers and distributiors in Japan and the United States, linked together behind their preferred standard.

Thus, as in the computer industry, the interaction of internal and external capabilities proved decisive. Like the computer industry, for instance, standards were decisively shaped by the external development of complementary products (software and pre-recorded tapes), which created bandwagon effects and network externalities, and the capacity of leading firms to relate to or ally themselves with these forces was vital. But the differences were perhaps even more important. First, unlike the computer industry, the mass production of video equipment was a demanding and complex product-engineering and manufacturing business — not a component assembly operation — and reliance on decentralized suppliers was hazardous. Second and most important, the nature of the product was fundamentally different. The microcomputer is really a system in a box; the VCR is ultimately an appliance. In this sense, the videocassette recorder industry did not have a "battle of the systems", but rather a duel between differentiated but essentially similar technologies. In this context, Sony's key mistake was to interpret a small technical advantage as a decisive lead in product definition and to leave itself vulnerable to a strategic coalition of producers that moved more decisively into mass production and distribution.

The third case is drawn from the early period of the American biotechnology industry. In this quintessentially research-driven industry the boundaries of the firm are a crucial issue. Firms need to generate innovations for continuing competitive success and they need to be part of a two-way flow of science, research and ideas. But, at the same time, they need to be able to control and appropriate the fruits of their innovations. In the telephone industry, AT&T's Bell Laboratories resolved a similar dilemma by basically pursuing a massive research monopoly over the industry and using its technical lead to 'close' the system[31]. In microcomputers, as we have

---

[31] Peter Temin with Louis Galambos, *The Fall of the Bell System: A Study in Prices and Politics* (Cambridge UP, 1987); Steve Coll, *The Deal of the Century. The Breakup of AT&T* (New York, 1986).

seen, several companies considered such a route, but clones and software piracy made this more problematic (though Microsoft may be an example of at least short-term success in this field).

A rather different solution to this problem emerged in parts of the American biotechnology industry. The example examined here draws on the work of Glenn Bugos on the chicken-breeding sector in the 1950s and 1960s[32], though analogous processes can be seen in the development of hybrid corn in Illinois in the interwar years[33]. Bugos shows that in chicken-breeding, the control of genetic variation through hybridization provided a route to control intellectual property that was more powerful than the patent system and which laid the basis for an industrial structure in which breeding remained a distinct and independent industry, separate from the otherwise vertically integrated chain of chicken-farming.

The central innovation was the development of hybridization from the 1950s. This not only created advantages of genetic uniformity and "hybrid vigor", but also created a "genetic lock" on the intellectual property of the industry, since chicken farmers could not reproduce the hybrid pattern through breeding, which now required complex control of trait selections and breeding sequences. The breeding industry became highly specialized, R&D-led, and hard to enter. It required relentless research and testing to respond to the needs of producers and to constantly shifting dangers from disease or unanticipated consequences of genetic changes. By the 1980s, 90% of US broilers came from the stock of half a dozen breeders.

This tight, specialized and research-led sector, however, also provided the basis of standardized genetic raw material, out of which a vertically integrated mass production chicken-farming industry developed. A highly vertically integrated system of hatching, supplying, housing, processing, branding and distribution grew up, dominated by firms like Tyson, Holly Farms, and Perdue, building on the opportunities for standardization and mass production provided by the genetic controls of the breeders and

---

32 Glenn Bugos. 'Intellectual Property Protection in the American Chicken-Breeding Industry'. *Business History Review* 66, 1, Spring 1992.

33 Deborah Fitzgerald. *The Business of Breeding. Hybrid Corn in Illinois, 1890-1940* (Cornell UP, 1990).

symbolized by the speedy and scientific slaughter of the chicken disassembly lines. In this industry at least, a key element of technology and innovation was provided externally and remained separate from the giant firms that developed the organizational capabilities of large-scale production and distribution in the sector.

These studies and others[34] raise intriguing questions about the large corporation and internal and external sources of innovation. In one case (chicken farming), large firms have depended systematically on innovations developed externally; in another (microcomputers), these external innovations have substituted for the development of large firms; in another (VCRs), the internal organizational capabilities of single firms had to be welded into a sort of global network in order to dominate the industry.

Though many major firms did succeed in basic invention, most have also continuously drawn on outside sources of invention and concentrated on effective commercialization. This extra-firm context of innovation has persisted strongly around the managerial firm, in the 20th century. In highly developed economies a wide variety of capabilities may be available on markets, through contracting or implicitly through the purchase of finished goods.

Contingency and Path-Dependency

The previous two sections have discussed various perspectives on how technological change and innovation is developed within and outside firms. But what of the content of the technologies themselves? The work of Chandler, Williamson and others implies that there is an immanent logic of technological development as

[34] Other recent work which deal with similar issues include studies of chemical design firms who played a role analogous to the chicken breeders in the chemical industry, see: Ralph Landau and Nathan Rosenberg, 'Successful Comercialization in the Chemical Process Industries', in Nathan Rosenberg, Ralph Landau and David C. Movery (eds.), *Technology and the Wealth of Nations* (Stanford UP, 1992); and Ross Thomson's studies of external networks in shoemaking, *The Path to Mechanized Shoe Production in the United States* (Chapel Hill, North Carolina University Press, 1989); and 'Crossover Inventors and Technological Linkages: American Shoemaking and the Broader Economy, 1848-1901', *Technology & Culture* October 1991.

more efficient technologies succeed less efficient ones, and as those firms which make the best-adapted technical choices survive and prosper. They are part of a broad tradition running from Marx to Landes that stresses the idea of technological development as a broad and mighty river, reshaping the economic and social landscape and sweeping puny economic actors in its path[35].

However, much recent work has tended to argue that technological outcomes are much less determinate and that the 'efficiency' of even successful technologies should be continually questioned. In the early stages of the development of many major industries, there were an abundance of competing solutions to key technical problems. Each solution was potentially better on some dimensions than others; and its advantages reflected the particular circumstances and favoured the interests of its sponsors over the other competitors. In the early days of the automobile, for example, it was by no means a foregone conclusion that the petrol engine would surpass the steam engine. McLaughlin has described the benign conjunction of circumstances that enabled the petrol engine to snatch a decisive lead in the early days (including droughts and horse diseases that forced the closure of horse troughs vital to the steam engine at crucial moments)[36]. And a recent CNRS-sponsored research project has reaffirmed the contention that if steam engines had had the same sort of developmental energies lavished on them as the petrol engine has received in the last century then the potential for comparable or superior steam engines for automobiles today would have been very strong.

Similarly, in a classic paper, Paul David has argued that the QWERTY typewriter keyboard is hardly the most efficient available: indeed it was created to be deliberately *inefficient*, to slow down the typist so that the keyboard mechanism would not persistently jam. There were numerous technical alternatives on offer in the 1890s (including embryonic 'golfball' systems and alternative keyboard

---

35 For overviews see: David Hounshell, 'On the Discipline of the History of American Technology'. *Journal of American History* 67, 4, March 1981; David S. Landes, 'Introduction: On Technology and Growth', in Higonnet *et al* (eds.), *Favorites of Fortune* (1991).

36 C. C. McLaughlin, 'The Stanley Steamer: A Study in Unsuccessful Innovation', in H. G. J. Aitken (ed.), *Explorations in Enterprise* (Cambridge MA, 1967).

configurations) but a series of chance circumstances and externalities, such as the emergence of a body of trained touch typists geared to the QWERTY system, pushed the typewriter into "premature standardization on the *wrong system*" which has subsequently been impossible to supplant because of its base of producers and users[37]. In computers, the 1950s computer language FORTRAN became established very early and then proved immensely difficult to dislodge. In telephone technologies, firms with a large installed base have been able to hold off latecomers possessing superior technologies[38].

Many of these technological debates have appeared at times to be closed and settled only to be reopened by later unexpected changes in the conditions of competition such as the upheavals of the 1970s and 1980s, the changing pattern of energy costs, or new concerns about the environmental impact of technologies. Many paradigms of technological development that have been taken for granted, including notably notions of mass production and the necessity of economies of scale, have been fundamentally challenged.

Reflecting this, theoretical work by Brian Arthur, Paul David, Michael Storper and others, has shown that the technology that wins out in any given contest is not necessarily the one with the greatest potential for long-term development[39]. Arthur has argued that once a technology is adopted it is generally caracterized by

---

[37] Paul David, 'Clio and the Economics of QWERTY'. *American Economic Review, Proceedings* 75, 1985; and 'Understanding the Economics of QWERTY: the Necessity of History', in W. N. Parker (ed.), *Economic History and the Modern Economist* (Oxford, Basil Blackwell, 1986).

[38] Michael L. Katz and Carl Shapiro, 'Technology Adoption in the Presence of Network Externalities'. *Journal of Political Economy* 94, 4, 1986; Joseph Farrell and Garth Saloner, 'Installed Base, Product Preannouncements, and Predation'. *American Economic Review* 76, 5, December 1986.

[39] W. Brian Arthur, 'Competing technologies, increasing returns, and lock-in by historical events'. *Economic Journal* 394, 99, March 1989; M. Storper, 'Big Structures, Small Events and Large Processes in Economic Geography'. *Environment and Planning. A.* 20, 1988; Paul David, 'Path-dependence and predictability in dynamic systems with local network externalities: a paradigm for historical economics', in Dominique Foray and Christopher Freeman (eds.), *Technology and the Wealth of Nations. The Dynamics of Constructed Advantage* (London, Pinter, 1993).

increasing returns. These include learning by doing, network externalities, production economies of scale, informational advantages and technological interrelatedness. Under these conditions, small historical 'events' may give one technology an initial edge which becomes cumulatively larger as additional adopters are attracted who might otherwise have gone along with one of its rivals, until the market 'tips' in its favour[40]. Where such increasing returns are unbounded, the dominant technology will drive out all others and create a monopoly, while under less extreme assumptions certain sequences of adoption could bid up the returns to both technologies simultaneously, leading to a shared market. In either case, however, it is the contingent outcome of historical events, which are themselves the results of the choices and expectations of historical actors, rather than current or potential efficiency which shapes the trajectory of technological development and the resulting market structure.

Robin Cowan's recent work on the history of the nuclear power industry, for example, demonstrates that a technology that improves rapidly as many people adopt it will have a better chance of surviving: but such early superiority is no guarantee of long-term fitness. In the mid-1950s, when the US embarked on its nuclear power program, a number of designs contented, including reactors cooled by gas, light water, heavy water and liquid sodium. It was a series of relatively trivial circumstances which locked virtually the entire US nuclear industry into light water. Light-water reactors were originally adapted from highly compact units designed to propel nuclear submarines. The role of the US Navy in early reactor-construction contracts, efforts by the National Security Council to get the first available reactor working as quickly as possible in the wake of the 1957 *Sputnik* launch, as well as the predilections of some key officials, all acted to favour the early development of light-water reactors. Construction experience led to improved light-water designs, and by the mid-1960s the technological trajectory of the industry had become fixed. Whether other designs would, in fact, have been superior in the long run is an open question: but many

[40] W. Brian Arthur, 'Self Reinforcing Mechanisms in Economics', in Philip W. Anderson, Kenneth J. Arrow and David Pines (eds.), *The Economy as an Envolving Complex System* (Addison-Wesley, 1988).

nuclear engineers argue that high temperature, gas-cooled reactors would have been better[41].

Such notions, under the general heading of path-dependency, have been most fully developed in Paul David's work on 'gateway technologies' and the role of 'hysteresis' in the "battle of the systems" (Edison vs. Westinghouse) between direct and alternating current in the early electrical industry. In both cases, he argues that the details of the timing of small historical events can have important and lasting consequences. In the case of the "Battle of the Systems" for example, the relatively minor technical innovation of the rotary converter had a profound and surprisingly far-reaching impact on the outcome of the duel. Big consequences can flow from petty events and small endogenous innovations or periodic fluctuations can serve to push the dynamics of a technological system in a particular direction[42].

Seen in this light, there seems little reason to assume that technological logics will at all times impose a narrow range of appropriate strategies on the enterprise. The criteria for choice and competitive survival may be much looser than is often assumed. A broad variety of managerial strategies and choices might produce comparable results and firms that perform poorly and make sub-optimal choices may often be able to survive indefinitely. In a world of indeterminate goals and results and path-dependency and lock-in, the exercise of power (economic, political or social) at particular moments may well be crucial. Outcomes that are sub-optimal may have triumphed.

---

41 Robin Cowan, 'Nuclear Power Reactors: A study of technological lock-in'. *Journal of Economic History* September 1990.

42 Paul David and Julie Ann Bunn, 'The Economics of Gateway Technologies and Network Evolution: Lessons from the Electricity Supply Industry'. *Information Economics and Policy* 3, Fall 1988; Paul A. David, 'The Hero and the Herd in Technological History: Reflections on Thomas Edison and the Battle of the Systems', in Higonnet et al (eds.), *Favorites of Fortune* (1991).

Conclusions

A strikingly wide variety of approaches are thus apparent in recent historical analysis of business and technology. The 'blank spot' of technology within the Chandler paradigm is being vigorously probed along a profusion of theoretical and empirical channels. Within the firm, the strengths and weaknesses of organizational capabilities in relation to innovation and incremental change are being examined and the relationship between firms and technologies reconceptualized on a more interactive basis. At the same time, a host of questions have been raised about 'internal' and 'external' sources of innovation which suggest that there is no necessary superiority of one form over the other, and indeed that it is their interaction that matters most. Finally, across a wide range of technological issues, the role of contingency, path-dependency and power have been re-asserted. These challenges link up to challenges to the Chandler paradigm in other fields, such as those of flexible specialization or the use of international comparisons mentioned earlier. They suggest that a selective focus on the institutions of big business (while a valid empirical strategy) may also create distortions, and they also cast doubts on the notion that a convergence on managerial structures, strategies and technologies will necessarily tend to override national contexts.

Pier Angelo Toninelli
Università di Milano and Fondazione ASSI

BUSINESS HISTORY AS A FIELD OF RESEARCH: THE EUROPEAN PERSPECTIVE

This paper will focus on the past tendencies and present trends of business history in a few European countries, namely Italy, Spain, France, Germany and the United Kingdom. Its purpose will be not so much to give a complete report or listing of publications in the field as to try to enlighten differences and similarities among the research experiences of each country as well as to evaluate if and how much these experiences reflect the real pattern of growth of firms and companies and the evolution of the business commmunity within different European economies.

The paper will also discuss if and to what extent business history, once asserted itself in these countries, has been showing the same approach that already basically characterized the discipline in the US — namely, the organizational. This approach may be the most suited to the pattern of growth of US enterprises, but does not look as completely appropriate to explain the business development and industrial growth of our countries, where giant enterprises, early separation between property and management, growth of firm burocracies have been the exception rather than the rule. Therefore, business history in Europe should, as in part it already does, address itself more to problems like the persistence of family capitalism, the role of state-owned companies and public enterprises, the growth (or decline) of small and medium-size business units, as well as to the relationship between the latter ones and a few big companies.

At a more general level, business history in Europe — as in the US and Japan — should try to overcome the narrow boundaries of today's exclusively microeconomic approach, by enlightening and explaining firms' microbehaviours and strategies, not *per se*, but as functional pieces of today's complex socio-economic systems.

I

The most evident aspect of differentiation among the patterns of evolution of business history in the European countries is related to the discipline's different timing of spread and performance. Borrowing from the history of economic growth, we may speak of first-comers and late-joiners also with regard to such historiography, either in its Schumpeterian approach (i.e, entrepreneurial history) or in the Chandlerian one (i.e, business history) . This taxonomy does nothing more than to reflect the actual pattern of economic growth of each country, as well as the development of their respective business communities. The UK and Germany should be placed among the former ones, Italy and Spain among the latter, with France staying somehow in between.

In England and in Germany the research tradition within the field goes back at least to the after World War I period, although the discipline cannot be said to have reached many major results before the 1950s and *1960s*, when the first journals devoted to business history — *Business History* in the UK (1958) and *Tradition* in Germany (1957) — were started, some twenty-five years after the American *Business History Review.*

However, with regard to the UK, there have been some major changes in the evolution of the discipline since the 1920s, when business histories were almost exclusively "official" company histories, "devoid of any scholarly value" and consisting "primarily of reminiscences and anedoctes". "The real change came when the idea emerged of *live* business firms commissioning academics to write their histories" (Coleman, 1987:142), the sources of which had to be mostly the firms' own private business records. It was however necessary to wait until the early 1950s to see the publication of the first commissioned major research — the *History of Unilever,* by Charles Wilson (1954).

In the meantime another symptom of change had already emerged: the renewed consciousness of the importance of preserving private business records, which resulted in the creation of the Council for the Preservation of Business Archives (1934), with professor G. N. Clark as its first chairman. This institution prospers nowadays under the name of Business Archives Council (Coleman:143, Williams 1989/90:534). Since the 1950s commissioned companies histories have been growing in number, although their quality is far from being homogenously high. In 1987 Donald Coleman enumerated the many "abuses" that were still afflicting a great part of the business history produced in his country: "anecdotal, soap opera history; unreadable academic company histories, which are wholly narrative and without any analysis of the involved issues; mere public relations purposes in commissioning company histories; and all unread histories" (Coleman, 1987:154).

Things had not much improved since another critical review of the British literature in the field, written ten years before by Roy Church. While observing that there was "probably no field of contemporary history so formidably dull as business history", he complained especially about the lack of conceptualization and the "too narrow focus" of business history in that country (Church 1976). Even so, one has to mention at least two major English contributions of the 1960s and 1970s: the first is Sidney Pollard's pathbreaking contribution to the analysis of business organization, accounting and finance at the time of the Industrial Revolution (Pollard 1965); and the second, Leslie Hannah's innovative research on the origins and evolution of corporate economy in Britain, the first study (even before Chandler's) to refer explicitly to Williamson's transaction cost analysis (Hannah 1976).

The creation in 1979 of the Business History Unit at the London School of Economics has been a further and potentially important development within the evolution of the discipline in the UK. It gathered business historians "who had formally proclaimed their intention to study business history in a wider, internationally comparative framework, with more attention to generalizations and to the kind of conceptual insights which Alfred Chandler had pioneered in America" (Hannah 1983:166). Unfortunately, during its first life period BHU has only partly succeeded in fulfilling its initial purposes. Unlike to the US, in Britain, business history has so far failed to define a sound and autonomous path of research, as well as to create its own institutional setting (Williams: 1989/90: 533-6).

By birth right, also Germany should be put among the first-comers with regard to the development of its own school of business history, the origins of which can be traced back to the second half of the nineteenth century. At that time, academic interest in the history of enterprise was spurred by Karl Marx's historical analysis of industrial capitalism, Max Weber's pathbreaking insights in the genesis of business attitudes and administrative organizations, as well as by the empirical case-studies approach developed by the German historical school of political economy. This school, in particular, would have a deep and lasting influence, as "its strong empirical bias" and "its reluctance to generalize on its findings are even today very influential in West Germany business history" (Wengenroth 1987: 410).

By 1914, some major contributions to the history of banks, cartels and heavy industry (although not strictly company histories) had already been published by leading scholars of the historical school, like Riesser, Stillich, Heymann, Jeidels and Liefmann. By then, however, also a number of official company histories had been produced, the so called *Festschriften.* If only few of them could be considered good examples of early business history, they all played an important role in preserving business records, since the writing of these *Festschriften* "usually marked the beginnings of what was to become the company's historical archives" (Wengenroth 1987: 412). Professor Richard Ehrenberg's undertaking of the history of Siemens marked the opening of company history to professional academics (Ehrenberg 1906), a practice which was to become more common during the interwar period, as witnessed by Walter Dabritz's studies on the Bochumer Verein, the Disconto-Gesellschaft and Hanomag.

Due to the long parenthesis of the war and after-war periods, it was only in the late 1950s that an actual revival of business history in Germany could be registered. An important development for it was the foundation in 1956 of the journal *Tradition,* specialized in the history of enterprise and entrepreneurial biography. In 1977, it was taken over by the newly created German Society for Business History, the GUG (Gesellschaft für Unternehmensgeschichte), and changed its title to *Zeitschrift für Unternehmensgeschichte.* Both in its first phase and in the following, this journal was charadterized by a strong historicistic approach and an explicit preference towards narration and description. Issues elsewhere widely discussed, like conceptualization and methodology, were not even mentioned in the rather disappointing report on the first decade of the Society's activities (Pohl 1987). Even if some recent contributions seem to escape this general rule, they most properly pertain to the fields of economic history, social history and financial history (see, for instance, Kocka 1969; Fremdling 1975; Hertner 1986; Wengenroth 1986). However, not a secondary exception can be found in Kocka's reasonable attempts to approach the growth of the modern German enterprise from a neo-institutionalist perspective (Kocka 1978 and 1980).

II

Business history has been a rather recent accomplishment in Italy (where it started in the 1970s) and in Spain (where it registered a further ten-years lag). The lagging of the discipline in the Mediterranean countries was primarily the consequence of their economic and industrial backwardness, but one should not undervalue also the effects of inadequate entrepreneurial capabilites, cultural provincialism, ideological as well as — in the case of Spain — political constraints (Tortella and Coll, 1992).

Since there actually are more similarities than diversities between the patterns of growth of these two countries (Prados and Zamagni, 1992), they show many common features in the evolution of their respective business historiographies. First of all, the cultural histories of the two countries have suffered from a lasting, subtle antindustrialist spirit — either in the form of a negative approach to the capitalist system, or of an underhand opposition to modernization and growth — whose roots can be traced back as far as to the Catholic Counter-Reformation. Secondly, after the last World War, a reciprocal distrust has emerged between historians and entrepreneurs. This can be explained, on the research side, by a tendency to point to the business enterprise as the central devil of capitalism, a tendency which in Italy grew out of two hegemonic cultures — the catholic and the marxist — while stemming in Spain from the prejudice that the only legimitate wealth is the inherited one. This has reflected in a reluctance of the entrepreneurs to disclose their archives, whose secrets, they feared, could be used as a negative propaganda (Segreto 1992:13; Tortella and Coll, 1992).

Therefore, during quite a long period, business history in both countries consisted only of few celebrating official firm-histories, with limited, if any, heuristic value. However, since the early seventies, things have changed in Italy, thanks to a few pathbreaking researches: a volume on Giovanni Agnelli, that was more a history of Fiat than a biography of its founder (Castronovo 1971); the history of a great iron and steel undertaking, Terni (Bonelli 1975); and the three-volumes research on the origins of the main Italian German-type bank, Banca Commerciale (Confalonieri 1974-76). Moreover, a very important contribution came paradoxally from younger students with Marxist background, previously involved in studying the evolution of the factory and plant's organization and technology, the history of industrial relations and of the class-struggle:

> "Many of us thought that the best way of explaining these issues was to go back to study the process by which Taylorism was introduced in the Italian manufacturing system: from here to a renewed attention to business history it was quite a short step". (Bigazzi 1990:20).

In 1983, a great part of these young scholars gathered around the Associazione di Storia e Studi Sull'impresa (later transformed in the Fondazione ASSI), directed by Giulio Sapelli. Its purposes were not only to stimulate empirical studies in business history, and to foster the cooperation between scholars and managers and entrepreneurs, but also to bridge the gap between historical research and other social sciences, particularly economics, business organization and sociology. In ten years of life the Foundation has produced more than twenty monographs published in ASSI series, and has been editing three periodicals — the *Annali di Storia d'Impresa,* a yearbook of business history, *Archivi e Imprese,* with a strong specialization in the matter of archives and business records, and *Industrial and Corporate Change,* an international publication with its focus on issues at the edge between theory and history. In can be said with certainty that, in this case, Italian business history has been enjoying the advantages of the late-comers, as it is trying to exploit the past experiences of the discipline in other countries.

Spanish business history, on the other hand, is still very young and has not reached important results so far — at least not as remarkable as the ones already got by quantitative economic history (Martin Aceña and Prados 1985). Therefore it seems too early to strike any balance (Puig Raposo and Torres Villanueva 1992:44).

On the whole, however, one can agree with Tortella and Coll (1992: 57) as they maintain that "the major connotations of Spanish business history are its extreme empiricism and its absolute lack of theory and conceptualization", even if this characteristic is mourned for almost everywhere in Europe. But, recent major exceptions can be found also in Spain, especially with regard to the history of banking (Tortella 1974; Tortella and Jimenez 1986; Tedde 1988; Lacomba and Ruiz 1990) and of public (state-owned) enterprises (Comin and Martin Aceña 1991a; 1991b).

Here again some connections can be found with the Italian experience, where studies in the history of state-owned companies are having a revival, partly as a consequence of the present discussions on privatization. Yet, the focus now is more micro-behavioral than it was in the past, dealing with subjects like the public management culture and power, the conditionining of strategy and structure by parties and politics, the actual reconstruction of the economic performance, namely on if and how economic performance can get along with the "public mission" of those institutions (Roverato 1991; Balconi 1991; Sapelli and Carnevale 1992; Sapelli et al., 1993).

Finally, there is the quite puzzling case of the French business history, of which it has been said recently that

> *"malgré l'éclosion de quelques belles oeuvres, il est incontestable que la France a alors pris un retard quantitatif, voire qualitatif"* (Daviet, 1987:429).

The puzzle is twofold. On the one hand, today's level of evolution and growth of the French economic and industrial system would deserve a more developed level of research in the field than has been actually reached. On the other, much of the delay which Daviet is talking about has emerged in the 1960s and early 1970s, at the very moment in which, in other countries, the discipline was reaching a sort of take-off. The explanations offered to the puzzle point mostly to same direction:

> *"Il y a aussi une raison plus spécifiquement française à la séparation qui existe dans notre pays entre l'histoire et la gestion. La connaissance historique s'obtient par la recherche... cette démarche n'est guère prise en considération en France dans la formation des gestionnaires; ici on*

préfère enseigner la résolution des problèmes à l'aide de techniques confirmées" (Doublet and Fridenson, 1988:1).

"La France a été caractérisée par un paysage intellectuel relativament original, de nature à infléchir la tournure de la recherche: pensée economique... plus portée à une analyse macro-économique de la croissance teintée de saint-simonisme qu'à la théorie de la firme (idéologie de la planification, du dirigisme à la française), pensée historique dominée par l'étude des conjonctures (Ernest Labrousse) et surtout divorce entre université et entreprises" (Daviet 1987:431).

Yet during the late 1950s a certain dynamism could be observed in French business history, which then seemed to be able to follow approximately what was happening in the UK and in Germany. It was probably linked to the economic growth of the country and to a renewed interest in technical progress, and was mostly the result of the initiative of Bertrand Gille. He created in 1955 the Centre de Recherches sur l'Histoire des Enterprises, which published its own bulletin. A little later the Centre became connected to the École Pratique des Hautes Études, and the bulletin was transformed into a quite remarkable journal *Histoire des Entreprises.* Unfortunately, however, these inititiatives were to clash with a cultural environment quite negative towards the history of enterprise, of the same kind to be found in Italy and Spain. After only five years, the journal was closed, and the Centre hardly survived. It was necessary to wait until 1992 to see the appearance of a new French journal, *Entreprises et Histoire,* thanks to the efforts of some leading business and economic historians. Therefore, up to the late 1970s business history in France was more the outcome of few scattered scholars — although of great value, like Jean Bouvier, François Caron, Pierre Léon and Maurice Lévy-Leboyer — than of an organized school. However, the climate changed again as leading companies — like Saint-Gobain, Pont-à-Mousson, Électricité de France, Renault, Rhône-Poulenc — began to open their archives and to encourage research in their histories. Remarkable studies like the ones on Saint-Gobain and Pont-à-Mousson could therefore be undertaken (Daviet 1983; Baudant 1980).

III

If one has to search for a common thread linking the research experiences sketched above this can be found in the empirical approach which has so far dominated European business history. And yet, almost everywhere, a need of conceptualization has been emerging recently, and efforts to produce "general" business history have been undertaken, in order to define an analytical framework useful to compare the different patterns of growth. Undoubtedly, a powerful influence to this development has been exerted by what was going on in the United States.

Since the early 1960s, American business history had become increasingly dominated by the "organizational" or "neo-institutionalist" approach, which Louis Galambos quite happily termed the "organizational synthesis" (Galambos 1970). Stemming out from Alfred Chandler's pathbreaking *Strategy and Structure*, this approach received its ultimate international consecration with the publication by the same author of the Pulitzer winner *The Visible Hand* (Chandler 1962 and 1977). Chandler's unrivalled contributions to business history were to allow the discipline extrapolation fron the narrow boundaries — of narration and description — within which it had been mostly confined until the early sixties, and to demonstrate that the discipline could be something better than a pure collection of biographies company studies, not rarely sponsored by the very firms of which the story was to be told. His efforts were pushing towards generalization: the identification of the mechanisms which explain the success and growth of American big entreprises into the efficient multidivisional big corporations of the twentieth century. As it is by now well known, these had to be searched for in the organizational revolution brought about by changes in technologies and markets, which allowed efficient managerial hierarchies to take the place "of the market mechanisms in coordinating the activities of the economy and allocating its resources" (Chandler 1977:1).

Besides its lasting influence on American business history, in the late 1970s and 1980s, the Chandlerian paradigm also won an increasing consensus outside the United States, favoured by the temporary coming to Harvard of younger European scholars — like Leslie Hannah, Jürgen Kocka, Patrick Fridenson and Franco Amatori — bound to become leading business historians in their respective countries. Articles which were Chandlerian in spirit, if not in substance, began to appear in the few European journals devoted to business history which were just mentioned. Some important collections of essays, focused on the evolution of the forms of entreprises in various European countries, as well as in Japan, were published, giving emphasis to another main aspect of the "Harvard paradigm", the comparative approach (Habakkuk and Postan 1988; Chandler and Daems 1980).

This in turn would soon become the basic methodology of Chandler's most recent large and ambitious comparative study (Chandler 1990). At the same time — as already said — centres and institutions for the study of business history, more or less distinct and separate from the academy, were created, somehow drawing inspiration from the Harvard Research Center in Entrepreneurial History. Such were the cases of the Business History Unit at the London School of Economics, and of the Associazione di Storia e Studi Sull'impresa (ASSI) in Milan.

Yet, similarly to what was occurring in economic history itself, Old Europe's cultural yielding to ideas and methods coming from overseas was far from being complete. To tell the truth, it doesn't seem that there is much agreement on this point — at least as far as the most developed European school of business history, the British one, is concerned. In the very same journal, *Business History*, at a distance of only three years, sentences like the following were published:

> "In Britain... the impact of the Chandlerian revolution has been less marked. Leslie Hannah, in the *Rise of the Corporate Economy*, makes use of some of Chandler's ideas... However, few British authors have followed Hannah in the application or testing of Chandlerian concepts" (Harvey and Jones, 1990:5).

> "Having read the 1991 business history literature, my abiding impression is of the enduring influence of Alfred Chandler" (Chick, 1993:1).

According to my own impression, the first proposition is more equilibrated than the second, it can be extended as well to much of European business history. Speaking again of the English case, resistance to Chandlerianism has been attributed to "an excessive attachment to the empirical method, innate conservatism, and an insularity of mind which breeds hostility towards innovative ideas originating abroad" (Harvey and Jones, 1990:5). Let us suppose that even if this were a sound enough explanation for the British experience, one should search for diverse but much as good reasons for fitting the behaviour of the remaining European countries, unless this explanation could hold for most of them too, which is, in part, probably true.

But there are perhaps other, more convincing, motivations — which should be traced back to the evolution of history and culture in Continental Europe, if not to the development of each of its leading countries. Looking at the history of the Western world in the last centuries, the model of growth of the United States seems more an exception than a rule. The size of the country, the abundance of its resources, the lack of a precise cultural identity — as a result of the continuous inflow of immigrants to check the country's structural shortage of workforce — the dynamics of the internal market and the relative isolation on the international one, the mildness of the conflicts arising from the industrial relations, all these, and other more, were the elements which combined to form an original and peculiar pattern of growth (Toninelli 1993).

The problem, then, is to evaluate to what extent historical approaches and methodologies best suited to such a different reality can be trasposed to our old and small countries. This was rather well understood by William Parker almost a quarter of century ago, when he tried to explain the different success of cliometrics in the two continents, namely the insistent American relying on neoclassic partial or general equilibrium models:

> "We [the Americans] have really very little experience outside the South with societies that are class structured in any obvious and fundamental way — class structured as a matter of theory and príncipe as well as practice. So we tend to think that social classes are a devilish invention of Karl Marx. We have really no intuitive grasp of why backward societies are backward, why defeated peoples are defeated, why people torn by social antagonism are so torn, though we are beginning to get this experience in this generation. I see all this very clearly in my own background and makeup... We have an incredibly optimistic and optimizing mentality and these mental traits have been set

in good part by our history, a history which has produced the ignoring of history as one of its prominent traits. It will be hard for us to hold ourselves back from studying either on the one end economic engineering or on the other the psychology of individual entrepreneurs, and to devote ourselves to studying how social organizations are created through human action and how in turn they mold and channel human action" (Parker, 1971, p. 12-13).

As a matter of fact, in recent years, it was out of the United States that economic history has been nurturing interesting new approaches, either on the side of quantitative research (time-series analyses, ARIMA models etc.) or on the one of the application of the new heteredox theories recently grown up outside the boundaries of the mainstream (for a discussion on this point, see Baccini and Giannetti 1990). However, we cannot undervalue the contributions also offered by a few American scholars, who tried to penetrate their macro-analysis whith problems and questions typical, of the microeconomic approach — like technological convergence, localized learning, path-dependence, bounded rationality, agency problems and so on (Rosenberg 1976, 1982; David 1975, 1985, 1992; Hughes 1993; Arthur 1989; Raff and Temin 1991). This is likely to tighten even more the links between economic history and business history with the two respective fields of research being probably bound to get at least partly superimposed. Perhaps business history has only to gain from this, both at the teorethical and the quantitative level, as it can push its conceptualization beyond the organizational synthesis and improve its efforts toward measurement and quantification (Hutchinson and Nicholas, 1988; Harvey, 1989; Lee, 1990a and 1990b).

IV

Chandler's sturdy framework has never looked more fragile than today, shaken as it was by concentric attacks coming both from the United States and Europe. Paradoxically the 1990 publication of what was so far the missing roof of the building, *Scale and Scope,* revealed itself as the weakest part of the construction. In fact, the powerful mechanisms of explanation of the performance of US big business, once transposed to non-American cases, are only marginally useful for enlightening the internal dynamics of the other countries examined in the volume — Great Britain, Japan and Germany. The weakness seemed more evident particularly in the first case, not to speak of other Wetstern countries to which it might be eventually applied (Church 1990; Morikawa 1990; Kocka 1990; Fishlow 1990; Hannah 1991; Supple 1991). Chandler's up-to-date version of the interplay between strategy and structure, and of the leading role of managerial hierarchies, focuses on the crucial process of the three pronged-investment (in production, distribution and managerial skills) and on the collateral enhancement of organizational capabilites within the firm. Large firms compete through what he calls 'functional and strategic effectiveness', and the first-movers tend to survive and prosper. This should hold particularly in the case of the US, where the pioneers of modern enterprise still remain among the outstanding and most succesfull businesses of today (Chandler, 1990, p. 8-17).

But the question remains of how useful these tools can be — formulated as they were within a context dominated by large enterprises — in countries where not only such enterprises were — and still remain — very few, but where the very process of separation between property and control is also still far from being completed? We might even accept this reformulation of the Chandlerian paradigm as a valid explanation of the performance of those sectors of the European economies more or less dominated by large enterprises, although it sill has to be demonstrated that, in those large undertakings, particularly in the Mediterranean countries, managerial capitalism has really replaced family capitalism. But this would be only a very partial contribution to the analysis of how the business system works, of what happens outside the world of the "happy few", and — above all — of what makes possible the transition from one form to another of business and of economic structure.

This takes us directly to what, in my opinion, is the heart of the problem: the inadequate dynamism of the Chandlerian model. This emerged already in previous works, especially in the second part of the *Visible Hand*, where the passage from the invisible to the visible hand stands out more as a problem of substitution by — or opposition to one other — than of growth and development, since the driving forces of its model, technology and market changes were considered exogenous. Does there not exist some intermediate form between market and managerial hierarchies? What about industrial districts, networks of firms, and the role of small and medium size enteprises? What about the action of State and finance in development, the two old-fashion Gerschenkronian factors of growth of the late-comers? All these remain undoubtedly very important elements to be counted for in any explanation of performance of the industrial and business systems of Europe.

Actually, according to some recent contributions, it seems that not all of those elements can be removed without problems even in analyzing the evolution and the performance of the American economy — namely of its business sector — from the last decades of nineteenth century onwards. Admittedly, attempts to remedy to these deficiencies in order to dynamize Chandler's model, and to overcome criticism concerning the implicit determinism of his vision of the growth of the enterprise have been made by some of his disciples. For istance, we can mention the highly meritorious effort by Bill Lazonick to conjugate Schumpeter's theory of innovation, Marx's dynamic conception of the capitalist economy and, more recently, Nelson and Winter's evolutionary theory of the firm with Chandler's organizational synthesis — an effort which looks quite promising (Lazonick 1991 and 1992).

Not surprisingly, the discussions about the methodology applied and the conclusions reached by the "Harvard School" have recently become more lively and compact, and criticisms more explicit, as a number of non-enthusiastic reviews of *Scale and Scape* in some leading American journals are likely to suggest (Parker 1991; Rosenberg 1991; Sherer et al. 1990). At the same time, during the last decade, a certain revisionism of the Chandlerian approach has emerged within the United States too, going so far as to propose alternative analytical frameworks. Here, I will mention them only to the extent they can be useful in explaining what, for the time being, looks as the most promising field of research for European business history.

First of all, I think that every scholar in the field should reflect upon the few questions recently put by Louis Galambos. He certainly does not reject the analytical framework that he himself had contributed to set up, but he feels that now the moment has come to enlarge that very framework in order to encompass "new methodologies and interests". In fact, by providing business history with "brilliant organizing principles", the Chandlerian framework marked "the climax of specialization", but failed "to develop a general synthesis" in which the findings of the new researchs in business history would fit: "If anything, it worked against that end by portraying America's central corporate institutions in relative isolation, separated from their social and political settings" (Galambos, 1992, p. 6).

In Galambos' opinion, there are few questions that business historians cannot anymore avoid to deal with. The main one are: *i)* the question of power, of its changing distribution, and particularly the question of the impact of business power upon society; *ii)* the question of how the development of business altered the distribution of income and wealth: "While our readers may or may not want to know a great deal about functional departments and structural decentralization, they will I assure you want to know how business has contributed to and detracted from the performance of the national economy" (Op. cit., 7); *iii)* the question of the "rationalization syndrome", one of the central myths of the discipline, strongly characterized by ex-post underlying functionalism which conceals the social as well as human problems always connected with rationalization policies; *iv)* finally, the question of overcoming the usual bias of the organizational approach of business history, which focuses on the internal top-management perspective. As a consequence, all transformations in business systems seem to take place without social frictions, while the implicit suggestion is that there are "no losers in business history, only winners over the long run" (Idem, p. 10).

The observations by Galambos were referred primarily to the American experience, and they can be read as a serious plea for a profound re-thinking of the discipline in the United States. But they also sound as an invaluable agenda for the research in the field of our Continent, an agenda in which organizational problems are brought back to their effective role within the wider framework of the evolution of the relationship between the socio-economic context and the enterprise.

As a matter of fact, there are to my knowledge, a few European studies which fulfill in great part Galambos's requirements. I am thinking of the volume by Alain Baudant (1980) on the evolution of the Pont-à-Mousson during the interwar period, of the research by Andrew Pettigrew (1985) on the role and influence of inherited cultures and traditional routines upon ICI recent experiences and evolution, as well as of the one by Duccio Bigazzi (1988) on the first twenty years of Alfa Romeo. The latter, especially, makes explicit a methodological approach which succesfully tries to conjugate business history and social history within the general framework of the evolution of the Italian economy, society and politics. Consequently, one can follow the interplay performed by entrepreneurs, managers, financiers, workers, trade-union-men in the take-off of the Italian automobile industry, and the difficult achievement of one of its leading branches.

V

If Galambos's agenda can act as a general framework of analysis for both European and US business historians, there are other American contributions that appear very appealing and useful in addressing specific paths of research in either continent. One, in particular, seems to me very suggestive, since, by evoking issues so far neglected by American business history, it actually raises problems of great relevance to the European experience. I am referring to a short essay by Philip Scranton, in which three fairly new axes for development of American business history are suggested: small business, family firms and batch production. Although these forms of enterprise are "intricately meshed within the workings of the business system" they have been "left in the shadows" and at most "treated as residual", particularly insofar studies and researches have centered on manufacturing.

> "Each of these realms for future research calls business historians to step outside the Chandler's motifs, outside the teleologies of triumphal managerialism and, with some exception, outside the format of the company history" (Scranton 1991a:100).

It is almost superfluous to point out that these subjects are actual and fundamental to European historians, even more than to the American, as the previous discussion has already suggested. Yet, one cannot forget the arduous problems arising along this path of research — for instance, the lack of adequate conceptualizations, and the difficulties in producing reliable quantifications, not to mention the sometimes insurmountable hindrances to the attaining to the appropriate business records. Let's pay attention for instance to what Maxine Berg has to say with regard to past tendenciers and present trends of British business history:

> "Our economic histories of Britain's industries have largely been written in the light of the view that bigger what better. Larger scale has been associated with greater efficiency, lower relative costs, and greater ability to develop and use new technology. (...). These analyses maintain a strong grip on our histories of industrial structures. Many of these histories are fundamentally teleologies, charting the emergence of the outstandingly large, wealthy and succesfull firms and entrepreneurs as the yardstick of industrialization. To some extent this is the bias encouraged by historical record. Few but large-scale producers left extensive business papers; and most official records, tax, government enquiry and legal records were biased towards wealthier producers. The result is a historical chasm between the known — the factory system and large-scale production — and the unknown — the artisan and the small — and medium-scale producer" (Berg 1993, p. 18).

However, in the last ten or fifteen years, some progress in the right direction has been made, both in Europe and in the United States, and both at the empirical and the conceptual levels. I am thinking, for instance, of the by now classic conceptualizations along neo-marshallian lines of the industrial districts by Becattini and Brusco; I am tinking as well of the discussion about historical alternatives to mass-production by Sabel and Zeitlin (Becattini 1979; Brusco 1982; Sabel and Zeitlin 1985). But see also, among others, Sabel 1982; Scranton 1983, 1989 and 1991b; Piore and Sabel 1984; Tolliday and Zeitlin 1985; ASSI/ISUC 1987; Magatti 1991; Sorrentino 1991; Berg 1993.

Most recently, Giulio Sapelli has raised a caveat against the conceptual dangers and disasters nowadays facing business history. In his opinion, economic reductionism has grown up out of a bad assimilation of Chandler's complex analytical fresco. This reductionism — that is the complete separation between the economy on one side, and society and politics on the other — is transforming business history into a redundant ornament, void of any heuristic value.

In order to overcome these perils, it becomes necessary to open the discipline to the issues and methods of sociology, anthropology and political thought: family and culture systems, social routines and behaviour, kinship, clan and clientele groups, political lobbies and parties, institutions, legislation and jurisprudence; all these are factors that help in moulding the way in which firms and businessmes behave (Sapelli 1993).

Fascinating as it is, this proposal has nevertheless to be taken with caution, being now exposed to dangers just opposite to those of reductionism: holism and wholeness. Excess of specialization as well as absolute lack of it end up in the same way: they don't explain anything. On the other hand, as we have already seen, a number of the issues that seem most relevant to European business history cannot be tackled *per se* though a strictly organizational, if not economic methodology. Where economics and organization cannot manage to arrive, other social sciences sometimes can; and, in this respect, Sapelli's suggestions hit the mark.

References

Arthur B. "Competing Technologies, Incresing Returns and Lock-in by Historical Events". *Economic Journal* 99. 1989.

ASSI/ISUC (eds.) *Piccola e Grande Impresa. Un Problema Storico.* Milano: F. Angeli. 1987.

Baccini A. & Giannetti R. *Cliometria.* Firenze, mimeo. 1990.

Baudant A. *Pont-à-Mousson 1918-1939, stratégies industrielles d'une dynastie lorraine.* Paris: Publications de la Sorbonne. 1980.

Balconi M. *La Siderurgia Italiana 1945-1990. Tra controllo pubblico e incentivi del mercato.* Bologna: Il Mulino. 1991.

Becattini G. "Dal 'settore' industriale al 'distretto' industriale". *Rivista di Economia e Politica Industriale,* n. 1. 1979.

Berg M. "Small Producer Capitalism in Eighteenth-Century England". *Business History,* n. 1. 1993.

Bigazzi D. *Il Portello. Operai, tecnici e imprenditori all' Alfa Romeo 1906-1926.* Milano: F. Angeli. 1988.

—— *La storia d'impresa in Italia. Saggio bibliografico 1980-1987.* Milano: F. Angeli. 1990.

Bonelli F. *Lo Sviluppó di una Grande Impresa in Italia. La Terni dal 1884 al 1962.* Torino: Einaudi. 1975.

Brusco S. "The Emilian Model: Productive Decentralization and Social Integration". *Cambridge Journal of Economics*. June. 1982.

Castronovo V. *Giovanni Agnelli*. Torino: UTET (reprint Torino: Einaudi 1977). 1971.

Chandler A. D. Jr. *Strategy and Structure. Chapters in the History of the American Industrial Enterprise*. Cambridge: Harvard Univ. Press. 1962.

—— *The Visible Hand: The Managerial Revolution in American Business*. Cambridge: Harvard Univ. Press. 1977.

—— *Scale and Scope: The Dynamics of Industrial Capitalism*. Cambridge: Harvard Univ. Press. 1990.

—— & Daems H. *Managerial Hierarchies. Comparative Perspectives on the Rise of Modern Industrial Enterprise*. Cambridge: Harvard Univ. Press. 1980.

Chick M. "British Business History: A Review of the Periodical Literature for 1991". *Business History*, n. 1. 1993.

Church R. "Business History in England". *Journal of European Economic History*. Spring. 1976.

—— "The Limitations of the Personal Capitalism Paradigm". *Business History Review*. Winter. 1990.

Coleman D. "The Uses and Abuses of Business History". *Business History*. April. 1987.

Comin F. & Martin Aceña P. (eds.) *Historia de la Empresa Pública en España*. Madrid: Espasa Calpe. 1991a.

—— *INI. 50 años de Industrialización en España*. Madrid: Espasa Calpe. 1991b.

Confalonieri A. *Banca e Industria in Italia 1894-1906*. Milano: Banca Commerciale Italiana (reprint Bologna: Il Mulino 1979-80). 1974-76.

David P. *Technical Choice, Innovation and Economic Growth*. Cambridge: Cambridge Univ. Press. 1975.

—— "Clio and the Economics of QWERTY". *American Econ. Review*. 75. 1985.

—— "Heroes, Herds and Hysteresis in Technological History. Thomas Edison and the 'Battle of the Systems' Reconsidered". *Industrial and Corporate Change*. n. 1. 1992.

Daviet J. P. *La compagnie de Saint-Gobain de 1830 à 1939, une entreprise française à rayonnement international*. Paris, mimeo. 1983.

—— "Existe-t-il une business history française?", *Annali di storia dell'impresa*, 3. 1987.

Doublet J. M. & Fridenson P. "L'histoire et la gestion: un pari". *Revue Française de Gestion*. Septembre-Octobre. 1988.

Ehrenberg R. *Die Unternehmungen der Brüder Siemens*. Jena. 1906.

Fishlow A. "Developing Countries and the Modern Firm". *Business History Review*. Winter. 1990.

Fremdling R. *Eisenbahnen und Wirtschaftswachstum 1840-1879.* Dortmund. 1975.

Galambos L. "The Emerging Organizational Synthesis in Modern American History". *Business History Review.* Autumn. 1970.

—— "What Makes Us Think We Can Put Business Back Into American History?". *Business and Economic History* 21. 1992.

Habakkuk H. J. & Postan M. (eds.) *Cambridge Economic History of Europe,* vol. VII. *The Industrial Economies: Capital, Labour, and Enterprise,* Cambridge: Cambridge Univ. Press. 1978.

Hannah L. *The Rise of the Corporate Economy.* London: Methuen. 1976.

—— "New Issues in British Business History". *Business History Review.* Summer. 1983.

—— "Scale and Scope: Towards a European Visible Hand?", *Business History.* April. 1991.

Harvey C. "Business History: Concepts and Measurement". *Business History.* July. 1989.

—— & Jones G. "Business History in Britain into the 1990s", *Business History.* January.

Hertner P. *Il Capitale Tedesco in Italia dall'Unità alla Prima Guerra Mondiale.* Bologna: Il Mulino. 1986.

Hughes T. *Networks of Power.* Baltimore: The Johns Hopkins Univ. Press. 1983.

Hutchinson D. & Nicholas S. "Theory and Business History: New Approaches to Institutional Change". *Journal of European Econ. History,* n. 3. 1988.

Kocka J. *Unternehmensverwaltung und Angestelltenschaft am Beispiel Siemens 1847-1914.* Stuttgart. 1969.

—— *Entrepreneurs and Managers in German Industrialization,* in Habakkuk and Postan (1978). 1978.

—— *The Rise of Modern Industrial Entreprise in Germany,* in Chandler and Daems (1980). 1980.

—— "Germany: Cooperation and Competition". *Business History Review.* Winter. 1990.

Lacomba J. A. & Ruiz G. *Una Historia del Banco Hipotecario de España.* Madrid: Alianza. 1990.

Lazonick W. *Business Organization and the Myth of the Market Economy.* Cambridge: Cambridge Univ. Press. 1991.

—— "Controlling the Market for Corporate Control:The Historical Significance of Managerial Capitalism". *Industrial and Corporate Change* 3. 1992.

Lee C. H. "Corporate Behaviour in Theory and History: I. The Evolution of Theory". *Business History,* n. 1. 1990a.

—— "Corporate Behaviour in Theory and History: II. The Historian Perspective". *Business History*, n. 2. 1990b.

Magatti M. *Mercato e Forze Sociali: Due distretti tessili: Lancashire e Ticino Olona 1950-1980.* Bologna: Il Mulino. 1991.

Martin Aceña P. & Prados de la Escosura L. *La Nueva Historia Economica en España.* Madrid: Alianza. 1985.

Morikawa H. "The View from Japan". *Business History Review.* Winter. 1990.

Parker W. N. "From Old to New to Old in Economic History". *Journal of Economic History.* January. 1971.

—— "The *Scale and Scope* of Alfred Chandler Jr.". *Journal of Economic History.* December. 1991.

Pettigrew A. *The Awakening Giant. Continuity and Change at ICI.* Oxford: Oxford University Press. 1985.

Piore M. J. & Sabel C. F. *The Second Industrial Divide.* New York: Basic Books. 1984.

Pohl H. "The Society for Business History: A Decade of Work". *German Yearbook on Business History 1987.* 1987.

Pollard S. *The Genesis of Modern Management.* Harvard: Cambridge Univ. Press. 1965.

Prados de la Escosura L. & Zamagni V. (eds.) *El Desarollo Economico en la Europa del Sur: España e Italia en Perspectiva Historica.* Madrid: Alianza. 1992.

Puig Raposo N. & Torres Víllanueva E. "La storia d'impresa in Spagna. Una rassegna bibliografica". *Annali di storia dell'impresa* 8. 1992.

Raff D. M. G. & Temin P. *Business History and Recent Economic Theory: Imperfect Information, Incentives and the International Organization of the Firm, in Inside the Business Enterprise* (ed. by P. Temin). Chicago: The Univ. of Chicago Press. 1991.

Rosenberg N. *Perspectives on Technology.* Cambridge: Cambridge Univ. Press. 1976.

—— *Inside the Black Box. Technology and Economics.* Cambridge: Cambridge Univ. Press. 1982.

—— "Review" to *Scale and Scope*, in *Journal of Political Economy*, n. 6. 1991.

Roverato G. *Nuovo Pignone. Le Sfide della Maturità.* Bologna: Il Mulino. 1991.

Sabel C. F. *Works and Politics: The Division of Labour in Industry*, Cambridge: Cambridge Univ. Press.

—— & Zeitlin J. "Historical Alternatives to Mass Production: Politics, Markets and Technology in Nineteenth Century Industrialization". *Past and Present.* August (also in ASSI/ISUC 1987). 1985.

Sapelli G. "Civilizzazione e Cultura per la Storia d'Impresa". LIUC Papers, Serie Storia Economica, n. 1, mimeo. 1993.

—— & Carnevali F. *Uno Sviluppo tra Politica e Strategia. ENI (1953-1995).* Milano: F. Angeli. 1992.

Sapelli G., Orsenigo L. & Toninelli P. A. *Continuità e Cambiamento: La Vicenda dell'Agip Petroli 1960-1990.* Bologna: Il Mulino (forthcoming). 1993.

Segreto L. "Dalla storia economica alla storia d'impresa. L'avvio del dibattito in Spagna". *Annali di storia dell'impresa* 8. 1992.

Sherer F. M. et al. *"Scale and Scope:* A Review Colloqium". *Business History Review.* Winter. 1990.

Scranton, P. *Proprietary Capitalism. The Textile Manufacture at Philadelphia 1800-1885.* New York: Cambridge Univ. Press. 1983.

—— *Figured Tapestry: Production, Markets and Power in Philadelphia Textiles, 1885-1941.* New York: Cambridge Univ. Press. 1989.

—— "Small Business, Family Firms, and Batch Production: Three Axes for Development in American Business History". *Business and Economic History,* vol. 20. 1991a.

—— "Diversity in Diversity: Flexible Production and American Industrialization, 1880-1930". *Business History Review.* Spring. 1991b.

Sorrentino T. "Appunti per una storia del distretto industriale di Sassuolo". *Annali di storia dell'impresa* 7. 1991.

Supple B. "Scale and scope. Alfred Chandler and the dynamics of industrial capitalism". *Economic History Review.* August. 1991.

Tedde P. *El Banco de San Carlos.* Madrid: Alianza. 1988.

Tolliday S. & Zeitlin J. (eds.) *Shoop Floor Bargaining and the State: Historical and Comparative Perspective.* Cambridge: Cambridge Univ. Press. 1985.

Toninelli P. A. *Schiavi, Pionieri, Macchine. Alle Origini dello Sviluppo Economico degli Stati Uniti 1780-1914.* Bologna: Il Mulino. 1993.

Tortella G. (ed.) *La Banca Española en la Restauración.* Madrid. 1974.

—— & Coll S. "Riflessioni sulla storia d'impresa: lo stato della questione in Spagna". *Annali di Storia dell'Impresa* 8. 1992.

—— & Jimenez J. C. *Historia del Banco de Credito Industrial.* Madrid: Alianza. 1986.

Wengenroth U. *Unternehmensstrategien und technischer Fortschritt. Die deutsche und die britische Stahlindustrie.* Gottingen. 1986.

—— "Business History in Germany". *Annali di storia dell'impresa* 3. 1987.

Williams M. A. "Storia d'Impresa nel Regno Unito: tendenze recenti". *Annali di Storia dell'Impresa* 5/6. 1989/90.

Carlos Marichal
Colegio de México

HISTORIOGRAFIA DE LA BANCA LATINOAMERICANA: SU DESPEGUE, 1970-1993

En la mayoría de las historias económicas generales de América Latina todavia se presta poca atención al papel de los bancos en la evolución económica a largo plazo. Ello resulta sorprendente si consideramos que los bancos se cuentan entre las empresas capitalistas más importantes y más antiguas en la mayoría de los países latinoamericanos; obsérvese, en este sentido, que un buen número de las instituciones financieras más grandes datan de hace más de un siglo. Pero, además, resulta todavía más extraño si tenemos en cuenta el lugar clave que han ocupado en la historia financiera y política de casi todos los países de la región, en especial en su función como bancos de los gobiernos.

¿Cuales pueden ser las razones que expliquen esta extraña laguna? Algunas pueden considerarse como técnicas. Por ejemplo, no ha sido sino hasta fechas recientes que se han podido consultar los archivos bancarios en profundidad. Sin fuentes de archivo, evidentemente resulta dificil para los historiadores explorar temas tan complejos como éste[1]. Pero existen, asimismo, otras explicaciones

---

[1] Entre los archivos bancarios más importantes en Latinoamérica de las que tenemos noticia se cuentan los del Banco de la Provincia de Buenos Aires, del Banco do Brasil y el recientemente creado archivo histórico del Banco Nacional de México En nuestro trabajo asesorando la creación de éste último archivo nos dimos cuenta que virtualmente todos los bancos cuentan con un gran archivo "muerto" por razones legales, lo cual induce a pensar que sería conveniente establecer una legislación para requerir que dichas empresas financieras cuiden de la conservación de la documentación antigua por razones de interés histórico nacional.

que se refieren más bien a limitaciones de tipo teórico o de enfoque. Ello se ha debido, en parte, a la falta de interés de los historiadores por compenetrarse con ciertos problemas de la teoría económica que se refieren a la esfera de lo monetario y lo financiero, problema que — debemos reconocer — comienza a corregirse. Pero también se puede atribuir a una falta de visión histórica por parte de algunos economistas teóricos.

Un ejemplo claro de lo segundo lo encontramos en la influencia poco afortunada de ciertas corrientes del pensamiento económico que insistieron en la virtual inexistencia de mercados crediticios y de capitales en los países "subdesarrollados". El influyente economista noruego Ragnar Nurske, entre otros, fundamentó una parte de su teoria sobre la formación de capitales en los países menos desarrollados en la supuesta debilidad o inexistencia de mercados financieros locales, lo que obstaculizaba el desarrollo del capitalismo. Por ello, de acuerdo con Nurske, era necesario descubrir la forma de canalizar los capitales ociosos hacia actividades productivas, pues, al movilizar los capitales atesorados (y por lo tanto inmovilizados), suponia que podria efectuarse una revolución económica en los países menos desarrollados.

Posteriormente, sin embargo, otros destacados economistas hicieron notar que había que matizar esta visión del problema en tanto era manifiesto que las estructuras financieras en los países menos desarrollados eran mucho más complejas de lo que Nurske sugería. Por ello, prestaron una atención preferente al problema del financiamiento del desarrollo, comparando esta problemática con la experiencias en diferentes tipos de economías. Fue Raymond Goldsmith, en particular, quien hizo enfasis en la importancia de estudiar la correlación entre el desarollo financiero y el crecimiento económico moderno, comparando las experiencias de países más y menos desarrollados en el largo plazo[2]. En este sentido, los estudios de Goldsmith sobre la evolución financiera de México y de Brasil son indicativos de la dirección en la que suponía debía dirigirse este tipo de investigación. También Edward Shaw planteó la

[2] Raymond Goldsmith. *Financial Structure and Development*. New Haven: Yale University Press. 1969. Véase asimismo su obra *Financial Intermediaries in the American Economy since 1900*. Princeton University Press. 1958.

necesidad de matizar este enfoque, haciendo hincapié en los límites del impacto del sector financiero sobre el crecimiento económico cuando el sistema financiero sufre "represión" o "cuellos de botella"[3]. A su vez, parece innecesario recordar la importancia que han tenido para los estudios en este terreno los trabajos historicos de teóricos monetaristas como Milton Friedman o de economistas del desarrollo como Alexander Gerschenkron.

Por otra parte, historiadores económicos de los Estados Unidos, Europa y Japón comenzaron a producir, desde el decenio de 1960, una cantidad de obras importantes sobre la evolución de los sistemas financieros y su impacto sobre el crecimiento económico. Quizás el más destacado exponente de los enfoques comparativos en el campo de la historia bancaria fue Rondo Cameron, quien coordinó una serie de volumenes colectivos que fueron ampliando las fronteras del debate en este terreno[4].

Coincidiendo con estas tendencias, en América Latina, en los últimos veinte anos, se han multiplicado los estudios por parte de historiadores que traspasan el marco de la historia bancaria institucional para entrar de lleno en una discusión que debe ser de interés tanto para aquellos que se interesan por la historia económica como por la teoría económica. Nos referimos en especial a los trabajos sobre banca y moneda de autores como Roberto Cortés-Conde, Samuel Amaral y Andrés Regalsky para el caso histórico de Argentina, de Carlos Pelaez, Wilson Suzigan, María-Barbara Levy y Flavio Saes para el caso de Brasil, de Alfonso Quiroz para Peru, y Antonio Mitre para Bolivia, entre otros que iremos citando a lo largo de este trabajo. En todo caso, existe ya una bibliografía amplia sobre la historia bancaria, monetaria y financiera de America Latina que obliga a repensar importantes aspectos de la historia económica del subcontinente.

Es precisamente a la revisión de las principales contribuciones de la pléyade de historiadores contemporáneos que han abierto el campo de estudios de la historia bancaria en Latinoamérica que dedicamos este ensayo, enfatizando siete ejes temáticos que han despertado debates especialmente intensos, y que abarcan desde el

---

3 Edward Shaw. *Financial Deepening in Economic Development*. New York: Oxford University Press. 1973.

4 R. Cameron (1967) y (1972).

análisis de las políticas monetarias y bancarias en el primer período independiente hasta la creación y funciones de los bancos centrales en Latinoamérica en el siglo XX.

Al entrar a estos temas y debates específicos, nos parece importante señalar que los trabajos realizados ya han obligado a la modificación de algunos estereotipos que eran comunes en la historiografía económica latinoamericana, estereotipos — dicho sea de paso — que son necesario que se cuestionen para lograr la renovación constante que requiere una disciplina que se desea dinámica y plural.

Las políticas monetarias desde la Independencia y el fracaso de los primeros experimentos bancarios, 1820-1850

Para el historiador de la banca latinoamericana, quizás el primer problema que se plantea — al analizar la evolución financiera en el siglo XIX — consiste en buscar una explicación del fracaso de los primeros experimentos bancarios en la región después de la Independencia. Entre estos primeros experimentos hay que destacar los casos del primer Banco do Brasil (1808-1829) y del Banco de Buenos Aires (1822-26), luego Banco Nacional (1826-35). En la historiografía tradicional se solía mencionar la temprana bancarrota de estas efímeras instituciones financieras como ejemplo claro del mal manejo de las finanzas públicas por los respectivos y flamantes gobiernos de Brasil y Argentina. Sin embargo, esta explicación — que sin duda tiene algo de validez — actualmente resulta insatisfactoria.

Profundizando en este terreno, investigadores como Samuel Amaral, Carlos Peláez, María-Barbara Levy & Ana Maria Ribeiro de Andrade han agregado una serie de elementos empíricos y analíticos que obligan a revisar las interpretaciones tradicionales sobre el tema. Para comenzar, han demostrado que no se puede entender estos experimentos bancarios sin vincularlos con el análisis de las políticas monetarias de los nuevos gobiernos. En toda Latinoamérica, pero en especial en aquellos países con escasez de medio circulante en metálico, resultó necesario desde la Independencia el buscar mecanismos para ofrecer fluidez a la circulación monetaria. Durante tres siglos, el régimen colonial había permitido el sostenimiento de un patrón monetario estable (en metálico) que, a pesar de sus defectos, había proporcionado seguridad a las elites locales y a los gobiernos metropolitanos de España y Portugal. Sin embargo, después de la Independencia, la unidad en los patrones monetarios se concluyó, y cada gobierno tuvo que buscar nuevas fórmulas que correspondieran, a su vez, con las respectivas reformas fiscales y financieras en marcha.

Los trabajos de María-Barbara Levy, Ana Maria Ribeiro de Andrade y Carlos Peláez nos hablan de la complejidad de estas políticas monetarias en los primeros decenios de la vida independiente de Brasil[5]. Mientras que las dos primeras autoras analizan los diferentes instrumentos monetarios y crediticios que fueron utilizados por comerciantes y hacendados, el tercero centra su atención en las políticas monetarias del Banco do Brasil. En este sentido, los estudios en cuestión nos remiten a un problema subrayado para otro caso histórico por Roberto Cortés-Conde, que consiste en señalar que la política monetaria no era determinada solamente por el gobierno sino que dicha responsabilidad recaía asimismo sobre los primeros bancos[6]. Para Peláez, no fueron solamente los deficits gubernamentales que llevaron a la bancarrota del primer Banco do Brasil, sino asimismo las dificultades en formular una política monetaria adecuada tanto para las demandas del sector público como del privado a partir de la Independencia en 1822.

A conclusiones similares llega Samuel Amaral en una serie de trabajos detallados sobre la economía financiera de Argentina en el decenio de 1820-30, que, metodológicamente, constituyen uno de los aportes más importantes a la temprana historia monetaria y financiera de cualquier país latinoamericano[7]. En dichos estudios, Amaral plantea la necesidad de relacionar y comparar una amplia gama de problemas que van desde el impacto de la introducción del papel moneda, la amplitud en la circulación de las letras de cambio y de los pagarés internos, al problema de la temprana deuda pública interna y externa, las consecuencias de la inflación provocada por la guerra argentino-brasileña de 1826-28 y por el manejo arbitrario de las politicas de emisión del único banco por el gobierno argentino.

Si bien los casos de Argentina y Brasil sean singulares por la

---

5 Levy & Andrade (1980 y 1985), Peláez (1975 y 1976).

6 Véase Cortés-Conde (1989) p. 10, al referirse a las políticas monetarias del gobierno de Buenos Aires a mediados del siglo XIX.

7 Véase Amaral (1977, 1982, 1989 y 1989b).

temprana fundación de bancos (efímeros, por cierto) y por la difusión de papel moneda desde la misma Independencia, también vale la pena indicar que en otros países latinoamericanos se llevaron a cabo algunas experiencias monetarias y financieras significativas. El caso de México, por ejemplo, es de interés en tanto que era un país firmemente atado al viejo patrón metálico colonial, el cual estaba basado esencialmente en el peso de plata. Entanto México era el principal productor de plata a nivel mundial, esta continuidad no resulta especialmente sorprendente, como tampoco lo era en otros países con riqueza argentífera u auréa, como era el caso de los países andinos.

Ocurre que, a pesar de contar con abundantes fuentes de metálico (en la forma de numerosas minas de plata), la economía mexicana pronto comenzó a sufrir de serios problemas monetarios desde las Guerras de Independencia en delante. Ello se debía fundamentalmente a tres factores. El primero era el alto nivel de exportación de moneda acuñada para pagar el súbito aumento de las importaciones a partir de 1820, lo cual provocó una creciente escasez de plata en circulación. Un segundo factor consistió en la retracción de la plata en circulación por sectores propietarios, que tendían a atesorar en vez de invertir por causa de la fuerte inestabilidad política y militar que sufrió México en la primera mitad del siglo XIX. En tercer lugar, la escasez de plata fue acentuada por la creciente acuñación de moneda de cobre, especialmente en el decenio de 1830, con lo que se dieron las condiciones para la puesta en marcha en México de la famosa Ley de Gresham, por la cual — como es bien sabido — la moneda mala expulsa a la buena.

Para contrarrestar esta situación de creciente escasez de capitales y de metálico de plata, las autoridades promovieron dos ensayos bancarios. El primero fue la creación del Banco de Avío (1830-40) cuyo objetivo consistió en utilizar fondos fiscales para promover un temprano proceso de industrialización. Las primeras fábricas textiles mexicanas del decenio de 1830 requerían capitales, pero dificilmente podían encontrarlos a raíz del atesoramiento de plata por los sectores propietarios del País. La historia del Banco de Avío — que proporcionó considerables sumas a los nuevos industriales — ha sido analizada en detalle en la sólida monografía de Robert Potash, recientemente reeditada[8]. En cambio, todavía no existe una

[8] Potash (1959 y 1985).

monografía importante sobre el Banco Nacional de Amortización del Cobre (1837-1841), el cual constituyó un esfuerzo financiero curioso por terminar con la abundante circulación de moneda de cobre en el "país de la plata".

Bancos libres versus bancos de gobierno a mediados del siglo XIX: el debate sobre modelos bancarios y politicas monetarias

Si bien los primeros intentos por crear bancos en los países latinoamericanos terminaron como fracasos, después de mediados del siglo XIX se desató una nueva ola de fundaciones bancarias que habría de ser más duradera. Por ello, los decenios de 1850 y 1860 pueden denominarse propiamente como la etapa de nacimiento de la banca latinoamericana. Quizá el factor más importante que indujo este "despegue" bancario fue la expansión del comercio exterior de varios países, en especial de Brasil, Argentina, Perú y Chile en los años 1850, lo que produjo un fuerte aumento de la demanda por nuevos servicios financieros. Dada la importancia del comercio, no fue extraño que, en la mayoría de los casos, los primeros bancos latinoamericanos se fundasen con base a los esquemas operativos de las casas de comerciantes-prestamistas que habían alcanzado un mayor nivel de desarrollo. Más concretamente, estos bancos noveles se montaron a partir de la red de intercambios mercantiles locales y externos que se habían forjado en los decenios inmediatamente procedentes. De allí también que las instituciones de crédito formasen sus primeras redes de corresponsales aprovechando las agencias y contactos que habían desarrollado las principales casas de comerciantes-prestamistas[9].

El surgir de los bancos, por otra parte, requirió una serie de innovaciones de tipo institucional, especialmente con respecto al tipo de legislación bancaria. La discusión sobre este punto en Latinoamérica se relacionó con el debate que se produjo a nivel internacional desde el decenio de 1840 sobre los méritos respectivos de los "bancos libres" en contraposición a los bancos de gobierno con monopolio de emisión. Los abogados de los "bancos libres" citaban, en particular, el exito, la flexibilidad y el dinamismo de los

[9] Véase Marichal (1986).

sistemas bancarios de Escocia y de los Estados Unidos, mientras que sus contrincantes citaban sobre todo a la solidez del Banco de Francia y del Banco de Inglaterra, como ejemplos de banca central que podían regular — en buena medida — la circulación de papel moneda. Como ha señalado Charles Jones, el modelo de la banca estatal con relativo control (aunque no-exclusivo) de la emisión fue aquel que tuvo mayor influencia en los países sudamericanos desde mediados del siglo XIX, especialmente en Argentina y Brasil[10]. Sin embargo, los abogados de los bancos libres no dejaron de ejercer un peso considerable en las politicas bancarias, especialmente en ciertos períodos cortos, como fue el caso del ministro de Finanzas de Brasil, Souza Franco, en 1857-60[11].

Aunado a la discusión sobre modelos bancarios, se inició un intenso y prolongado debate en casi todos los países latinoamericanos sobre las políticas monetarias desde mediados del siglo. De nuevo, este debate se vinculó estrechamente con la discusión que se había iniciado en Europa, más especificamente entre los partidarios de la llamada *currency school* y los de la *banking school*, a raíz de las reformas bancarias y monetarias en Inglaterra en el decenio de 1840-50. Por lo general, en America Latina los campos se dividieron entre los abogados de la emisión de papel moneda con limitado respaldo en metálico (los que se conocían en algunos países como los "papelistas") y los defensores de medidas mas estrictas de emisión, con total respaldo en oro (conocidos como "metalistas"). Dicha división tuvo una larga duración, y el seguimiento de esta problemática resulta fundamental para la comprensión de las políticas financieras del resto del siglo en diversos países como lo demuestran los trabajos de Cortés-Conde (1989) para Argentina, el estudio clásico de Subercasseaux (1922) para Chile y diversos trabajos para Brasil[12].

---

[10] Jones (1977). Sobre este tema véase también Marichal, "Modelos y sistemas bancarios en América Latina en el siglo XIX: 1850-1880", en *La Economía Financiera...* (1993).

[11] Sobre la influencia de los abogados de los bancos libres en Argentina y Brasil y Chile en este período véase Cortés-Conde (1989), Levy & Andrade (1985).

[12] Véase Peláez (1976), por ejemplo. Asimismo tenemos noticia de una tesis de Ana Maria Ribeiro de Andrade sobre el tema de la política monetaria en Brasil en el siglo XIX.

El papel de la banca extranjera en Latinoamérica y el supuesto predominio de la banca británica en el siglo XIX

Un tercer órden de cuestiones en el que han avanzado sustancialmente los historiadores contemporáneos de la banca latinoamericana se refiere al papel de la banca extranjera en la región desde mediados del siglo XIX. De acuerdo con un paradigma tradicional, la banca británica ejerció un papel central en el establecimiento de la banca latinoamericana. De hecho, en la historiografía económica latinoamericana ha sido tan fuerte la aureola del "imperio informal británico" del siglo XIX en Latinoamérica que no resulta sorprendente encontrar textos básicos contemporáneos en los que siguen haciéndose afirmaciones categoricas acerca del predominio de las firmas británicas en el sector financiero en los países de este subcontinente durante el siglo XIX. Esta visión encontró un punto de apoyo en textos como el magnífico estudio de David Joslin sobre la evolución de la banca británica en América Latina en el siglo XIX, el cual fue de los primeros estudios modernos a basarse en la revisión de archivos históricos bancarios[13].

Este enfoque, sin embargo, ha oscurecido el hecho de que los bancos "nacionales" generalmente tuvieron un papel mucho más destacado que los bancos "extranjeros" dentro de los sistemas financieros de los países del subcontinente a lo largo del siglo XIX. Los estudios sobre el Banco de la Provincia de Buenos Aires y el Banco de la Nación de Argentina, sobre el papel del Banco do Brasil y sobre el Banco Nacional de México nos indican que estas instituciones "nacionales" dominaban los mercados financieros de su época[14]. En segundo término, el enfasis puesto en el papel de la banca británica ha oscurecido otros hechos importantes como fue

---

[13] El trabajo de Joslin (1963) fue uno de los pioneros en la moderna historia bancaria latinoamericana, en especial porque se basaba en un detallado estudio de los archivos bancarios de los bancos británicos que se guardan en la biblioteca de la University of London. Un estudio inédito pero más detallado sobre la banca británica en Argentina en el siglo XIX es el de Jones (1973), trabajo que debiera traducirse y publicarse.

[14] Sobre los bancos argentinos ver Cortés-Conde (1989); sobre la banca brasileña Peláez y Suzigan (1976) y Melo Franco (1979); y sobre la mexicana Hilda Sánchez (1983).

la intensa competencia con la banca germánica desde fines del siglo hasta 1914. Los estudios de George Young son sugerentes en este sentido, al igual que los clásicos estudios de Diouritch y Lough[15].

Por otra parte, numerosos estudios recientes han demostrado que un considerable número de bancos latinoamericanos de la época eran instituciones que combinaban capitales nacionales y extranjeros. El Banco de Londres y Mexico, por ejemplo, que podríamos suponer controlado por capitales británicos hasta fines del decenio de 1880, después pasó a ser una firma con mayoría de capital mexicano, y con participaciones minoritarias de capitalistas ingleses, franceses y españoles. Por su parte, el Banco de Perú y Londres, que ha sido magistralmente estudiado por Alfonso Quiroz, pasó a ser un banco con muy fuerte participación de capital doméstico desde 1895, cuando se fusionó con el Banco de Callao, convirtiéndose en la mayor institución financiera del Perú durante unos veinte años[16].

A su vez, no era despreciable la participación de capitales franceses en una variedad de instituciones, especialmente las de caracter oficial. En el Banco Nacional de México, por ejemplo, la participación de los accionistas franceses fue mayoritaria a mediados del decenio de 1880, pero luego fue creciendo la participación de los capitalistas mexicanos así como — en menor grado — la de capitalistas españoles, británicos, alemanes y norteamericanos[17]. Algo diferente fue el caso del Banco Francés del Rio de la Plata, analizado en detalle por Regalsky (1992) el cual tenía una mayoría de capitales de comerciantes radicados en Buenos Aires, al igual que el Banco de Italia y Rio de la Plata o el Banco Español y Rio de la Plata. En estos casos (como en los anteriores), observamos que las investigaciones recientes modifican la visión maniquéa de una necesaria contraposición entre capital nacional y capital extranjero, cuando la realidad histórica nos revela un cuadro mucho más complejo y matizado.

---

15 Lough (1915), Diouritch (1909), Young (1990 y 1991).

16 Quiroz (1989) está basado en una parte importante en los archivos históricos del Banco de Peru y Londres que fueron abiertos hace pocos años.

17 Ludlow (1986 y 1990).

El *boom* bancario de los años 1880 y la crisis de 1890

Una cuarta problemática que ha llamado la atención de los historiadores de la banca latinoamericana en los últimos años ha sido la explicación del "boom bancario" de los años ochenta y las causas de las crisis financieras de 1890-1893 en varios países de la región. El decenio de 1880-90 fue una de las épocas más importantes en la expansión de la banca en los países mayores como Argentina, Brasil, Chile y México[18]. Lo importante de este período consistió no solamente en que se crearan mayor número de bancos sino además en dos factores adicionales: 1) la creciente especialización — desarrollo de bancos hipotecarios, mineros, de ahorro, etc.; 2) la creación de extensas redes de sucursales de los bancos más importantes en cada uno de los países mencionados[19]. Con respecto al segundo punto, puede argumentarse que fue entonces que el sistema conocido como *branch banking* (dominante en Inglaterra, Francia o Canadá, por ejemplo) se impuso en buen número de paises latinoamericanos, a pesar de la influencia de los modelos bancarios de los Estados Unidos, en el cual el *unit banking* era más común.

La proliferación de bancos se acentuó notablemente hacia 1888-90, coinciendo con un breve, pero febril, momento de especulación financiera en Buenos Aires, Rio de Janeiro, Santiago de Chile y otras ciudades latinoamericanas. No obstante, poco después comenzaron a producirse una serie de crisis financieras y bancarias de gran severidad, en la mayoría de los casos acompañadas por crisis politicas de primer orden. En Argentina la crisis de 1890 fue tan profunda que sacudió a los bancos ingleses que tenían mayores compromisos en la zona del Rio de la Plata, desatando el famoso "pánico Baring" en Londres. Dicha crisis ha sido objeto de numerosos estudios recientes, los cuales nos hablan de la transcendencia internacional de esta crisis financiera argentina[20].

[18] Para estudios de la relación entre el auge bancario en Argentina y Brasil y la especulación financiera por parte de la banca internacional véanse Marichal (1984), Regalsky (1987) y Colson (1983).

[19] El mejor estudio "institucional" para el período es la monografía de Quiroz sobre la banca peruana.

[20] Marti (1989), Cortés-Conde (1987), Ferns (1993), Marichal (1989) cap. 6, Joslin (1963) passim, y Jones (1973) passim.

Pero la intensidad de la crisis argentina no debe opacar otras crisis financieras igualmente importantes que tuvieron lugar poco despues, entre ellas la provocada por el "Encilhamento" en Brasil. El *boom* financiero de 1889-90, provocado en parte por el cambio de régimen político, pero de manera más específica por una politica monetaria y financiera expansiva, ha sido motivo de intensos debates en la historiografía brasileña. En un reciente y documentado trabajo Stephen Topik ha cuestionado la interpretación tradicional de las politicas del ministro republicano, Rui Barbosa, como "industrialistas", y argumenta que en la práctica correspondieron a los intereses de la elite mercantil y financiera de la capital[21].

En su conjunto estos estudios nos hablan de la creciente complejidad de las economías de los mayores países latinoamericanos, en los cualés las respectivas esferas financiera y bancaria ya eran fundamentales — tanto en determinar algunas de las principales tendencias económicas a nivel interno, como en las vinculaciones con las fluctuaciones en el comercio y las finanzas internacionales.

La banca y el desarrollo económico regional

Quizás el campo de investigación de historia bancaria latinoamericana en el cual se haya avanzado más rapidamente y de manera más innovadora en los últimos años sea aquel que centra su atención en el análisis de la relación entre banca y crecimiento económico regional. En este sentido, es menester tener en cuenta la diferencia entre aquellos trabajos que enfatizan el estudio de la banca en un ámbito urbano especifico y aquellos que centran la antención en la relación entre banca y la evolución económica de una región más amplia. En todo caso, los planteamientos que surgen del análisis de archivos bancarios y fuentes de documentación financiera regional están en proceso de modificar la forma en que los historiadores interpretan el desarrollo económico en espacios más precisos y delimitados que el marco nacional.

---

[21] Sobre las politicas monetaria y financiera en los años 1880/90 véase el estudio de G. H. B. Franco (1983) y un ensayo de Colson (1983). Para la crisis subsiguiente véanse Topik (1988) y contrastar con Peláez & Suzigan (1976).

En el caso de México, país de tardío desarrollo bancario, los últimos años han sido testigos de avances importantes en el estudio de la relación entre formación de burguesías regionales y constitución de banca regional a finales del siglo XIX. Los trabajos de Mario Cerutti sobre Monterrey, por ejemplo, demuestran como los principales grupos de comerciantes-prestamistas regionales fueron sentando las bases para el surgir de mercados de capitales locales que darían pie al despegue de la industrialización en esa zona del norte de México a fines del siglo XIX[22]. En este proceso, la creciente concentración de capitales y la subsiguiente creación de una serie de bancos regionales constituyeron elementos fundamentales. De manera similar, Ricardo León ha analizado los primeros bancos en Chihuahua, establecidos desde el decenio de 1870 en estrecha consonancia con la expansión ganadera y con el despuntar de una serie de nuevos ejes de actividad económica de caracter minero e industrial[23]. En cambio, Stephen Haber ofrece una interpretación algo distinta al analizar las primeras grandes industrias mexicanas de la época — especialmente en el centro de México — al argumentar que los bancos ejercieron un papel relativamente poco importante en el financiamiento de la mayoría de las empresas industriales que él analiza[24]. Dicho enfoque obliga a reconsiderar hasta que punto las perspectivas de la historiografía europea sobre la relación entre banca e industria (que se afirma estrecha) es válida para muchas regiones latinoamericanas[25].

---

22 Cerutti (1992a y 1992). En la primera de estas obras el Autor realiza el mejor estudio de historia económica regional del México del siglo XIX que se haya publicado hasta la fecha. Por otra parte, proporciona una referencia casi exhaustiva de los trabajos realizados en México sobre historia del crédito regional en los últimos dos decenios.

23 León (1992).

24 El libro de Haber (1989) ofrece un análisis detallado de los problemas de financiamiento, mercados y tecnología de las grandes empresas industriales del centro de México. Su ensayo (1991) tiene la ventaja adicional de proporcionar un marco de referencia comparativo con Brasil.

25 Nos referimos al hecho de que durante algunos decenios la historiografia bancaria europea ha enfatizado el problema analítico de la relación entre desarrollo bancario y desarrollo industrial. Autores tan diversos como Rondo Cameron (1967 y 1972), Bertrand Gille (1970), Gabriel Tortella (1973), Jean Bouvier (1973) o Richard Tilly (1966) han abierto un amplio debate acerca del papel de la banca en la industrialización europea en el siglo XIX.

En el caso brasileño tambien se ha producido una considerable cantidad de obras sobre el desarrollo de la banca a nivel regional y en ciertas ciudades. Los trabajos de Lagemann sobre la banca en el sur de Brasil y de Azevedo sobre Bahía son ejemplos de dos estudios regionales de tipo institucional. Por su parte, sobre el caso de la banca en Rio de Janeiro son muy conocidos los importantes trabajos de Eulalia Lobo sobre la elite financiera y los de María-Barbara Levy, tanto sobre el mercado de capitales como sobre la banca. Asimismo, debe destacarse la obra de Flávio Saes sobre la conformación de la banca en São Paulo entre fines del siglo XIX y principios del siglo XX. En este excelente trabajo se vincula el análisis institucional con el desempeño de la economia regional, revelando en primer término la estrecha vinculación entre la banca y el sector cafetalero y, en segundo lugar, su relación con el despegue industrial en São Paulo desde principios del siglo[26].

Para el caso argentino se cuenta actualmente con un número creciente de estudios que vinculan la historia bancaria con el desarrollo económico regional, aunque debe puntualizarse que la mayoría se centran sobre la província de Buenos Aires. Estos estudios demuestran que la banca estatal o semi-estatal ejerció un papel fundamental en el financiamiento de la expansión ganadera y agricola de la pampa húmeda, aunque hay ciertas discrepancias en cuanto al impacto de este tipo de financiamiento sobre distintos sectores sociales y económicos. Por ejemplo, en un estudio por Mariluz Urquijo sobre las políticas crediticias del Banco de la Provincia de Buenos Aires a mediados del siglo, se argumenta que esta institución (la mayor de Argentina, en esa época) contribuyó de manera casi indiscriminada a la promoción de la ganaderia, el transporte, la industria, etc. En cambio, en estudios por Adelman sobre el sistema bancario argentino hacia fines de siglo, se argumenta que la banca estatal tendió a favorecer de manera cada vez más notoria a los grandes ganaderos y las mayores empresas comerciales en perjuicio de agricultores e industriales. Por su parte, en un importante estudio sobre el conjunto de las operaciones crediticias del Banco de la Nación, Tulchin ha realizado un análisis geográfica de la distribución del crédito bancario al doblar el siglo, en el cual demues-

[26] Lagemann (1985), Azevedo (1969), Lobo (1978), Levy (1979, 1980, 1985) y Saes (1986).

tra una fuerte concentración del mismo en las zonas pampeanas del País[27].

Por último, púede mencionarse que sobre la historia monetaria y bancaria de los países andinos existen una serie de excelentes trabajos por Antonio Mitre y Alfonso Quiroz, que han abierto importantes y nuevas perspectivas sobre economías que anteriormente contaban con muy escasos trabajos históricos sobre la esfera financiera. En sus estudios sobre la moneda y la banca boliviana del siglo XIX, Mitre aclara la estrecha relación que existe entre la minería, las políticas monetarias y la banca temprana en la económia minera. Por su parte, Quiroz en sus trabajos históricos sobre la banca peruana nos ha proporcionado uno de los mejores estudios institucionales de la banca que existen para cualquier país latinoamericano, vinculando el estudio de la banca con los procesos de desarrollo económico regional en una época marcada por profundos cambios en los vínculos de Perú con la economía internacional[28].

La creación de los bancos centrales en el primer tercio del siglo XX

Para concluir, es necesario comentar la eclosión relativamente reciente de una serie de estudios sobre los origenes de la banca central en Latinoamérica. Es importante tener en cuenta que, si bien los principales bancos de gobierno en países como Argentina, Brasil y México ya cumplían algunas de las funciones de bancos centrales, no fue hasta el decenio de 1920 que comenzó a crearse formalmente este tipo de institución bancaria, con monopolio de emisión, control de las reservas, etc. La evolución paulatina hacia la banca central en América Latina refleja algunas de las tendencias que han remarcado historiadores que han trabajado el tema para el caso europeo, pero con matices propios[29].

27 Adelman (1990 y 1992), Mariluz Urquijo (1969), Tulchin (1978) y Castillo y Tulchin (1986).

28 Mitre (1981) y Quiroz (1989).

29 Para un excelente análisis de la evolución gradual en la formación de la banca central en Europa véase Goodhart (1988).

Sobre la creación de la banca central en los países andinos entre 1922 y 1930, ya es de consulta obligatoria la obra de Paul Drake, quien ha documentado la influencia del economista norteamericano Edwin Kemmerer, en el establecimiento de la banca central en Bolivia, Chile, Colombia, Ecuador y Perú. Su modelo consistió en la aplicación de una serie de reformas fiscales y administrativas del respectivo ministerio de finanzas, con la creación de los bancos centrales, todo ello dentro del patrón oro.

La influencia norteamericana, en cambio, fue menos importante en los tres mayores países de la región. En México, por ejemplo, el establecimiento del Banco de México en 1925 respondió esencialmente a una serie de presiones internas para lograr el equilíbrio financiero, trás el largo período revolucionario de 1910-20. El estudio detallado de Eduardo Turrent sobre este banco ilustra el predominio de factores domésticos en las reformas financieras, monetarias y bancarias emprendidas en México en esta época[30]. En cambio, en Argentina y Brasil, las autoridades financieras eran más reacias al establecimiento de bancos centrales. Como es bien sabido, no fue hasta 1935 que se estableció el Banco Central de Argentina, cuyo primer presidente fue Raúl Prebisch hasta 1945. La constitución de este banco fue fuertemente influenciado por los consejos de la misión Niemeyer (del Banco de Inglaterra) en 1933, que coincidió asimismo con una serie de intentos de reformas bancarias en Brasil, pero con menos exito[31]. En todo caso, la experiencia de los distintos países en lo que se refiere a la creación de la banca central es sintomática de una serie de particularidades que reflejan las diferencias bastante notables en cuanto a sus estructuras financieras en el largo plazo[32].

---

30 Turrent (1989 y 1992).

31 Sobre el caso argentino véase Banco Central de Argentina (1972) y sobre el caso brasileño Paiva Abreu (1979).

32 Para una visión comparada de los origenes de la banca gubernamental y central en América Latina pueden consultarse los ensayos en Marichal y Tedde (1989).

Bibliografia consultada

Adelman, Jeremy. "Agricultural Credit in the Province of Buenos Aires, 1890-1914", *Journal of Latin Anerican Studies*, 22, 70-92. 1990.

—— "Financiamiento y expansión agricola en la Argentina y Canadá 1890 -1914". *Revista Ciclos en la Historia, Economía y Sociedad* (Buenos Aires), 2, 3, p. 3-21. 1992.

Amaral, Samuel. "Comercio y crédito: el Banco de Buenos Aires, 1822-1826". *América*, II, n. 4 (Buenos Aires), 9-49. 1977.

—— "El Banco Nacional y las finanzas de Buenos Aires. El curso forzoso y la convertibilidad del papel moneda en 1826" en *VI Congreso Internacional de Historia de América*. Buenos Aires, Academia Nacional de la Historia, V, p. 415-29. 1982.

—— "Alta inflación y precios relativos en el pago de las obligaciones en Buenos Aires, 1826-1834". *Trimestre Económico*, lvi, n. 221, p. 163-91. 1989.

—— "La deuda pública argentina, 1800-1850", trabajo presentado a la conferencia sobre "La deuda pública latinoamericana" IberoAmerikanisches Institut, Berlin, actualmente en prensa. 1989b.

Azevedo, Thales de. *Historia do Banco da Bahía, 1858-1958*. Rio de Janeiro. 1969.

Banco Central de Argentina. *La Creación del Banco Central y la experiência monetaria argentina. 1935-1943*. Buenos Aires, 2 vols. 1972.

Barman, Roderick J. "Business and Government in Imperial Brazil: The Experience of Viscount Mauá". *Journal of Latin American Studies*, 13, n. 2, 239-64. 1981.

Bouvier, Jean. *Un siécle de banque française*. París. 1973.

Cameron, Rondo. *Banking in the Early Stages on Industrialization: A Study in Comparative Economic History*. Londres: Oxford University Press (véase la edición en español publicada en Madrid por la Editorial Tecnos en 1974). 1967.

—— (Ed.) *Banking and Economic Development: Some Lessons of History*. London: Oxford University Press. 1972.

Castillo, Hugo & Tulchin, Joseph. "Développement capitaliste et structures sociales des régions en Argentine, 1880-1930". *Annales, E.S.C.* (noviembre-enero), n. 6, 1359-84. 1986.

Cerutti, Mario. *Burguesía, Capitales e Industria en el norte de México: Monterrey y su ámbito regional, 1850-1910*. México: Alianza/Universidad Autónoma de Nuevo León. 1992.

—— "Comerciantes y generalización del crédito laíco en México (1860-1910): experiencias regionales". *Anuario del IEHS* (Universidad del Centro, Tandil, Argentina) vii, 211-36.

Colson, R. F. "European Investment and the Brazilian Boom, 1886-1892: The Roots of Speculation". *Ibero-Amerikanisches Archiv*, N. Folge 9, 314. 1983.

Cortés-Conde, Roberto. *Nuevos aspectos en la crisis de 1890*. Buenos Aires: Cuaderno del Instituto Torcuato Di Tella. 1987.

—— *Dinero, deuda y crisis: evolución fiscal y monetaria en la Argentina, 1862-1890*. Buenos Aires: Editorial Sudamericana / Instituto Torcuato Di Tella. 1989.

Cuccorese, Horacio Juan. *Historia del Banco de la Provincia de Buenos Aires*. Buenos Aires. 1972.

Diouritch, Georges. *L'expansion des banques allemandes a l'étranger*. París/ Berlín. 1909.

Drake, Paul. *The Money Doctor in the Andes: Edwin Kemmerer and the Establishment of Central Banks in South America, 1920-1930*. Princeton: Princeton University Press. 1989.

Ferns, H. S. "The Baring Crisis Revisited". *Journal of Latin American Studies*. 1993.

Fontenla, Vicente Paz. *Historia dos Bancos no Brasil*. Rio de Janeiro. 1965.

Franco, Gustavo Henrique Barroso. *Reforma Monetária e Instabilidade durante a Transição Republicana*. Rio de Janeiro. 1983.

Granziera, R. G. *A Guerra do Paraguai e o Capitalismo no Brasil*. São Paulo, Campinas. 1979.

Gille, Bertrand. *La banque en France au XIXe siècle*. París: Droz. 1970.

Goodhart, Carles. *The Evolution of Central Banks*. Cambridge, Mass.: The MIT Press. 1988.

Haber, Stephen. *Industry and Underdevelopment: The Industrialization of Mexico. 1890-1940*. Stanford. 1989.

—— "Industrial Concentration and Capital Markets: A Comparative Study of Brazil, Mexico and the United States, 1830-1930". *Journal of Economic History*, 51, 3, 559-80. 1991.

Jones, Charles. "British Financial Institutions in Argentina, 1860-1914". Tesis doctoral. University of Cambridge. 1973.

—— "The Transfer of Banking Techniques from Britain to Argentina, 1862-1914". *Revue Internationale d'Histoire de la Banque*, n. 26-7, 251-64. 1983.

—— "Commercial Banks and Mortgage Companies" en D.C.M. Platt (éd.). *Business Imperialism, 1840-1930: An Inquiry Based on British Experience in Latin America*. Oxford: The Clarendon Press. 1977.

—— "European Bankers and Argentina, 1880-1890". Working Paper n. 3. Business Imperialism Series, Centre of Latin American Studies. University of Cambridge. 1973.

Joslin, David. A *Century of Banking in Latin America*. Londres: Oxford University Press. 1963.

Lagemann, Eugenio. *O Banco Pelotense & O Sistema Financeiro Regional*. Porto Alegre, R. S. 1985.

Leon, Ricardo. "La banca chihuahuense durante el porfiriato". *Siglo XIX. Cuadernos de Historia*. México / Monterrey: Instituto Mora / Universidad de Nuevo León, p. 211-34.

Levy, María Barbara. *História da Bolsa de Valores do Rio de Janeiro*. Rio de Janeiro. 1979.

—— & Andrade, Ana Maria Ribeiro de. "A Gestão Monetária na Formação do Estado Nacional", en *Revista Brasileira do Mercado de Capitais*. Rio de Janeiro, 6, n. 17, 138-52 (maio-agosto). 1980.

—— "Fundamentos do Sistema Bancário no Brasil: 1834-1860", en *Estudos Econômicos*, 15, n. especial, 17-48. 1985.

Lobo, Eulalia María. *História do Rio de Janeiro (Do capital comercial ao capital industrial e financeiro)*. Rio de Janeiro, 2 vols. 1978.

Lough, William. *Banking Opportunities in South America*. Washington: Department of Commerce. Special Agents Series n. 106. 1915.

Ludlow, Leonor. "La construcción de un banco: el Banco Nacional de México, 1881-1884", en C. Marichal & L. Ludlow (eds.). *Banca y Poder en México. 1800-1925*. p. 299-346. 1986.

—— "El Banco Nacional Mexicano y el Banco Mercantil Mexicano: radiografia social de sus primeros accionistas, 1881-1882", en *Historia Mexicana*. 39, 4, p. 979-1028. 1990.

Marchant, Anyda. *Viscount Mauá and the Empire of Brazil: A biography of Irineu Evangelista de Sousa (1813-1889)*. Berkeley: University of California Press. 1965.

Marichal, Carlos. "Los banqueros europeos y los empréstitos argentinos: rivalidad y colaboración, 1880-1890". *Revista de História Econômica*. II, n. 1 (Madrid, 1984), 47-82. 1984.

—— "El nacimiento de la banca mexicana en el contexto latinoamericano", en C. Marichal & L. Ludlow (eds.). *Banca y Poder en México. 1800-1925*. México, p. 231-65. 1986.

—— & Tedde, Pedro (co-eds.). *La Economía Financiera y la formación de la banca central en España y Latinoamérica (siglos XIX y XX)*. Madrid: Banco de España. 1993 (en prensa).

Mariluz Urquijo, José María. "Fomento industrial y crédito bancario en el Estado de Buenos Aires". *Trabajos y Comunicaciones*, n. 19. Facultad de Humanidades. Universidad de La Plata, p. 105-44. 1969.

Marti, Gerardo Marcelo. "Argentina: La Crisis de 1890. Endeudamiento externo y crack financiero". *Trimestre Económico*, 57, n. 228, p. 933-68. 1990.

Melo Franco, Afonso Arinos de. *História do Banco do Brasil* [Rio de Janeiro] 5 vols. 1979.

Mitre, Antonio. *Los Patriarcas de la Plata. Estructura socioeconómica de la mineria boliviana en el siglo XIX*. Perú, Lima: Instituto de Estudios Peruanos. 1981.

Neuhaus, Paulo. *História Monetária do Brasil, 1900-1945*. Rio de Janeiro. 1975.

Paiva Abreu, Marcelo de. "The Niemeyer Misson: An Episode of British Financial Imperialism in Brazil". Centre of Latin American Studies: University of Cambridge, working papers, num. 10, p. 1-30. 1979.

Peláez, Carlos Manuel. "The Establishment of Banking Institutions in a Backward Economy: Brazil, 1800-1851". *Business History Review*, vol. 49, n. 4. 1975.

—— & Suzigan, Wilson. *História Monetária do Brasil: análise da política, comportamento e instituições monetárias*. Rio de Janeiro: IPEA/INPES. 1976.

Potash, Robert. *El Banco de Avio de México*. México. Reed. por Fondo de Cultura Económica. 1985.

Quintero Ramos, Angel. *A History of Money and Banking in Argentina*. Rio Piedras, Puerto Rico. 1965.

Quiroz, Alfonso W. *Banqueros en Conflicto: Estructura financiera y economía peruana, 1884-1930*. Lima: Centro de Investigación de la Universidad del Pacifico. Versión en inglés. 1989.

Regalsky. "Las exportaciones de capital hacia paises nuevos: los bancos franceses y las finanzas públicas argentinas, 1881-1887". *Revista de Historia Económica* (Madrid) 5(1):73-97. 1987.

—— "La evolución de la banca privada nacional en la Argentina, 1880-1914", en C. Marichal & P. Tedde (eds.). *La economía financiera* y *la formación de la banca central en España y America Latina (Siglos XIX y XX)*.

—— "El Banco Francés del Rio de la Plata y la emergencia de nuevas formas de crédito, 1886-1914" ms. en "Jornadas de Historia Económica, Asociación de Historia Económica de Argentina". Mendoza. 1992.

Ricardina de Magalhães, Beatriz. "Investimentos Ingleses no Brasil e o Banco Londrino e Brasileiro" *Revista Brasileira de Estudos Políticos* (49):233-52. 1979.

Sabato, Hilda. *Capitalismo y ganadería en Buenos Aires: la fiebre del lanar, 1850-1890*. Buenos Aires: Editorial Sudamericana. 1989.

Saes, Flávio Azevedo Marques de. *Crédito e Bancos no Desenvolvimento da Economia Paulista, 1850-1930*. São Paulo. 1986.

Sanchez, Hilda. "La banca mexicana en el porfiriato, 1880-1910", en Jose Manuel Quijano (coordinador). *Banca, pasado y presente: problemas financieros mexicanos*. México, CIDE. 1983.

Stallings, Barbara. *Banker to the Third World: US Portfolio Investment in Latin America, 1900-1986*. Berkeley: U. of California Press. 1988.

Subercasseaux, Guillermo. *Monetary and Banking Policy of Chile*. Oxford: Clarendon Press. 1922.

Tilly, Richard. *Financial Institutions and Industrialization in the Rhineland, 1815-1870.* Madison: Wisconsin University Press. 1966.

Topik, Stephen. "A empresa estatal em um regime liberal: O Banco do Brasil, 1905-1930". *Revista Brasileira do Mercado de Capitais*, 7, n. 19, 70-83. 1981.

—— "La revolución republicana en Brasil: ¿la burguesía en el poder?" *Siglo XIX*, 3, n. 5 (enero-junio de 1988), p. 9-44. 1988.

Tortella, Gabriel. *Los origenes del capitalismo en España: banca, industria* y *ferrocarriles en el siglo XIX*. Madrid: Tecnos. 1973.

Tulchin, Joseph. "El crédito agrario en la Argentina, 1910-1926". *Desarrollo Económico*, n. 71 (octubre-diciembre), 381-408. 1978.

Turrent, Eduardo. *Historia del Banco de México*. México: Banco de México, 2 vols. 1989 y 1992.

Vieira, Evaldo Amano. "Considerações históricas sobre a expansão da rede bancária brasileira". *Revista de Historia*, 47, 96, n. 2, 409-52. 1973.

Vieira, Dorival Teixeira. *Evolução do Sistema Monetário Brasileiro*. São Paulo: Instituto de Pesquisas Econômicas. 1981.

Young, George. "Anglo-German Banking Syndicates and the Issue of South American Government Loans in the Era of High Imperialism, 1885-1914". *Bankhistorisches Archiv* (West Germany) 16(1):3-38. 1990.

—— "British Overseas Banking in Latin America and the encroachment of German Competition, 1887-1914". *Albion* 23 (1):75-99. 1991.

II
TRAJETÓRIAS DAS EMPRESAS MULTINACIONAIS

Mira Wilkins

THE EVOLUTION OF MANUFACTURING MULTINATIONAL ENTERPRISE*

The title of this essay was chosen by the Conference sponsors to differentiate "manufacturing multinationals" from those in agriculture, banking, and other sectors. For this business historian, the title posed a major difficulty, since the lines are often obscure, especially with today's multiproduct firms. Ford Motor Company — which manufactures in the United States and abroad (a manufacturing multinational) — at one time also owned a rubber plantation in Brazil. Japanese trading firms with no manufacturing at home participate in manufacturing abroad (I presume they are nonetheless "trading multinationals"). There are manufacturing enterprises whose distribution network worldwide has for years been more important than their foreign manufacturing (BMW, for example); are they manufacturing multinationals? Then, there is BAT Industries, PLC, which does not manufacture at home in Britain, but has an extensive chain of cigarette factories abroad (going back to 1902); today, at home, in the United Kingdom, BAT Industries owns a large insurance firm and also has a sizable overseas business in insurance (through direct investments). Is it a manufacturing multinational?

For simplicity, I will assume "manufacturing" as defined by what is done in the *home* (headquarters) nation, and relate "multinational" to expansion abroad through direct investments; by direct investments, I mean those made by the firm that are directly connected

* Comments by Lou Wells, Al Chandler, Geoff Jones, and Harm Schröter on recent, albeit related, essays have greatly enriched this paper.

with its business *operations*[1]. I will, however, exclude "oil multinationals" (even though the most important U.S. one, EXXON, started as a refiner — i.e. processor/manufacturer — at home). In short, this essay on the evolution of manufacturing multinationals will consider manufacturing enterprises as they undertook international operations. Not until the nineteenth century were there manufacturing companies extending themselves over borders with direct investments. Accordingly, this paper will deal with the manufacturing multinational from the nineteenth century to the present.

When does a firm qualify to be called a "multinational"? Since I am looking at the growth of the firm, the evolution of the manufacturing multinational, the process begins in my mind when the manufacturing company makes its first foreign direct investment, however small. We assume a process — i.e. that multinational enterprises as we know them today did not obtain their complex multinational operations instantaneously. Even when a company became multinational "overnight", through the takeover of an existing multinational, the latter's activities can be seen as having a history grafted on to that of the acquirer. Indeed, as this essay will demonstrate, in the evolution of the manufacturing multinational, a single company's multinational business may be based on the international business of many individual firms that have been built up independently only to be very recently combined. In terminology, I make no distinction between "transnational corporations", "multinational enterprises" and "multinationals"[2].

---

[1] In recent decades, for statistical conformity, the US Department of Commerce has defined a US direct investment abroad as a business outside the United States in which at least 10 per cent of the equity is owned by a US investor. A nineteenth century British manufacturing firm that employed its spare cash to invest in a portfolio of American railroad securities would not qualify as a British manufacturing multinational; the manufacturing firm must make *direct* investments to fit the definition.

[2] The United Nations has adopted the term "transnational corporation". I prefer "multinational enterprise", or alternatively, "multinational". My preference is because I do not believe that the multinational enterprise "transcends" nations. Yet, in the literature *now* the words — multinational and transnational — are used interchangeably; what is important is that we are considering manufacturing firms that extend through direct investments over national boundaries.

In my *The Maturing of Multinational Enterprise*, I provided a *general* model of the evolution of US multinationals and argued therein that the general model applied specifically to the evolution of US *manufacturing* corporations (as well as to other types of US businesses) that became multinational[3]. The evolution of US manufacturing multinationals, as charted in that 1974 volume, was based on the study of hundreds of such enterprises.

Herein, I want to ask whether now — roughly two decades later — I am satisfied with that model, whether that model, derived solely on evidence on the evolution of US companies, fits manufacturing firms headquartered in nations other than the United States, whether any of the subsequent fresh theoretical insights developed by economists would alter the fundamental argument, and whether the events (the empirical happenings) of the last twenty years fit comfortably into the framework presented in 1974. In short, how, if at all, should the model be revised or amended to encompass other nationalities aside from US manufacturing multinationals, new theoretieal insights, and recent occurrences? Since *The Maturing* was published, substantial research has been undertaken on the history of manufacturing enterprises headquartered in many different countries that became multinationals; at the same time, manufacturing multinationals have become a popular topic and the literature has exploded. There is much new grist for the mill of the historian of multinational enterprise.

The US model

Since the framework for my analysis will be the "US model", as I presented it in 1974, I will give a summary[4]. I began with the

3 Mira Wilkins, *The Maturing of Multinational Enterprise: American Business Abroad from 1914 to 1970*. Cambridge, Mass.: Harvard University Press. 1974, 414-36. The general model was based not only on the materials presented in this volume, but also on data collected for an earlier work, Mira Wilkins, *The Emergence of Multinational Enterprise: American Business Abroad from the Colonial Era to 1914*. Cambridge, Mass.: Harvard University Press. 1970.

4 Based on Wilkins. *The Maturing*, 414-36, and especially 431-36, wherein the general model was applied in particular to manufacturing firms.

proposition that it was essential to look at the evolutionary process as a dynamic one, developing over time out of the requirements of innovative business enterprise. The growth of the firm had to be considered, along with the numerous diverse external factors (political, economic, and military) that influenced its course. I saw the expansion of the firm's global operations as an aspect of — as arising from — the development of its business at home[5]. Alfred D. Chandler had in *Strategy and Structure*, in 1962, documented the rise in the United States of enterprises from the single-plant, single-product businesses, to multidivisional corporations[6]. He had not yet applied this to the multinational enterprise[7]. I found what Chandler wrote on the history of domestic US business coincides with my own studies of US business abroad[8]. I was very influenced, as will be evident, by his findings. My model insisted on "the evolutionary, cumulative, nature of direct foreign investment"[9].

It was clear to me (as it had been to Chandler) that not every US manufacturer grew large — became national, or multinational. In certain industries, manufacturers continued to serve only local markets, as they had from time immemorial. It seemed evident that to succeed internationally, a firm had to have some kind of advantage[10]. Thus, I had emphasized the "innovative" business enterprise.

---

5 Ibid., 436.

6 Alfred D. Chandler. *Strategy and Structure*. Cambridge, Mass.: MIT Press. 1962.

7 He would do so in *The Visible Hand*. Cambridge, Mass.: Harvard University Press. 1977.

8 In the late 1950s and early 1960s, I had prepared a history of Ford Motor Company's international business, based on extensive documents in the Ford archives in Dearborn and worldwide. Ford exported its sixth car; in its second year of existence, it had invested in manufacturing abroad. See Mira Wilkins & Frank Ernest Hill. *American Business Abroad: Ford on Six Continents*. Detroit, Mich.: Wayne State University Press. 1964. As I wrote that book, I sought a theoretical framework to understand the vast amount of archival data that I collected on this manufacturing multinational. My intensive Ford study was what stimulated me to look at the general issue of the history of American multinational enterprise.

9 Wilkins. *The Maturing*, 414.

10 Here I was accepting the views that were current in the 1960s: those of Stephen Hymer in his 1960 MIT Ph.D. thesis (still unpublished when I

In concluding my exposition, I wrote: "In a sense the five aspects of the Schumpeterian entrepreneur — the development of new products, new markets, new production methods, new sources of supply, and new forms of organization — seem to have been present in the US entrepreneurial enterprises that expanded over borders. In the process, US corporate leaders have interrupted the continuity of economic processes *abroad* and in a true Schumpeterian sense caused economic development outside their own country[11]. I was, however, in my work,more interested in the evolution of the firm than in documenting all the details of its impact.

My model, I insisted, applied to US businesses — whether the expansion across borders started in the 1850s or the 1960s. As I noted, "The timing in moving through this configuration [the one that I would present], the size of each foreign investment, and the specific reason why a corporation moved from one stage to the next varied greatly among US companies — depending on such factors as (1) the company's technological, product, managerial, or marketing advantage; (2) its concern with national versus local or regional markets in the United States; (3) the actions of customers and competitors; (4) the extent to which its resource requirements could be met at low cost through domestic investment or domestic or foreign purchases. Likewise, there failed to be uniformity in direct foreign investment *within* a single company, since the course of the investment depended on a multiplicity of factors, including: (1) where the foreign investment was made, (2) the type of investment, (3) when the decisions were made, and (4) who made the decisions[12]. Thus, I warned that I was in no way minimizing the vast variety in experience.

Before I put forth my model, I introduced one more key caveat: I did not want to imply inevitability; nothing in growth-of-the-firm pattern that I was presenting was deterministic. Some companies started on the route to becoming multinational and fell by the

---

was writing, but I had — as had all serious students of multinationals — read the unpublished thesis), Charles Kindleberger in his *American Business Abroad*, New Haven: Yale University Press, 1969, and, of course, in the work of Raymond Vernon and his students at Harvard Business School. Vernon's work was an inspiration to me.

11 Wilkins. *The Maturing*, 437.

12 Ibid., 415.

wayside; some retreated from individual countries. Some exited for many years from foreign business, and then resumed multinational activities with new vigor. While I searched for a pattern, I did not want to pigeon-hole. I felt very strongly on the individuality of particular decision making in specific circumstances; yet, I believed one could find general explanations[13]. My goal was to seek a general model of the evolution of multinational enterprise, one that could be applied to US manufacturing multinationals and all other US multinationals. My stages were part of a continuous process, not discrete, separate steps. Here, in the present article, I am only indicating how my model pertained to US manufacturing multinationals, as defined above[14].

At the start of the growth of the American multinational enterprise, the US manufacturing company invested abroad with little complexity. In what I called stage one, the firm's approach was monocentric. "The American company reached out to sell or to obtain and in doing so felt the necessity or saw the opportunity to cross over borders". American manufacturing companies with innovative technologies and unique products began to invest abroad — some as early as the 1850s. After preliminary use of independent foreign agents, they often established sales outlets abroad. They did so for marketing reasons, such as the need to keep inventores, have warehouses, display products, provide service, and so forth. Some firms, however, confronted with tariffs, patent laws, nationalism, high costs of transportation and existing or potential competition, moved rapidly into manufacturing abroad in order to reach certain foreign markets. They might license a manufacturer abroad and obtain a small interest in the licensee. They might buy the stock or assets of one or of several foreign manufacturers to penetrate an alien market. Or they might make "greenfield", new investments.

---

13 Ibid.

14 At the start of this essay, I indicated that my topic assignment was manufacturing multinationals. When I wrote *The Maturing*, manufacturing multinationals were the "rage". One of the unique, original, contributions of *The Maturing* was that it included discussions of non-manufacturing multinationals, of service multinationals (now the most topical of subjects), and, in fact, of companies that invested in all sectors. It argued that *all* US multinationals could be analyzed within the identical institutional frame of reference.

The initial stakes of US manufacturers abroad were usually part of a marketing strategy. At the same time, "a few, exceptional" manufacturers invested abroad to obtain low-cost, reliable sources of raw materials. Direct foreign investments by US manufacturing firms began as "spokes on a wheel", with the parent company at the hub. Usually, the chief executives in the parent firm were directly involved in the establishment of the foreign units, in decisions related to the financing of them, and in their staffing[15].

Then, over time, each of the existing foreign units (whether a sales outlet, a *factory* to serve foreign customers, or a *supply-related* stake) came to have its own history *outside* the United States. In each case, the affiliate abroad developed business at a different pace. Some units abroad failed to grow — they were not profitable and were sold off; others were expropriated. A *sales* outlet could remain such for years, remitting its profits back to the parent. Alternatively, it might reinvest profits and seek to cover new markets. It might undertake assembly, mixing, bottling, packaging, or a small amount of fabrication. It might persist for years (even decades) receiving no financial aid from the parent company, and then the parent might determine that within the particular foreign country, manufacturing was desirable, because the market was large enough to support a plant and/or because of politically imposed restraints on trade. Several options were available: (a) licensing an independent foreign firm to manufacture within the host nation; (b) manufacturing through its existing foreign sales unit; or (c) buying a foreign manufacturing plant in the same nation.

Meanwhile, the parent company's already established stakes in *factories* abroad would also be changing, becoming over time more integrated and diversified operations. These (along with the transformed sales outlets) acquired added functions and products. At first, foreign manufacturing subsidiaries had personnel consisting mainly of salesmen, accountants, and production executives and depended heavily on the parent firm for technology, engineering, product plans, research and development, and added imports (of machinery, components, and related final products). Over time, they grew less reliant on the parent and began to take on their own identities as ever more complete enterprises. Sometimes, they

---

[15] Wilkins. *The Maturing*, 416, 431-32.

served more than the host nation market. So, too, the supply-related investments abroad adopted their own character and histories.

And as the changes occurred abroad, at home, the US parent in its growth, might introduce new products, start new facilities, participate in mergers and acquisitions, and these new activities might in turn be reflected in new international operations. By this time, what had emerged was a growing international business and within the parent company there might develop some kind of an administrative organization to handle foreign business[16].

At this point, we enter, into what I called stage two. The earlier monocentric relationship no longer remained. While new and distinct foreign units would continue to be established or acquired by the parent company, radiating from the parent, as in stage one, what characterized stage two was the presence of foreign units with their own separate histories and their own satellite activities. In stage two, each major foreign unit of the US parent continued to assume additional functions, integrating its activities, and introducing new products. "It might acquire other firms; it might recruit its own product planning staff; in time, it might come to do its own research; it might make its own *foreign* (third country) investments. In its growth, the foreign unit might expand out of reinvested profits; it might borrow abroad." Within a single multinational enterprise, foreign units progressed at varying paces, while some were detached from the cluster — through bankruptcy, divestment, or expropriation[17].

Each of the principal foreign affiliates that persisted adopted its own distinct role within a foreign industry, operating in an economic and political environment different from that of its parent. The management of each made certain decisions on its own, not requiring approval from the parent; other decisions, however, were made exclusively in the United States. I compared the process to a purely domestic US enterprise, wherein certain decisions were made at headquarters and others made in the field. At the same time, I insisted that there were profound differences. The first related to geographical distance; usually, the foreign operation was farther from the home office than a domestic facility, which gave the foreign

---

[16] Ibid., 416-7, 432-3.

[17] Ibid., 417.

operation more independence. The second related to political distance; because the foreign unit was in another country, operating under a different sovereignty, far more than a domestic field office, it had to formulate unique responses. And, as it did so, and as it began to possess its own distinctive business history, what evolved in stage two to replace the original monocentric structure was a polycentric industrial relationship, characterized by heterogeneous foreign centers, each with diverse trading, administrative, and corporate relationships with the American parent[18].

At home the parent company continued to expand, deciding on new entries into foreign markets with existing products and more recent ones. At a certain point, if efficient, it would be likely to create a new administrative structure, adopting a multidivisional organization. Often, an international division was among the earliest set up by a multidivisional company[19].

The third stage in the evolution of the multinational enterprise — as I described it in 1974 — might come quickly after stage two or be long delayed. The awesome complexities of the third stage resulted from two sets of happenings: those involving (1) the parent

---

[18] Ibid., 418. I borrowed the *words* monocentric and polycentric from Hans Thorelli, who had employed them in a 1965 speech in relation to organizational structures, whereas I applied them to industrial structures. Ibid., 565n. 13. I did not name my third stage. Others had adopted variations of Thorelli's concept. Howard Perlmutter in a 1969 article contrasted ethnocentric, polycentric, and geocentric firms, in terms of management. In Perlmutter's view the first type firm issued detailed instructions from headquarters; the second involved a loosely linked group of decentralized subsidiaries; while the third, the genuine multinational in Perlmutter's view, was a stateless super-giant, with global objectives. For the lasting impact of Perlmutter's views, see "Howard's Perfect Multis", in Alex Rubner, *The Might of the Multinationals: The Rise and Fall of the Corporate Legend*. New York: Praeger. 1990, 39-44. My usage was *not* that of Perlmutter's; unlike Perlmutter, I had no normative overtones in my designations; my stages were sequential (i.e. historical); my third stage bore little resemblance to his "vision", for I never accepted the notion of "stateless" enterprises; in my view sovereignty was never at bay. Wilkins, *The Maturing*, 439. What my ideas shared with Thorelli and Perlmutter was attention to managerial structures, albeit I added concerns over trading, corporate, and financial structures.

[19] Wilkins. *The Maturing*, 418-9.

firm and (2) the existing foreign branches, subsidiaries, and affiliates. First, as the parent company grew, it continued, as in stage one and stage two, to expand abroad, starting new foreign units radiating from the parent company in its traditional products, but now going to more countries. Since at home, it introduced new products, these could be presented abroad, often requiring added foreign investments. So, too, the parent company might require more raw materiais from outside the United States. Thus, in stage three, as the parent company had new products and new needs, it continued its move abroad. The parent firm not only grew internally, but often through domestic and foreign mergers and acquisitions. Both its domestic and its foreign merger partners and takeovers might have their own international business operations. Accordingly, as a consequence of its mergers and acquisitions, a new monocentric or polycentric *foreign* business structure would be introduced, superimposed on its existing activities.

The implications were clear in the question that faced the parent firm: What was to be the legal, administrative, trading, and financial relationships between (1) the established parent company's units abroad (with their ramifications developed through time); (2) the new units initiated abroad, generally covering an even broader geographical range; (3) the new foreign units representing new products and new raw material needs of the expanding parent; and (4) the pre-existing international operations obtained as a consequence of domestic and foreign mergers and acquisitions. In short, there came into being abroad as an outcome of the US company's growth at home a collection of distinct foreign units to be merged or not merged (grouped or not grouped) abroad according to corporate choices.

And, if the added complexity occasioned by domestic growth and diversification were not sufficient, *abroad* in stage three, all the enduring established foreign affiliates and subsidiaries, through their own continued development, added to the tangle within the cluster. For a wide range of reasons, internal and external to the enterprise, the old relatively simple polycentric industrial structure of stage two, with the parent company as the sun and the subsidiaries as planets with satellite moons, disintegrated — and the imperatives for organizational innovation became overwhelming.

The numerous reasons internal to the enterprise included everything from the aggressiveness of the management of a particular foreign unit (that resulted in the directing more resources to that locale), to efficiencies (a foreign unit could only achieve economies of scale if it exported). The reasons external to the firm included, for example, US antitrust policy that forbade divisions of markets when there was an effect on US commerce — which meant that companies could not neatly divide world markets. Likewise, the establishment of the European common market (with the Treaty of Rome in 1957) made it more appropriate to supply a sales subsidiary within the community with a plant in Germany than one in the United States[20]. For many reasons, *foreign* affiliates altered their behavior in the course of growth and took on more activities and also activities different from those envisaged at their foundation.

Overtime, certain foreign subsidiaries and affiliates became full-fledged, fully integrated, multiprocess, multiproduct, multiplant, enterprises with engineering, product planning, and research staffs, with a continuity of employee, supplier, dealer, consumer, and banking relationships, and with their own prominent role in foreign industries, with their own staff to deal with the host government, and with their own third country investments that entailed similar relationships. Such subsidiaries and affiliates became centers not of limited but of extensive international trade, selling and buying from independent firms as well as from their own daughter firms and other firms within the multinational enterprise. Major foreign subsidiaries and affiliates recruited their unskilled, skilled, and managerial personnel not only in the countries where they were established, or in the United States, but in third countries. They raised capital wherever it was available, and were able to do so without the help of their parent. Certain foreign operations specialized in particular components, providing intermediate products to businesses in third countries. Networks of company associations emerged abroad, and the parent company could be to a large extent, or even completely excluded from the trading relationships.

By the time stage three was reached, the US parent manufacturing enterprise was no longer confined to several foreign countries, to a few products, or to one or two major processes, but existed in numerous foreign nations, in a range of different products and production processes, and with a proliferation of plants. Complica-

---

[20] Many more reasons were given in Wilkins. *The Maturing*, 420.

ted multi-faceted relationships replaced simple bilateral connections. Legal, administrative, trading, and financial structures no longer corresponded and thus could not be easily charted — and each, for different reasons, might follow a different design.

In the process of moving from stage two to stage three, the extent of managerial control by the parent company might loosen and then retighten as managements changed at home and abroad. At home, faced with the new and formidable complexities of stage three, US businesses might radically revise their organizational structures to cope with and control the new intricacies. Such reorganizations meant that the old "isolated" international divisions were eliminated, and firms restructured their corporate administration on a worldwide basis, relating to product, geographical areas, a combination of both, or overlapping grid structures. It was clear there would be experiments with other different organizational forms and lines of reporting in an attempt to rationalize the awesome complexity.

In stage three, there was introduced a new element of choice. Multinational enterprises could decide where to place productive activities, where to extend and where to contract them. They had unprecedented flexibility in using resources. They could alter patterns of production and trade. Financing and personnel recruitment were no longer national. The totally, fully, multinational enterprise, I concluded, would probably have dividend payments as multinational as plants, research and development, trade, financing, and employment. Yet, American multinationals still intended to return to the United States as high dividends and royalties as possible; the headquarters was still in America; and in that sense such firms were still national.

As I charted the growth of American headquartered manufacturing multinationals, I found that some, few, had passed out of stage one and into stage two by the early twentieth century; some were still in stage one by the end of the 1960s. I discovered a 1907 letter from H. B. Thayer, Vice President of Western Electric (then as now the manufacturing subsidiary for American Telephone & Telegraph) to an agent in Bangkok, Thailand. Thayer wrote:

> "You speak of anti-American attitude on the part of the [Government] Commission. We have offices and factories making our standard apparatus in Great Britain, Belgium, Germany, France, Russia, Austria, Italy, and Japan so that so far as this

matter goes we are international rather than American. If there were time we could arrange to have the order go to any one of those countries that might be preferred."[21]

Clearly, global sourcing was not confined to post-World War II American business abroad. In 1918, Western Electric set up a 100 per cent owned international subsidiary, International Western Electric Company, to own and to administer its international business[22].

In the 1920s, a number of American companies had reached stage two, with the world divided into territories and foreign manufacturing affiliates prepared to serve these allocated areas; some were by decade's end, in or approaching stage three, already having trade and ownership links among key foreign subsidiares and affiliates (located in different countries), with the parent excluded partly or totally from that trade. Thus, for example, the Timken Roller Bearing Company, an American enterprise, in 1927 acquired a majority interest in a formerly independent British manufacturer, British Timken Ltd. The US firm licensed the British one to use its know-how and gave it the rights to the Timken trademark. The next year, 1928, the American Timken and the managing director of the British Timken participated in founding French and German Timken companies. Each Timken firm manufactured the same product; each agreed to sell in a delineated territory and not to compete with one another. An orderly arrangement was established. Such partial ownership arrangements and division of market territories were not atypical[23].

After the Second World War, foreign dollar shortages meant that US companies with overseas factories often used them to export to markets that lacked dollars; this meant the expansion of a foreign manufacturing subsidiary, beyond its originally intended market.

---

21 Wilkins. *The Emergence*, 200.

22 Wilkins. *The Maturing*, 147. This was the company that would be sold to International Telephone & Telegraph in 1925. Western Electric in 1925 became a purely domestic manufacturer — an example of a retreat from international business. It was not until the 1980s that American Telephone & Telegraph — as both public utility and manufacturer— once again embarked on large scale international business!

23 Wilkins. *The Maturing*, 151.

American antitrust rulings made it clear that US companies could not assign territories to particular overseas plants; pre-war arrangements that divided world markets were terminated; they could not be renewed. In the 1950s, many third-world countries insisted on industrialization; US manufacturing multinationals that could not reach these markets through exports made investments within the confines of major third-world host countries. As European postwar recovery occurred, technologically advanced American enterprises sought to invest, to take advantage of the new opportunities. Especially in the 1960s, US investments in Europe multiplied. J. J. Servan-Schreiber's *The American Challenge* was a best-seller. It documented the spread of American technological achievements to Europe — through US manufacturing multinationals. Some American companies that had set up plants in times past to fill European market needs exported to the United States. More and more often plants were established in Europe to fill common market requirements, rather than individual national demand[24].

In the years 1945 to 1970, most US manufacturing companies — as in earlier times — invested abroad to obtain foreign sales. Some integrated backward into raw material procurement. New to the 1960s were the growing number of supply-related manufacturing plants in Hong Kong, Taiwan, South Korea, and Mexico. These factories were based on the availability of cheap labor and lower *US* tariffs. Many were in the new electronics industry and in components. In the 1960s, such stakes were still small compared with that

[24] Raymond Vernon's product life cycle sought to explain the investment in Europe and then the European exports back to the United States. Vernon argued that products had life cycles; that US companies developed innovative goods; that they exported them; then they made direct investments, producing the products abroad where with lower wages they could make them cheaper; in time, the lower-cost goods were in turn exported back to the United States. I was never happy about the idea that Americans invested in European plants to obtain cheap labor; my research never suggested that. I also was uncertain whether it was the identical products that had once been exported from the United States that were in the 1960s imported. Vernon's product cycle dealt with products and not firms; I wanted to discuss firms. Often, the US imports in the broad product category were not by American investors abroad, but by foreign-headquartered firms that had copied US methods and had also innovated with fundamental product variations.

same industry's market-directed foreign factories. In the 1950s and particularly in the 1960s, American manufacturing companies grew in size and complexity, and more moved from stage two to stage three.

What was original about my model was that it focussed on the multinational firm (rather than dealing with nations or industries or products, and the firm second); it was not bilateral (it assumed the growth of complexity — multicountry relationships); it did not look at isolated single decisions but rather at cumulative behavior; it was dynamic, dealing with change through time (while all economic and business historians do this, I was the first to apply an historical analysis to the overall growth of American multinational enterprise); it addressed changes in operations of the firm at home *and* abroad as the individual firm's multinational business evolved; it demonstrated conclusively that multinationals were not new to the post-Second World War period; and it considered the advantages of the whole firm — especially the multifunctional, multiplant, multiproduct, multidivisional, multinational enterprise — as it expanded internationally[25]. It appears to have been the first attempt to shape an ecumenical model of the development of the US multinational manufacturing enterprise.

The European, Japanese, and Canadian experience

Since my 1974 book was published, substantial research has been done on the history of British, Continental European, and Japanese manufacturing multinationals[26]. The history of Canadian manu-

---

[25] I am not sure I should claim originality on this last point; I was certainly original in putting the concept of "advantage" in an historical context, yet many economists were exploring the advantatves of the multinational firm and in that sense my work was obviously derivative (see note 10 above). In addition, as indicated, it was original in that my model dealt with all multinationals — not simply manufacturing multinationals.

[26] The best work on the history of British manufacturing multinationals has been done by Geoffrey Jones: see in particular, Geoffrey Jones, ed., *British Multinationals: Origins, Management and Performance.* Aldershot: Gower. 1986. Stephen Nicholas has long been studying the subject and

facturing multinationals has, however, not been treated systematically[27]. Third-world headquartered manufacturing multinationals are in the main of recent vintage — and thus have not attracted the attention of historians[28].

How does the US model, as presented above, fit? In many ways it fits very well — albeit its application to British multinationals had some curious consequences. The US model assumed a large business at home in the biggest of national markets; this gave the firm the "learned" advantages that allowed it to succeed abroad. In the British case, there were several findings: (1) A number of the late nineteenth-early twentieth century British direct investors in

---

has had a book pending for a number of years. A major contribution to the literature on continental European multinationals is Geoffrey Jones and Harm G. Schröter, eds., *The Rise of Multinationals in Continental Europe.* Aldershot: Elgar. 1993. Alfred Chandler, *Scale and Scope.* Cambridge, Mass.: Harvard University Press, 1990, deals with the history of American, British, and German manufacturing multinationals. Likewise, Mira Wilkins, *The History of Foreign Investment in the United States to 1914,* Cambridge, Mass.: Harvard University Press, 1989, has substantial data on European manufacturing multinationals in the United States. Major contributions to the study of the history of European multinationals have been made by Peter Hertner, Patrick Fridenson, Alice Teichova, Ragnhild Lundström, Harm Schröter, Keetie Sluyterman, to mention, but a few of the numerous economic and business historians. See also Mira Wilkins, "French Multinationals in the United States: An Historical Perspective". *Entreprises et Histoire,* n. 3 (May 1993), 14-29. In addition, much valuable work has been done on the history of Japanese manufacturing multinationals. Mira Wilkins, ed., *The Growth of Multinationals,* Aldershot: Elgar, 1991, contains a survey of the recent literature on the history of multinationals and some reprints.

27 Practically all the studies have been of Canadian manufacturing companies in the United States — and there have been several of these.

28 They have however, spurred books on their contemporary activities. The latest list of *Fortune 500* — the world's largest industrial companies — contains 166 from the United States, 128 from Japan, 40 from Britain, 32 from Germany, 30 from France, 14 from Sweden, *12 from South Korea* (historians take note), 9 from Australia, 9 from Switzerland, and 8 from Canada. See *Fortune,* July 26, 1993, 188-9. (Most "industrials" are "manufacturers", but the terms "industrial" does not exactly correspond with "manufacturing", as used in this paper, since oil companies, for example, *are* included.) There are also contemporary studies of "second world" multinationals — which do not rank among the major firms.

manufacturing abroad had *no* manufacturing at home whatsoever — and thus would not qualify at all for inclusion in this paper as a "manufacturing multinational" and were in fact generally excluded from studies of British manufacturing multinationals[29]. (2) A number of British manufacturing multinationals were very unsuccessful abroad; because a firm was a multinational did not necessarily mean that it would succeed[30]. (3) A number of British manufacturing multinationals — from Lever, to Courtaulds, to J & P Coats — fit the pattern described above to a tee.

While no British or continental European manufacturing firm had a direct investment abroad before the nineteenth century, there were direct investments in sales outlets that preceded those of American firms. Thus, Jean-Pierre Daviet found that the French glass-maker Saint Gobain had established a US sales branch in 1832[31].

Studies of the history of Swiss and Swedish multinationals revealed another difference that my model had not addressed. In the case of American multinationals, throughout the largest single market for American firms (even in stage three), was the home one. By contrast, very quickly Nestlé and Swedish Match, for instance, had greater business outside Switzerland and Sweden than within. SKF almost from the start had larger sales (and production facilities) in Germany than in Sweden.

In stage one, American companies virtually always had only a single plant in each host country abroad; dissimilarly, many Eu-

---

[29] There were British companies that invested in manufacturing cotton textiles in India, meatpacking in Argentina, breweries in the United States and South Africa, steel companies in the United States, and so forth that had *no* manufacturing in Great Britain. I called these "free standing companies". See Mira Wilkins, "The Free Standing Company, 1870-1914: An Important Type of British Foreign Direct Investment". *Economic History Review* 2nd ser. 33 (May 1988) 259-82. Applying the "American model" to British manufacturing abroad excluded all these direct investments!

[30] This point was made by Geoffrey Jones, in his introduction to *British Multinationals.*

[31] Jean-Pierre Daviet. *Un Destin International: La Compagnie de Saint-Gobain de 1830 a 1939.* Paris: Eds des Archives Contemporaines. 1988, 216. Even earlier, in the 1820s, some of British manufacturers' "agents" in the United States may have been controlled from the United Kingdom and tantamount to a direct investment in a sales outlet. See Wilkins, *The History of Foreign Investment in the United States to 1914*, 59.

ropean companies when they came to the United States — even in stage one — started several plants, to serve the greatly extended market[32]. Thus, they very rapidly became multiplant operations in a single host nation.

The concept of "advantage" seemed crucial to the US model. The advantage was derived from influences at home. It could be technological, organizational, or other advantage — but there had to be an advantage *if the firm was to succeed (to persist) abroad*[33]. This applied very well to non-US multinationals, albeit there were differences. American advantage was always "home grown"; by contrast, a number of Swedish companies adopted German technologies and expanded on the basis of these technological accomplishments[34]. In the Swedish case, the advantage was taken over and then extended abroad.

My model had no trouble with the notion that the earliest Japanese manufacturing multinationals were in textiles — since that was where in the first decades of the twentieth century the Japanese had been most innovative and had a true advantage[35].

What became very evident was that, historically, manufacturing multinationals headquartered in different countries had different advantages. There was not a uniformity in the historical pattern on which companies went abroad; yet just as in the American case so in the case of companies headquartered in other countries, there was a selection process; some companies did and other companies did not become multinational enterprises. Clearly, the home economy influenced everything from the industry to the method of business abroad to the direction of the investment (what locales were the first choices for investment and which places followed;

---

32 See Wilkins. *The History of Foreign Investment in the United States to 1914.*

33 Companies, US and non-US, often ventured abroad, assuming advantage; they failed when the advantage was not in evidence.

34 Mira Wilkins. "European and North American Multinationals, 1870-1914: Comparisons and Contrasts". *Business History* 30. January 1988, 55.

35 Mira Wilkins. "Japanese Multinational Enterprise before 1914". *Business History Review* 60. Spring 1986, 199-231. There were some other early (pre-1939) Japanese manufacturing multinationals: Kikkoman, Japanese match companies (about which we know little), and others in Korea, Taiwan, and Manchuria.

where abroad the investment was concentrated), to the pace of international investment. Thus, not only the advantages, but the pattern of moving abroad by manufacturing companies depended on the domestic environment in which the particular manufacturing unit originated[36]. And, just as experiences abroad shaped American multinationals, so too economic and political conditions in host countries molded the course of non-US multinational enterprise expansion.

The intermediaries that assisted in the earliest stages of the multinational process differed by country. Perhaps, American companies became more vertically integrated (forward integration) at home and abroad earlier than firms from other (at least some other) countries. While traders assisted US companies to move into stage one investments, the traders (with some few exceptions) bore little resemblance to the big Japanese *sogo shosha* that served as important sources of information for the first Japanese manufacturing companies to venture abroad[37].

There were clear differences by nationality in inter-firm, inter-industry linkages. The United States was alone in having had for years a strong antitrust tradition that shaped American business enterprise[38]. There may be a unique role of banks vis-à-vis international business patterns. In the case of US business abroad, manufacturing companies made the decisions: banks were always peripheral. We asked this question in relation to other foreign industrial multinationals. Rondo Cameron was prepared to conclude recently that, to his surprise, this was true of the 1870-1914 history of European multinational enterprise as well: "Banks were *not*", Cameron wrote, "with few and minor exceptions, responsible for the emergence of multinational industrial enterprises"[39].

---

[36] I made this point in Wilkins, "European and North American Multinationals". This was true even in the Swiss and Swedish cases, where business abroad quickly exceeded that at home.

[37] On this see, Shin'ichi Yonekawa and Hideki Yoshihara, eds., *Business History of General Trading Companies*. Tokyo: University of Tokyo Press. 1987.

[38] Jones and Schröter, ed., *The Rise of Multinationals*, 19, make this point about "Anglo-Saxon" versus Continental multinationals; Japanese multinationals also had different inter-firm, inter-industry relationships.

[39] Rondo Cameron and V. I. Bovykin, eds., *International Banking, 1870-*

Once non-US manufacturing multinationals set up businesses abroad, there were on occasion some notable differences in the path followed from that found in the US case. For example, when American business first organized marketing organizations abroad, and then subsequently decided to manufacture in the same country, the typical pattern was immediately to integrate the two functions (marketing and manufacturing) within the host country. I was thus surprised that certain Japanese investors in the United States, which had an established marketing network, organized the manufacturing facilities separately (and had each function report back along distinct administrative lines to Japan); as I predicted, over time, the two US affiliates began to have closer contact with one another, first on routines, and then on more substantive matters; they dealt with one another rather than each going through Japan[40].

In short, research on the history of non-US manufacturing multinationals has been fruitful. The attempt to apply the American model has brought out differences — and also remarkable similarities[41]. My model, however, was a US one — and does need certain modifications to become general.

Applying other research of the last two decades

Would I write the *US model* differently, based on new theoretical developments and on the new historical research on *American* business abroad of the last two decades? Fundamentally, the answer is "no". I think the model is still sound. My vocabulary would, however, be different — and I might address more explicitly certain issues. Thus, concepts relating to path dependencies, experience curves, transaction costs, internalization, boundaries of the firm,

---

1914. New York: Oxford University Press. 1991, 526-7; yet see Jones and Schröter, ed., *The Rise of Multinationals,* 19, which suggests not responsibility but a differing role by country.

40 Professor Tetsuo Abo's research project on Japanese manufacturing multinationals in the United States stimulated this finding.

41 I was amazed at how appropriate it was when I started to study the history of Japanese business in the United States. See Mira Wilkins. "Japanese Multinationals in the United States: Continuity and Change, 1879-1990". *Business History Review* 64. Winter 1990, 585-629.

contestable markets, and competitive performance, would undoubtedly be included in a newly written model. I might use the term "firm-specific" advantages to characterize more precisely the advantages that I have been considering essential. The phrases, strategic decisions and strategic alliances, have become fashionable, and I probably would employ them (although in the case of strategic decisions I would employ the phrase differently from its contemporary game-theoretic usage).

I think path dependencies and learning curves are inherent in my model as I perceived the growth of the firm. I did in a footnote cite R. H. Coase's classic article, "The Nature of the Firm", and I might have said more. I really had never thought very clearly about choices at the margin and the limits of expansion. In fact, when I did my research on the history of American multinationals, I had specifically looked at capital constraints and found to my surprise that with most American companies, that these were never in the long run (and only occasionally in the short run) major influences on decisions. American multinational companies if they did not have in-house capital could always borrow.

As for organizational constraints, I knew that firms reorganized for efficiency and that the organizational structure was important. Yet, I had not thought through the limits to organization, per se, or the fact that it was sometimes more efficient to do things within the firm and sometimes more efficient to deal with outsiders. This I think is a crucial insight of students of internalization — and here the work of Oliver Williamson is germane[42].

The notion of "core competencies" is useful, as one considers the boundaries of the firm[43]. I think we understand that the alternatives are not the bipolar, firm and market. The firm often has

---

42 For the particular influences of Oliver Williamson's work on mine, see notes to Mira Wilkins, "Defining a Firm: History and Theory", in Peter Hertner and Geoffrey Jones, eds. *Multinationals: Theory and History*. Aldershot: Gower. 1986, 80-95. Jean-François Hennart and I have had many long discussions on this subject, and he has been very influential in my thinking.

43 See Giovanni Dosi. "Sources, Procedures, and Microeconomic Effects of Innovation". *Journal of Economic Literature* XXVI. Sept. 1988, 1133. Michael Porter also writes of "core competencies".

rough edges[44]. There are within the national and multinational firm many types of special relationships that are not arms-length: these include licensing of otherwise independent firms and various types of supplier-dealer contracts. These relationships have different organizational requirements[45]. Then, of course, there are the separate independent outsiders — suppliers and customers. There has been an extensive literature on when firms make direct investments and when they license others; clearly, historically, direct investments and licensing are not always alternatives; sometimes they complement one another.

The concept of contestable markets is very attractive to me; the multinationals that I have been describing are able to move into new markets[46]. They make markets contestable. Alfred Chandler, whose work was influential in my original model, has added new insights and continues to be highly pertinent and enriching[47]. The volume of Richard Nelson and Sidney Winter on the evolutionary nature of the firm is completely in consonance with my approach, although I find myself a bit cautious about the biological analogies[48]. My own research has led me to put more explicit emphasis on trade marks as firm-specific advantages[49].

In the last twenty years, students of multinational enterprise have been heavily influenced by and have also influenced the field of industrial organization. They have enlarged on the earlier work of Hymer, Kindleberger, Vernon, and Richard E. Caves. F. T. Knickerbocker wrote a thesis on oligopolistic rivalries; Monty Graham

---

44 Wilkins. "Defining a Firm". On this subject I find myself very influenced by the work of Mark Casson.

45 On this, Jean-François Hennart has been particularly stimulating.

46 William J. Baumol, John C. Panzar & Robert D. Willig. *Contestable Markets and the Theory of Industry Structure*. New York: Harcourt Brace Jovanovich. 1982.

47 Chandler, *Visible Hand*, and Chandler, *Scale and Scope*.

48 Richard R. Nelson & Sidney G. Winter. *An Evolutionary Theory of Economic Change*. Cambridge, Mass.: Harvard University Press. 1982.

49 Mira Wilkins. "The Neglected Intangible Asset: The Influence of the Trade Mark on the Rise of the Modern Corporation". *Business History* 34. Jan. 1992, 66-95, and Mira Wilkins. "When and Why Brand Names in Food and Drink", in Geoffrey Jones & Nicholas Morgan, eds. *Adding Value*, forthcoming.

discussed exchange-of-threats; Caves published a splendid full length book on multinational enterprise and economic analysis. Jean Tirole elaborated, adding oligopolistic responses to the mainstream of the industrial organization literature[50]. I have read carefully all this work and found it of great interest.

One of the most significant contributions of recent research is the spreading acceptance of the view that firms can become large and profitable through efficiency rather than through predatory practices. There had long been in the economics literature, and in the inspiration behind antitrust policy, the belief that big businesses made monopoly profits, "economic rent", gained at the expense of workers and consumers. Consumers got less and paid more than with "perfect competition". What has emerged is the recognition that bigness is not necessarily bad; that economies of scale and scope create efficiencies; that big firms reinvest profits in research and development and new technologies; that technology is embodied in firms and that understanding how the firm innovates is important; that the management of giant enterprises matters; and that learned organizational capabilities were worth studying. None of this is new to the last two decades (and it was certainly implicit in my model), yet the ideas have gained in acceptability[51].

---

[50] See Richard E. Caves, *Multinational Enterprise and Economic Analysis.* Cambridge, Eng.: Cambridge University Press. 1982. And Jean Tirole. *The Theory* of *Industrial Organization.* Cambridge, Mass.: MIT Press. 1989. Recently, David Yoffie, in concluding his edited *Beyond Free Trade* (Boston: Harvard Business School Press, 1993), 434, wrote that the multinational firms his contributors studied were greatly influenced by the moves and countermoves of direct global competitors: *"firms invested heavily in competitors' markets, regardless of the profitability of such investments.* ... they wanted to prevent their competitors from having safe havens, they wished to pre-empt new entrants, or they wanted to create or maintain industry discipline and stability" (italics in the original). Unlike Vernon's earlier work on defensive investments, Yoffie's perception was of "aggressive" rather than "defensive" behavior.

[51] In 1932, Adolf Berle and Gardiner Means published *The Modern Corporation and Private Property,* arguing that the owner-managed firm was increasingly being replaced by impersonal shareholder equity in large scale managerial enterprises, making for a division between ownership and control. In a revised edition, in 1967, Berle's introduction noted that the modern corporation with its managerial organization

Today, there is new attention placed on what makes a firm "competitive". Countries and firms are looked at together, and comparative advantage is thought of not solely in country but in corporate terms[52]. Questions are asked can a firm be competitive but a nation not?[53] I am not sure how my model can or should incorporate such thoughts; persistence implies some form of competitiveness, and if my model shows how firms have survived in an international environment, perhaps that is enough. On the other hand, this line of thinking does press one to look more closely at performance as distinct from mere existente. John Dunning's OLI (ownership, location, internalization) stimulates this historian to be sure her model incorporares all these dimensions[54]. As for strategic alliances, these are far from new and my model is all about these interrelationships.

The last twenty years — the events

In the last twenty years, more multinational manufacturing firms

---

had resulted in tremendous increases in productivity (rev'd. ed., New York: Harcourt, Brace & World, 1967, xxv). Others such as Joseph Schumpeter had suggested efficiencies in large-scale enterprise. Chandler, however, more than any other single individual has contributed to this view, and the proponents are now joined by many economists, including Harold Demsetz, Oliver Williamson, and others. See for example, Demsetz, *Efficiency, Competition and Policy: The Organization of Economic Activity Vol. 2.* Oxford: Oxford University Press. 1989. The new work on technological innovations is extremely relevant. See Dosi, "Sources, Procedures and Microeconomic Effects of Innovation", 1.120-71.

52 Yoffie. *Beyond Free Trade*, is particularly good on this.

53 See Irving B. Kravis & Robert E. Lipsey. "Technological Characteristics of Industries and the Competitiveness of the US and its Multinational Firms". Working Paper no. 2933, National Bureau of Economic Research. Cambridge, Mass. April 1989.

54 John Dunning, who has been writing on multinational enterprise since the 1950s, has had immense impact on everyone (and I am no exception) who studies multinational enterprise. His most recent work, *Multinational Enterprises and the Global Economy* (Wokingham, Eng.: Addison-Wesley, 1993), provides a summary and an introduction to his numerous contributions.

(American and non-American) have moved into what my model called stage three[55]. I do not see a need for a stage four. Manufacturing multinationals are investing in more countries, in more functions, in more products, in more physical facilities, and the ways in which these activities are coordinated and controlled has undergone substantial change The complexities in the trade, legal, financial, and managerial relationships have increased.

In the last twenty years, there has been greater cross-border trade within manufacturing multinational enterprises in intermediate products; I anticipated the expansion of trade between and among affiliates, but did not say nearly enough about the differences between intermediates (tangible and intangible) and end-products. With lower barriers to trade (and reductions in relative transportation costs), it is less necessary that all components be produced or assembled within a single nation[56]. Likewise, products have become more complex and inputs more numerous. How information moves between and among the many units of a multinational enterprise is extremely important.

As new industries have evolved, stimulated by new technologies, we see a changed industrial horizon. My model was dynamic in nature; it emphasized advantage; there is nothing in it that cannot incorporate the rise of new manufacturing multinationals; in fact, this would be predicted and it would be forecast that those with new advantages would become involved in business abroad. The relaxation of American antitrust rulings has opened the way for a large number of partial alliances between companies that are product specific, technology-specific, country-specific, or even plant-specific. A recent *Wall Street Journal* article referred to the emerging alliances (that included Japanese and Dutch manufacturing multinationals in the United States) as American *keiretsu* — after the

---

55 In the splendid United Nations, *World Investment Report 1992*, 254-255, there is a wonderful description of Asea Brown Boveri, a perfect example of the complexities of a firm, in my "stage three".

56 By contrast, sometimes barriers to trade have *resulted* in third-country transactions. When US voluntary export restraints against Japanese goods emerged and when the United States imposed antidumping duties, some Japanese companies used as sources to supply the US market their owned factories in East Asia. See Dennis Encarnation, *Rivals Beyond Trade*. Ithaca: Cornell University Press. 1992, 168-70.

Japanese pattern of linkages[57]. Such associations exist in the United States and other markets around the world. In form, none of these strategic alliances is new and all can be encompassed within stage three of my model.

There are many more countries in the world than ever in history. Some companies operate in 140 or 150 different nations. The span is awesome. At the same time, the literature has noted the concentration of investment in the developed world. Why? This is where the opportunities are the largest, because of the high per capita income. This is where political stability prevails. This is where demand is similar to that at home. This is where the barriers to trade are lowest, so there can be cost advantages in specialization. And, this is where as in the past, so today, managers of manufacturing multinationals have put their major resources[58].

In the last two decades there has been a substantial increase multinational research and development; this would be predicted by my model that argues that over time as firms operate in stage three, more functions are placed where they can best enhance the appropriate units abroad.

The multiproduct, multiplant, multifunctional, multinational structures of the modern American (and non-American) manufacturing firm has introduced immense stresses on organizational capabilities as companies have grown with mergers and acquisitions. As a result, there has been a recurring need for organizational innovation: one sees business groups, regional configurations, and other organizational forms newly juxtaposed on the complexities. Lines of command, lines of control, lines of authority, within multinationals have to be redrawn to create efficiencies. The experimentation with such administrative structures that I predicted has come to pass.

The costs of generating and moving information — with fax machines; cheap international telephone calls; and computers — has fallen dramatically since 1974. The implications for multinational

[57] See fascinating story on the new digital media market: *Wall Street Journal*. July 14, 1993. The Dutch manufacturing multinational involved was Philips.

[58] Manufacturing multinationals have always historically had larger investments in developed than less developed countries, despite a literature that concentrares on the latter.

enterprise are profound, although the actual impact on the extent of internalization is not entirely clear.

What does seem new and very evident is that there appears to be a limit on size. General Motors got up to 800,000 employees — and has been cutting back rapidly. Generally, the peak seems to be about 350,000. Some few other companies reached 400,000, but above 350,000 there may well be major limits on organizational ability. Divestment and "downsizing", in the interests of rationalization, have become as much a part of the story of manufacturing multinational enterprises as "growth" per se[59].

My dynamic model did include divestment (through bankruptcies, reorganizations, and expropriations) so the closing down of facilities and the resorting of corporate assets between and among companies is easy to incorporate in the model that I have presented.

On a global scale, manufacturing technologies have changed; productivity in many industries has risen rapidly as a result of the application of new relationships between the worker and the machine, relationships that have been dramatically altered as the computer is able to direct many "production" tasks that had once required human beings. New industries and new social and mechanical technologies affect the growth of manufacturing multinationals; advantages change; location decisions alter. Yet, my model is surely sufficiently adaptable to incorporate such developments.

Whereas, in the 1950s and 1960s, American headquartered manufacturing multinationals held the spotlight, today it is apparent that although in many industries American multinationals remain in the lead, there are new challenges from Japanese and European manufacturing multinationals. There are also rising third-world manufacturing multinationals, generally still minor players in the world arena[60].

---

[59] In 1992 GM employed 750,000; Siemens 413,000; IRI 400,000, Daimler-Benz 376,000, Pepsico 371,000. No other industrial company had over 350,000. Ford, which had 427,000 employees in 1980, had 325,000 in 1992; IBM: which had 341,000 in 1980, had 308,000 in 1992. *Fortune,* July 26, 1993, for 1992 figures; United Nations Centre on Transnational Corporations, *Transnational Corporations in World Development. Third Survey,* New York: United Nations, 1983, 357, for 1980 figures.

[60] Of the 12 South Korean companies that ranked in *Fortune 500* in 1992, none ranked among the top ten industriais, although two did make the top fifty. *Fortune,* July 26, 1993, 229.

Unilever was the exception as a dual-parent headquartered manufacturing multinational enterprise of long-standing; Asea Brown Boveri is a newer entry. Will there be more? Alliances notwithstanding, there are no significant US multinationals sharing "headquarters". We can continue to discuss US manufacturing multinationals as based in a single country. The separation between a US and non-US multinational is still legitimate — the popularity of the "Who is 'us'?" notion notwithstanding[61].

Conclusions

My 1974 model on the growth of manufacturing multinationals seems to hold up very well to the test of time. Were I to revise it today, so as to generalize on the growth US *and non-US* manufacturing multinationals, to take into account the new research, and to comprise the events of the last twenty years, how would I change the format? In some of my most recent work, I have introduced five parameters that managers of multinationals (irrespective of nationality) use to make decisions to invest or not to invest in any particular foreign nation[62]. These include (1) the opportunity para-

---

[61] See Robert B. Reich. *The Work of Nations.* New York: Random House. 1992. Ben P. A. Gales & Keetie E. Sluyterman, "Outward Bound. The Rise of Dutch Multinationals", in Jones and Schröter, *The Rise of Multinationals*, 74, in a splendid article, suggest that Unilever was not an exception, that AKU was a joint Dutch-German venture (which indeed it was), and that Philips in the 1920s had attracted a 30 per cent interest from General Electric. Gales and Sluyterman conclude that "already in the 1920s, there was a tangle of interlocking interests across borders, which makes it difficult to speak of purely 'Dutch' multinationals". I wonder. Unilever did last with its joint headquarters; AKU, however, and its successor, AKZO, became in my mind definitely Dutch. General Electric sold its interest in Philips in 1952, but even before that Philips was clearly no t a jointly-headquartered company. Yet, their point is well taken, for interlocking alliances have long existed.

[62] Mira Wilkins. "Hosts to Transnational Investments — A Comparative Analysis", paper delivered in Munich in 1988, forthcoming in a volume to be edited by Hans Pohl, and "Comparative Hosts", forthcoming in *Business History.* Much of which follows comes directly from these two contributions.

meter; (2) the political parameter; (3) the familiarity parameter; (4) the third-country parameter; and (5) the corporate parameter. These parameters apply to all multinationals, including manufacturing multinationals. Nothing in my earlier model explained the sequencing of particular host countries (those that are recipients of foreign direct investment) in the evolving investment pattern, yet in considering the growth of multinational activities and the limits to expansion (not only do multinationals not go on expanding ad infinitum, but they do not expand everywhere), this seemed an obvious omission.

The opportunity parameter is straightforward: businesses invest at home or abroad where there are opportunities to sell and to obtain sources of supply. For the manufacturing enterprise, instead of the home nation being the frame-of-reference, the world becomes the basis for the search for opportunities. Yet, choices have boundaries. The larger a market, the more tempting, the sooner a firm will invest — either to sell its products through a distribution network or make its products within the host nation. In determining the size of the market, the number of customers *able* to purchase the company's specific goods or services is critical (large numbers of poor people do not, for example, provide a promising market for automobiles). How a market is currently being filled may also be relevant. If there are already firms (domestic or international ones) that fill the needs as well or better than a particular multinational, then there may be no opportunity. Alternatively, if a competitor perceives an opportunity, a firm may follow. Likewise, skilled cheap labor in a locale abroad may provide a good opportunity for investments in products that will be exported from the host country. The opportunity parameter relates to the *economic* allocation of a firm's resources.

Location theory that deals with where economic activity occurs is helpful in explaining not only the choice of a host country, but where within a host country an investment is made. Location theory is not useful in explaining the firm-specific aspects of opportunity, since it tells us nothing about whether this is an opportunity for a domestic or for an international firm, or for which particular international firm. In my 1974 model, I wrote firms "felt the necessity or saw the opportunity" to invest abroad, a rendition in keeping with the large contemporary literature on "defensive investment" that argued multinationals invested abroad to defend markets and to respond to oligopolistic rivals[63]. Indeed, critics of my new five parameters, drawing on the newer industrial organization literature and their own research, have asked whether I should have included a parameter on "rivalistic behavior", "exchange of threats", or "strategic interactions". I have felt that the "opportunity" parameter along with the corporate one (see below) were broad enough to encompass such motivations for direct investments. A company does not invest to defend a market, unless it perceives some kind of opportunity; companies in the same industry may see the same opportunity in the same or in different terms.

The second parameter is the political one. Depending on the political circumstances in a particular country, the economic opportunity may or may not exist. Government policies make a difference in investors' decisions. Huge opportunities existed for American cigarette manufacturers in the 1950s and 1960s in China; none invested; political circumstances made such investments impossible, economic opportunities notwithstanding. I include under the rubric of political conditions, nationalistic considerations.

The familiarity parameter comes next. *Ceteris paribus*, the nearer to the home country from a physical standpoint, the greater the shared cultural values, the closer the political relationships, the more congenial the business arrangements, the earlier and greater will be the multinationals' interests. The costs of extending a firm rise as that entity operates under circumstances less familiar. Faced with the same economic opportunities and the same political conditions, companies from different countries, within the same industry, make disparate investment choices for familiarity reasons.

The fourth parameter relates third-country issues. When a firm is in stage two or stage three of the model that I presented earlier, third-country matters are increasingly important. When the European Economic Community was formed, for example, the location of plants came to be based not only on national but on Community determinants.

Finally, the fifth parameter is the corporate one. This takes into account the enterprise's history, advantages, experiences, and strategies. It addresses to how managers perceive economic opportunities and judge political conditions; it considers how familiar mana-

---

[63] See text above. Vernon for as long as I can remember has been talking about defensive investments, as have his students.

gers themselves are with particular markets abroad and how they evaluate third-country circumstances. The marginal costs of expansion to alternative locales and in diverse products and process can vary greatly by firm. Core competencies are differently maintained in diverse environs. Managerial restructuring can enhance advantages, reduce uncertainties, and enlarge options. Integrated multinational aluminum companies have bauxite mining properties, refineries (bauxite to alumina), and smelters (alumina to aluminum). Where the facilities have been located, however, diverged substantially by manufacturing multinational — and the variation depended on the "corporate parameter"[64]. Managers are influenced by the behavior of other firms within their industry; firms lead, and follow[65].

These five parameters can be seen as providing an overlay on my existing dynamic model of corporate growth. Opportunities change (as economic development occurs; as purchasing power rises; as circumstances alter). Political conditions change (countries closed to investments become open, and vice versa; political regimes rise and fall). Familiarity increases with more contacts (jet airplanes, for example); it also decreases, as political changes can, for example, make a familiar country unfamiliar (Cuba, once very familiar to American multinationals, became after the Castro regime took power unfamiliar). Third-country relations alter (with wars and new political and economic alignments).

---

[64] See the absolutely wonderful article by Louis Wells, in David B. Yoffie, ed. *Beyond Free Trade.*

[65] There is no question that multinationals are aware of what competitors do. They operate in imperfect markets; they are price-makers not price-takers. I would *not*, however, include oligopolistic rivalry as part of a *general* theory of the growth of multinational firms. There are undoubtedly many cases where this explanation for foreign direct investment holds, but also many instances where it fails entirely to explain business strategies. Much of the literature on exchange-of-threats and oligopolistic rivalries discusses "cross-investments", where firms invest in their rivals' markets. My own research has found asymetry in the history of multinational enterprise rather than a persisting pattern of cross-investments, although there are clearly cases where cross-investment motives such as those described in Yoffie, ed. *Beyond Free Trade* (see note 50 above) prevailed. Most important, today's multinationals are engaged in much more than cross-investments; their sphere is much broader — as all students of multinationals recognize.

So too, corporate managements change; corporate strategies evolve, sometimes gradually and sometimes they take radical turns; advantages of any particular firm shift; new experience (and learning) arise within a firm; corporate memories dim. Moreover, a firm in stage one or stage two or stage three in its growth is confronted with new circumstances that pose differing requirements. Existing facilities and technologies create path dependencies. The major multinational enterprises are now multiproduct, multiplant, multiprocess, multifunctional units — with complex structures — and vast geographical spans. They are continually investing *and* divesting.

In sum, it is easy to stretch my US model to include other nationalities. To do so, the model considers the entire firm as it grows over borders, through time, and recognizes that the process is dynamic, uneven, and by no means deterministic, although experiences and past decisions set constraints on future ones. While the firm's growth is shaped by conditions in its home country; its evolution is also importantly influenced by circumstances in the countries in which it does business. I said this of American firms in 1974; it is true of all multinationals, yet those from different countries and those with different configurations of facilities and technologies will obviously behave in manners that are not identical. Throughout managers have choices, but the choices are restricted. If a manufacturing multinational is to succeed, if it is to persist and remain competitive, it must have some sort of advantage and retain that advantage (or gain new advantages). The advantages can be in technology, knowledge of products and processes, awareness of markets and sources of supply, and organizational structures. The advantages are ofte reflected in a trade name (brand name, trade mark, or company name) that identifies the firm's reputation and the quality of its output[66]. Overtime the advantages that sustain a multinational enterprise are typically in a package of attributes associated with the learned experience of the individual firm[67].

---

66 Wilkins. "The Neglected Intangible Asset".

67 This is very important. Often, third-world countries in the past thought that they could "unbundle" the firm's attributes, buy the technology, license the process, etc. What they failed to realize was that often the whole was greater than the sum of its parts and that the advantages of the multinational enterprise lay in the intangible "package" of experience along with products, processes, and so forth.

The firm may, as many British multinationals did, perceive advantage — and then find that the advantage was not there. Internalization (doing something within the enterprise) is not always the best approach. Sometimes, it makes economic sense not to expand a firm. There appears to be limits on how large an efficient firm can become — with the limits based principally on organizational capabilities.

With greater information flows, lower transportation costs, and lower barriers to trade, there has been and can be more trade in intermediate products. Yet, given political and economic uncertainties (along with the limits on organizational flexibility), full regional, much less global, rationalization is neither probable nor possible. Language barriers create communications obstacles. Nation states persist. Sovereignty is not at bay. The multinational enterprise must conform to national rules and regulations. Rational "economic" decisions must take into account uncertainties (no matter what the basis for the uncertainty); history teaches us that political surprises are common and that these "surprises" affect multinational enterprise.

The dynamics of multinational enterprise growth is not linear. There will be adjustments, divestment, reorganizations, an alliances. A firm will be expand where there is economic growth and opportunity and where it has a competitive advantage — assuming the barriers to investment are not too high. There will be contraction where there are long-term losses (where profits are not being made) and where the firm's particular operations do not contribute to the efficiency of the whole[68]. There will be retreats when political condi-

[68] It is very difficult for an outsider to measure a multinational's "successfull performance in any single host country without having a great deal of inside information. A company in a particular national market may report low profits or losses over long periods of time and this may be indicative of unsuccessful performance, *or* alternatively, the affiliate may be in a high tax nation (so the profits are taken elsewhere), or corporate strategy may for political reasons want to show low profits (a foreign company with large profits is often seen as an exploiter), or corporate strategy might want for other political reasons to allocate profits to another constituency (to be seen as a particularly good taxpaying citizen there), or the absence of profits of the particular operation may be unimportant for the unit is an essential part of an integrated process and overall there are profits. The multinational enterprise is a profit making organization; if over a long period of time

tions in host countries create too great obstacles. Companies will sell off businesses and buy others. Priorities are shaped by the five parameters given above. More firms will move into stage three. The evolution of multinational enterprise is a continuous, vital process; the successful firm must be innovative; advantages change with new competitive pressures, and with new technologies and economic growth.

---

an affiliate is not profitable, either it is unsuccessful *or* the student of multinational enterprise must find another reason for its continuing existence.

Peter Hertner
European University Institute, Florence (Italy)

GLOBAL ENTERPRISE BEFORE THE SECOND WORLD WAR: THE EXAMPLE OF THE ELECTRO-TECHNICAL INDUSTRY

An essential part of what has been called the "Second Industrial Revolution" was the production and distribution of electric energy and its application to transport, illumination and the production of heat and power[1]. The first private and public power stations, built in 1882/83 in New York, Milan and Berlin, were still very small direct current producers which supplied lighting to a few blocks in the heart of these cities[2]. Increasing demand and the subsequent growth of the electric generators' size created a load problem, since illumination peak hours occurred only twice a day in the early morning and during the evening hours. The electrification of public urban transport — and that meant normally: the electrification of tramways — seemed to offer a solution to this problem since it helped to increase electricity sales during day hours and thus helped to improve the power plants' efficiency.

By the middle of 1890, one sixth of United States tramways had already switched to electric traction; three years later 60 percent

---

1 Cf. for instance D. S. Landes. *The Unbound Prometheus. Technological Change and Industrial Development in Western Europe from 1750 to the Present*. Cambridge. 1969, p. 4, 196, 235.

2 Cf. T. P. Hughes. *Networks of Power: Electrification in Western Society, 1880-1930*. Baltimore/London. 1983, p. 41 ff.; C. Pavese. *Le Origini della Società Edison e il suo Sviluppo fino alla Costituzione del "Gruppo" (1881-1919)*, in B. Bezza (ed.). *Energia e Sviluppo. L'Industria Elettrica Italiana e la Società Edison*. Torino. 1986, p. 23-169, and particularly p. 48; C. Matschoss, E. Schulz & A.Th. Gross. *50 Jahre Berliner Elektrizitätswerke*. Berlin. 1934, p. 11 ff.

and by the end of 1903, 98 percent of US tramways had been electrified. In Europe, these changes took more time: by the end of 1895, a quarter of the German tramway network had adopted electric traction, by the end of 1902 practically all German tramways were electrified, whereas in Britain only 38 percent of the network had undergone the same change[3].

A second element which could improve the load factor was the supply of power to machines in artisanal workshops and factories. This process took considerable time to develop; it started by the middle of the 1890s and came to a certain conclusion only by the end of the 1920s. By 1909 barely a quarter of industrial power had been electrified in the United States; in Germany, this had been the case with 19.5 percent two years earlier[4].

A decisive technological break-through had made these developments possible: long distance transport of high-voltage alternating current as demonstrated by the pioneering experiment, done in 1891, of connecting a power plant at Lauffen on the Neckar river to Frankfurt/Main over a distance of not less than 179 km[5]. As a consequence, and with subsequent technological development, energy production and consumption could take place at sites which remained hundreds of kilometers distant from each other. Electricity production could thus move directly to the coal or lignite mines and, as far as the use of water power was concerned, dams and artificial storage reservoirs could be built high up in the mountains in order to tap all available resources.

Financing these power plants of steadily growing size and the expanding regional grids of distribution required a rapidly increa-

---

[3] Cf. J. P. McKay. *Tramways and Trolleys. The Rise of Urban Mass Transport in Europe*. Princeton: N. J. 1976, p. 50, 73; K. T. Jackson. "The impact of technological change on urban form", in J. Colton & S. Bruchey. *Technology, Economy, and Society: The American Experience*. New York. 1987, p. 156.

[4] Cf. W. D. Devine. "From Shafts to Wires: Historical Perspective on Electrification", *Journal of Economic History*, 43 (1983), p. 347-72, and particularly p. 354; S. B. Saul. "The American impact on British industry 1895-1914", *Business History*, 3 (1963), p. 129-38, and particularly p. 36, note 1.

[5] Cf. T. P. Hughes. Op. cit., p. 129 ff.; B. A. Behrend. "The debt of electrical engineering to C. E. L. Brown", part IV, in *Electrical World and Engineer* 38 (1901/II), p. 932-4, part V, p. 1.015-8.

sing share of national income which, in the case of Britain during the first decade of the 20th century, has been estimated at amounting to about 10 percent of gross domestic capital formation[6]. The swift growth of electrification, at least in the industrialized countries of Europe and in North America, was accompanied by an equally dynamic development of the electro-technical industry which produced the equipment necessary for creating and distributing this new source of energy.

The 1880s and the following decade were characterized by a relatively large number of small and medium-sized electro-technical firms active in practically all industrialized countries, but by the end of the 1890s conditions had changed. First of all and particularly in the high-voltage sector, most of the products had reached a certain level of technical maturity which awarded a premium to those firms able to switch over to standardized mass production. This was true especially for goods like light bulbs or small electric motors which found a fast growing market among a public of small enterprises and final consumers. The erection of power plants, which constantly grew in scale since the middle of the 1880s, favoured on the other hand "full-line" producers who could offer solutions for an entire system, as Harold C. Passer has expressed with great clarity:

> "Electrical products had to be part of a system — a lighting system, a power system, or a transportation system. To ensure that the component parts would operate together in a satisfactory manner, manufacturers found it advantageous to produce all, or nearly all, of the components of any system they chose to market. They also found it advantageous to sell and install the complete system"[7].

Thus, standardized mass production on the one hand and the advantages connected with "full-line" manufacturing on the other created the conditions for a rapid concentration process in this branch. Finance was another factor which accelerated this deve-

---

[6] I. C. R. Byatt. *British Electrical Industry 1875-1914: The Economic Returns to a New Technology*. Oxford. 1979, p. 5.

[7] H. C. Passer. "Development of large-scale organization. Electrical manufacturing around 1900", *Journal of Economic History* 12 (1952), p. 378-95 (quotation on p. 392).

lopment: fast growth during the 1890s required increasing amounts of capital which could be mobilized either via the Capital market or via the banking system. Actually both ways were interdependent and normally the banks provided credit and acted as intermediaries for eventual-debt consolidation via the placing of equity titles and bonds. There were firms like General Electric or AEG which were "public companies" with a wide-spread shareholders ownership and with close links to the banks right from their foundation[8]. There was a typical family enterprise like Siemens & Halske, founded already in 1847, which, as a result of pressure stemming from the Deutsche Bank, became a joint-stock company in 1897 with the Siemens family, however, owning the majority of stock for the next few decades. George Westinghouse, founder of the second largest US company in the high-voltage sector equally needed bank support on several occasions and received it, but he never really collaborated with these credit institutions in a satisfactory way. The result were recurrent financial instabilities of the Westinghouse company which lasted for decades[9]. There were, finally, smaller but still very important firms like Schuckert of Nuremberg or medium-sized German companies like Helios or Kummer which did not have sufficient backing from banks. After a rapid expansion in the 1890s, the latter two disappeared from the market as a consequence of the crisis of 1901/02, or were forced to merge as Schuckert did in 1903 with the high-voltage branch of Siemens & Halske[10].

By 1902/03, when the concentration process had reached its first climax, a world-wide oligopoly had been firmly installed and there

---

[8] Cf. W. B. Carlson. *Innovation as a Social Process. Elihu Thomson and the Rise of General Electric, 1870-1900.* Cambridge. 1991, p. 271 ff.; P. A. David. "The hero and the herd in technological history: Reflections on Thomas Edison and the Battle of the Systems", in P. Higonnet, D. S. Landes & H. Rosovsky (eds.). *Favorites of Fortune. Technology, Growth and Economic Development since the Industrial Revolution.* Cambridge. Mass./London. 1991, p. 72-119, particularly p. 94 ff.; *50 Jahre AEG* (privately printed, Berlin, Allgemeine Elektricitäts-Gesellschaft, 1956), p. 21 ff.

[9] Cf. J. Kocka. *Unternehmensverwaltung und Angestelltenschaft am Beispiel Siemens 1847-1914.* Stuttgart. 1969, p. 319 ff.; H. C. Passer. *The Electrical Manufacturers 1875-1900.* Cambridge, Mass. 1953, p. 279.

[10] Cf. J. Loewe. "Die elektrotechnische Industrie", in *Die Störungen im deutschen Wirtschaftsleben während der Jahre 1900 ff.*, III (*Schriften des Vereins für Sozialpolitik*, CVII). Leipzig. 1903; J. Kocka. Op. cit., p. 327 ff.

were two US firms and two German companies which together dominated the world market: General Electric, founded in 1892 through a merger of Edison General Electric Company, Thomson-Houston Electric Company and Thomson-Houston International Electric Company, as the biggest US firm, followed by the Westinghouse Electric and Manufacturing Company, created in 1891 by the merger of the Westinghouse Electric Company, itself founded in 1886, with two smaller firms. For the time being these two were the only "full- line" manufacturers of high-voltage equipment in the United States[11]. The two big German firms were Siemens, founded, as we have already seen, in 1847 and merged, for its high-voltage business, with Schuckert in 1903, with the Siemens family remaining control of the new Siemens-Schuckert branch. On the other hand there was the Allgemeine Elektricitäts-Gesellschaft (AEG), founded in 1883 as Deutsche Edison-Gesellschaft by the industrialist Emil Rathenau and a group of Frankfurt and Berlin banks. In 1887 it changed its name to AEG and managed to free itself from technical dependence on Edison and Siemens gradually until 1894[12].

As to the size of these four companies we could eventually compare their sales in 1913, converted, for the sake of comparison, into German marks, and we would find out, astonishingly enough, that the two German firms were slightly bigger than their American competitors: the Siemens group numbered sales of 472 million marks, of which however 23 percent were being done by its low-voltage branch; AEG reached 453 million, General Electric 447; the Westinghouse group being last with sales of about 160 million[13]. Siemens and AEG dominated the national German market: in 1913 their share in total sales of the German electro-technical industry

---

[11] Cf. the detailed description in US Senate, 70th Congress, 1st Session, Document n.° 46. *Electric Power Industry: Supply of Electrical Equipment and Competitive Conditions*. Washington, D.C. 1928, p. 15 ff.

[12] For a brief description of these developments, see P. Hertner. "Financial strategies and adaptation to foreign markets: the German electro-technical industry and its multinational activities: 1890s to 1939", in A. Teichova, M. Lévy-Leboyer & H. Nussbaum (eds.). *Multinational Enterprise in Historical Perspective.* Cambridge/Paris. 1986, p. 145-59.

[13] I. C. R. Byatt. Op. cit., p. 166; for General Electric in 1913 cf. US Senate, *Electric Power Industry*, cit., p. 46.

amounted to about 58 percent; the remaining part was produced by a group of about 350 small and medium-sized firms. In 1930, the share of the two big companies in the German market had slightly shrunk to a figure of about 53 percent[14].

General Electric's share of total US electro-technical production in 1914 has been indicated as being 24.8 percent[15]. On a world-wide scale, the German electro-technical industry's share of world production in 1913 approximated, according to one estimate, to 35 percent, compared to the United States' 29 percent[16]. Another estimate gives 31 percent to the German industry and 35 percent to the American[17]. It is agreed, however, that German industry, with its comparatively limited home market, dominated world exports of electro-technical goods with a share of 46 percent, followed by the British and US industries with shares of 22 and 16 percent respectively[18]. According to a contemporary observer, German electro-technical industry exported 22 percent of its production in 1913 whereas the Americans with their huge home market remained at a level of about 7 percent[19].

After 1918 the once dominant position held by the German electro-technical industry on the world market could not be reestablished: its share of world exports fluctuated around 25-28 percent during the second half of the 1920s. Only in 1931, at the height of the world economic crisis, did it reach the exceptional percentage of 32.7. The corresponding share of American industry amounted to 24.9 percent in 1925 and 26.5 percent in 1929[20]. Since 1914 the

---

[14] H. Homburg. *Rationalisierung und Industriearbeit. Arbeitsmarkt-Management-Arbeiterschaft im Siemens-Konzern Berlin, 1900-1939.* Berlin. 1991, p. 350.

[15] US Senate. *Electric Power Industry,* cit., p. 66.

[16] P. Czada. *Die Berliner Elektroindustrie in der Weimarer Zeit.* Berlin. 1969, p. 138.

[17] G. Jacob-Wendler. *Deutsche Elektroindustrie in Lateinamerika: Siemens und AEG (1890-1914).* Stuttgart. 1982, p. 11; "Die Elektrizität auf dem Weltmarkt", in *Elektrotechnische Zeitschrift*. 1913, p. 1.016.

[18] P. Czada. Op. cit., p. 137 ff.; G. Jacob-Wendler. Op. cit., p. 11.

[19] "Die Elektrizität auf dem Weltmarkt", cit.

[20] P. Czada. Op. cit., p. 317; A. Glardon. *Die deutsche Elektroindustrie und der Absatz ihrer Erzeugnisse in der Nachkriegszeit*. Hamburg. 1933, p. 61.

development of the US electro-technical industry had been clearly more dynamic: in 1927 the total volume of its production amounted to 7 billion marks against 2.7 billion marks for the German output in this sector. This means that American production had grown almost fivefold since 1912 whereas in the German case it had only somewhat more than doubled[21]. In 1929 Siemens' sales volume amounted to 850 million marks and AEG had a corresponding figure of 580 million. Both of them were largely left behind not only by General Electric, but also by Western Electric — the latter one producing above all telephone equipment — with 1,744 and 1,722 million respectively, whereas the second US producer of high-Voltage material, Westinghouse, was not so far removed from the two German firms with its sales volume of 909 million marks[22].

The two big German firms could easily be called prototypes of multinational enterprises[23]. Each of them had so-called "technical offices" at home and abroad which were responsible not only for most of the sales but also for after-sale service wich was particularly important given the technical complexity of these investment goods and the necessity to keep, for instance, power plants running around the clock. Exports amounted to 33 percent of total sales by Siemens-Schuckert in 1913/14, to 35 percent in the case of Siemens & Halske and to about 40 percent in the case of AEG[24]. These proportions did not undergo considerable changes in the post-war era: in 1929/30 these shares amounted to 44, 33 and 38 percent respectively[25]. Furthermore, increasing tariff and non-tariff protectionism forced these two companies to establish producing subsidiaries abroad,

---

21 Calculated on the basis of A. Glardon, op. cit., p. 15; cf. also F. Gapinski, *Die Stellung der deutschen Elektroindustrie innerhalb der internationalen Elektro-Wirtschaft in der Gegenwart* (doctoral thesis, University of Cologne; published Berlin 1931), p. 85, 90.

22 A. Gebhardt. *Die Expansion der amerikanischen Elektro-Konzerne in Europa* (doctoral thesis, University of Heidelberg, published Wertheim am Main 1932), p. 8.

23 Cf. P. Hertner. "Financial strategies", cit., p. 146; idem, "German multinational enterprise before 1914: Some case studies", in P. Hertner & G. Jones (eds.). *Multinationals: Theory and History*. Aldershot. 1986, p. 113-34.

24 H. Homburg. Op. cit., p. 362.

25 Ibidem.

and especially in the principal European markets: Siemens employed 82.900 persons, of which almost 17.000 worked in the factories which had been set up in France, Britain, Russia, Spain and in both parts of the Austro-Hungarian Empire. AEG had 70.162 persons employed in 1912; 6.551 of them belonged to its factories in Vienna, Milan and Riga[26].

As to the two big American companies, we do not possess data on the relative importance of exports in their total sales before World War I. In 1923, this share amounted to 6 percent for General Electric, and to 6.9 percent for Westinghouse, whereas it was 4.7 percent for the entire US electro-technical industry during the same year[27]. It is by no means probable that this percentage could have been higher before 1914. The American firms had also founded subsidiaries abroad: General Electric, via its subsidiary British Thomson-Houston, which had been created in 1894, and since 1901 with the help of its new works at Rugby, dominated the market for the electrification of British tramways, but it had also a comparatively strong position for the equipment of new power plants of which it had supplied 16 percent of the capacity installed between 1909 and 1913[28]. In France General Electric held a participation — even if its size shrank rapidly after 1894 — in the Compagnie Française Thomson-Houston, the largest electro-technical producer in that country[29]. On the contrary, the international expansion of Westinghouse met with recurrent difficulties due to the mother company's chronic undercapitalization which also left its subsidiaries too often with urgent liquidity problems. When, in 1907, the US mother firm went into receivership, Westinghouse could count on producing subsidiaries in Britain, France, Russia, Italy and Canada[30].

---

26 Cf. P. Hertner. "Financial strategies", cit., p. 145.

27 US Senate. *Electric Power Industry,* cit., p. 78.

28 I. C. R. Byatt. Op. cit., p. 33 ff., 138; cf. also H. A. Price-Hughes, *B.T.H. Reminiscences. Sixty-years of Progress.* Leicester/London [1946], p. 9 ff.; M. Wilkins. *The Emergence of Multinational Enterprise: American Business Abroad from the Colonial Era to 1914.* Cambridge, Mass. 1970, p. 94.

29 Cf. P. Lanthier. *Les constructions électriques en France: Financement et stratégies de six groupes industriels internationaux, 1880-1940* (Thèse de doctorat, Université de Paris-Nanterre). 1988, p. 40 ff.

30 Cf. *The Westinghouse Companies in the Railway and Industrial Fields.* Chicago/New York. 1905, p. 43; P. Lanthier. "Westinghouse en France:

So far we have agreed that the "four electro-technical sisters" formed a world-wide oligopoly at least until 1914. We have also seen that they were full-line, multinational producers, the only other firm which fulfilled these conditions, although on a quite smaller basis, being the Swiss Brown Boveri group with subsidiaries — already before 1914 — in Germany, France, Italy, Norway and Austria-Hungary[31]. But could we go a step further and talk of the electro-technical industry, during the period which ran up until the Second World War, as of a "global industry" in the sense of Michael E. Porter's definition? Porter defines, as a matter of fact, an industry "... as global if there is some competitive advantage to integrating activities on a worldwide basis"[32]. He distinguishes these "global industries" from what he calls "multidomestic industries" where "... competition occurs on a country-by-country basis" or where "... the competitive outcome over time is ... determined by conditions in each country". While, according to Porter, "multidomestic industries" "... can choose to remain domestic or can expand internationally", "... a global competitor must view its international activities as an overall system" maintaining, nevertheless, "some country perspective"[33].

If we accept this approach, could we then call the electro-technical industry a "global industry", and — if yes — which were the competitive advantages that allowed its international presence? International competition on a practically global scale was compelling particularly for those producers who had "gone full-line" for five clearly distinguishible reasons[34]:

Histoire d'un échec (1898-1920)". *L'Information historique* 47 (1985), p. 212-9; M. Wilkins. Op. cit., p. 96.

31 Cf. W. H. Ziegler. *Die wirtschaftliche Entwicklung der A. G. Brown Boveri & Cie., Baden, des Brown Boveri-Konzerns und der A. G. Motor-Columbus* (doctoral thesis, University of Berne). Brugg. 1937, p. 93 ff.

32 M. E. Porter. "Competition in global industries: a conceptual framework", in his *Competition in Global Industries.* Boston, Mass. 1986, p. 15-60, quotation p. 19.

33 Idem, p. 18 f.

34 These reasons have been developed in detail in P. Hertner. "Espansione multinazionale e finanziamento internazionale dell'industria elettrotecnica tedesca prima del 1914", *Studi Storici.* 1987, p. 819-60, and particularly p. 826 ff.

(1) The *technical quality* of much of the high-voltage equipment and its system character which, at least during the first two decades of development, made it difficult for customers to change producers;

(2) The *quality of service* which started with assembly of the plants and ended with a reliable after-sale service;

(3) *Innovation of production processes* which led, as already described, to standardized mass-production combined with economies of scale accessible only to large firms which could boast the necessary capital and access to large markets;

(4) *The organizational structure and the quality of management* which only the large firm could achieve; according to Alfred D. Chandler, " ... the structure built at General Electric became and still remains today a standard way of organizing a modern integrated industrial enterprise"[35]. Practically, that meant steady control from the top combined with "a surprising degree of independence" of the individual factories"[36]. A high degree of centralization was also guaranteed in the case of AEG with the undiscussed leadership of Emil Rathenau, founder and director-general of the enterprise[37]. As to Siemens, there were at least several attempts, not all of them totally convincing, to overcome the typical organization of a family enterprise and to create a responsible body of managers without letting the family lose control over its firm[38];

(5) Finally there were important advantages in *financing not only electro-technical production itself but also in financing the expansion of the market*. The latter problem meant concretely that electro-technical producers established local and regional power, tramway and lighting companies in those countries (especially of the European periphery and of Latin America) and for those customers (particularly local public authorities) which suffered from chronic lack of capital and showed little initiative. Newly created companies were then forced by contract or statute to buy their electro-technical

---

35 A. D. Chandler. *The Visible Hand: The Managerial Revolution in American Business*. Cambridge, Mass./London. 1977, p. 433.

36 H. C. Passer. "Development of large-scale organization", cit., p. 385.

37 Cf. F. Pinner. *Emil Rathenau und das elektrische Zeitalter*. Leipzig. 1918, p. 350 ff.

38 Cf. the fundamental analysis of J. Kocka. Op. cit., p. 233 ff., 390 ff.

supplies from their big industrial founders[39]. These electro-technical producers found themselves, however, with the risks stemming from the accumulation of a growing volume of equity capital which they had to keep in their portfolios and which threatened to reduce their liquidity quite dangerously. By creating financial holdings together with the great banks the producers managed to solve this problem.

The financial holding companies were supposed to take over the shares and bonds of the newly created public utility companies, to keep them in their portfolios during the period of construction and initial development, and to sell most of these securities to the general public as soon as they had "matured" and were able to yield a profit. Each of the German electro-technical producers controlled such intermediate financial holdings; those earmarked for international business were often based in Switzerland or Belgium for legal and fiscal reasons[40]. Probably the oldest one was the United Electric Securities Company, founded by Edison General Electric in 1890. In 1904 General Electric created the Electrical Securities Corporation and in 1905 the Electric Bond & Share Company[41].

Any of these five groups of advantages tended to favour global strategies, but the strongest pressure probably came from two of them: technology and finance. Global strategies *vis-à-vis* the other competitors could run from fierce rivalry to close collusion. An intermediate solution seemed to offer attempts to delimitate neatly each one's market, either by product or by territory as AEG and General Electric did in 1903 when they split up the world among themselves and decided for the exchange of patents and licenses. Other agreements of this kind followed and became much more sought after in the inter-war period, again between AEG and GE but also between Siemens and Westinghouse[42]. These phenomena cannot be treated

---

39 Cf. above all the important contemporary study by R. Liefmann. *Beteiligungs — und Finanzierungsgesellschaften. Eine Studie über den modernen Kapitalismus und das Effektenwesen.* Jena. 1913, p. 103 ff.

40 Cf. P. Hertner. "Financial strategies", cit., p. 151.

41 Cf. R. Liefmann. Op. cit., p. 389 ff.

42 Cf. H. Schröter. "A typical factor of German international market strategy: agreements between the US and German electro-technical

in detail in this context but they could certainly be judged as good indicators for the fact that this particular industry had "gone global" well before any economist started to discuss the matter.

industries up to 1939", in Teichova, A., Lévy-Leboyer, M. & Nussbaum, H. (eds.). *Multinational Enterprise,* cit., p. 160-170.

Hubert Kiesewetter
Katholische Universität Eichstätt (Germany)

THE INTERNATIONAL HARVESTER COMPANY IN EUROPE (1902 TO 1918)

Until the end of World War I, the International Harvester Company (IHC) occupied a unique position, not only within the harvester business in the United States, but also among the leading industrial corporations at home and abroad. The hostility towards large foreign corporations, and against the "American invasion" was most severely felt in Europe. The analysis of trade activities, which functionally and strategically competed for market shares of multinational enterprises like IHC, can possibly clarify how differences in trade conditions in foreign countries may have changed the selling policy of multinational corporations. My paper deals with four aspects concerning the business methods of International Harvester in Europe: (1) the formation and consolidation of the Company, (2) the selling strategy and structure of IHC in Europe until 1914, (3) the confrontation with European competition, and (4) the conduct of the Company during World War I.

I

The beginning of the twentieth century was not very promising for the American agricultural implements industry. In 1901/02 an economic crisis at home and in Europe sharpened the competition between the hundreds of establishments all over the United States[1].

[1] See *Twelfth Census of the United States, Taken in the Year 1900. Manufactures*, Part I, Washington, US Census Office, 1902, p. 66, where 715 establishments with a capital of $157, 707, 951 are registered.

This led McCormick Harvesting Machine Co. of Chicago, Illinois, to consider combining the principal harvesting implement manufacturers in the United States[2]. On June 24, 1902, P. D. Middlekauff, an agent of the McCormick Company, secured an option on the stock and plant for $3,123,691.90 of the Milwaukee Harvester Company of Milwaukee, Wisconsin. The next day Middlekauff went to New York to assign this option to J. P. Morgan & Co., and remainded there until July 30, 1902. During that month, representatives of the McCormick Company, the Deering Harvester Company of Springfield, Ohio (called "Champion") and the Plano Manufacturing Company of West Pullmann, Illinois, were all in New York. They stopped at different hotels and avoided seeing one another. All of them, however, talked with George W. Perkins. On July 28, 1902, these representatives seperately met with William C. Lane, a New York banker and later president of the Standard Trust Company, who was acting upon the suggestion of his counsel, Guthrie, Cravath & Henderson. Lane agreed to sell all their tangible property and specified portions of their bills receivable. "These agreements all contained a recital that the purchaser, upon his acquisition of the property, intended to transfer the same to a corporation to be organized under the laws of Illinois, or some other State, called the 'purchasing company'."[3] The total amount of the four vendors' stock were valued at $76, 451,721.48, leaving 49.27% for McCormick, 40.32% for Deering, 6.31% for "Champion", and 4.10% for Plano.

On August 11, 1902, the day before the International Harvester Company was officially organized under the laws of New Jersey with a total capital of $120,000,000, a new contract was made; all the companies signed an agreement for the immediate devilery of the plants and property. On August 12, the board of directors agreed that the five companies, McCormick, Deering, Milwaukee, Plano, and Warder, Bushnell & Glessner furnished $60 million of working

[2] See McCormick Archives, Madison (Wisc.). Nettie Fowler McCormick Papers, Box No. 29 A, where Stanley wrote on March 5, 1901, to his brother Cyrus H. McCormick "that it will be useless for us to attempt to make any progress [in the consolidation, H. K.] if we lay down the ultimatum that we must retain control in any event".

[3] Federal Anti-Trust Decisions 1890-1917. Compiled by John L. Lott and Roge, Shale, vol. 5, Washington, Government Printing Office, 1917, p. 642.

capital which was to be represented by accounts and bills or in cash. A day later, it was accepted that the capital stock of the new company would be $120 million, even though it seemed to be an over-capitalization. In pursuance of the agreement of August 12, 1902, International Harvester shortly afterwards acquired all the stock of the Milwaukee Harvester Company, reduced its capital to $1million, and changed its name to International Harvester of America. In the following year the properties and business of four other companies were acquired: (1) D. M. Osborne and Company of Auburn, New York, (2) the Aultman & Miller Buckeye Company of Akron, Ohio, (3) Keystone Company of Sterling, Illinois and (4) Minnie Harvester Company of St. Paul, Minnesota.

The objects and reasons of International Harvester organization were stated in the articles of incorporation as follows: "To manufacture, sell, and deal in harvesting machines, tools, and implements of all kinds, including harvesters, binders, reapers, mowers, rakes, headers, shedders, machinery, engines, wagons, motor vehicles, and vehicles of all kinds; agricultural machinery, tools, and implements of all kinds, binder twine, and all devices, materials, and articles used or intended for use in connection therewith, and all repair parts and other devices, materials, and articles used, or intended for use, in connection with any kind of harvesting of agricultural machines, tools, or implements, or any gasoline, electric, or other vehicles. To engage in the manufacture or production of, and to deal in, any materiais or products which may be use in, or in connection with, the manufacture of harvesting or agricultural machines, tools, and implements."[4]

This, however, was not the whole truth. On May 20, 1907, the president of the Company, C. H. McCormick, made a confidential statement that its organization "was the outgrowth of the abnormal conditions which had obtained in the harvester trade for several years"[5]. The result of these trade conditions was not only a strong competition between the manufacturers of harvesting machinery, but ultimately the financial ruin of many small producers, who could not stand the increasing costs of labour and raw materials along

---

[4] Idem, p. 640 f.

[5] McCormick Archives, Madison (Wisc.). McCormick Collection, IHC Papers, Box No. 1.

with falling prices and the need for large financial resources. The effort of the Company was directed to increasing profits by reducing the cost of production and selling its products; and not through higher prices. This goal was not accomplished. Nevertheless, total sales rose from $53,012,823 in 1903 to $129,573,820 in 1913, and the net profit from $5,641,181 in 1903 to $15,070,779 in 1913. This represented an increase of 144.4% and 267.2% respectively. The foreign sales (except in Canada) grew between 1903 and 1913 from $9,484,000 to $38,730,000, and were equivalent to 75% of the increase of all sales. The sales in Europe totalled $33,119,000 in 1913.

II

The firm's European business connected to the *International Harvester* trust did not start with the foundation of this multinational enterprise. Since the middle of the nineteenth century, McCormick[6], "Champion", Deering, Milwaukee, and Plano had all built up divisions in different European towns. Table 1 shows the approximate sales accounts of the five companies in 1902 in four European countries. The total was more than $4.22 million. We do not know the exact number of machines sold to each country during that year, as the figures probably include machines still unsold or those purchased by other countries. For example, the McCormick division in 1902 sold at the German market 3,981 mowers[7], 2,226 reapers, 523 binders, and 446 rakes. In 1902, the number of machines sold to Eastern and Western Europe amounted to 140,464 with a value of $5.682 million, and in 1906 the quantity rose to 253,950, worth $11.458 million.

[6] Take, for example, the agencies of McCormick. In 1900 the McCormick Harvesting Machine Company had agents in Copenhagen for Denmark, in Alexandria for Egypt, in London for England, in Helsingfors for Finland, in Paris for France, in Athens for Greece, in Groningen for Holland, in Budapest for Hungary, in Grosseto for Italy, in Christiana for Norway, in Bucarest for Rumania, in Odessa for Russia, in Malmø for Sweden, in Lausanne and Niederwenigen for Switzerland, in Bilbao for Spain, in Constantinople for Turkey, and in Hamburg for Germany. See McCormick Archives, Madison (Wisc.). Cyrus H. McCormick Papers, Box No. 115.

[7] Price f.o.b. New York for the type "Big Four" $42.50.

TABLE 1
Sales of American Harvesting Machines in Europe in 1902 (in $)

	McCormick	Deering	Plano	Champion	Milwaukee
England	170,318.00	265,435.82	137,000.00	3,645.00	75,000.00
France	543,359.00	395,878.47	143,835.00(1)	15,000.00	62,000.00
Germany	377,297.50	227,581.59	120,000.00(2)	11,935.00	93,500.00
Russia	608,577.00	765,937.09	150,514.52	36,200.00	19,000.00
	1,699,552.00	1,654,832.97	551,367.52	66,780.00	249,500.00

Source: International Harvester Archives, Chicago. Doc. No. 00208-LA1-01.
Notes: (1) For only 35 of the 80 Departments of France. (2) Estimation.

By 1903, W. V. Couchman was stationed in Hamburg as the European manager of the McCormick division. He headed the entire business except in France. The European manager of "Champion", Oscar Schweitzer, had his office in London, and made contracts and canvasses for orders in England, France, Germany and Russia. T. A. La Porte, the European sales manager of Deering, was in Paris, and made contracts with the same and other European countries, except with Russia, where other Deering representatives were stationed. The organization of Milwaukee's European division was two-headed: while in London, S. D. Conrey managed the business for the United Kingdom, George H. Bartlett was located in Hamburg as an European traveler. The Plano division was similarly organized: William B. Birge in London managed the United Kingdom's business and H. W. Zimmerman(n) handled the business in Russia. The French and the German importers of agricultural implements from Plano dealt with the Chicago office directly. McCormick's manager estimated that about 65 per cent of the machine business in Germany was done by the five divisions. Therefore, if International Harvester could have ninety per cent or more of the business, the manufacture of machines in Germany could lead to the lion's share of the trade possible in other European countries as well. Of course, all these European managers also handled, if necessary, business in Finland, Norway, Sweden, Denmark, Holland, Belgium, Austria, Italy, Spain, Turkey, Algiers, Syria and other countries.

The foreign, specially the European, business of The International Harvester Co. had to be reorganized after 1903, and new selling structures and strategies were to be introduced. In a report of his observations in Europe, Mr. Robert Walker, "an impartial observer", stated after his return to New York that "the legal questions in most of the European countries in which the products of the International Harvester Company are sold proved to be less complicated than was expected"[8]. Nevertheless, the legal as well as the business side of the Company's future policies abroad had to be (re-)considered and adapted to the new situation[9]. The procedures of the above mentioned divisions in every European country were clearly marked and two-folded: (1) to sell the machines in a given country, either to an importing house of that country or to two or more importing firms; and (2) to maintain a branch office and warehouse in the respective country for the division. While the first procedure relieved the division from the labour and expense of exploiting its machines, maintaining an office or warehouse, and of paying tariff and taxes, the second assigned all responsibility to the division and its managers. All the work of selling the machines, paying taxes and tariff duties, keeping connections with local dealers, and acting as agents, was done at the division's expense. Due to the fact that the division received all the profits, agents' failures and unreliability, which rarely occurred, were risked. The Deering division typically followed the first procedure while the latter method was used by McCormick except in the Russian division. In 1900, McCormick opened a German corporation called "McCormick Harvesting Machine Company, m.b.H.". The corporation had offices and a warehouse in Berlin[10], and was very profitable for German conditions. It was estimated that on a higher scale of prices, sales brought yearly returns $100,000 to $200,000 — greater than the same volume of business done through an importer.

Suggestions for future actions to improve the European business

---

[8] International Harvester Archives, Chicago. Doc. No. 00208-LA1-01. Report from Guthrie, Cravath & Henderson, New York, April 25, 1903.

[9] For example, with regard to taxation. In 1903 a share company in Germany with a capitalization of $50,000 and five per cent of divided earnings would have to pay $25 trade tax, $22.5 Imperial tax, $75 city tax, and four per cent income tax if the income exceeded $25,000, while a company m.b.H. (a company with limited liability) had to pay $25 trade tax and $75 members' taxes.

[10] See Hubert Kiesewetter: "Mein Vater ist mit seinen McCormick Ma(s)-chinen sehr zufrieden." Verkaufsstrategien eines internationalen Unternehmens in Deutschland, in: *Zeitschrift für Unternehmensgeschichte*, vol. 34. 1989, p. 91-123.

of International Harvester included a better financial standing, more aggressive salesmanship, a central office, the unification of shipment between the five divisions to save on freights, joint warehouses, reforms in the sales department by reducing the number of divisions operating in a given country; and the building up of a European force of representatives who were excellent mechanics and also good linguists — in one word: hustlers. The selling of American harvesting machines had been organized in two ways: on the one hand, the quality of American machines was as good as, or even better than, those of other makes, but by charging a lower price for them. This way was especially effective when the business was new in a country, a "stool-pigeon". The competitors could possibly be driven out of the market. The second method was to maintain the same, or even a higher, level of prices, but also by selling the machines through vigorous canvassing. The latter strategy seemed to be, in the long run, vastly more effective for International Harvester in Europe. As Walker put it:

> "The canvassers gradually wean away the customers of the low-price company, or destroy his business by developing support for their machines by virtue of advertising their merits liberally. The company that has been selling cheaply eventually gets into an uncomfortable position."[11]

As assumed, the higher prices, even though slower at the beginning, more than payed for the exploitation. In order to sell his machines, the competing seller had to raise his prices and thereby lost many customers. In fact, the Company secured higher prices in its foreign trade than it did in the United States.

III

The first ten years after the formation of International Harvester were a great success in foreign, and especially, European sales. As table 2 demonstrates, total sales more than doubled between 1903 and 1914 (+ 111.3 per cent), while net profits rose by 107.9 per cent.

---

[11] International Harvester Archives, Chicago. Doc. No. 00208-LA1-01, p. 4.

The same seems to be true for nearly every European country between 1903 and 1911. Even if the total foreign sales of the Company rose during the same period by 245.5 per cent, the European sales still increased 189.8 per cent (see table 3). Around 1912, 53 foreign branch-houses had been established, and the foreign sales of International Harvester represented 44.3 per cent of total sales[12].

TABLE 2
International Harvester Company
Invested Capital, Sales, and Net Profits, 1903 to 1914

Years	Invested Capital(1) Dollars	Sales Dollars	Net Profits Dollars	Percentage(2) Capital %	Sales %	Earnings (3) Dollars
1903	120,000,000	53,012,823	5,641,181	4.7	10.3	4.70
1904	122,041,180	51,314,752	5,658,535	4.6	11.0	4.72
1905	122,899,715	55,687,978	7,479,187	6.1	13.4	6.23
1906	125,578,902	67,589,056	7,346,947	5.8	10.9	6.12
1907	128,125,849	78,206,890	8,080,458	6.3	10.3	6.47
1908	132,006,307	72,541,771	8,885,682	6.7	12.2	7.81
1909	136,691,989	86,614,550	14,892,740	10.9	17.2	17.82
1910	147,384,729	101,166,359	16,084,819	10.9	15.9	14.86
1911	156,069,549	108,033,596	15,521,398	9.9	14.4	14.15
1912	163,390,946	125,438,104	16,395,597	10.0	13.1	15.25
1913	171,586,544	129,573,820	15,070,779	8.8	11.6	13.59
1914	178,457,322	115,205,431	11,725,826	6.6	10.2	9.41

Source: McCormick Collection, International Harvester Company Papers, Box No. 2, June 5, 1930.
Notes: (1) At the beginning of each year (capital stock and surplus); (2) Percent of Net Profits to Invested Capital resp. Sales; (3) Per share of Common Stock (after preferred dividends).

In 1903, the Russian market took in 42.1 per cent of all International Harvester's European sales; while in 1911, it roughly had half of all sales (49.7 per cent). Already on August 4, 1903, the president of McCormick and later of International Harvester, Cyrus H. McCormick, received a letter from a Russian agent of McCormick, W. S. Krebs, who was convinced that in Alexandrovsk, "practically

[12] See Cleona Lewis: *America's Stake in International Investments,* Washington, D.C., 1938, p. 184. Howard B. Schonberger: *The Foreign Business of the McCormick Harvesting Machine Company,* MA-Thesis, University of Wisconsin, 1964, p. 228. Mira Wilkins: *The Emergence of Multinational Enterprise: American Business Abroad from the Colonial Era to 1914 (1970),* third Printing, Cambridge (Mass.), London, 1981, p. 103, says that by 1911 the foreign busines constituted 40 per cent.

the Chicago of Russia", about 30,000 *Lubbuckrakers* were manufactured and about 65,000 sold in Russia. Therefore: "In Russia ... the need of a simple combined reaper and mower is a crying one, and the manufacturer who first presents a simple practical reaper and mower to the trade, will reap a fortune."[13]

At the beginning, lack of money and the traders' caution after an economic crisis made it difficult for the Company to change the rather stagnant business conditions in Europe, especially in Germany. Another important problem was that the American company was too far away from the German customers, which gave local firms the possible advantage of rising national feelings, while copying American machines successfully. Nevertheless, for the American optimism, this was only a natural obstacle. They were, however, afraid of the fact that, in Germany, trade relations were a matter "of blood relationship and social ties". Therefore, the importers' agents had to be paid a handsome profit to work for a new company. In 1903, the Company believed: "Germany is a fine field for the sale of machines, and will not be fully stocked for years to come. There is not much local competition. The existing makers have only a small output and seem to do less each year."[14]

The assumed initial outlay necessary to produce agricultural machines on the American scale, frightened German entrepreneurs and capitalists. But, in fact, there was a miscalculation, and the optimistic expectations were not realized[15]. The German agricultural machines industry had traditionally concentrated on building and producing plows and harrows, because most of the agricultural fields in Germany were small — except in Eastern Prussia, where however the Junkers avoided, or reduced, extended mechanization until the late 19th century, by employing cheap seasonal Polish labourers. Compared to the United States or Russia, there was no urgent need to engage in producing harvesting machines. But the situation changed completely in the late nineteenth and early twen-

---

13 International Harvester Archives, Chicago. Doc. No. 01228-BB4-03, p. 1 f.

14 International Harvester Archives, Chicago. Doc. No. 00208-LA1-01, p. 40.

15 See also Elvis L. Eckles: *The Development of Oligopoly in the Farm Implement Industry*, Ph. D. Thesis, University of Illinois at Urbana-Champaign, 1953, p. 122 f.

tieth centuries, when agricultural labour became scarce and expensive, and when Germany began to rely more and more on imports of grain from the USA and Russia. The rising of agricultural import tariffs in 1879 made it rewarding for the Junkers to mechanize, as well as for the agricultural implements industry to pick up competition. In 1905 in Germany, the duties on imported machines were $11.41 for harvesters, $5.21 for reapers, $3.45 for mowers, and $4.64 for rakes. In Austria the duties were much higher: in 1906, $35.58 for harvesters, $20.48 for reapers, $12 for mowers, and $6.91 for rakes.

The introduction and competitiveness of new lines of production took time to occur. Factories had to be extended or new factories had to be built in order to readily produce harvesting machines. By 1907, at the time of another economic crisis, International Harvester felt the actions of European and German competitors more strongly. Between 1907 and 1908, its total European sales fell by 2.87 per cent, the German sales by 7.14 per cent, and this trend continued until 1910 (see table 3). In a personal letter of July 4, 1908, W. V. Couchman wrote from Hamburg to C. H. Haney: "We must be prepared to meet local competition, but we cannot do this until we have the entire business in our hands."[16] And he added, with caution, that during the first two years after the establishment of a German plant, the Company should not expect too favourable results, even if the Company is prepared to make "an aggressive fight".

The Vereinigte Maschinenfabriken at Augsburg (before Epple & Buxbaum) had sales in 1904 of 1, 500 rakes, 400 mowers, 260 reapers, and 40 binders. Four years later the estimate of their sales in Germany were 2,500 mowers, 2,500 rakes, 1,500 tedders, and 1,000 reapers. They paid a 22.5 per cent dividend. Another company Chr. Wery'sche Maschinenfabriken, at Zweibrücken, sold in 1903 three hundred mowers and two hundred rakes. A report of July 18, 1908, showed that its sales in Germany amounted to 4,000 tedders, 2,000 mowers, 600 reapers, 400 rakes, and 25 binders. Many other smaller firms produced harvesting machines of all kinds (see table 4).

---

[16] International Harvester Archives, Chicago. Doc. No. 17323-DC7-07. Exhibit "B", p. 1. Next quotation on p. 2.

TABLE 3

Sales of the International Harvester Company in European Countries, 1903 to 1911

Years	1903	1904	1905	1906	1907	1908	1909	1910	1911
Countries (1)	in $	in $	in $	in $	in $	in $	in $	in $	in $
Russia(2)	2,964,347.48	3,952,773.25	3,997,648.33	5,009,336.79	5,729,631.76	5,959,875.57	6,912,925.56	8,761,511.31	10,131,233.76
France	1,764,573.86	2,165,885.36	1,959,489.36	2,045,360.27	2,747,595.82	2,551,766.32	2,847,289.23	2,563,468.34	2,823,103.69
Germany	737,242.33	820,322.75	1,089,012.67	1,559,394.69	2,113,170.65	1,962,307.01	1,596,740-36	1,526,583-39	2,766,752.04
"Scandinavia"(3)	515,259.28	408,350.31	544,359.81	747,666.80	1,056,510.94	1,320,077.91	1,193,783.87	1,093,475.70	1,242,768.70
Austria-Hungary	79,123.65	117,537.37	117,093.33	429,482.39	622,620.11	517,030.36	811,559.45	1,033,160.09	1,226,582.09
Great Britain	618,081.04	836,128.89	643,886.49	753,248.68	706,448.36	598,685.93	504,477.83	669,430.20	749,598.90
Roumania	118,729.01	200,152.91	78,380.27	381,528.61	497,764.80	147,209.92	188,458.55	223,220.45	631,821.54
Italy	126,116.80	58,144.64	138,610.04	251,092.36	354,839.39	381,694.13	340,125.46	311,850.62	313,517.51
Spain	63,619.88	105,854.40	101,017.67	47,223.90	82,290.67	87,249.50	142,655.09	110,880.66	141,412.46
Finland	-	-	36,563.49	63,182.23	107,055.88	146,582.21	153,865.75	101,396.72	122,654.83
Switzerland	14,854.30	63,031.13	78,040.87	102,171.90	121,548.28	118,659.54	143,094.60	156,429.29	122,644.24
Bulgaria	-	-	-	1,827.03	16,213.29	10,027.77	47,268.50	70,476.07	62,071.67
Turkey	16,804.54	11,688.12	586.23	14,827.48	30,374.92	16,450.65	8,747.83	10,309.80	53,321.05
Greece	460.17	-	1,844.14	2,083.16	3,411.90	4,874.55	11,102.09	7,367.06	16,661.57
Portugal	387.43	224.46	861.84	2,027.97	5,511.64	7,832.97	10,077.02	4,851.52	2,501.86
Belgium	-	-	6,916.17	9,775.81	10,695.96	13,356.82	14,343.97	9,345.16	307.72
The Netherlands	21,783.86	35,205.67	28,824.76	35,977.90	66,111.33	18,495.98	14,221.92	6,003.41	300.00
1. Total Europe	7,041,383.63	8,775,299.26	8,823,135.47	11,456,207.97	14,271,795.70	13,862,177.14	14,940,737.08	16,659,759.79	20,407,253.63
2. Total World (4)	12,246,012.73	15,349,364.48	16,941,706.04	20,199,313.71	24,478,544.17	24,746,688.86	28,134,375,76	34,196,055.60	42,314,678.67
Percentage of 1.:2.	57.50	57.17	52.08	56.72	58.30	56.02	53.10	48.72	48.23

Source: International Harvester Archives, Chicago. Doc. No. 15767-FA2-09, "Sales by Coutries. 1900 to 1911 Inclusive. Foreign."

Notes: (1) Ordered according to height of sales in 1911; (2) Including Siberia; (3) Sweden, Norway, and Denmark; (4) Excluding the United States, but including Canada.

TABLE 4
Estimates of Machines Sold
in Germany Manufactured by German Makers in 1908

Maker	Mowers	Reapers	Binders	Rakes
1. Vereinigte Maschinenfabriken, Augsburg (vorm. Epple & Buxbaum)	2,500	1,000	-	2,500
2. Chr. Wery'sche Maschinenfabriken, Zweibrücken	2,000	600	25	400
3. R. Dollberg, Rostock	1,500	500	-	-
4. J. G. Fahr, Gottmadingen	800	-	-	500
5. C. F. Richter, Brandenburg	600	300	20	-
6. F. Zimmermann, Halle	400	200	-	350
7. L. Neuner, Leutkirch	400	-	-	300
8. A. Speiser, Göppingen	300	-	-	-
9. C. Krätzig & Söhne, Jauer	250	75	-	200
10. Gebr. Botsch, Rappenau	250	100	-	-
11. W. Siedersleben & Co, Bernburg	200	150	-	400
12. H. F. Eckert, Berlin	200	50	-	1,500
13. Meys & Co., Hennef	200	-	-	-
14. Ruppe & Sohn, Apolda	150	100	-	-
15. B. Holthaus, Dinklage	100	50	-	400
16. Joh. Baur, Niederraunau	100	50	-	-
17. H. Hanauer Söhne, Winnweiler	100	50	-	-
18. J. F. Jacoby, Hennef	100	-	-	-
19. Mich. Ködel, Lauingen	75	-	-	-
20. Gebr. Hanke, Potschappel	50	50	-	-
21. August Dauber, Breslau	-	5	-	-
22. Ernst Köttner, Lossnitz Gross & Co., Leipzig	-	-	-	3,000
23. Ventzki, Graudenz	-	-	-	2,500
24. Franz Richter, Döbeln	-	-	-	1,500
25. Carl Beermann, Berlin	-	-	-	1,000
Other small German Manufacturers	-	-	-	15,000
Total	10,275	3,325	45	29,550

Source: International Harvester Archives, Chicago. Doc. No. 19090-1/2. "Harvesting Investigation", p. 108-10.

This development was alarming to International Harvester. After a conference on foreign manufacturing held in Chicago on November 10, 1908, Cyrus H. McCormick stated on this problem:

> "Taking the situation in Germany for example, we certainly cannot expect but that everything possible will be done to supply the German needs with German products. All influences work to that one end, and a brief review of the situation will show that the German maker of harvesting machines is forging ahead, and we cannot afford to ignore the situation or

wait too long before doing something for our own protection."[17]

In 1904, IHC estimated the number of mowers made in Germany as 3,693, while in 1908, the estimate covered over 10,275. McCormick believed that after producing harvesting machines in Germany, "we expect to take the large share of the trade from the German makers, and in this way retard their growth and limit the sphere of influence"[18].

A second obstacle for the sales of American harvesting machines in Germany was the rise and extension of the *Genossenschaftswesen.* This was a cooperative organization which was also active in agriculture. It bought, for example, agricultural machinery and turned it over to the farmers, either for a low cost or sometime even without costs to paying members of the *Genossenschaft.* Even though the former divisions, for instance Plano, sold machines to these organizations, the managers of the International Harvester Company refused to do so. Yet these obstacles were not unsurmountable. It was believed that a good American machine could be sold in Germany without fail if American energy was put into the work.

On May 11, 1905, the International Harvester Company received a notice that the Ministry of the Interior in Russia planned to build a factory for the manufacture of agricultural implements. As a result of this threat for future competition on a most lucrative market with nearly $4 million of sales in 1904 and 1905, G. F. Steele, the general manager of the manufacturing department of IHC in Chicago, proposed to Cyrus H. McCormick on June 9, 1905, whether it would be wise for the company "to establish a number of separate small plants in various parts of Europe, or, ultimately, whether it would be better to establish only one or two large plants to supply all of our foreign trade, when we are forced into supplying our foreign trade abroad"[19].

To find the best solution, a representative of International Harvester interviewed several companies which had already established foreign factories. Because the problem of manufacturing in Europe depended on the tariffs in the European countries, James Deering,

[17] Idem, p. 1. Chicago, November 10, 1908. Sent to the members of the Board of Directors and other responsible people of IHC.

[18] Idem, p. 4.

[19] International Harvester Archives, Chicago. Doc. No. 01228-BB4-03.

the Vice President of International Harvester, concluded on July 14, 1905:

> "What we want in Europe, I take it, is the nearest thing to a monopoly in our line of business that the laws or public sentiment will tolerate. (sic) Changes of tariff among the European nations are common enough and at this moment, since most of the commercial treaties have expired or are expiring, there is great activity in Europe in making new tariffs."[20]

As long as the Company would have the capacity to supply the demand in foreign countries, a manufacturing plant should not be built. Yet because of the danger, especially from Swedish competitors, lied in the fact that they were stretching out to foreign countries, the task of International Harvester should have been to make their business so unprofitable through very low prices so that they were driven out of business. Or in the words of Mr. Deering: "The Swedish competitor must be killed."

At the same time, the Sales Department, and then later the Executive Committee, was convinced that the only effective thing to do was to establish a factory in Sweden. Others, like G. F. Steele, believed that if the Company would only have one factory in Europe and ship machines from there to several countries, then Germany would be the most favourable country to locate in. At a conference held in London, on August 1, 1905, it was agreed that it would be absolutely necessary to build mowers and rakes in Sweden, as the Arvika Company had such an advantage and supremacy in the Scandinavian trade. It was as strong in the territory it commanded as any American factory of International Harvester, so that a successful competition would be impossible. The establishment of a Swedish factory was, therefore, seen, as indispensable. To secure the future growth and stability of the Company's foreign (European) business, a manufacturing plant was necessary. The cost involved in building a plant in Sweden was estimated at a conference in Paris, on September 4, 1905, with a total outlay of $300,000[21]. The de-

---

[20] Ibid.

[21] The total plant investment at Norrkoping as of December 31, 1907, amounted to $264,707.55, and the factory inventory as of August 1, 1907, amonted to $87,298.36, making a total investment of $352,005.91.

cision to erect a plant at Norrkoping made International Harvester, "a foreign manufacturing company instead of an exporting company" according to Richard F. Howe, the Company's treasurer, in a letter to James Deering. Howe's statement was correct, as Norrkoping during the 1907 season, manufactured 8,132 mowers, 2,020 rakes, and 1,400 reaping attachments along with about $4,000 in same parts. Thus it became what we now call a multinational company.

The Swedish plant did not fulfil the various requirements to compete against a growing European market in agricultural implements. This was already clear in 1905, but became more apparent after the economic crisis of 1907. The profit from European sales during the 1907 season was $2,461,114.48 or 28.6% per cent of the Company's total profit. Even though the financial condition of IHC in 1908 was quite satisfactory, Cyrus McCormick wrote in a letter to Couchman on October 14, 1908, that the subject of foreign manufacture "is one of the most fundamental questions which has been under consideration for a long time."

The cost of building and equipping a plant in Germany to manufacture mowers, rakes, binders, and reapers, was estimated a total of $1 million. If this investment's savings compared to manufacture in Chicago, plus freight and duty, were calculated, according to the Swedish case, a profit of about 20 per cent would have been obtained. The situation in France was similar, although the cost of equipping a plant to manufacture mowers and rakes would have been approximately "only" $600,000. The pressing situation of a losing trade was stated in a letter by C. H. Haney, manager of the Foreign Sales Department, on April 28, 1908:

> "The French manufacturer of mowers is going to be stronger competition each year, and we will probably each year receive a less percentage of the total French business, unless we do prepare to put ourselves on a basis to actually compete with him in prices, which we can only do, in my opinion, by putting ourselves on the same basis as the French maker and manufacturer in France".[22]

---

[22] International Harvester Archives, Chicago. Doc. No. 17323-DC7-07. Exhibit "B".

The Swedish cost to produce a mower unit was $8.39. Therefore, the savings compared to manufacture in Chicago and shipping to France would amount to roughly $9.21 per mower unit, or in absolute terms, approximately $280,000 a year.

The situation in Russia has been mentioned above. In 1907, the total sales of International Harvester machines in Russia amounted to 97,178 mower units, compared to 48,427 in Germany and 72,803 mower units in France. Manufacturing in Russia at as low a cost as in Sweden with a net saving of approximately $250,000 was possible. The estimated outlay for plant investment, including the production of binders, reapers, mowers and rakes, was $1.5 million, with an additional cost of roughly $500,000 for raw material and work in progress inventories. All in all, by 1908, there were no more doubts. Cyrus H. McCormick wrote in a statement on June 3, 1908, to the Board of Directors that,

> "the experience which the Company has already had in manufacture at Norrkoping has been most satisfactory and helpful, and it is because of the success that has thus far been attained in Sweden that I commend to your attention with great confidence the extension to France, Germany and Russia of the policy you have thus far pursued in Sweden".[23]

At the end of July 1908, several locations for the French factory were discussed and some of the places even visited. Especially attractive were four or five sites close to Lille with water, rail, electric power, cheap labour, etc. As the French company Puzenat sold tedders cheaper than IHC, and had taken the rake, harrow and tedder trade — not of mowers — away from International Harvester, it was important to find a going concern that could be converted into the Company's line of manufacturing.

In Germany, 36 different locations had been investigated, but none was found with suitable buildings, very few had the desired combination of water, rail, electric power and favourable labour conditions. Ultimately, the terms were most promising at Neuss, near Düsseldorf, which was situated in a more thickly populated manufacturing district than in Hamburg, Wittenberg or Magdeburg. Twenty-five acres of ground were available near Neuss at a price of

[23] Idem, p. 11.

$4,000 per acre or four Marks for the square metre. Neuss had at the time 35,000 inhabitants, and was at ten minutes by train from Düsseldorf.

In June, 1911, four European plants of IHC — and one in Canada — were being established or built: (1) A/B International Harvester Company, Norrkoping, Sweden; (2) Compagnie Internationale des Machines Agricoles, Croix, Nord, France; (3) International Harvester Company, m.b.H., Neuss, Germany; (4) International Harvester Company in Russia ("Lubertzy Works"), Moscow, Russia[24]. Reorganizations took place in the United States as well as in Europe both on personal and functional levels. With the General Advice No. 13 of December 23, 1912, from the division manager in Chicago, B. A. Kennedy, the formation of a new foreign experimental organization was announced. J. A. Hutmacher, sales manager in Berlin, took charge of this department with its headquarters in Brussels.

All experimental matters of general interest in the European business were to be coordinated by a new work committee in Brussels and by the division manager in Chicago. Joint actions regarding all machines manufactured in the foreign works were made final and effective at once. Nevertheless, the experimental department in Chicago tried to have the situation well in hand by upholding the final decision on whether or not changes could have been made and would not interfere with machines for domestic and foreign countries[25]. This reduced autonomy for the experimental organization in Brussels and proved detrimental to the different requirements of the countries for which the machines were furnished.

Instead of using European practice for the increase of domestic sales, as well as foreign sales outside of Europe, the Chicago office insisted, not only on receiving full information, but also on keeping the responsibility for the general results. Quite often the president or directors visited Europe to get an impression of the trade and to give advice. On September 25, 1913 Cyrus H. McCormick wrote from Paris to his mother: "The greatest prospect for the Company's

---

[24] On May 22, 1912, the number of employees at the Neuss works was 685, and in the twine mill 135, e. g. a total of 820 employees, while in the Norrkoping works the number of employees was 279.

[25] See International Harvester Archives, Chicago. Doc. No. 05478-DE2-02.

future business in any country in the world is undoubtedly in Russia and we are building up a fine organization at the new works at Lubertzy."[26] Time, however, was running out: the shadows of the First World War also darkened the European trade of International Harvester. But in May, 1914, Haney still wrote:

> "Conditions generally in Europe are good. In France the present outlook is that we will not have mowers enough in time. Croix seem to be behind in their production and not catching up. Our prospective mower trade in France is so big that one cannot credit it, — about one-third of our entire foreign mower trade."[27]

IV

The outbreak of World War I on July 28, 1914, took the managers of International Harvester by surprise. More than two years elapsed before the president of the Company considered at a meeting with IHC-managers in Chicago, in order to avoid further uncertainty, the necessity of finding a new location for the European General Office. The secretary's minutes of this portion of the meeting on September 29, 1916, read as follows:

> "Mr. McKinstry [the general manager of IHC, H. K.] brought up the question of a definite location for the European general office, stating that some of the organization favored Copenhagen as a permanent place, while others did not. He stated he thought it would have a good effect on the organization if some permanent arrangement was made, as at present most of our people are living in hotels and he felt that the atmosphere was probably not as conducive to the satisfaction of the individual as a more permanent resident would be. It was felt that it was undesirable te determine upon a definite location at this time. It was decided, however, that the organization at Copenhagen would be notified

---

[26] McCormick Archives, Madison (Wisc.). C. H. McCormick Jr. Papers, Box No. 111.

[27] International Harvester Archives, Chicago. Doc. No. 17397-FD7-03.

that they were at liberty to make leases for living arrangements for a three year period and that if any change in the location of the general office took place before the expiration of that time the Company would take off their hands the unexpired leases."[28]

Obviously, the IHC-people were not aware of the consequences of the War on European business, even though they did not expect an early end of the fighting. Instead, Mr. Couchman at the meeting brought up the question of 1915 bonuses for the selling organizations in belligerent countries, and it was decided that all employees in those countries should be paid a war allowance of 25 per cent of their salary for the year 1915, and then later also for 1916[29]. In a letter to C. H. Haney on October 6, 1916, Couchman favoured Brussels as a central location, if, after the War was ended, conditions in Europe remained similar to what they were before the outbreak! Couchman believed that a final decision on a permanent location could be postponed until after the close of the War.

After occupying Belgium and parts of the French territory, the military authorities in Germany gave orders to take part of the Croix Works, even though they knew that it was legally a French concern; the shareholders were, however, Americans. Most of the stock had been removed by German soldiers, but the prices were evaluated and receipts were given. The IHC-people tried to keep everything in order and in good condition to prevent damage or rusting of machines. The German military authorities did not allow the selling of any goods or machines directly, but permitted only the delivery of the machines upon requisitions properly filled out and signed by them. As many goods as possible were shipped to Neuss, but in November, 1915, it was very questionable whether or not the Neuss Works could continue to operate. By December, everything was becoming more problematic at Neuss, partly because German workers were drafted, partly because some kinds of material were very difficult to obtain or were delayed. Many women and Russian prisoners, 61 at the time, were hired. As Halverson wrote to Chica-

28 Idem, Doc. N°. 01386-BA2-01.

29 In 1915 the average prices on IHC-mowers (4½, Reg. Bar) were 278.32 Marks in Bucarest, 228.23 in Riga, 226.25 in Paris, 201.58 in Königsberg, and 193.51 Marks in Neuss, e. g. approximately 10 per cent more than in 1914.

go on December 6, 1915: "There is one great advantage in having these, and that is they cannot quit after they are broken in, but they are well treated there, and seem to be satisfied."[30]

Early in May, 1917, an article appeared in the Berlin paper in which a committee, appointed by the manufacturers of agricultural implements in Germany, had addressed a letter to the Reich's Counselor. In this letter it was stated that International Harvester had accepted a contract to produce motor trucks for Germany's ennemies. Therefore, the German government was forbidden to assign further material to the International Harvester Company at Neuss until a German inspector had been placed in charge. In about the middle of May, the *Vergleichungsstelle für landwirtschaftliche Maschinen* asked the sales department at Neuss to send a few machines to a section near Kleve. An officer from the *Vergleichungsstelle* visited the plants at Neuss and thoroughly inspected the factory. Two of the management men at Neuss were called to the War Department in Berlin and were accused of a disposition on the part of the Company to curtail production.

After the United States declared war to Germany, the German government took over the factory, by the socalled *Zwangsverwaltung*. In November 1918, the production of the factory came to a standstill because of lack of iron and melting coal. On April 23, 1920, the German custodian wrote a letter which began: "By order of the Minister for Commerce and Trade of January 11th, 1920 the coercive administration of the firm Deutsche Internationale Harvester Company *mit beschränkter Haftung* has been cancelled."[31] The total war losses of the Company amounted to $56,830,000, including $44,996,000 (79.2%) in Russia, $5,462,000 (9.6%) in Germany, $3,962,000 (7.0%) in Austria-Hungary, $1,514,000 (2.7%) in Rumania, and $896,000 (1.6%) in France. The war claims awarded for the losses in Germany and the damages in France were $4,428,000, that is 7.79 per cent of all war losses.

---

30 International Harvester Archives, Chicago. Doc. No. 01477-BA4-01. Out of a total of 631 employees, there were 461 German men, 76 German women, 61 Russian prisoners, 11 Americans, six Danes, five Belgians and Dutch each, four Poles, and two Swiss.

31 Idem Doc. No. 17189-FB4-01. Translation. A demand for the return of the property in the total a mount of Marks 15,791,040.98 was being administred by the Custodian for Enemy Property.

To sum up, we can conclude from our analysis what Chandler[32] has shown for other American machinery companies. The rapid expansion of International Harvester in Europe between 1902 and 1918 was the result of successful efforts to centralize administration, rationalize production, and building plants in countries where the tariff barriers and the competition were most severe. By using these advantages of scale and scope the exploitation of comparative savings of expenses could be acquired for a rather long time, even if governments patronized domestic firms. Since European enterprises were able to produce farm implements at comparable quality and prices, IHC was forced to adapt to domestic needs of the respective country. As Couchman had already written on July 4, 1900, to Cyrus H. McCormick:

> "It is of utmost importance that we study carefully the conditions that prevail in Europe. They are different from what they are in America, and were we make the machines fit the conditions that exist here, and do so without any more cost to ourselves in making the machines, it certainly seems that we should pursue the wisest cource, and, under these circumstances, give the people what they want."[33]

[32] See Alfred D. Chandler, Jr.: *Scale and Scope: The Dynamics of Industrial Capitalism*, Cambridge (Mass.), London, 1990, p. 194-201.

[33] McCormick Archives. Cyrus H. McCormick Papers, Box No. 115.

Appendix I
Total World and Total Europe Sales of the International Harvester Company (1903-1911)

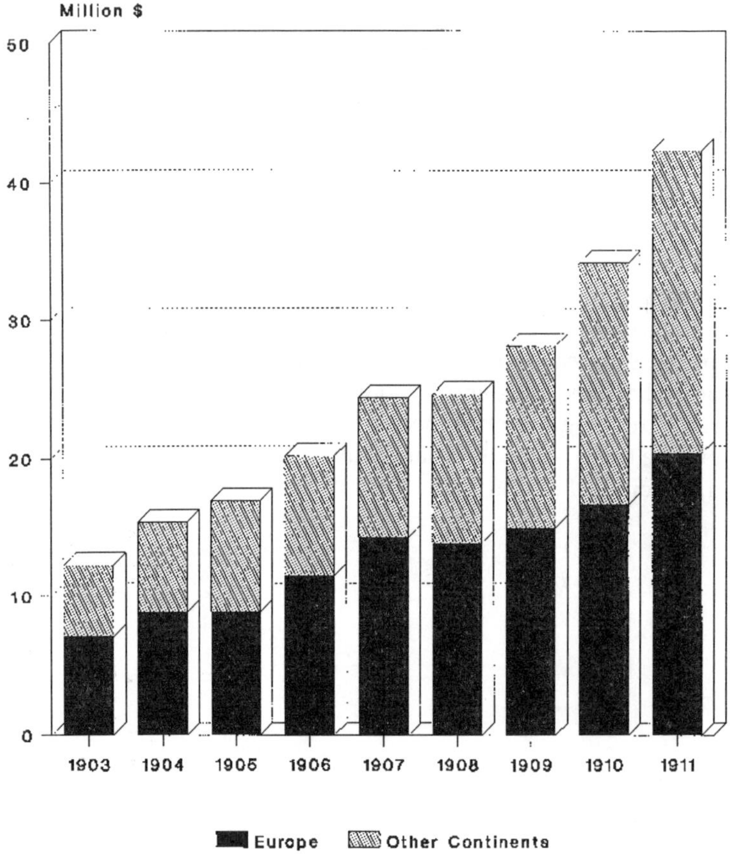

Appendix II
Sales of the International Harvester Company in Europe (1903-1911)

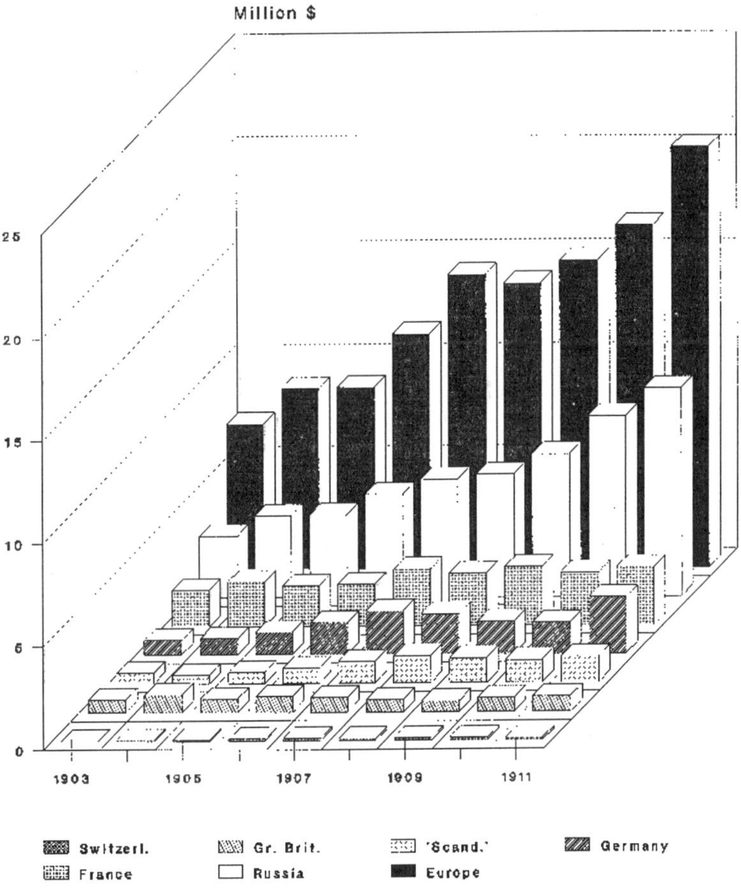

III
EMPRESÁRIOS E TRABALHADORES NUM MUNDO EM TRANSFORMAÇÃO

Luiz Carlos Bresser Pereira
Fundação Getúlio Vargas, SP

EMPRESÁRIOS, SUAS ORIGENS E AS INTERPRETAÇÕES DO BRASIL

Há certos momentos em que a visão dominante dos intelectuais sobre um determinado problema contraria frontalmente os dados existentes sobre o assunto. Este fato ocorreu nos anos sessenta e setenta, no Brasil, em relação ao problema das origens étnicas dos empresários industriais paulistas. No início da década de 1960 publiquei na *Revista de Administração de Empresas* pesquisa demonstrando de forma clara que os empresários não se haviam originado em famílias brasileiras ligadas ao café, mas em famílias de imigrantes de classe média (Bresser Pereira, 1964). Não obstante, no final da década, depois da publicação do ensaio de Caio Prado Jr. *A Revolução Brasileira* (1966), tornou-se voz corrente entre os intelectuais brasileiros que a origem do empresariado industrial estava na oligarquia cafeeira. Nesse livro o grande historiador afirma peremptoriamente, embora sem nenhuma base em pesquisa, que "em São Paulo, por exemplo, muitas das primeiras e principais indústrias são de fazendeiros que empregam os lucros auferidos na cultural do café, em iniciativas industriais (1966:198). E o livro de Warren Dean sobre a industrialização de São Paulo, publicado no Brasil em 1971, embora confirmasse minha pesquisa sobre as origens dos empresários, acabou por agravar a confusão. Depois de dar grande ênfase à importância do café para o surgimento da indústria em São Paulo, mostrou, com base em cuidadosa pesquisa, como os primeiros industriais eram originalmente imigrantes que se dedicavam à importação. Isto não o impediu, entretanto, de empenhar-se em negar a tese de que os latifundiários se constituíram em obstáculo político à industrialização, e afirmar que "os proprietários rurais não somente sobreviveram como classe, mas também dirigiram a passagem de uma cultura rotineira de cana-de-açúcar, do princípio do século XIX, para um complexo sistema industrial nos meados do século XX" (1971:41)[1].

Como explicar este fato? Devido ao grande prestígio intelectual de Caio Prado Jr.? Sem dúvida esta é uma razão. Por que não leram meu artigo? Ou por que não concordaram com suas conclusões? Entre essas duas hipóteses, a primeira deve ser mais verdadeira, já que o artigo raramente foi citado?[2] Mas, evidentemente, estas não são explicações suficientes. Deve haver um problema maior, de caráter ideológico, que explica como uma interpretação histórica sem nenhum fundamento na realidade, sem nenhuma pesquisa para convalidá-la, ganhou foros de verdade indiscutível, sendo, provavelmente, até hoje dominante.

Neste artigo inicialmente apresentarei de forma sumária os dados de minha pesquisa. Em seguida farei uma tentativa de explicar o equívoco ocorrido, a partir de uma análise baseada em aspectos ideológicos e de psicologia social. Argumentarei que o ressentimento ao nível da esquerda provocado pelo golpe militar que resultou na Revolução de 1964 levou seus intelectuais a uma interpretação da história do Brasil — a "interpretação funcional-capitalista ressentida" — oposta à "interpretação nacional-burguesa" que fora dominante nas esquerdas no período imediatamente anterior, e que explicava o projeto nacional de industrialização a partir de uma coalizão de classes entre a burguesia industrial nascente e os trabalhadores urbanos.

Fique claro, entretanto, que a crítica presente neste artigo não se

---

[1] Fernando Henrique Cardoso, que escreveu o primeiro livro importante sobre os empresários industriais no Brasil, reconheceu implicitamente que não se originavam das famílias ligadas à produção e ao comércio de café, ao afirmar que os empresários industriais foram recrutados "nas camadas médias da população urbana: descendentes das famílias 'de tradição', mas sem posses, que se ligaram ao funcionalismo público...; descendentes de imigrantes... imigrantes" (1963: 160-1).

[2] Mesmo no extraordinário trabalho de Suzigan (1986), em que o problema da origem e do desenvolvimento da indústria brasileira foi amplamente analisado e todo o debate resenhado, não há menção à minha pesquisa. Um dos poucos historiadores que a utilizaram foi Sergio Silva (1976).

refere às relações econômicas entre o café e o início da industrialização, mas apenas aos equívocos relacionados com as origens étnicas e sociais dos empresários. Enquanto estas origens são simples e claras, lineares mesmo, mas foram objeto de uma grande confusão, aquelas relações são complexas e contraditórias, eminentemente dialéticas, mas encontraram uma interpretação adequada. A industrialização brasileira jamais teria ocorrido sem a criação de um excedente como aquele proporcionado pelo café, mas isto não impediu os cafeicultores de se oporem politicamente à industrialização na grande maioria das ocasiões.

Volto ao tema das origens étnicas e sociais dos empresários, não apenas porque o problema não foi resolvido, mas também porque, trinta anos depois dos equívocos cometidos, as paixões devem estar amainadas e será possível uma avaliação mais objetiva por parte dos historiadores, aos quais este trabalho é dirigido.

A pesquisa

A pesquisa sobre as origens étnicas e sociais dos empresários foi realizada por Zaíra Rocha Awad e por mim em 1962. Nosso universo era constituído pelos empresários vivos ou mortos de empresas industriais paulistas com mais de cem empregados no momento da pesquisa. Foram adotados todos os cuidados estatísticos para garantir resultados isentos de viés, com margem de erro pequena e elevada probabilidade de acerto[3]. Para a definição da origem étnica foi adotado um critério patriarcal. Era considerado de origem estrangeira todo empresário que fosse ele próprio nascido no exterior, ou cujo pai ou avô paterno fosse estrangeiro. Empresário cujo avô paterno já havia nascido no Brasil era considerado de origem brasileira. Para a determinação da classe social, dividiu-se a sociedade em seis classes. A classe alta superior foi identificada à burguesia mercantil envolvida na produção e comercialização do café, havendo no questionário uma pergunta específica a respeito. A classificação nas demais classes foi realizada a partir, principal-

[3] Para um nível de segurança de 95 por cento, as margens de erro variavam de 6,30 por cento em uma distribuição 50-50% para 3,76 por cento em uma distribuição 90-10 por cento.

mente, de dados sobre a situação econômica da família na época da infância ou adolescência do empresário e sobre a profissão e nível de educação do pai. O caráter histórico do *survey* foi garantido porque em 1962 estávamos ainda próximos ao início da industrialização brasileira, que realmente deslanchou em São Paulo após 1930; e principalmente porque indagávamos sobre o empresário que havia fundado ou desenvolvido decisivamente sua empresa. Dos 204 empresários sobre os quais se levantaram dados, cerca de 10 por cento estavam mortos ou aposentados na época da pesquisa; 82,8 por cento fundaram a empresa.

Os resultados em relação às origens étnicas dos empresários paulistas foram claríssimos. Conforme se pode observar na Tabela 1, apenas 15,7 por cento tinham origem brasileira. Entre os de origem estrangeira, somando 84,3 por cento, 49,5 por cento do total eram eles próprios estrangeiros; os demais 34,8 por cento, filhos ou netos de estrangeiros. Pela Tabela 2 verificamos que, quanto à origem nacional ou étnica, predominaram os empresários de origem italiana, com 34,8 por cento. Em seguida vêm os de origem brasileira (15,7 por cento), alemã ou austríaca (12,8 por cento), portuguesa (11,8 por cento) e árabe (9,8 por cento).

As origens sociais dos empresários industriais paulistas são também claras. Apenas 3,9 por cento tiveram origem nas famílias "aristocráticas" ligadas ao comércio e à produção do café. Originados na classe alta inferior, constituída por famílias ricas mas sem origens nos barões do café, tivemos 21,6 por cento dos empresários. Na classe média superior, definida pela situação econômica média da família na época da infância ou adolescência do empresário e pela educação de nível superior do pai, tivemos apenas 7,8 por cento. Nas classes médias propriamente ditas, formadas principalmente por pequenos e médios empresários, originaram-se 50 por cento, enquanto apenas 16,7 por cento originavam-se na classe baixa, constituída principalmente por famílias pobres nas quais o pai tinha geralmente uma profissão braçal.

Esta pesquisa não deixa, portanto, qualquer dúvida. Os empresários industriais do Estado de São Paulo, onde se concentrou a industrialização brasileira, não tiveram origem nas famílias ligadas ao café. Originaram-se em famílias imigrantes principalmente de classe média.

Tabela 1
Origens étnicas dos empresários paulistas

Origens	N.º		%	
Brasileira (3 gerações)		32		15,7
Estrangeira		172		84,3
* Netos de imigrantes	23		11,3	
* Filhos de imigrantes	48		23,5	
* Imigrantes	101		49,5	
Total	172	204	84,3	100,0

Tabela 2
Origens por país dos empresários paulistas

País de origem e grandes grupos étnicos	N.º		%
1. Itália		71	34.8
2. Brasil (3 gerações)		32	15.7
3. Alemanha	21		
Áustria	5	26	12.8
4. Portugal		24	11.7
5. Líbano	13		
Síria	5		
Armênia	2	20	9.8
6. Rússia	6		
Polônia	2	9	4.4
Checoslováquia	1		
7. Suíça	5		
Hungria	3		
Espanha	3		
Dinamarca	2		
França	2		
Estados Unidos	2		
Grã-Bretanha	2		
Uruguai	2		
Grécia	1		
Romênia	1	22	10.8
Total		204	100.0

Tabela 3
Origens sociais dos empresários paulistas

Social class	N.º	%
Alta-superior	8	3.9
Baixa-superior	44	21.6
Média-superior	16	7.8
Média-média	44	21.6
Média-inferior	58	28.4
Baixa	34	16.7
Total	204	100.0

Estes dados deixam claro a falta de relação entre as famílias de cafeicultores e as dos empresários industriais. Nada dizem, porém, sobre as relações econômicas, muito menos sobre as relações políticas entre esses empresários e os cafeicultores. Como uma das causas do fato de que os resultados desta pesquisa tenham sido ignorados está na relação — e na confusão — entre as origens étnicas dos empresários e as relações econômicas entre a indústria e o café, farei agora uma breve análise deste problema. Em seguida me concentrarei no problema ideológico e político, onde se encontra a meu ver explicação fundamental.

Está claro que a industrialização de São Paulo jamais teria ocorrido na forma que ocorreu não fosse a acumulação de riqueza provocada pelo café. As primeiras tentativas de industrialização do Brasil tiveram lugar no Nordeste e no Rio de Janeiro. Abortaram porque faltava-lhes um excedente que permitisse, de um lado, a formação de um mercado interno, de outro, o surgimento de uma infra-estrutura econômica que viabilizasse a indústria. Warren Dean (1971), no primeiro capítulo de seu livro afirma a relação causal direta entre café indústria no próprio título do primeiro capítulo de seu livro, sugestivamente denominado "O Comércio do Café Gera a Indústria". Villela e Suzigan (1973) e Robert C. Nicol (1974) também se empenharam em demonstrar essa relação positiva. Na mesma linha de pensamento estão Carlos Manuel Peláez (1972) e João Manoel Cardoso de Mello (1975).

Esses trabalhos, entretanto, tiveram uma clara preocupação em criticar a interpretação clássica, desenvolvida principalmente nos anos cinqüenta, que salientava a oposição entre a industrialização e o café. Esta interpretação estava, de um lado, baseada na análise definitiva de Celso Furtado (1959) sobre o extraordinário desenvolvimento industrial ocorrido nos anos trinta, exatamente a partir da crise do café[4], e de outro, nas análises políticas, que enfatizavam os conflitos entre os cafeicultores e a burguesia industrial nascente

---

[4] Esta tese foi contestada de forma explícita, à direita, por Peláez, e, implicitamente, à esquerda, pelos representantes da "interpretação funcional-capitalista". Estudos realizados por Maria da Conceição Tavares (1963), Fishlow (1971), Suzigan (1976) e Marcelo de Paiva Abreu (1990) confirmaram a tese de Furtado.

pelo controle do Estado. Segundo esta análise, que teve em Nícia Vilela Luz (1961) sua mais documentada representante, os cafeicultores, embora não se opusessem à diretamente industrialização, opunham-se ferrenhamente à proteção à indústria nacional, a qual chamavam de "artificial", em contraposição à agricultura, que seria "natural" para a economia brasileira[5]. Os cafeicultores percebiam que a proteção à indústria, além de prejudicar diretamente os consumidores, teria que, em última análise, ser financiada ou subsidiada pela própria produção cafeeira. Este fato, que nem sempre estava claro quando essas lutas se desencadeiam, no início do século, tendo Joaquim Murtinho como principal defensor do liberalismo cafeeiro e Amaro Cavalcanti e Serzedelo Correa como importantes orientadores do movimento protecionista[6], torna-se claríssimo com a luta dos cafeicultores contra o "confisco cambial", e com a disputa entre Roberto Simonsen e Eugênio Gudin nos anos quarenta[7]. O confisco cambial — um imposto sobre a exportação de produtos primários sob a forma de taxas de câmbio diferenciadas — será nos anos quarenta e cinqüenta a forma por excelência através da qual o Estado transferirá renda da agricultura exportadora para a indústria.

Furtado, por sua vez, mostra como havia uma relação cíclica inversa entre o café e a indústria, em função, principalmente, dos movimentos da taxa de câmbio[8]. Quando o preço do café subia no mercado internacional, o valor das exportações brasileiras aumentava, realizava-se um superávit comercial, e em conseqüência a taxa de câmbio baixava (a moeda nacional valorizava-se), reduzia-se a proteção cambial à industria local, aumentando as importações de manufaturados. Não escapava, porém, a Furtado, que havia tam-

---

5 Ver também Hélio Jaguaribe (1962) e Nelson Werneck Sodré (1964).

6 Ver Nícia Vilela Luz (1961: capítulo II).

7 Eugênio Gudin colocava-se contra o planejamento econômico e considerava artificial a indústria brasileira. Nas décadas de 1950 e 1960 ele seria, no Brasil, o líder da reação contra as idéias da Cepal. Roberto Simonsen, em nome dos empresários, defendia a indústria nacional e a intervenção do Estado na economia. Sobre essa disputa ver Magalhães (1961), Sola (1982), Bielschowsky (1988) e Loureiro (1992). Os textos originais do debate foram republicados em Gudin e Simonsen (1977).

8 Suzigan chamou esta análise de "teoria do choque adverso" (1986: 23-8).

bém uma relação positiva entre o café e a indústria. Era óbvio que o complexo cafeeiro produzia um excedente econômico e divisas estrangeiras que permitiam a constituição de uma infra-estrutura de energia e transportes essencial para a industrialização, o estabelecimento de um sistema bancário, e o surgimento de um mercado interno para a indústria.

Imaginou-se, também, que o capital cafeeiro tenha sido essencial para o financiamento dos investimentos na indústria nascente. A pesquisa que realizei, entretanto, não confirma esta hipótese. Conforme demonstra a Tabela 4, diante da pergunta sobre o financiamento dos investimentos iniciais, 78,4 por cento informaram que os fundos haviam sido próprios ou da família.

TABELA 4
Origens dos investimentos iniciais das empresas industriais paulistas[9]

Origem dos investimentos	N.º	%
Fundos próprios ou da família do empresário	160	78,4
Fundos próprios e de capitalistas privados	13	6,4
Fundos próprios e de fontes regulares de crédito privado	11	5,4
Fundos próprios e de fontes oficiais de crédito	2	1,0
Fundos de capitalistas privados	18	8,8
Total	204	100,0

O debate sobre as relações econômicas entre o café e a indústria foi afinal satisfatoriamente resolvido por Sergio Silva (1976), seguindo a linha que Celso Furtado esboçara. Não apenas reconheceu a origem dos empresários industriais entre os imigrantes, afirmando claramente que "a burguesia industrial nascente encontra suas origens na imigração européia" (1976:91), mas principalmente percebeu ele o caráter eminentemente contraditório ou dialético do café com a indústria no Brasil. Silva é explícito a respeito:

> "Na verdade, ao examinarmos os diferentes aspectos da questão concluímos que as relações entre o comércio exterior e o café de um lado, e a indústria nascente, de outro, implicam, ao mesmo tempo, a unidade e a contradição. A unidade está no fato de

[9] Essa tabela foi originalmente publicada em um breve *Anexo de Empresários e Administradores no Brasil* (Bresser Pereira, 1974:211).

que o desenvolvimento capitalista baseado na expansão cafeeira provoca o nascimento e um certo desenvolvimento de indústria; a contradição, nos limites impostos ao desenvolvimento da indústria pela própria posição dominante da economia cafeeira na acumulação de capital" (1976: 103)[10].

Uma explicação: a "Interpretação Funcional-Capitalista"

As relações econômicas e políticas contraditórias, de apoio e negação, entre o café e a indústria nascente, podem nos ajudar a explicar a confusão sobre as origens étnicas e sociais dos empresários. Aqueles que viam uma relação positiva direta entre café e indústria tendiam a ver os cafeicultores como os fundadores da indústria no Brasil[11], enquanto que os que viam uma relação negativa entre café e indústria estariam mais inclinados a atribuir esse imigrantes. Eu, por exemplo, quando realizei a pesquisa de 1962, influenciado pelo pensamento do ISEB (Instituto Superior de Estudos Brasileiros), particularmente pelas idéias de Hélio Jaguaribe e Ignácio Rangel, inclinava-me para esta segunda alternativa. Mais tarde, entretanto, ficou claro para mim a relação eminentemente dialética entre café e indústria.

Minha questão fundamental, entretanto, continua sem resposta? Por que a análise das relações entre café e indústria, que tendiam a enfatizar o caráter negativo até os anos cinqüenta, muda-

---

10 Análise dialética semelhante encontra-se em Liana Aureliano. Para ela "a acumulação cafeeira se faz sob o signo do capital mercantil, e, no seu movimento contraditório, impulsiona o surgimento da grande indústria" (1981:10-1). Mais adiante assinala a importância de 1930: "a crise política da década de 1920 culmina com a Revolução de 1930: a burguesia cafeeira é definitivamente deslocada de sua posição de controle sobre o aparelho do Estado" (1981:98). Na mesma linha Sônia Draibe, apesar de insistir nas relações positivas entre café e indústria, e de identificar-se com a crítica à "economia politica da Cepal", admite o conflito entre o café e a indústria, afirmando que "a nível de seu projeto de industrialização, a burguesia industrial enfrentaria a oposição dos setores ligados ao café" (1985:37). Sua análise da industrialização brasileira significativamente começa em 1930.

11 Zélia Cardoso de Mello, em sua tese de doutorado (1981), empenhou-se em demonstrar que no século XIX muitas das indústrias foram criadas por cafeicultores.

ram para enfatizar o aspecto positivo a partir de meados dos anos sessenta? E, conseqüentemente, por que prevaleceu um amplo equívoco sobre as origens étnicas e sociais dos empresários industriais, principalmente entre aqueles que dominantemente passaram a enfatizar as relações positivas entre café e indústria?

A meu ver, estes equívocos decorreram do surgimento, após o golpe de Estado de 1964, de uma "interpretação funcional-capitalista" ressentida da realidade brasileira, a partir do ensaio inaugural de Caio Prado Jr. (1966)[12]. Quando ocorreu o golpe militar, a esquerda, que havia proposto — através do Partido Comunista e do ISEB, de forma clara, e , através da CEPAL, implicitamente — a aliança com a burguesia industrial, sentiu-se traída. E diante dessa traição, não bastava apenas culpar o adversário externo, a própria burguesia, mas aqueles que, dentro da esquerda, haviam formulado a "interpretação nacional-burguesa" e apoiado o pacto populista nacional-desenvolvimentista, que prevaleceu entre 1930 e 1960 sob a liderança de Getúlio Vargas.

É esta a tese central do ensaio de Caio Prado, Jr. Como o grande historiador havia sido comunista, seu alvo fundamental é o próprio partido. Seu objetivo é claro: criticar a tese de uma aliança com a burguesia, a partir da negação de que essa burguesia tivesse qualquer caráter "nacional" , e que de alguma forma se distinguisse da burguesia ou oligarquia agrário-mercantil que muitos haviam chegado a equivocadamente classificar de "feudal"[13]. Através dessa estratégia era possível a Prado Jr. negar a própria existência do pacto populista nacional-desenvolvimentista — o pacto que, entre a Revolução de 1930 e a derrota do candidato do PSD (Partido Social-Democrático) e PTB (Partido Trabalhista Brasileiro), general Henrique Teixeira Lott, em 1960, uniu empresários, trabalhadores, classes médias tecnocráticas e a parte da oligarquia que Ignácio Rangel

---

12 Desenvolvi inicialmente essas idéias em "Seis interpretações sobre o Brasil" (1982), onde identifiquei duas interpretações pré-1964 — a "interpretação da vocação agrária" em conflito com a "interpretação nacional-burguesa" -, e quatro pós-1964 — a "interpretação autoritário-modernizante", a "interpretação da superexploração capitalista", a "interpretação funcional-capitalista" e a "interpretação da nova dependência". Pessoalmente identifiquei-me com a segunda antes de 1964, e com a última a partir de então.

13 Ver, por exemplo, Alberto Passos Guimarães (1964).

(1980) chamou de "substituidora de importações", em torno de um projeto de industrialização[14].

Caio Prado Jr. começa por criticar, corretamente a meu ver, a tese da existência de um feudalismo ou de um semifeudalismo no Brasil pré-1930, para, em seguida, negar qualquer "distinção política e de categoria social entre, de um lado, os fazendeiros, estancieiros, senhores de engenho e usineiros... e de outro lado a burguesia industrial, comercial ou qualquer outra" (1966:106). E, em função desta análise, ou seja, de entender a burguesia brasileira como uma única burguesia mercantil desde o período colonial até o momento em que escrevia, em 1966, conclui, no plano político, que "a idéia de uma 'burguesia nacional, progressista e contrária ao imperialismo por sua posição específica de classe, causou à linha política da esquerda os mais graves danos" (1966:112)[15].

Dessa forma, Caio Prado Jr. inaugurava a "interpretação funcional-capitalista". Era uma abordagem ressentida do Brasil, indignada com o golpe militar, que definia para os intelectuais de esquerda brasileiros uma tarefa: revisar a história do Brasil e particularmen-

---

[14] Rangel observa que a Revolução de 1930 chefiada por Getúlio Vargas foi produto de um movimento à frente do qual "encontravam-se — como hoje sabemos e como poucos o suspeitávamos então — duas forças muito díspares, mas idênticas num ponto, a saber: o latifúndio *substituidor de importações* (principalmente gaúcho) e a indústria *substituidora de importações* (principalmente paulista)" (1980:47, grifos do Autor).

[15] Escrevendo dois anos antes, e portanto não estando sob o impacto do ressentimento causado pela derrota de 1964, Fernando Henrique Cardoso admitia a existência do pacto político entre empresários, intelectuais tecnocráticos e trabalhadores, e, ao mesmo tempo, assinalava o rompimento desse pacto de uma maneira mais serena e objetiva: "os grupos sociais que organizaram movimentos pela emancipação econômica não suspeitavam que, no momento seguinte, a burguesia nacional poder-se-ia aliar aos 'interesses estrangeiros'..." (1963:85). Um pouco mais adiante, entretanto, ele esquece o processo histórico de dividira as elites e as reunificara e afirma, simplesmente, que o Estado "continuou a ser controlado nas decisões fundamentais pela aliança entre e burguesia industrial e os grupos agrários e financeiros tradicionais" (1963: 90). Esta segunda afirmação estava mais de acordo com a reação ideológica paulista às idéias do ISEB e do Partido Comunista sobre o pacto nacional desenvolvimentista, que Prado Jr. encarnaria um pouco depois.

te a história da industrialização brasileira, para reduzir o significado da crise econômica de 1929 e da Revolução de 1930. A economia e a sociedade brasileiras deixavam de ser duais: haviam sido sempre capitalistas. O que havia de não-capitalista era funcional ao capitalismo. O momento decisivo de desenvolvimento e consolidação da indústria brasileira deixava de ter como marco fundamental a depressão dos anos trinta e a Revolução de 1930, sendo transferido para o final do século XIX, quando as primeiras indústrias são instaladas no Brasil[16]. Os empresários industriais deixavam de ser um grupo étnico e social distinto dos cafeicultores mas identificavam-se com eles. Os interesses dos dois grupos eram identificados ou pelo menos seus conflitos colocados em segundo plano. A dinâmica industrialização brasileira deixava de ser dependente dos fatores externos, como Celso Furtado tão bem enfatizara, e passava a depender de fatores internos, particularmente da própria burguesia[17].

Esta análise representou uma reação às análises anteriores que haviam exagerado a ruptura representada pela Revolução de 1930[18].

---

16 Segundo Cardoso de Mello (1975:109), "o período que se estende de 1888 a 1933 marca, portanto, o momento de nascimento e *consolidação* do capital industrial" (grifos meus).

17 A grande maioria dos intelectuais de esquerda adota na segunda metade dos anos sessenta essas posições a partir da análise de Caio Prado Jr. Entre eles — embora nem todos adotem todas as idéias enumeradas — merecem menção especial Luciano Martins (1968, 1973), Francisco de Oliveira (1972), Lúcio Kowarick (1973), Boris Fausto (1972), Fernando Novais (1973), Caio Navarro de Toledo (1974), João Manoel Cardoso de Mello (1975). A respeito do tema ver as excelentes resenhas de Wilson Suzigan (1986) e de Eli Diniz (1981), esta última especificamente sobre a Revolução de 1930. Suzigan comete a meu ver um erro ao colocar Sergio Silva nesse grupo, quando ele, na verdade, representa um passo adiante na linha de Celso Furtado. Nos anos setenta essa interpretação seria paulatinamente substituída pela "interpretação da nova dependência" (Bresser Pereira, 1982), que, embora representasse uma crítica ao funcionalismo e ao ahistoricismo da "interpretação funcional-capitalista", permaneceu com ela confundida por muito tempo, talvez até hoje.

18 Nesta linha merecem especial menção os trabalhos de Hélio Jaguaribe (1956, 1958, 1962), mas esta era a visão geral nos anos quarenta e cinqüenta dos representantes do que chamei "interpretação nacional-burguesa" (Bresser Pereira, 1982).

Mas, uma reação radical e, a meu ver, ressentida em relação ao desastre político que representou o golpe de 1964. Em conseqüência, uma reação equivocada. Realmente a sociedade e a economia brasileira jamais foram feudais. A classe dominante na Colônia, no Império e na Primeira República foi uma burguesia, mas uma burguesia mercantil, como Caio Prado Jr. enfatizou em suas obras clássicas (1933, 1942, 1945)[19]. De fato, antes de 1930, a incipiente indústria nacional estava intimamente ligada ao café[20]. Sem dúvida, a tese da "burguesia nacional" foi exagerada pelos intelectuais-tecnocratas que analisaram o pacto nacional-desenvolvimentista populista, como também foi exagerada a divisão no seio da burguesia. Havia uma burguesia industrial, mas que jamais conseguiu assumir plenamente seu papel de burguesia nacional. Mas estes erros não justificavam o erro inverso de ignorar o papel fundamental dos anos trinta para o deslanche e consolidação da industrialização brasileira, de considerar a Revolução de 1930 mais um mero episódio de conciliação de elites, de ver na relação café-indústria apenas o aspecto, positivo esquecendo todos os conflitos de interesse subjacentes, de afirmar que essas elites eram basicamente unas, não havendo distinção nem de interesses, nem de origens entre a aristocracia cafeeira e os industriais.

Fatos novos ignorados

Na verdade, esta análise viesada do sentido da Revolução de 1930, da relação econômica entre café e indústria, do momento fundamental em que ocorre a nossa "revolução industrial", e das origens étnicas e sociais dos empresários paulistas aconteceu, e até

---

[19] Desenvolvi mais extensamente esta oposição entre o capital mercantil, dominante até 1930, e o capital industrial, dominante a partir de então, em Bresser Pereira (1981).

[20] Conforme assinala Suzigan, "o investimento na indústria de transformação estava diretamente relacionado ao desempenho do setor exportador até 1913, e, em menor grau até 1929. Essa relação foi interrompida em 1930, quando o crescimento da renda interna nas atividades econômicas ligadas ao mercado interno substituiu a demanda externa como principal determinante da acumulação de capital industrial" (1986:345).

hoje mantém seus efeitos[21], porque os intelectuais de esquerda no Brasil não foram capazes de perceber que o colapso do pacto populista nacional-desenvolvimentista no início dos anos sessenta, que acabou resultando no golpe de 1964, não podia ser atribuído a uma traição dos empresários que participaram desse pacto, muito menos a um erro de avaliação dos intelectuais de esquerda que patrocinaram o mesmo. Se, ao invés de adotarem essa atitude de busca dos responsáveis, houvessem procurado entender os novos fatos históricos que inviabilizaram a grande coalizão de classes que Getúlio Vargas tão bem costurara, poderiam ter compreendido muito melhor a dinâmica da sociedade brasileira naquele momento. E estariam mais condizentes com o método histórico, que ao invés de buscar culpados para o fracasso de pactos políticos, procura as razões objetivas do colapso.

Este reconhecimento só ocorreu quando, no final dos anos sessenta, começa a se definir mais claramente a "interpretação da nova dependência"[22]. Eu fiz uma análise dos fatos novos que iriam dar origem a essa nova interpretação no momento das eleições presidenciais de 1960. Estava então estudando nos Estados Unidos e li no *New York Times* uma pequena notícia sobre as eleições presidenciais que se avizinhavam no Brasil: o jornal dizia aproximadamente o seguinte em sua primeira página: "No Brasil, o candidato de direita é apoiado pela esquerda, e o candidato de esquerda é

---

[21] Wilson Suzigan (1986), por exemplo, em sua notável análise das origens e desenvolvimento da indústria brasileira, deixou o problema das origens étnicas e sociais razoavelmente em aberto. É interessante, entretanto, como, passados os anos e o ressentimento, a "interpretação funcional-capitalista" perde importância, e fenômenos como a Revolução de 1930 recuperam seu lugar na história. Francisco Weffort, por exemplo, afirma em 1985: "O Estado brasileiro como Estado moderno, isto é, como Estado nacional, passa a existir depois de 1930" (1985:166).

[22] A "interpretação da nova dependência" tornar-se-ia dominante nos anos setenta, a partir das contribuições de Fernando Henrique Cardoso e Enzo Faletto (1969), F. H. Cardoso (1972, 1977), Antônio Barros de Castro (1969), Bresser Pereira (1970, 1973, 1977), Maria da Conceição Tavares e José Serra (1971), Edmar Bacha (1973), Peter Evans (1979) e muitos outros. Esta interpretação não deve ser confundida com a "interpretação da super-exploração imperialista" de Gunder Frank (1966, 1969), Theotônio dos Santos (1967, 1970) e Ruy Mauro Marini (1969, 1973).

apoiado pela direita". A notícia era curiosa e parcialmente equivocada: Lott, de fato, era um candidato de direita apoiado pela esquerda por ser nacionalista e desenvolvimentista; Jânio Quadros, porém, não era um candidato de esquerda, mas um candidato populista e autoritário apoiado pela direita. O importante na notícia, entretanto, era que ela assinalava bem a grande confusão política que imperava no Brasil naquele momento — confusão que decorria do vácuo político existente a partir do colapso do pacto nacional-desenvolvimentista. Escrevi então uma carta a um amigo, desenvolvendo minha análise[23]. Estava claro para mim que o pacto político de Vargas, juntando burguesia industrial, setores da oligarquia substituidora de importações, tecnoburocratas no aparelho do Estado, e trabalhadores, se tornara inviável na segunda metade dos anos cinqüenta porque, de um lado, já se manifestava naquele ano a crise da estratégia de substituição de importações e do financiamento inflacionário do déficit público que fora levada ao paroxismo nos cinco anos do Governo Kubitschek (1956-1960), de outro, porque fatos históricos novos levaram as elites, que haviam se dividido em torno da industrialização e do confisco cambial, a novamente se unir e a romper sua aliança com a esquerda.

Identifiquei, então, seis fatos históricos novos: primeiro, a consolidação do desenvolvimento industrial, ocorrida na década, que terminava de vez o debate sobre o "caráter artificial" da indústria brasileira, tão comum ainda na primeira metade dos anos cinqüenta; segundo, a vertiginosa queda, entre 1954 e 1960, dos preços internacionais do café, que enfraquecia os cafeicultores e encerrava na prática sua luta contra o confisco cambial; terceiro, a entrada maciça de empresas multinacionais manufatureiras no Brasil, que liquidava com o argumento — parcialmente válido no passado — de que "o imperialismo se opunha à industrialização"; quarto, a

[23] A carta foi escrita em 1960 a Luiz Antônio de Almeida Eça e data de 14 de dezembro. Com base nela escrevi um primeiro artigo sobre os empresários industriais e a política (Bresser Pereira, 1963). Em 1968 publiquei uma versão mais completa dessa análise dos fatos novos que haviam inviabilizado o pacto de Vargas no quarto capítulo de *Desenvolvimento e Crise no Brasil* (1968). Este capítulo, que não alterei nas edições subseqüentes do livro, correspondia a um artigo escrito em 1963 e destinado à *Revista Brasileira de Ciências Sociais*, da Universidade de Minas Gerais, que não chegou a publicá-lo devido à suspensão da própria publicação da revista em função do golpe de Estado.

aprovação de Lei de Tarifas, de 1958, que oferecia uma proteção estável à indústria nacional, isentando-a de continuar a defender idéias nacionalistas já que o principal — o protecionismo — estava assegurado; quinto, o recrudescimento do movimento sindical, com a tentativa de formação de centrais sindicais intersetoriais e a realização de greves importantes, levando empresários a reconsiderar seu acordo com as esquerdas; sexto, a revolução em Cuba, em 1959, que apavorou a burguesia brasileira e convenceu-a de vez da necessidade de se unir "contra o inimigo comum".

Estes fatos novos, que depois seriam a base da "interpretação da nova dependência", liquidavam a grande coalizão de classes — o pacto populista ou nacional-desenvolvimentista — que Getúlio Vargas arquitetara, e que durante trinta anos dominara o Brasil. A consolidação da indústria e o enfraquecimento do café uniam as duas classes. O próprio café era, agora, produzido e comercializado de forma crescente por imigrantes e seus descendentes. A entrada das multinacionais na indústria, que efetivamente só ocorreu nos anos cinqüenta, liquidava com a tese de que "o capital estrangeiro se opunha à industrialização. Os empresários industriais, agora defendidos de importações por uma lei de tarifas, que seria um pouco mais tarde complementada pela Lei do Similar Nacional, podiam associar-se, tornar-se fornecedores e distribuidores dos bens produzidos localmente pelas empresas multinacionais manufatureiras. O recrudescimento da luta sindical e principalmente a revolução em Cuba, levando a um aumento da pressão política das esquerdas, indicavam que era mais cauteloso para a burguesia brasileira se unir. O pacto nacional-desenvolvimentista perdera, portanto, sua razão de ser. Os analistas e defensores desse pacto político no seio da esquerda estavam corretos quando o identificaram, e não é possível condená-los por lhe terem dado seu apoio. Não era sua análise que havia sido errada. Ela simplesmente fora superada por fatos históricos novos.

Com o colapso do pacto populista produz-se, então, um vácuo político, ao mesmo tempo que a esquerda e a direita radicalizavam seu discurso e sua ação. As eleições de 1960, particularmente o apoio dado ao general Lott, que era um homem de direita, pelas forças de esquerda, revelava esse vácuo e esse impasse. Sua derrota leva Jânio Quadros ao poder. Com sua renúncia, entretanto, João Goulart, o herdeiro por excelência de Getúlio Vargas, sobe ao poder. A reação contrária da burguesia e dos militares explica-se dessa forma. Jango chegava ao poder quando já naufragara o pacto político que deveria dar-lhe sustentação. O golpe militar de 1964 é a conseqüência deste fato.

A esquerda não se enfraqueceu, como afirmou Caio Prado Jr., por ter-se associado aos empresários nacionais. Ela foi derrotada quando insistiu em uma estratégia política em um momento em que as bases para essa estratégia — a aliança nacional-desenvolvimentista com o empresariado industrial — haviam sido minadas por fatos objetivos. Entretanto, a partir de *A Revolução Brasileira*, de Caio Prado Jr., a esquerda, ao invés de fazer essa análise, imobilizou a história — ou seja, em última análise a ignorou — e chegou à conclusão que toda a análise anterior de uma burguesia industrial relativamente aliada aos trabalhadores e em conflito com a burguesia mercantil cafeeira havia sido historicamente errada e politicamente enfraquecedora da esquerda. Felizmente, porém, isto não impediu essa mesma esquerda, dez anos depois, a partir de meados dos anos setenta, participasse de uma nova coalizão política com a burguesia, principalmente com a burguesia industrial — coalizão que tenho chamado de "pacto democrático-populista de 1977" — para lutar pela restauração da democracia no Brasil[24].

Conclusão

Neste trabalho me propus a responder uma questão muito simples: como explicar que, não obstante tenha demonstrado, em uma pesquisa publicada em 1964, que os empresários industriais paulistas se originavam em sua grande maioria de imigrantes de classe média, e apesar de essa tese ter sido comprovada na pesquisa histórica de Warren Dean, a idéia ainda hoje dominante é a de que

[24] Pacto democrático, porque seu objetivo fundamental era restaurar a democracia; pacto populista, porque, uma vez no governo, retomou as teses dos anos cinqüenta; de 1977, porque consolidou-se em 1977, após o "pacote autoritário de abril", através do qual o Presidente Geisel fechou o Congresso provisoriamente, causando profunda indignação na burguesia. Esse pacto entraria em colapso dez anos depois, em 1987, em função do fracasso do Plano Cruzado, que pôs a nu o caráter populista e arcaico das idéias econômicas nele embutidas. Desde então o Brasil vive novamente um vácuo político.

esses empresários originaram-se da aristocracia cafeeira. Minha resposta assumiu um caráter de crítica das idéias. O equívoco nascera da justa indignação de Caio Prado Jr. com o golpe de Estado de 1964, que o grande historiador transformou em indignação contra os intelectuais de esquerda que haviam diagnosticado o pacto nacional-desenvolvimentista, unindo empresários industriais, trabalhadores, classes médias tecnocráticas e setores substituidores de importação da oligarquia mercantil, e apoiado a participação da esquerda nesse pacto. Ao invés de admitir que o pacto realmente existira — embora possa ter sido exagerado pelos analistas —, Caio Prado Jr. negou-o, e considerou aqueles que o diagnosticaram e apoiaram entre os culpados pela derrota da esquerda em 1964. Ao negar a existência do pacto, era necessário também demonstrar que a classe dominante no Brasil sempre fora unida, que não havia distinções significativas de caráter social ou étnico separando empresários industriais dos cafeicultores. Logo, isto foi enfaticamente afirmado, embora contrariasse as evidências. Era necessário também demonstrar o caráter não de oposição mas de forte consistência entre a economia cafeeira e a industrialização, quando, na verdade, o que havia era uma relação dialética de oposição e reforço.

Embora equivocada porque ressentida, essa análise do grande historiador encontrou campo fértil nas esquerdas. Deu origem ao que chamei de "interpretação funcional-capitalista" do Brasil. A partir do início dos anos setenta, entretanto, uma outra abordagem mais consentânea com a realidade — a interpretação da nova dependência passou paulatinamente a substituí-la, e facilitou, a partir do final da década, a formação de uma nova coalizão política unindo empresários e esquerdas — o pacto democrático-populista de 1977. Este pacto chegaria ao poder em 1985, com a Nova República, e entraria em colapso em 1987, com o fracasso do Plano Cruzado, quando se evidenciou o caráter arcaico e populista de muitas das idéias da esquerda naquele momento. A partir daí a esquerda no Brasil e na América Latina entra em uma profunda crise, das qual vai aos poucos emergindo nos últimos anos, na medida em que vai se tornando capaz de criticar não apenas a onda conservadora, neoliberal, que atingiu o Brasil no final dos anos oitenta, mas também o esgotamento da estratégia nacional-desenvolvimentista. Na medida em que, pragmaticamente, recuse dogmatismos ideológicos e afirme a possibilidade de uma esquerda moderna, crítica do populismo, aliada aos setores progressistas e dinâmicos dentro do empresariado, que certamente não serão os mesmos dos anos cinqüenta ou dos anos setenta. Na medida em que, definindo a atual crise como essencialmente uma crise do Estado, aceite as idéias de disciplina fiscal, liberalização e privatização não como uma via para o Estado mínimo dos neo-conservadores, mas como uma condição para a reforma do Estado[25].

Referências

Abreu, Marcelo de Paiva. "Crise, crescimento e modernização autoritária: 1930-1945". In M. P. Abreu, org. *Ordem e Progresso: Cem Anos de Política Econômica Republicana.* Rio de Janeiro: Campus. 1990.

Bacha, Edmar L. "Sobre a dinâmica de crescimento da economia industrial subdesenvolvida". *Pesquisa e Planejamento Econômico* 3(4) dezembro. 1973.

Aureliano, Liana Maria. *No Limiar da Industrialização.* São Paulo: Brasiliense. 1981.

Bielschowsky, Roberto. *O Pensamento Econômico Brasileiro.* Rio de Janeiro: IPEA/INPES. 1988.

Bresser Pereira, Luiz Carlos. "O empresário industrial e a revolução brasileira". *Revista de Administração de Empresas 2(8)* julho 1963. Republicado em Bresser Pereira (1972). *Empresários e Administradores no Brasil.* São Paulo: Brasiliense. 1963.

—— "Origens étnicas e sociais do empresário paulista". *Revista de Administração de Empresas 3(11)* junho, 1964. Republicado em Bresser Pereira (1972). *Empresários e Administradores no Brasil.* São Paulo: Brasiliense. 1964.

—— "Desenvolvimento político", capítulo 4 de *Desenvolvimento e Crise no Brasil: 1930-1967.* Rio de Janeiro: Zahar. 1968. Este capítulo não foi alterado nas edições subseqüentes do livro.

—— "Dividir ou multiplicar: a distribuição de renda e a recuperação da economia brasileira". *Visão,* dezembro 1970. Republicado na terceira edição de Bresser Pereira (1972). *Desenvolvimento e Crise no Brasil.* São Paulo: Brasiliense, (p. 211-21) e nas edições subseqüentes.

[25] Examinei a crise e renovação da esquerda na América Latina em Bresser Pereira (1990). Em todos os meus trabalhos escritos a partir de minha experiência no Ministério da Fazenda (1987) venho procurando desenvolver uma interpretação nesse sentido, que chamo de "interpretação da crise do Estado", mas que também poderia ser chamada de "interpretação pragmática" ou "interpretação social-democrática". Ver, especialmente, Bresser Pereira (1993).

—— *Empresários e Administradores no Brasil.* São Paulo: Brasiliense. 1972. Tese de doutoramento com o título original *Mobilidade e Carreira dos Dirigentes de Empresas Paulistas.* São Paulo: Universidade de São Paulo, Faculdade de Economia e Administração. 1972.

—— "O novo modelo de desenvolvimento". *Dados,* n. 11, sem mês. 1973.

—— "Três hipóteses sobre o início da industrialização brasileira e a economia cafeeira". Anexo II de Bresser Pereira (1972). 1974.

—— *Estado e Subdesenvolvimento Industrializado.* São Paulo: Brasiliense. 1977.

—— A *Economia Brasileira: uma Introdução Crítica.* São Paulo: Brasiliense. 1982.

—— "Seis interpretações sobre o Brasil". *Dados* 25(3), sem mês, 1982.

—— "Crise e renovação da esquerda na América Latina". *Lua Nova,* n. 21, outubro de 1990. Republicado em Bresser Pereira (1991). A *Crise do Estado.* São Paulo: Nobel. 1990.

—— "Economic reforms and economic growth: efficiency and politics in Latin America". In Bresser Pereira, Maravall and Przeworski (1993). *Economic Reforms in New Democracies.* Cambridge: Cambridge University Press. 1993.

Cano, Wilson. *Raízes da Concentração Industrial no Brasil.* São Paulo: Difusão Européia do Livro. 1977.

Cardoso, Fernando Henrique. *Empresário Industrial e Desenvolvimento Econômico.* São Paulo: Difusão Européia do Livro. 1964.

—— O *Modelo Político Brasileiro.* São Paulo: Difusão Européia do Livro. 1972.

—— "O consumo da teoria da dependência nos Estados Unidos". *Ensaios de Opinião,* n. 4, 1977.

—— & E. Faletto. *Dependência e Subdesenvolvimento na América Latina.* São Paulo: Difusão Européia do Livro. 1970.

Castro, Antônio Barros de. "Agricultura e desenvolvimento no Brasil", *in* Antônio Barros de Castro (1969). 7 *Ensaios sobre a Economia Brasileira,* vol. 1. Rio de Janeiro: Forense. 1969.

Dean, Warren. A *Industrialização de São Paulo (1980-1945).* São Paulo: Difusão Européia do Livro. 1971.

Diniz, Eli. "Estado Novo: estrutura de poder e relações de classe", *in* Boris Fausto (org.). *História Geral da Civilização Brasileira: III — O Brasil Republicano.* São Paulo: Difusão Européia do Livro. 1981.

Draibe, Sônia. *Rumos e Metamorfoses.* São Paulo: Paz e Terra. 1985.

Evans, Peter. *Dependent Development: the Aliance of Multinational, Local and State Capital in Brazil.* Princeton University Press. 1979.

Fishlow, Albert. "Origens e conseqüências da substituição de importações no Brasil". *Estudos Econômicos* 2(6) dezembro, 1972.

Frank, Gunder. "Development and underdevelopment", *in* Robert I. Rhodes (org.). *Imperialism and Underdevelopment.* New York: Monthly Review Press. 1970.

—— *Capitalism and Development in Latin America.* New York: Monthly Review Press. 1969.

Furtado, Celso. *Formação Econômica da Brasil.* Rio de Janeiro: Fundo de Cultura. 1959.

—— *Subdesenvolvimento e Estagnação na América Latina.* Rio de Janeiro: Civilização Brasileira. 1966.

Guimarães, Alberto Passos. *Quatro Séculos de Latifúndio.* Rio de Janeiro: Paz e Terra. 1964.

Gudin, E. & R. Simonsen. A *Controvérsia do Planejamento na Economia Brasileira.* Rio de Janeiro: IPEA/INPES. 1977.

Jaguaribe, Hélio. "Sentido e perspectivas do governo Kubitschek". *Cadernos do Nosso Tempo,* n. 4, janeiro 1956 (artigo não assinado). 1956.

—— *O Nacionalismo na Atualidade Brasileira.* Rio de Janeiro: Instituto de Estudos Brasileiros — ISEB. 1958.

—— *Desenvolvimento Econômico e Desenvolvimento Político.* Rio de Janeiro: Fundo de Cultura. 1962.

Luz, Nícia Vilela. *A Luta pela Industrialização do Brasil.* São Paulo: Difusão Européia do Livro. 1961.

Loureiro, Maria Rita. "Economistas e elites dirigentes no Brasil". *Revista Brasileira de Ciências Sociais* 7(20) outubro. 1992.

Magalhães, João Paulo de A. *A Controvérsia Brasileira sobre Desenvolvimento Econômico.* Rio de Janeiro: Gráfica Récord Editora, sem data. Publicada originalmente em 1961 pela Confederação Nacional da Indústria.

Martins, Luciano. *Industrialização, Burguesia Nacional e Desenvolvimento.* Rio de Janeiro: Saga. 1968.

—— *Pouvoir et Développement Economique.* Paris: Editions Anthropos. 1976.

Mello, João Manoel Cardoso de. O *Capitalismo Tardio.* São Paulo: Brasiliense. 1982.

Mello, Zélia Cardoso de. *São Paulo, 1845-1895: Metamorfoses da Riqueza.* Tese de doutoramento. São Paulo: Universidade de São Paulo, Faculdade de Economia e Administração. 1981.

Nicol, Robert C. A *Agricultura* e a *Industrialização no Brasil.* Tese de doutoramento. São Paulo: Universidade de São Paulo, Faculdade de Filosofia e Ciências Humanas, Departamento de Ciências Sociais. 1974.

Novais, Fernando A. *Portugal e Brasil na Crise do Antigo Sistema Colonial — 1777-1808.* São Paulo: Hucitec. 1979.

Peláez, Carlos Manuel. *História da Industrialização Brasileira.* Rio de Janeiro: APEC. 1972.

Prado Jr., Caio. *Evolução Política do Brasil.* São Paulo: Brasiliense, segunda edição, 1957 (primeira edição, 1933).

—— *Formação do Brasil Contemporâneo.* São Paulo: Brasiliense, quinta edição, 1957 (primeira edição, 1942).

—— *História Econômica do Brasil.* São Paulo: Brasiliense, quarta edição, 1956 (primeira edição, 1945).

—— A *Revolução Brasileira.* São Paulo: Brasiliense. 1966.

Rangel, Ignácio M. "Revisitando a 'questão nacional'". *Encontros com a Civilização Brasileira,* n. 27. 1980.

Sodré, Nelson Werneck. *História da Burguesia Brasileira.* Rio de Janeiro: Civilização Brasileira. 1964.

Sola, Lourdes. *The Political and Ideological Constraints of Economic Management in Brazil, 1945-1963.* Tese de doutoramento. Universidade de Oxford. 1982.

Silva, Sergio S. *Expansão Cafeeira e Origem da Indústria no Brasil.* São Paulo: Editora Alfa Omega. 1976.

Tavares, Maria da Conceição. "Auge e declínio do processo de substituição de importações no Brasil", *in* M. C. Tavares (1972). *Da Substituição de Importações ao Capitalismo Financeiro.* Rio de Janeiro: Zahar.

—— & J. Serra. "Além da estagnação". In M. C. Tavares (1972).

Toledo, Caio Navarro de. *ISEB: Fábrica de Ideologias.* São Paulo: Atica. 1977.

Suzigan, Wilson. *Indústria Brasileira: Origem e Desenvolvimento.* São Paulo: Brasiliense. 1986.

Weffort, Francisco. "Nacionalismo, populismo, e o que restou do legado político de Getúlio Vargas". In T. Szmrecsányi e R. Granziera (orgs.). *Getúlio Vargas e a Economia Contemporânea.* São Paulo: Editora da UNICAMP. 1985.

Villela, A. & W. Suzigan. *Política do Governo e Crescimento da Economia Brasileira: 1989-1945.* Rio de Janeiro: Fundação Getúlio Vargas. 1973.

Ary Cesar Minella
Universidade Federal de Santa Catarina

EMPRESARIADO FINANCEIRO: ELEMENTOS DISCURSIVOS NA DÉCADA DE 1980

Os anos oitenta têm sido caracterizados como "década perdida" considerando-se, em termos gerais, a persistência de um contexto de crise econômica e social. No entanto, a crise ou as crises do período afetaram de forma diferenciada os diversos segmentos sociais e, dentre os empresários, parece não existir dúvidas que o empresariado financeiro no Brasil consolidou sua posição econômica. Assim, o setor financeiro teria passado praticamente incólume pela crise, ou mais que isto, teria sido um dos grandes beneficiados pelo desfavorável contexto econômico e social.

Consolidando tendências existentes nos anos anteriores, o sistema financeiro brasileiro manteve um alto grau de concentração, diversificou suas inversões no setor não-financeiro, estreitou vínculos com o capital internacional, modernizou seu aparato operacional, manteve alta rentabilidade, diversificou sua estrutura de representação político-corporativa e manteve sob seu comando mais de meio milhão de trabalhadores bancários.

A partir dessa constatação, parece até supérfluo enfatizar a necessidade de acompanhar de forma sistemática a evolução deste sistema financeiro e a influência que seus agentes — privados ou estatais — possam ter na definição de políticas econômicas e de alternativas sociopolíticas para o País. Este trabalho contribui, em alguma medida, para atender essa necessidade, identificando e examinando posicionamentos expressos pelo empresariado do setor em torno de questões relevantes, considerando-se o contexto mais geral do período.

Dois temas foram selecionados para a análise: *a)* o posicionamento do empresariado financeiro acerca do liberalismo ou neoliberalismo; *b)* suas manifestações em relação aos próprios pares empresariais, especialmente durante o primeiro lustro da década de oitenta, considerando-se o conflito em torno à taxa de juros e as ações corporativas e políticas conjuntas[1].

Na impossibilidade de investigar todo o universo de empresários financeiros, centrou-se a análise nos líderes que ocuparam a direção dos órgãos de representação do setor: Associação dos Bancos no Estado de São Paulo (ASSOBESP), Federação Brasileira de Associações de Bancos (FEBRABAN), Federação Nacional dos Bancos (FENABAN), Confederação Nacional das Instituições Financeiras (CNF) e Associação Brasileira de Bancos Comerciais e Múltiplos (ABBC).[2]

Sistema Financeiro Brasileiro: algumas características e tendências do período

Apenas a título de referência mais geral, é necessário indicar algumas das características e tendências apresentadas pelo sistema durante o período em estudo.

a) Os bancos mantiveram uma rentabilidade elevada em termos comparativos aos demais setores durante a década de 1980 e início dos anos noventa. Tal rentabilidade se mostrou especialmente alta em 1981 e 1982 (período de crise econômica) e em 1989 (final do governo Sarney). Tomando-se como indicadores o custo do finan-

---

[1] Embora não incluídas diretamente no trabalho, resgatamos nas conclusões elementos indicativos do posicionamento do empresariado financeiro sobre os trabalhadores bancários e sua ação coletiva.

[2] Em termos gerais, tais entidades revelam um baixo grau de rotatividade em suas lideranças destacando-se, portanto, alguns poucos nomes: Roberto Konder Bornhausen, Pedro Conde, Antônio de Pádua Rocha Diniz, Léo Wallace Cochrane Junior, Elmo Camões e José Carlos Jacintho de Campos. As *fontes básicas* consultadas para esta avaliação (preliminar) foram artigos e entrevistas publicados na grande imprensa, em publicações especializadas, e textos de palestras em eventos do setor empresarial. Por limitações de tempo e de disponibilidade de dados, deixamos de incluir na análise o banqueiro Theophilo de Azeredo Santos, que ocupou a presidência da FENABAN e que, desde 1967, dirige o Sindicato dos Bancos do Estado do Rio de Janeiro.

ciamento do capital de giro e do desconto de duplicatas no período (ver tabela na página seguinte) pode-se entender melhor as "tensões" intersetoriais que se manifestariam no discurso empresarial. Esta alta rentabilidade dos bancos está associada também ao padrão de financiamento adotado pelo Estado, que favoreceu a manutenção da chamada "ciranda financeira". O contexto inflacionário resultou em poderoso mecanismo de transferência de renda para o setor financeiro.

b) Durante a década de 1980, os bancos intensificaram o processo de automação bancária e criaram uma maior diversidade de serviços. Essa diversidade se expressou, por um lado, em uma tendência de atendimento massivo (leve-se em conta a quantidade de operações) e, por outro, em um processo de "elitização" através do atendimento privilegiado a clientes selecionados.

c) Uma característica marcante do sistema, e que se aprofundou no contexto do processo de privatização ocorrido nos últimos anos, foi a participação dos bancos em investimentos nos setores não-financeiros. É importante destacar que esta relação não ocorre apenas com os grandes bancos (e suas *holdings*) mas, também, com os chamados médios e pequenos bancos[3]. A eliminação da carta patente e a criação do banco múltiplo em 1988 foram fatores que favoreceram essa diversificação. No início dos anos noventa, portanto, o empresariado financeiro parece ter consolidado um conjunto bastante complexo de interesses econômicos, com implicações que se manifestam em nível da estrutura e dinâmica da representação de interesses empresariais no campo corporativo e também político.

d) O número de instituições financeiras ampliou-se a partir de 1988, mas o sistema mantém como característica um alto grau de concentração das operações e da força de trabalho. Algumas poucas instituições de controle estatal e privado são responsáveis por cerca de 90% de todo o sistema. O conjunto de pequenos e médios bancos respondem por apenas 5 a 6% das operações.

e) O número de trabalhadores bancários cresceu de 440 mil em

---

[3] Em 1991/1992, pelo menos 14 bancos médios e 21 bancos pequenos estavam vinculados a grupos nacionais classificados entre os trezentos maiores do País. Nove entre os bancos médios se vinculam a grupos classificados entre os cem maiores.

Taxas de juros, inflação e rentabilidade empresarial dos Bancos, Brasil (%)

Anos	Financiamento - Capital de giro (*)	Desconto de duplicatas (*)		Resolução 63 (*)	Libor	Micro-, pequenas e médias empresas (*)		*Over night* (2)	CDB (pós-fixado) (3)	Tx. de câmbio: variação	Inflação	Rentabilidade (4)	
		S/R	C/R (1)			S/R	C/R					Empresas	Bancos
1973	10.6	4.1	9.8	5.9	9.24	-7.3	-3.8	-	-	0.1	15.5	15.2	16.2
1974	7.0	-8.3	0.0	16.9	11.15	-8.5	-5.1	-11.9	-	19.5	34.6	-	-
1975	4.1	-2.1	10.0	12.7	7.86	-15.7	-12.6	-5.7	-	22.0	29.3	-	-
1976	4.4	-9.4	8.0	9.2	6.26	-18.3	-15.2	-2.9	-	36.1	46.3	16.0	24.4
1977	16.8	3.7	19.1	8.0	6.44	-15.2	-12.1	3.3	-	30.0	38.8	-	-
1978	18.4	1.4	19.8	12.3	9.19	-21.5	-18.6	4.7	-	30.3	40.9	-	-
1979	0.1	-15.7	4.6	47.9	12.14	-39.8	-37.6	-18.2	-	103.3	77.2	7.9	11.6
1980	-13.4	-27.1	-1.8	-5.2	13.94	-41.7	-38.9	-29.6	-	54.0	110.2	-	-
1981	25.7	5.5	34.5	36.4	16.45	-28.1	-22.6	-1.5	-	95.1	95.2	9.2	28.3
1982	24.6	23.2	60.7	64.3	13.74	-32.8	-26.2	11.8	9.0	97.7	99.7	-	-
1983	13.4	0.8	20.9	34.7	9.89	-28.9	-18.5	-2.5	-2.9	289.4	211.0	-	-
1984	36.4	42.4	-	22.9	11.21	7.6	27.3	-1.5	14.9	223.6	223.8	12.7	10.6
1985	32.1	86.5	-	22.2	8.64	-0.2	15.0	4.1	12.3	229.5	224.4	-	-
1986	6.4	17.3	-	11.0	6.82	6.2	-	-5.5	-	42.4	62.4	14.5	13.6
1987	30.7	64.9	-	22.2	7.88	6.8	-	6.5	12.5	380.0	336.0	-	-
1988	9.7	34.2	-	-6.8	8.02	-28.9	-	1.7	-0.8	955.0	933.6	-	-
1989	116.1	232.5	-	-	-	-	-	81.8	-	1401.3	1764.9	14.0	20.8
1990	142.3	368.3	-	-	-	-	-	-10.5	-	1397.3	1198.5	-	-
1991												-3.0	9.1
1992												2.2	9.5

FONTES: Taxas de juros no Brasil, edição especial da revista *Análise Financeira*. 3.ª ed. 1991.
Revista *Exame*, edição 456, 27 junho 1990, p. 40; e edição 534, 23 junho 1993, p. 65 (para dados sobre rentabilidade).

OBSERVAÇÕES: (*) Custo efetivo real. (1) S/R; C/R: Sem/Com Reciprocidade. (2) Taxa líquida real. (3) Taxa média líquida real. (4) 500 maiores empresas brasileiras e 30 maiores bancos. Para os anos de 1973, 1981, 1989, 1991 e 1992: rentabilidade média das 500 empresas não-financeiras e 50 maiores bancos.

NOTAS EXPLICATIVAS da revista *Análise Financeira:*

1) Nos empréstimos, o custo efetivo inclui, além dos juros, os impostos, taxas comissões e eventuais reciprocidades exigidas pelos bancos.

2) Nas aplicações, a taxa líquida corresponde a remuneração nominal depois de deduzido o imposto de renda.

3) Para chegar à taxa real, ao ano, tomou-se a taxa no período da operação, descontou-se a inflação nesse mesmo período e atualizou-se o resultado. Isso é feito para permitir a comparação entre operações com prazos diferentes.

4) As médias anuais correspondem à média aritmética do ano.

5) Financiamento do capital de giro: o custo efetivo inclui reciprocidade, conforme as práticas de mercado.

6) Desconto de duplicatas: o custo efetivo com reciprocidade considera a retenção de saldo médio entre 20% e 50% da operação, conforme práticas de mercado na época da operação.

7) Micro-, pequenas e médias empresas: a série do custo com reciprocidade admite a exigência constante de um saldo médio equivalente à do valor da operação. Na prática, porém, essa taxa deve ter variado ao longo do tempo, mas tornou-se virtualmente impossível recuperar a informação. A partir de 1986, inclusive, as operações passaram a ser feitas, na maioria das vezes, sem a exigência de reciprocidade.

8) *Overnight:* a série histórica da taxa leva em conta o papel mais negociado em cada período.

9) Inflação: série encadeada a partir dos índices oficiais de inflação em cada período.

(Para maiores detalhes sobre estas notas consultar a fonte citada.)

1979 para 724 mil em 1985. A partir de 1986, no entanto, com a adaptação dos bancos ao Plano Cruzado, o sistema diminuiu sensivelmente o número de bancários (para 649 mil) mantendo-se a partir daí um crescimento muito lento. Além da automação, os bancos privados adotaram como estratégia a não-reposição da rotatividade normal do sistema. Assim, em inícios dos anos noventa, o contingente de trabalhadores não alcançava a mesma magnitude verificada em meados da década passada. Pode-se observar, no entanto, que algumas poucas instituições financeiras concentram a maior quantidade de trabalhadores. Em 1989, apenas sete bancos empregavam 441 mil bancários[4]. Ao longo do período, em termos gerais, os sindicatos que representam os trabalhadores bancários recuperaram sua capacidade organizativa e, em alguns grandes centros urbanos (especialmente em São Paulo), montaram uma moderna infra-estrutura operativa e agilizaram suas formas de mobilização. Nas negociações trabalhistas, os bancários buscaram estabelecer estratégias globais, mas os impasses com os banqueiros levaram freqüentemente a greves locais ou nacionais do setor.

f) No período que estamos considerando, ampliou-se o processo de internacionalização do sistema — seja pela atuação no exterior, seja pela associação interna com o capital estrangeiro, no segmento financeiro e em outros segmentos — como, também, pela maior participação dos bancos estrangeiros dentro do sistema[5].

g) Na mesma década, verifica-se uma diversificação de estrutura de representação de interesses do empresariado financeiro, através da criação de novos órgãos como a Associação Brasileira de Bancos Comerciais e Múltiplos ABBC (1983), a Confederação Nacional das Instituições Financeiras — CNF (1985) e a Associação Brasileira de Bancos Internacionais — ABBI (1988). Os bancos comerciais estatais fortaleceram a Associação Brasileira de Bancos

---

[4] Bancos e números de trabalhadores em 1989: Banco do Brasil: 134.308; Bradesco: 102.934; Itaú: 75.985; Bamerindus: 40.622; Banespa: 38.277; Unibanco: 26.356; Real: 23.220. (Fonte: Dados publicados pela FEBRABAN a partir de informações do Banco Central.)

[5] Em janeiro de 1993, o Banco Central do Brasil contabilizava: 17 bancos estrangeiros e 17 privados nacionais com controle estrangeiro. (Dados do Banco Central, *apud* publicação da Assessoria de Marketing Financeiro da Febraban, sem título)

Comerciais Estaduais (ASBACE), criada em 1979, e que passaria a exercer importante papel na articulação operacional e política dos interesses deste segmento do sistema financeiro.

Estas referências parciais dão conta de algumas características e tendências do sistema financeiro nos últimos anos. Uma análise detalhada das mesmas escapa à delimitação deste trabalho, mas é necessário tê-las presentes para contextualizar melhor o posicionamento dos líderes empresariais do setor.

O discurso (neo) liberal

O discurso liberal ou neoliberal ganhou espaço no meio empresarial e tendeu a ser hegemônico no período. Em termos gerais, ele se manifesta com diferente intensidade entre o empresariado financeiro. Por um lado, constatamos a existência de manifestações sistemáticas e conseqüentes com uma certa ação, pelo menos no campo do terreno doutrinário e ideológico. Por outro, ele se manifesta de forma dispersa ou conjuntural, sem um grau maior de elaboração e vinculação (pelo menos aparentemente) com uma ação político-doutrinária mais conseqüente.

Uma matriz de produção e ação a favor do liberalismo

Um exemplo significativo do primeiro caso é o empresário Roberto Konder Bornhausen, do grupo Unibanco, que foi presidente da ASSOBESP e da FEBRABAN no período 1977-80 e da ASSOBESP, FEBRABAN e FENABAN entre 1983 e 1986, e que comandou ainda a primeira diretoria da CNF (1985-87). É importante destacar a participação de Bornhausen na direção do Instituto Liberal de São Paulo, organização que se propõe exatamente a divulgar e defender os princípios liberais[6].

---

[6] Uma das características básicas deste empresário é a de associar à atividade de direção empresarial, uma especial "produção intelectual", que abrange tanto os problemas conjunturais como as diretrizes de mais longo alcance da grande burguesia bancário-financeira. Esta produção se traduz em palestras, entrevistas e artigos, que possibilitam uma análise mais sistemática do seu posicionamento. Para uma análise do Instituto Liberal no Brasil ver Gros, 1993.

O Unibanco é controlado pelo grupo Moreira Salles, que se caracteriza por uma série de elementos particulares: complexo entrelaçamento de interesses com o capital internacional e grupos locais; diversidade de investimentos; vínculos no campo político e trânsito na área estatal[7].

O apoio de Bornhausen ao liberalismo se manifestou desde fins da década de setenta, quando sintetizava seu posicionamento na expressão "liberalismo social", através do qual defendia o "princípio da responsabilidade social e do compromisso da empresa para com os valores da comunidade a que pertence". Contudo, este liberalismo "defende, igualmente, a primazia da oferta e da demanda, a liberdade de mercado e a eficiência como critério de concorrência". Este liberalismo social — afirma o empresário — "não é contrário a qualquer forma de planejamento que se sobreponha às leis do mercado". (Bornhausen, 30.08.79; a defesa de um certo poder regulatório do Estado aparece também em 29.9.82.)[8]

No contexto da crise que o País vivia em 1982, Bornhausen sustentava a validade do liberalismo, atribuindo os desajustes a fatores externos ao mesmo: limitação do conhecimento humano e egoísmo humano (Bornhausen 29.9.82)[9]. Em 1988, atuando no Ins-

---

[7] O Unibanco é controlado por E. Johnston Administração de Bens e Empresas e pela Cia. Brasileira de Metalurgia e Mineração (ambas controladas pelo grupo Moreira Salles, embora na última participe a International Mining Corp. dos Estados Unidos com 46% do capital). Desde que se constituiu como Banco Múltiplo em 1989, a participação estrangeira no banco ficou assim constituída: The Dai Ichi Kangyo Bank (Japão), um dos maiores bancos do mundo (com 11,72%), Commerzbank A.G. (Alemanha, com 10,17%) e Security Pacific National Bank (Estados Unidos, com 2,63%). Cf. *Gazeta Mercantil*, 9/2/90, p. 25.

[8] Outro membro do grupo Unibanco era forte aliado na divulgação do liberalismo: Marcílio Marques Moreira, que se manifestou em artigos editados na época (Moreira, 1981:14). Esta defesa do "liberalismo social", ao que tudo indica, não foi aprofundada ao longo dos anos oitenta, embora Bornhausen voltasse a usar a expressão em artigos de 1984 (Bornhausem, março 84; 13.4.84).

[9] Na concepção mais geral do liberalismo, a produção e os investimentos da empresas "estão intimamente ligados à obrigatoriedade de satisfazer as mais diversas necessidades dos consumidores, e o equilíbrio e o funcionamento correto do processo produção/distribuição estão assegurados a longo prazo" (Bornhausen, 29.9.82).

tituto Liberal, Bornhausen seguiu defendendo o liberalismo como única alternativa para o País[10].

Na concepção liberal, amplamente enfatizada por este empresário, o Estado não deve intervir no processo econômico, salvo quando interessar à segurança nacional ou "quando não for viável o envolvimento de capitais privados", mas sempre em caráter de complementaridade (Bornhausen, 30.08.79). A crítica e a oposição à intervenção do Estado na economia se manteriam ao longo de todo o período, assumindo em determinadas conjunturas um caráter de centralidade no discurso. (Bornhausen, março 1983; 8.5.89; e especialmente em artigos de 1984: março 1984, 13.5.84; 15.7.84; julho/agosto 1984; junho 1984; e palestras: 6.4.84; 24.10.84. Ver ainda Bornhausen, outubro 1985; 4.12.85; 16.8.88; 7.6.91 e 19.6.91.)

Já em 1979, Bornhausen considerava que o processo de intervenção estatal chegara longe demais e era o "momento de alterá-lo" (Bornhausen, 30.8.79). As esperanças de que tal processo pudesse ser revertido durante o governo do General Figueiredo desapontaram o lider empresarial e o levaram a afirmar em 1984, que "a iniciativa privada brasileira espera que o esforço para a contenção do expansionismo estatal passe do plano retórico (...) para o plano das ações concretas" (Bornhausen, 12.12.84)[11]. Mas, este banqueiro esperaria ainda alguns anos para ver concretizado, pelo menos em parte, seu anseio de privatização: o plano de privatização adotado pelo governo Collor, no qual os bancos passariam a ter uma significativa participação.

---

[10] "O Brasil somente alcançará o grau de desenvolvimento que todos desejamos, se seguir os caminhos liberais, na política e na economia" (Bornhausen, 16.8.88; ver também discurso pronunciado em novembro daquele ano na Câmara Americana de Comércio com o Brasil (Bornhausen 22.11.88).

[11] O governo Figueiredo (1979/84) se propôs a executar um plano de privatização de várias empresas e, nessa época, os grupos financeiros estavam interessados em adquiri-las, inclusive o próprio Unibanco, conforme declarações de Bornhausen (14.3.79). Em maio de 1982, este empresario indicava que o governo Figueiredo era o "primeiro que havia tomado iniciativas claras" para a contenção e modificação do processo estatizante, mas lamentava que os resultados alcançados não eram os desejados (Bornhausen, maio 1982).

Outros discursos — os mesmos temas, novas ênfases

O posicionamento liberal mantido por Bornhausen à frente da ASSOBESP/FEBRABAN teve continuidade na gestão de Pedro Conde, do Banco de Crédito Nacional — BCN (1980-83)[12]. Nesse período, a crise econômica se manifestou de forma mais aguda (1981-82) e os banqueiros passaram a ser alvo de sérias críticas por parte de empresários de outros setores. Além de procurar responder às críticas de seus pares burgueses, o empresariado financeiro passou a enfatizar em seu discurso as alternativas para superar a crise.

As questões centrais do discurso do presidente da ASSOBESP/FEBRABAN em 1982 giravam em torno de dois eixos: primeiro, um chamado ao empresariado no sentido de unir forças na defesa do liberalismo; e, segundo, a defesa dos bancos em relação a sua responsabilidade na crise econômica do País.

Conde reconhecia a gravidade da situação: "estamos passando pela maior crise do Brasil industrial moderno" e sugeria que "a luta dos empresários é uma só (...) pela livre-iniciativa". Para ele, a saída da crise passa pela concretização da proposta liberal. E propõe um postura mais agressiva dos empresários, os quais devem assumir um papel decisivo na sociedade brasileira. A "proposição maior" é "defender a livre iniciativa" que, segundo Conde, "está, de certa forma, órfã" (Conde, 26.6.82).

O reconhecimento da crise, no entanto, não podia ocultar o fato de que o setor financeiro obtinha alta rentabilidade comparativamente aos demais setores. Pedro Conde adotou, em seu discurso, uma tática dispersiva em relação às críticas dirigidas ao setor financeiro, conclamando os empresários à unidade em torno da livre iniciativa. Durante as eleições de 1982, Conde sugeriu que os empresários só deveriam apoiar candidatos comprometidos com os valores liberais e, ainda, que a formulação de propostas de política econômica do candidato deveria ter a participação do empresariado através de suas entidades representativas (Conde, 31.10.82).

Note-se que, em Bornhausen, a fundamentação da proposta liberal ganhara contornos mais sofisticados e sistematizados (tanto

---

12 Banco considerado de médio porte, tendo a família Conde investimentos diversificados em vários ramos de economia, com forte atuação na Bolsa de Valores.

em seu aspecto doutrinário quanto no que se refere a propostas efetivas). A expressão "liberalismo social" não se apresentava no discurso de Conde. A "livre iniciativa", no entanto, ganhou centralidade (Conde, 8.2.83 e 17.3.83).

A partir de 1986, o discurso da liderança empresarial retomava as críticas a uma intervenção estatal específica: a do setor financeiro. A partir da Nova República, algumas instituições financeiras de controle estatal adotaram uma política mais agressiva de atuação no mercado, gerando o que os banqueiros iriam chamar de "concorrência desleal" (Diniz, 21.5.88). Segundo o presidente da FEBRABAN/FENABAN/CNF, "na luta por parcelas crescentes de poder, as diferentes agências do Estado tendem a buscar apoderar-se crescentemente de parcelas da atividade possível, suprindo o espaço em que a iniciativa privada pode florescera" (Diniz, 8.11.86)[13].

As críticas dos banqueiros neste período não se dirigiam apenas à participação do Estado no setor financeiro, mas também ao papel regulador do mesmo dentro do sistema: a *desregulamentação* passou a ser uma demanda central do empresariado financeiro. Assim, para ele, o Estado se envolve "demasiado na atividade financeira, quer por participação excessiva, quer por ordenação desnecessariamente rígida do setor bancário privado" (Diniz, 8.11.86). A "burocratização" excessiva do sistema era, também, incluída entre os argumentos dos banqueiros para explicar os altos custos financeiros[14]. Além do mais, segundo este empresário, a regulamentação existente estaria beneficiando os bancos estatais (Diniz 29.9.87; 21.5.88).

Dessa forma, o discurso segundo o qual o Estado deve apenas traçar a regulamentação mais geral da economia encontra, aqui, uma ressonância específica: a desregulamentação do sistema financeiro, afetando portanto a capacidade regulatória do Estado. O contexto deste discurso neoliberal pela "desregulamentação" estava informado ao menos por dois elementos conjunturais. Por um lado,

---

[13] Para Diniz, era necessário preservar a participação das instituições financeiras privadas, "para que o financiamento aos empresários possa guardar critérios flexíveis, a agilidade e a capacidade de inovar, que são características do setor empresarial" (Diniz, 8.11.86).

[14] "(...) assegurada aos bancos privados maior liberdade e flexibilidade, toda a ação empresarial dela se beneficiaria, e os custos dos fluxos financeiros (...) reduzidos, porque são fruto, em grande parte, da burocratização das finanças"(Diniz, 8.11.86; ver também 29.8.87).

a discussão dentro da Assembléia Nacional Constituinte sobre o sistema financeiro nacional. Por outro, os contatos gestados pelo Banco Mundial e o governo brasileiro no sentido de injetar um apreciável volume de recursos (US$ 1,5 bilhão) para o processo de reformulação do sistema financeiro do País. A pauta dessas negociações incluía a desregulamentação e a reavaliação da presença dos bancos estatais dentro do sistema (Banco Mundial, 1989).

A demanda pela desregulamentação do sistema manteve-se de forma intensa no discurso de Léo Wallace Cochrane Junior (Banco Noroeste), presidente da FEBRABAN/FENABAN/CNF para o período 1989/92. Deve-se ter presente que, então, o Congresso Nacional deveria ter aprovado a legislação complementar sobre o sistema financeiro. Para este fim, foi criada uma Comissão Especial, a qual, até o momento, não apresentou uma proposta para votação.

Assim, o discurso de Cochrane Jr., parecia ter endereço certo: "Os bancos vivem submetidos a um excesso de regulamentação que lhes tolhe a liberdade de agir. E grande parte do que lhes é imputado é devido ao cumprimento dessas normas do Poder Executivo (...)" (Cochrane Jr., abril 1989). No ano seguinte voltaria a insistir: "a melhor Lei Bancária é aquela que somente disser o que é o sistema financeiro. Na verdade, há muito poucos problemas que devem figurar na lei (...)" (Cochrane Jr., janeiro 1990).

No discurso do presidente das Federações bancárias — já no contexto do Governo Collor — a desregulamentação é considerada sinônimo de modemidade: todos queremos passar ao primeiro mundo e isto significa menor regulamentação. E o que se vê em todo o mundo atualmente: modernidade no sistema financeiro é desregulamentação: a melhor norma é não ter norma, exceto, naturalmente, as que implicam fiscalização e controle" (Cochrane Jr., outubro 1990). Avaliando o sistema financeiro brasileiro, este banqueiro concluia que "não há nada de intrinsecamente errado" com o mesmo, "embora aperfeiçoamentos importantes possam ser imaginados". O "diagnóstico dos males do sistema resume-se a três pontos fundamentais: *a)* estatização; *b)* descontrole monetário-fiscal; e *c)* regulamentação excessiva" (Cochrane Jr., 23.8.89).

O discurso dos "pequenos e médios" banqueiros

Em termos gerais, e nos limites dos artigos analisados, não encontramos no discurso dos presidentes da ABBC no período 1987 a

1992 (Elmo Camões e José Carlos Jacintho de Campos) uma reflexão mais sistematizada sobre o liberalismo ou o neoliberalismo[15]. Contudo, os posicionamentos assumidos e as políticas sociais e econômicas propostas por tais empresários indicam uma adesão em maior ou menor grau aos postulados liberais, mesclando defesa de abertura econômica com privilégios específicos. Em nível discursivo, no entanto, foi Campos quem assumiu uma defesa mais contundente do liberalismo.

Em 1986, Camões (Banco Sogeral) considerou o Plano Cruzado coerente, realista e com capacidade de equilibrar a economia do País mas, também, que o corte do déficit público seria crucial para o sucesso do plano (Camões, 16.3.86). Em meados de 1986, Camões defendia a extinção do "Estado-empresário e a desburocratização da economia" (Camões, 11.5.86). Defendia assim a privatização e, além disso, manifestava claro apoio à internacionalização da economia brasileira (Camões, 20.7.87). Em março de 1988, Camões deixou o comando da ABBC para ocupar a presidência do Banco Central do Brasil.

O sucessor de Camões à frente de ABBC, Jacintho de Campos, participava da direção de um banco que, ainda que seja de médio porte (Bozano Simonsen), está integrado a um dos maiores grupos privados do país, que, recentemente, assumiu o controle de empresas estatais privatizadas (USIMINAS e CST)[16].

Em 1988, durante os trabalhos da Assembléia Nacional Consti-

---

15 As posições defendidas pela ABBC ao longo de sua história podem ser sintetizadas em cinco pontos: *a)* reivindicação de um tratamento diferenciado para os pequenos e médios bancos; *b)* denúncia da crescente concentração e formação de monopólios dentro do sistema financeiro; *c)* defesa da participação do capital estrangeiro dentro do sistema — associação em até 1/3 do capital volante; *d)* oposição às tentativas de tabelamento de taxas de juros; *e)* oposição à moratória da divida externa.

16 O grupo Bozano Simonsen está constituído por cerca de cinquenta empresas que incluem ramos como madeira, fertilizantes, ferro, nióbio, níquel, ouro (a Mineração Morro Velho é considerada a maior empresa de mineração de ouro do Brasil) e shopping centers (*Gazeta Mercantil*, 28.3.89 p.44; Banco Bozano, Simonsen, Relatório Anual, *Gazeta Mercantil*, 20.4.89). Além da presidência da ABBC, outro executivo do grupo (Cristiano Buarque Franco Neto) participou da direção de órgãos de representação do empresário financeiro: Associação de Bancos de Investimentos (ANBID) e da CNF.

tuinte, Campos defendia uma alternativa liberal para os rumos do país. "A livre atuação das forças econômicas promove o desenvolvimento e a justiça econômica e social". Campos argumentava que "quando as forças econômicas interagem, buscando uma posição melhor, promovem a justiça econômica e social" (Campos, 4.8.88).

Semelhantemente a outros banqueiros (Bornhausen, por exemplo), Campos atribuía ao imenso déficit público a causa básica da inflação e desenvolveu intensa militância pela livre iniciativa através de palestras, artigos e reuniões a nível governamental (Campos, fevereiro 1990).

Convergindo com anteriores presidentes da ABBC, este empresário defendeu um tratamento diferenciado para os pequenos e médios bancos. "O governo vem tratando todos os bancos como se fossem iguais (...) é preciso que haja tratamento desigual para instituições desiguais" (Campos maio 1990; ver também: fevereiro 1990; julho 1990; outubro 1990). No entanto, havia diferenças importantes entre a FEBRABAN e a ABBC na questão dos pequenos e médios bancos, pois o presidente da Federação defendia em janeiro de 1990 (Revista *Banco Hoje*) um "tratamento igual para os bancos, independentemente do tamanho e da nacionalidade" (Cochrane Jr., janeiro 1990; ver também Informativo FEBRABAN/FENABAN, abril 1990, p. 5).

Em março de 1991, Campos reafirmava seu credo liberal e sua convicção de que a equipe econômica do governo precisava mudar. "O caminho liberal é a solução para a crise brasileira com uma economia de mercado, e não o dirigismo econômico. O que se precisa é a reformulação do pensamento econômico da equipe econômica passando de heterodoxa e dirigista para uma economia liberal" (Campos, 15.3.91). O recado estava dado. Pouco tempo depois, a equipe econômica do governo seria trocada, passando o comando a um histórico defensor das idéias liberais e cuja trajetória se vinculava ao setor financeiro (Marcílio Marques Moreira).

Empresários em conflito (?)

Em que medida é possível caracterizar a existência de um conflito entre diferentes segmentos do empresariado e o empresariado financeiro? Por um lado, parece difícil entender ou captar esta problemática, considerando a existência de grandes grupos econômicos cujos interesses se vinculam a muitos setores. Considere-se ainda a existência de espaços de articulação político-corporativa que abrigam empresários dos mais variados segmentos. Agregue-se a isto a dificuldade de analisar de forma correta a relação discursiva com a prática efetiva, muitas vezes de difícil percepção pública.

Por outro lado, como deixar de reconhecer alguns indicadores tão explícitos como, por exemplo, a persistente vantagem de rentabilidade comparativa das instituições financeiras, que gera tensões permanentes com o setor não-financeiro? Como ignorar que os empresários financeiros acumularam intensamente nas últimas décadas, e que mostraram um apetite voraz nos investimentos fora do seu próprio setor, passando, inclusive, a controlar empresas estatais privatizadas? Como ignorar o confronto de propostas alternativas para a saída das crises econômicas, confronto no qual os empresários financeiros se posicionam, via de regra, em propostas rigidamente ortodoxas? Como interpretar a ausência de um órgão de representação empresarial amplo que agregue todos os segmentos como os existentes em outros países?

Uma análise da ação coletiva do empresariado financeiro no País, levando em conta um processo complexo de relações que os mesmos estabelecem, não se pode deixar de reconhecer a existência de ações ou tentativas de ações coordenadas no campo econômico e político. Mas, ao mesmo tempo, deve se constatar a existência de importantes conflitos conjunturais, cujos reflexos no processo de governabilidade e legitimação do Estado capitalista merecem uma análise aprofundada. Não é o caso de nos propormos esta tarefa aqui. Trataremos, portanto, de identificar e analisar de forma sucinta alguns elementos discursivos do empresariado financeiro que, de alguma forma, traduzem pontos de conflito e alianças, especialmente no início dos anos oitenta.

Até 1985 (início da Nova República), podemos identificar pelo menos dois momentos de ênfases discursivas diferenciadas. O primeiro inclui os três anos iniciais, quando a crise econômica se agudiza, as taxas de juros efetivas alcançam os níveis mais elevados em muitos anos (ver quadro anexo), o sistema financeiro é objeto de uma CPI (Chamada CPI dos Juros) e o discurso de alguns órgãos de representação do setor industrial radicalizam sua crítica ao setor financeiro. O segundo momento se caracteriza por um discurso que busca enfatizar os pontos de convergência mais gerais do empresariado, tratando de garantir (não sem dificuldades) uma unidade mínima durante a transição para o governo civil.

Um discurso crítico ao sistema financeiro partia de Confederação Nacional da Indústria (CNI). Em 1982, o presidente da mesma considerava que "Os bancos, fortalecidos pela limitação da oferta de crédito, exercem o seu *poder discriminatório na determinação do nível da taxa de juros* vigente na economia." (Albano Franco, fev. 1982:12). Segundo este empresário, o poder especial do Sistema Financeiro "é particularmente reforçado pelo *elevado nível de concentração bancária* existente na economia brasileira" (idem). O processo de concentração — afirmava ele — não teria trazido reduções dos custos bancários, nem economias de escala e maior eficiência. E concluía que o Sistema Financeiro "tem estabelecido *especial resistência aos ajustes* que ora se sucedem na economia brasileira, *transferindo parcelas da sua cota de contribuição para os demais agentes econômicos*" (ibid. p. 15, grifos nossos).

Em janeiro de 1983, a CNI encaminhou um estudo ao Ministro da Fazenda, alertando-o para o "esgotamento da capacidade das empresas industriais, sobrevivem a mais um ano com taxas reais positivas superiores a 40% a.a" e demandando uma "nova política em relação à taxa de juros" (*Indústria e Produtividade,* núm. 166, fev 1983). Durante 1983, editorias da publicação oficial da CNI caracterizavam a existência de uma "crise dos juros", assinalando que a mesma ameaçava o processo de abertura política[17].

Embora em discurso menos enfático, o então novo presidente da Federação das Indústrias do Estado de São Paulo (FIESP) reconhecia o alto custo financeiro e a proteção histórica que o Estado havia dispensado ao sistema financeiro. (Vidigal Filho, 21.6.81)[18]. O discurso deste empresário faria coro posteriormente ao empresariado financeiro, cuja ênfase explicativa básica para as altas taxas de juros era o déficit público (Vidigal Filho, 29.9.83; 11.6.85).

Pedro Conde, então presidente da FEBRABAN/FENABAN rebateu as críticas que apontavam os bancos privados como um dos principais responsáveis pela crise, argumentando que o governo é

---

17 *Indústria e Produtividade,* núm. 166, fev 1983; e núm. 168, abril 1983.

18 Ver ainda editorial do *Jornal do Commércio,* Rio de Janeiro, 1 e 2.3.81 "A Fiesp e a recessão", *Folha de São Paulo,* 25.3.81. "Algo de Novo na Fiesp"(editorial).

o "maior banqueiro", além de regular as atividades dos bancos privados (Conde, 31.8.82)[19].

O discurso do empresariado financeiro atribuía ao Estado grande responsabilidade no elevado custo do dinheiro. Segundo Bornhausen, este custo seria determinado por: *a)* cobrança de impostos diretos pelo governo e *b)* limite de expansão do crédito, que reduziria a competitividade do mercado e elevaria os juros. Para baixar a taxa de juros, seria necessário, portanto, liberar as instituições financeiras dos entraves às suas operações (Bornhausen, 21.10.82).

A partir de maio de 1983, no entanto, é possível identificar uma nova orientação no discurso: identifica-se no *déficit público* a origem de "todos os nossos grandes problemas atuais: inflação (...), endividamento interno e o desequilíbrio do balanço de pagamentos" (Bornhausen, maio 1983). Este novo enfoque discursivo — que iria se acentuar nos anos seguintes atendia a duas necessidades prementes dos banqueiros. Por um lado, não era possível ignorar os dados da crise que vivia o País e manter um discurso otimista sobre o capitalismo vigente; por outro, fazia-se necessário encontrar uma explicação básica para os problemas do País. E, como já vimos, o empresariado encontraria no déficit público o novo vilão (Bornhausen, 6.5.84; 24.10.84; 18.11.84; 12.12.84; outubro 1985; discurso de posse na CNF; e 25.9.85). Deslocava-se, assim, o foco das críticas para o déficit público e os empresários passaram a encontrar uma unidade discursiva.

Neste contexto discursivo, os líderes dos órgão de representação do empresariado industrial, comercial e financeiro de São Paulo lograram um consenso mínimo para assinar um documento de apoio a Sarney em maio de 1985[20]. Para a imprensa, os empresários

---

19 Conde buscou diluir a responsabilidade pela crise: não é toda da responsabilidade do governo, nem na iniciativa privada (Conde, 31.8.82). Pelo menos a partir dos textos analisados, este banqueiro não assumiu explicitamente o "déficit público" como elemento básico na explicação da crise. Ao que tudo indica, seria na nova gestão de Bornhausen à frente dos órgãos de representação (1983-1986) que o mesmo ganharia esta ênfase explicativa.

20 Assinaram este documento: Roberto K. Bornhausen, ASSOBESP; Abram Szajman, Federação e Centro do Comércio do Estado de São Paulo; Guilherme Afif Domingos. Associação Comercial de São Paulo; Luiz Eulálio de Bueno Vidigal Filho, Federação e Centro das Indústrias

explicitaram questões que o documento levado ao presidente não mencionava claramente. "Destas, o déficit público é a que está no centro de tudo" (*Indústria e Produtividade*, abril 1985: 5). Segundo essa publicação, o empresariado tomava uma atitude crítica em relação ao "papel do Estado-empresário" e fazia um "apelo por um retorno às origens", ou seja, ocupar-se da segurança pública, da saúde e de outras áreas sociais (*Indústria e Produtividade*, abril 1985:6). Nesse momento, as estatais apareciam como as grandes responsáveis pelo déficit, o controle sobre as mesmas seria o "único caminho para um efetivo combate à inflação"(idem).

Os empresários reconheciam a existência de *divergências setoriais*, mas que também existia uma "*unidade de enfoque nesse movimento* que visa à redução das atuais taxas inflacionárias". E, segundo declarações de Euclides Carli (presidente em exercício da Federação do Comércio do Estado de São Paulo) não haveria motivos para "colocar-se contra o setor financeiro". Segundo este empresário: "já passamos da época em que se acusava o setor financeiro pelas altas taxas de juros". E concluia: "hoje, somos todos vítimas de uma política errada que mantém um governo voraz" (ib., p. 7).

Em fins de 1985, o empresariado financeiro organizou sua Confederação (CNF) e Bornhausen, no discurso de posse, fez um chamado ao empresariado no sentido de convergir sua ação na defesa dos interesses comuns. Os empresários de todos os setores deveriam "atuar conjuntamente, de forma coesa e unificada" na defesa dos objetivos da iniciativa privada "numa economia" de mercado socialmente responsável" (Bornhausen, 4.12.85). Tenhamos presente que, em 1986, o empresariado buscou uma articulação mínima através de União Brasileira de Empresários para defender seus interesses na elaboração da Carta Magna. Embora tivessem logrado consenso em torno de alguns princípios mais gerais, os empresários não lograram vencer divergências em questões mais pontuais.

Em 1988, algumas críticas do presidente da FEBRABAN/FENABAN a certas definições adotadas pela Constituinte indicavam também divergências com outros posicionamentos empresariais. Segundo Diniz, tais definições eram "contrárias ao progresso do País,

---

do Estado de São Paulo; Fábio de Salles Meirelles, Federação da Agricultura do Estado de São Paulo; e Flávio Teles Menezes, Sociedade Rural Brasileira). (*Indústria e Produtividade*, v. 28, n. 4, abril 1985.) O Documento foi entregue a Sarney no dia 9 de maio de 1985.

como as distinções insustentáveis entre empresa nacional e estrangeira, a consagração do princípio da reserva de mercado e outras decisões que afastam o capital estrangeiro do Brasil" (Diniz, 28.8.88). Diniz repudiou veementemente a limitação da taxa de juros reais em 12% ao ano estabelecida pela Constituição (Diniz, 5.7.88). Posicionamento reforçado por Cochrane em 1990: "limitação de juros não pode ser matéria constitucional" (Cochrane Jr., janeiro 1990).

A crítica à reserva de mercado, especialmente o de informática, seria mantida também por Cochrane Junior. Contudo, este posicionamento não era compartilhado por outros empresários, até mesmo do setor financeiro, que encontravam exatamente na reserva de mercado um de seus campos de investimento e acumulação (as instituições financeiras que mantém empresas de informática).

Considerações conclusivas

Uma primeira ressalva necessária diz respeito à possibilidade de se generalizar esta análise ao conjunto do empresariado financeiro. Que os líderes dos órgãos de representação tenham assumido — em maior ou menor grau — um discurso liberal ou neoliberal, não indica necessariamente, que o mesmo possa ser atribuido aos demais empresários financeiros. Mesmo entre os banqueiros analisados, podemos encontrar ênfases diferenciadas sobre o tema.

Contudo, foram esses empresários que assumiram o comando dos órgãos de representação e, portanto, em alguma medida, sugerem uma certa influência ou hegemonia do pensamento liberal no setor financeiro durante os anos oitenta. A análise de um caso particular (Bornhausen/Unibanco), revela um persistente discurso e militância no campo do liberalismo, tanto a partir do comando dos órgãos de representação corporativa e extracorporativa, como através de organizações político-ideológicas (Instituto Liberal).

É interessante observar que dois empresários (Bornhausen e Campos), que assumiram de forma mais explícita o discurso e a ação dentro do campo do (neo)liberalismo, apresentam algumas características comuns em relação à sua prática e ao grupo empresarial ao qual estão vinculados: constante participação na gestão das entidades de representação do setor, significativa rede de relações políticas, fortes investimentos no setor não-financeiro constituindo-se em grandes grupos privados, estreitos laços com o capital financeiro internacional, e participação direta no processo de privatização das empresas estatais. O discurso em defesa da privatização, portanto, representava muito mais do que simples coerência com um corpo doutrinário liberal.

A relativa convergência em torno das linhas gerais do modelo (neo)liberal não afastam, porém, as "divergências setoriais e os desencontros entre discurso e prática política" quando são necessárias definições "das políticas relativas às diferentes áreas" (Diniz, 1991:353-354). No caso particular de alguns grandes empresários do setor financeiro, tais desencontros revelam a diversidade de interesses setoriais das próprias inversões. A defesa de tratamento diferenciado para pequenos e médios bancos não é, necessariamente, estendida às empresas de tal porte no setor não-financeiro, em que o grupo atua como grande empresa. O ataque à reserva de mercado — especialmente da informática — dividiu os empresários financeiros, pois foi exatamente nessa reserva que alguns deles encontraram um importante campo de acumulação.

O discurso do empresariado financeiro sugere ainda três outras ordens de observações. Em primeiro lugar, constata-se uma "idealização" da estratégia (neo)liberal, apresentada como alternativa para resolução de todos os problemas do capitalismo no país (Diniz, 1991: 350).

Em segundo lugar, pode-se observar a dificuldade do empresariado financeiro em reconhecer — mesmo a nível discursivo — a existência e a legitimidade de outros interesses e sujeitos sociais. Em relação aos seus pares burgueses, parece interessante assinalar dois elementos revelados pelo discurso. Por um lado, a incapacidade de abrir espaços para qualquer reconhecimento em relação a sua possível responsabilidade na condução econômica e política que tivesse contribuído para aumentar os problemas do País e a negação de que tivesse obtido benefícios neste mesmo contexto. Pelo outro, a forma como rejeita a crítica do setor não-financeiro, negando evidências de sua participação na manutenção de condicionantes do sistema de crédito, passando ao governo a responsabilidade pelos "desvios" do mesmo[21].

---

[21] Em relação aos assalariados, e em especial aos trabalhadores bancários — embora o espaço deste trabalho não tenha permitido incluir a transcriação discursiva — podemos constatar uma baixa freqüência de ma-

Como terceira observação, constata-se que o empresariado adota um discurso de tendência nitidamente *unicausal* (o déficit público) para explicar um fenômeno complexo de crise econômica e social. A consequência desta interpretação é uma proposição ortodoxa simplista para a saída da crise. Talvez inspirados na concepção da ideologia liberal, segundo a qual a crise econômica é considerada apenas um desequilíbrio passageiro, em que as fontes perturbadoras dos "agentes naturais do mercado" — geralmente o Estado — são responsabilizados (Brunhoff, 1991:7-18), o empresariado "comodamente" evita realizar ou admitir uma análise mais profunda da crise do País.

A convergência discursiva em torno a uma explicação unicausal revela debilidade analítica sobre uma realidade complexa. Ao mesmo tempo, tende a gerar um artificialismo discursivo que oculta e posterga uma negociação efetiva em torno de interesses corporativos e políticos sobre os quais nenhum os segmentos ou grupos empresariais parece fazer qualquer concessão. Tudo isso, somado à dificuldade em reconhecer as demandas e a legitimidade de outros sujeitos sociais, talvez ajude a entender a debilidade e os fracassos dos "acordos" ou "pactos sociais".

Em termos gerais, parece importante reconhecer que o empresariado financeiro — ou pelo menos alguns de seus principais representantes—, tem adotado um posicionamento (neo)liberal e uma postura ativa quanto a sua divulgação. Além disso, tem pressionado o Governo no sentido de adotar políticas econômicas condizentes com os postulados mais gerais deste liberalismo, embora muitas vezes suas demandas específicas se afastem do mesmo. E, sem dúvida, este empresariado dispõe de apreciáveis instrumentos de poder, recursos financeiros e capacidade organizacional para atuar em defesa de seus interesses.

---

nifestações sobre o tema. As breves referências que aparecem nos artigos tendem a desqualificar certos segmentos como os trabalhadores do setor público (Bornhausem, 3.5.88; 30.8.88; 6.9.88), deslegitimar as demandas e a formas de ação dos bancários (Bornhausen, janeiro 1986; 3.5.88) ou a conclamar à colaboração entre o capital e trabalho (Campos, 4.8.88; Diniz, 13.11.88).

Bibliografia citada

Banco Mundial. *Relatório sobre o Desenvolvimento Mundial.* Rio de Janeiro: Fundação Getúlio Vargas. 1989.

Bornhausen, Roberto Konder. Entrevista, *Exame,* núm. 171. 14.3.79.

—— "Empresários e Estado na Economia Brasileira", Palestra na ADVB. 30.8.79.

—— "Dificuldades econômicas: sua causa básica". FENABAN, palestra na ADVB, Porto Alegre, maio 1982.

—— Palestra. 29.9.82.

—— Discurso de posse na FEBRABAN/FENABAN, março 1983.

—— "Estatização dos bancos ou mudança de regime?". *Folha de São Paulo.* 8.5.83.

—— Palestra no VII Seminário das Indústrias de Cortume. RS, mimeo. 6.4.84.

—— "Como revigorar a iniciativa privada". Revista *Legenda,* março 1984.

—— "O Estado e a livre iniciativa". *Jornal do Brasil.* 13.5.84.

—— "Estado e iniciativa privada: as relações ambíguas". *Jornal do Brasil.* 15.7.84.

—— "Os diversos enfoques sobre as relações Estado-livre empresa". *Digesto Econômico,* julho/agosto 84.

—— "Estado e iniciativa privada, Movimento Nacional pela Livre iniciativa", junho 1984.

—— "A questão dos juros". Revista *Parceiro Econômico,* núm. 4, outubro 1985.

—— Discurso de posse no CNF, Superintendência das Relações Externas de CNF. 4.12.85.

—— Discurso de término de mandato, FEBRABAN, *Relatório de Atividades,* janeiro 1986.

—— "Gesto público e cidadania". *Folha de São Paulo.* 3.5.88.

—— "As idéias liberais e a economia brasileira", palestra de posse na diretoria do IBEF. 16.8.88.

—— "A favor ou contra a sociedade". *Folha de São Paulo.* 30.8.88.

—— "Menos impostos, mais serviços". *Folha de São Paulo.* 6.9.88.

—— "Liberalismo: Alternativa para a economia". Conferência na Câmara Americana de Comércio para o Brasil. 22.11.88.

—— "O Brasil é viável?". Palestra no Instituto Brasileiro de Executivos Financeiros. 7.6.91.

—— "Reflexões sobre o Brasil". *Cadernos do IRS,* núm. 18. 19.6.91.

Brunhoff, Suzanne de. *A Hora do Mercado: Crítica do Liberalismo.* São Paulo: UNESP. 1991,

Camões, Elmo. "Devemos ser confiantes". 16.3.86.

—— "A Reforma Monetária e os bancos médios e pequenos. *O Globo.* 11.5.86.

—— "Privatização e Internacionalização da economia". *Jornal do Brasil.* 20.7.87.

Campos, J. C. Jacintho de. "Constituinte — o 'menos' ou o 'mais'". *Gazeta Mercantil.* 4.8.88.

—— "ABBC defende a integração dosetor financeiro (entrevista), *Banco Hoje.* maio 1990, "Bancos reagem aos CPs" (mesa redonda), Banco *Hoje.* fevereiro 1990.

—— Declarações. Carlos Dias, "Bancos: a luta por uma presença menor do Estado na economia brasileira", *Gazeta Mercantil.* 15/03/91.

Conde, Pedro. "A responsabilidade do empresário", *Folha de São Paulo.* 26.6.82.

—— "O nosso maior banqueiro". *Jornal do Brasil.* 31.8.82.

—— "Os empresários e as eleições". *Folha de São Paulo.* 31.10.82.

—— "Juros, um equívoco a ser esclarecido". *Folha de São Paulo.* 8.2.83.

—— Discurso, FEBRABAN, *Relatório de Atividades da Gestão 1980/1983.* 17.3.83.

Cochrane Jr., Léo Wallace. "Os erros não são nossos" (entrevista). *Banco Hoje,* abril 1989.

—— "Os desafios econômicos brasileiros", pronunciamento no Seminário Economia Brasileira — a Retomada do Desenvolvimento. Federação do Comércio do Estado de São Paulo, mimeo. 23.8.89.

—— "Os bancos estão mudando". *Banco Hoje,* janeiro 1990.

—— "Febraban quer menos inflação e menos normas". *Banco Hoje,* outubro 1990.

Diniz, Antonio de Pádua Rocha. "Bancos se definem e apóiam institucionalização". *O Estado de Minas.* 8.11.86.

—— "Bancos discriminados". *Folha de São Paulo.* 29.9.87; e *O Globo.* 17.10.87.

—— "A vantagem de quem faz as regras". *Folha de São Paulo.* 21.5.88.

—— "Os bancos e a realidade econômica". *O Estado de S. Paulo.* 5.7.88.

—— "É preciso vencer o imobilismo". *Folha de São Paulo.* 28.8.88.

—— "Os bancos e o pacto social". *Folha de São Paulo.* 13.11.88.

Diniz, Eli. "Empresariado e Projeto Neoliberal na América Latina: uma avaliação dos anos 80". *Dados,* v. 34, núm. 3. 1991, p. 349-77.

Franco, Albano. (Pronunciamento na CPI). *Moeda e Finanças.* "Taxas de juros no banco dos réus", fevereiro 1982, p.11-6.

Gros, Denise Barbosa. "Liberalismo, empresariado e ação política na Nova República", in Eli Diniz, *Empresários e Modernização Eoconômica: Brasil anos 90.* Florianópolis: Editora da UFSC/IDACON. 1993, p. 133-53.

Indústria e Produtividade. "A CNI e a questão dos juros", núm. 166. fev. 1993, p. 4-6.

—— Editorial, a. 15, núm. 166, fevereiro 1983.

—— "É preciso repensar o Brasil". Editorial, a. 15, núm. 168, abril 1983.

Informativo FEBRABAN/FENABAN, abril 1990.

Jornal do Commércio. Rio de Janeiro: Editorial "A FIESP e a recessão". 1 e 2.3.81.

Folha de São Paulo. Editorial "Algo de novo na *FIESP*". 25.3.81.

Moreira, Marcílio Marques. "Estará o Liberalismo obsoleto?". *Tempo Brasileiro,* núm. 65/66. 1981, p. 3-16.

Vidigal Filho, Luis Eulálio. "O papel do lucro e a importância da livre iniciativa" palestra da Escola Superior de Guerra. 21.6.81. *Indústria e Desenvolvimento,* núm 9, setembro 1986.

—— "Em defesa da livre iniciativa", discurso de posse no segundo mandato na FIESP/CIESP. 29.9.81. *Indústria e Desenvolvimento,* núm. 9, setembro de 1986.

—— "As perspectivas da indústria", palestra na ESG. 11.6.85. *Indústria e Desenvolvimento,* núm 9, setembro 1986.

Elisabeth von der Weid
Fundação Casa de Rui Barbosa

CARACTERÍSTICAS DO MERCADO DE TRABALHO INDUSTRIAL NO RIO DE JANEIRO E EVOLUÇÃO DA MENTALIDADE OPERÁRIA (1870-1930)

A formação do mercado de trabalho industrial no Rio de Janeiro é um estudo fascinante, pela originalidade da composição das classes populares nesta cidade e pelas dificuldades encontradas pelo próprio trabalhador em se assumir como operário neste contexto. O período escolhido talvez seja um pouco longo, mas tentaremos saltar da compreensão do meio social no início do processo de industrialização da cidade para o momento em que se estrutura entre os trabalhadores fabris alguma consciência de classe. Tentaremos observar e comparar setores diferentes, dando ênfase ao processo de formação do operário da indústria têxtil, que era o setor fabril mais representativo, com mão-de-obra mais numerosa.

As primeiras indústrias e o Rio de Janeiro

O Rio de Janeiro, capital do Brasil desde os tempos coloniais, passou pela experiência de hospedar a Corte portuguesa no início do século XIX durante doze anos, antes da Independência. Seu desenvolvimento se deu com base no fato de centralizar desde então a administração e as relações comerciais e políticas com o exterior, o que lhe possibilitou tornar-se também, a partir da década de 1880, o principal centro de expansão industrial do País.

As primeiras fábricas tinham-se estabelecido já como empresas industriais, no seio de uma sociedade agrária e escravista, durante as décadas de 1850 a 1870, na Bahia, em Minas Gerais e no Rio de Janeiro. Quase sempre na zona rural, e muitas delas empregando mão-de-obra escrava junto a trabalhadores livres (Stein, Giroletti).

A transição para o trabalho assalariado não correspondeu ao processo tradicional europeu. Havia artesãos, proprietários de suas ferramentas, que atuavam em diversos setores: sapateiros, carpinteiros, oleiros, etc. Mas os escravos, além de trabalharem nas fábricas, muitas vezes eram também bons artesões (Hardman & Leonardi). Essa convivência dificultava a formação de um mercado de trabalho livre -- tanto por parte dos empresários, habituados ao sistema escravista, quanto por parte dos homens livres, que desprezavam o trabalho braçal.

Considerando que, em 1872, o número de indivíduos vivendo em aglomerações urbanas (5,9% do total) correspondia a pouco mais de 600 mil habitantes, percebe-se que somente o Rio de Janeiro concentrava quase a metade da população urbana do País. A densidade demográfica era crescente, e o processo se intensificou na virada do século.

Tabela 1
Crescimento da população urbana no Brasil

Censos	População total	População urbana % (50 mil hs. ou mais)	População do Rio de Janeiro
1872	9.930.478	5,9	275.000
1890	14.333.915	6,8	522.000
1900	17.438.434	9,4	691.000
1920	30.635.605	10,7	1.150.000

Fonte: Brandão Lopes, Juarez Rubens. *Desenvolvimento e Mudança Social.* São Paulo: Nacional. 1972,p. 16. Ver para o Rio, Ibge, *Recenseamentos Gerais e Estatísticas Históricas do Brasil.*

Esta expansão se dava, graças à atração exercida pela capital política, econômica e cultural do País. Apesar de ter sido o eixo inicial da atividade cafeeira, no começo do século XIX, o Rio não conseguiu capitalizar essa posição. A economia cafeeira fluminense era predatória, levando à rápida decadência da produção regional. À medida que as terras iam sendo exauridas, as fazendas de café avançavam para o Interior. Os cafeicultores se apegavam ao sistema escravista e às lavouras envelhecidas, sem procurar diversificar ou modernizar o processo produtivo. A abolição da escravatura foi apenas a gota d'àgua para a falência da cafeicultura na região.

Características da população do Rio de Janeiro

O retrocesso da lavoura regional e a libertação dos escravos tiveram como conseqüência uma explosão demográfica do Rio de Janeiro, decorrente do êxodo rural. Entre 1872 e 1890, a população da cidade teve um crescimento de 90% em menos de duas décadas (ver Tabela 1). Houve também um fluxo razoável de imigrantes europeus, principalmente portugueses. Em 1890, havia 28% de estrangeiros, 26% de imigrantes de outras regiões do País e apenas 46% de cariocas (Carvalho). Essa intensa imigração trazia um desequilíbrio entre os sexos, pois era muito mais freqüente a migração de homens solteiros do que de mulheres ou famílias. A Tabela 2 mostra a expansão demográfica desse período. A taxa mais alta deu-se na década de 1880, correspondendo ao período de decadência dos cafezais e à imigração dos ex-escravos após a Abolição. Essa população veio engrossar a massa de trabalhadores livres da Capital, não-inseridos no mercado de trabalho da cidade.

TABELA 2
Crescimento anual da população do Rio de Janeiro: 1872-1906

Anos	Crescimento anual (%)
1872-1880	3,84
1880-1890	4,54
1890-1900	3,23
1900-1906	2,91

Fonte: *Anuário Estatístico do Brasil* (1908-1912), v. l, p. XVIII. *Apud* José Murilo de Carvalho. Op. cit.

A composição racial e de nacionalidades, resultante dessa imigração, pode ser observada na Tabela 3. Chama a atenção a redução proporcional dos pretos entre 1872 e 1890, depois da avaliação anterior. Como vimos, o crescimento demográfico do período foi enorme.

Além da grande imigração européia, que ampliou a proporção de brancos no conjunto, as transferências locais de população foram intensas. No inicío do período, houve uma tentativa de diversificação agrícola na região próxima, visando o mercado consumidor carioca em expansão, o que teria absorvido uma parte razoável dos escravos urbanos da Capital. Após 1888, a libertação provocou o retorno em massa para a cidade, mas, dentro do período, a etapa da migração "campo-cidade" foi muito curta, e na estatística o resultado final aponta para uma redução no número de negros (Damazio).

TABELA 3
Componentes raciais, nacionais e regionais da população do Rio de Janeiro — 1872-1940 (%)

	1872	1890	1906	1920	1940
Cariocas		46	75	53	50
Outras regiões		26		26	38
Estrangeiros		28	25	21	12
Brancos	55	63			71
Mestiços	21	25			17
Pretos	24	12			11
População total (habs.)	275.000	515.559	805.355	1.147.599	1.749.368

Fontes: Brasil. *Recenseamento:* 1872,1890,1920,1940. Rio de Janeiro, Diretoria Geral de... e Estatística. *Recenseamento do Distrito Federal.* 1906. *Apud* Sylvia F. Damazio. Op. cit., e Eileen Keremitsis. Op. cit.

A formação do mercado de trabalho fabril teve problemas específicos no Rio de Janeiro, em virtude dessa composição social que acabamos de analisar. O grande número de ex-escravos rurais era dificilmente absorvido nas atividades produtivas urbanas. A Tabela 4 dá idéia da distribuição da população economicamente ativa da Capital durante essa fase de expansão.

Nota-se por esta tabela que, na virada do século, os setores intermediários e o que estamos qualificando de operariado estavam mais ou menos equilibrados. O que chama a atenção é o grande número de "domésticos, jornaleiros e outros", que representam a metade da população economicamente ativa da cidade. Era uma massa crescente de trabalhadores não-qualificados, que se distribuía em inúmeras modalidades alternativas de trabalho urbano — como vendedores ambulantes, empalhadores, consertadores de panelas, biscateiros em geral, além de uma série de ocupações indefinidas como trapeiros, tatuadores, ratoeiros, e outras. Seu espaço de atuação eram as ruas da cidade, e conseguiam organizar-se, prestando serviços e formando freguesias. Esses trabalhadores autônomos se sustentavam com sua atividade e abasteciam-se mutuamente de alimentos, roupas e serviços a preços módicos, o que criava um imenso subsistema econômico fora do controle do Estado (Damazio).

Tabela 4
População Economicamente Ativa do Rio de Janeiro, 1890-1906

		1890	%	1906	%
Classe alta	Banqueiros	44			
	Capitalistas	517			
	Proprietários	2.267			
Subtotal		2.828	1,1		
Setores intermediários	Profissionais liberais	3.395		12.050	
	Funcionários públicos	18.226		28.921	
	Profissões técnicas	2.885		-	
	Comércio	48.048		62.775	
Subtotal		72.554	27,4	103.746	24,4
Operariado	Artistas	5.859		-	
	Extração	703		893	
	Manufatura	48.661		77.450	
	Transporte	10.733		22.807	
Subtotal		65.956	25,0	101.150	23,8
Proletariado	Serviço doméstico	74.785		117.904	
	Jornaleiros	-		29.933	
	Outros*	48.100		72.087	
Subtotal		122.885	46,5	219.924	51,8
Total		264.233	100,0	424,820	100,0

Fontes: Censos de 1890 e de 1906. Excluídos inativos e empregados na agropecuária (1890); os sem profissão, empregados na agropecuária, classes improdutivas e os que vivem de renda (1906).
* Inclui os sem profissão declarada (1890) e os de profissão desconhecida e mal definida (1906).
Apud José Murilo de Carvalho. Op. cit., p. 75.

A cidade era dividida em zonas: Cidade Velha (centro comercial e financeiro, junto ao porto); Zona Sul (residencial e industrial); Zona Norte (cidade nova, residencial e industrial) e Subúrbios (originalmente zona rural, que se incorporava à cidade) (Abreu). O Centro era, ao mesmo tempo, local de moradia e trabalho. Ao lado de habitações das classes remediadas, havia as casas de cômodos e os cortiços. E havia as oficinas artesanais, o pequeno comércio e as casas atacadistas de secos e molhados, pequenas manufaturas e lojas de confecções. O trabalhador autônomo agia nesse meio, paralelo ao sistema capitalista, que começava a se afirmar (Damazio).

O mercado de trabalho industrial

Ao final do século XIX, o Rio de Janeiro já se caracterizava como o mais importante centro industrial do País. A Tabela 5 mostra a distribuição de operários por setor industrial em 1890.

TABELA 5
Número de operários no Distrito Federal por setor industrial — 1890

Setor industrial	Número de operários
Alimentação	1.383
Vestuário	3.463
Têxteis	10.281
Bebidas	1.496
Metalurgia	2.066
Fumos	274
Material de construção	1.512
Material de transporte	1.345
Móveis e marcenaria	2.583
Papel	374
Vidros	450
Calçados	3.781
Construção naval	2.729
Sabão e velas	706
Couros	335
Produtos químicos	563
Outros	1.386
Total	34.727

Fonte: IBGE. *Estatísticas Históricas do Brasil.* Séries Econômicas, Demográficas e Sociais de 1550 a 1985. *Séries Estatísticas Retrospectivas,* vol. 3. Rio de Janeiro. 1987.

Destaca-se o setor têxtil, que concentrava um terço das fábricas de tecidos do País. Nas décadas seguintes o setor se expandiu, mantendo-se o Rio e seus arredores como principal pólo industrial têxtil até a década de 1920, quando começou a perder terreno para São Paulo (Weid & Bastos).

Mas o número crescente de fábricas e pequenas manufaturas não garantia a presença de uma "classe operária"na cidade. A principal característica da população do Rio era sua extrema mobilidade. Na verdade, esses "operários"dos censos não eram estáveis. A maioria permanecia pouco tempo nos empregos. Como quase todas essas indústrias estabelecidas não exigiam mão-de-obra qualificada, os "operários"podiam facilmente trocar de fábrica, ou trabalhar no comércio, ou ainda ganhar a vida livremente como ambulantes ou biscateiros. Sua dificuldade de adaptação a um regime disciplinar de trabalho fazia com que a permeabilidade entre o mercado de trabalho assalariado e o subsistema econômico paralelo tornasse seus limites indefinidos, não havendo mais do que uma ampla massa fluida de trabalhadores não-qualificados que representavam aproximadamente dois terços da população economicamente ativa da capital (Damazio, Keremitsis, Weid). Essa massa de população que sobrevivia nas ruas assustava as classes dominantes, pelo limite em que viviam entre o legal e o marginal. "Era uma sociedade em que a escravidão impedira o desenvolvimento de uma forte tradição artesanal e facilitara a criação de um vasto setor proletário" (Carvalho).

Em 1890, 70% dos estrangeiros que viviam na cidade eram portugueses. Sua participação no mercado de trabalho estava bastante setorizada eram 40% dos artesões, 51% dos empregados do comércio e 53% dos empregados nos transportes. O próprio embaixador de Portugal na época avaliou em 90% a presença dos portugueses entre carroceiros e cocheiros (Carvalho).

No caso da indústria, os estrangeiros em geral assumiam as tarefas mais especializadas, em parte pelo mito empresarial da Europa como centro de desenvolvimento. Alguns estrangeiros eram realmente qualificados, como os mestres e técnicos ingleses das fábricas têxtis. Mas, em geral, a qualificação era adquirida no próprio trabalho, e os estrangeiros, na maioria portugueses de origem rural, eram escolhidos pela sua postura diante do trabalho. Como imigrantes, transferiam-se para melhorar de vida. Nesse sentido, eram mais engajados com o trabalho, e mais disciplinados (Maram). Havia também, por parte dos empresários, um preconceito contra o trabalhador brasileiro, o qual se originava por sua vez na relação deste com o trabalho pesado, que para ele era trabalho de escravo.

Trabalhadores e artesãos — a transição para o mundo fabril

O processo de transição para a ordem industrial seguiu caminhos bastante diversos, dependendo do setor. A imensa maioria da população era formada por trabalhadores sem qualificação e sem um emprego fixo, que ora trabalhavam nas ruas, ora no comércio estabelecido, ora nas fáricas. Na Cidade Velha concentravam-se também as pequenas oficiais de artesães, que eram uma minoria de trabalhadores qualificados com uma produção independente. Os artesãos tinham uma transição de trabalho corporativo, que já não funcionava como na Europa pré-industrial, pois as guildas tinham sido abolidas em 1824. Entretanto, eles mantinham uma identidade e um auto-conceito, que os destacava dentro do sistema desestruturado das classes populares cariocas.

Vamos tomar como amostra no processo de transição três categorias de trabalhadores que representavam três caminhos distintos — os trabalhadores da grande indústria fabril, moderna e racional, representados pelo setor têxtil, com maior oportunidade de emprego; o setor de serviços urbanos, representado pelos motorneiros dos bondes, que tiveram um progressivo processo de qualificação e uma posição privilegiada; e os artesãos, representados pelos sapateiros, com um processo inverso, de desqualificação e marginilização. A maior parte dos dados sobre motorneiros e sapateiros foram obtidos da tese de Eileen Keremitsis. Quando aos têxteis, a parte da tese referente à Bangu completou o estudo feito anteriormente sobre as fábricas Pau Grande e Cruzeiro, da Companhia América Fabril, permitindo ampliar as informações sobre este setor.

Composição dos setores

Os trabalhadores têxteis eram em sua maioria brasileiros. O contingente de estrangeiros no total das fábricas do Rio era de 13% em 1907 e 23% em 1920. No caso da fábrica Bangu, que era uma comunidade no subúrbio da cidade, a proporção diminuiu de 19% em 1903 para 11% em 1927 (Keremitsis). Já a fábrica Cruzeiro, na Zona Norte, tinha em torno de 19% de estrangeiros durante a década de 1920, sendo 16% da força de trabalho formada por portugueses (Weid e Bastos).

A distribuição dos estrangeiros na fábrica comprova a avaliação anterior. Os portugueses tinham 55% do contingente concentrado entre a tecelagem e a conservação da fábrica, que era um setor com tarefas especializadas, como marcenaria e cantaria. Italianos e espanhóis estavam 70% concentrados entre a tercelagem e a conservação da fábrica e das máquinas. Os ingleses tinham uma presença residual, mas 97% se distribuíam entre a administração, a fabricação e a conservação de máquinas, e nas seções mais especializadas da produção têxtil; 78% dos outros estrangeiros estavam entre a tecelagem e conservação das máquinas e da fábrica (Weid e Bastos).

Os trabalhadores dos transportes do Rio tinham uma alta proporção de estrangeiros: 54% em 1890, 61% em 1906 e 51% em 1920.

Nas companhias de bondes, a presença era sobretudo de portugueses. Na Cia. Ferrocarril do Jardim Botânico, entre 1897-1911, 38% eram portugueses e 13% espanhóis e italianos. Na Light, que abrangeu um período mais amplo e absorveu companhias anteriores, 57% eram portugueses e 9% italianos e espanhóis (Keremitsis).

Os sapateiros, também, tinham 42% de estrangeiros. Havia maior número de homens adultos estrangeiros (81%) do que brasileiros (65% segundo dados de 1908). Os técnicos estrangeiros eram contratados por algumas fábricas para treinar os brasileiros no uso adequado das máquinas.

Do ponto de vista racial, o processo de inserção do ex-escravo no mundo do trabalho assalariado foi difícil, apesar de já terem trabalhado, enquanto escravos, em indústrias e como artesãos. Na indústria têxtil, os pretos eram empregados nos trabalhos pesados, sem qualificação. Entre os cocheiros e motorneiros, havia preferência para contratação de brancos ou mulatos, com forte presença de estrangeiros.

Com referência a sexo e idade, as fábricas têxteis tinham forte presença de mulheres e crianças, apesar da maioria da força de trabalho ser de homens adultos. Na fábrica Cruzeiro, por exemplo, havia 33% de mulheres, para 67% de homens, na maior parte concentrados em seções complementares à produção têxtil — atividades mecânica e metalúrgica, conservação da fábrica, gravação, administração. Na produção têxtil a proporção era de 57% de homens para 43% de mulheres. As crianças estavam presentes desde o início, freqüentemente com muito pouca idade. Apesar da suspensão, em 1917, da contratação de menores de 8 anos e da redução do número de menores de 14, a fábrica Cruzeiro tinha contratado 9,8% da sua força de trabalho, nos anos 1920, com menos de 14 anos. Com relação ao trabalho fabril, as crianças, ou eram aprendizes em seções diversas, ou estavam concentradas na fiação, onde havia tarefas específicas para seu tamanho e agilidade.

A composição dos cocheiros ou motorneiros de bondes era simples: somente homens adultos podiam conseguir licença para conduzir a geralmente eram contratados com mais de 20 anos, freqüentemente com mais de 35. Uma vez conseguida a licença para dirigir, passavam a ter uma profissão de prestígio, e não mudavam mais de trabalho, mesmo que mudassem de emprego.

Os sapateiros tiveram um processo mais complexo. Tradicionalmente, eram todos homens adultos. O sapateiro artesão fazia todo o trabalho, inclusive as vendas. Era importante, para ter uma freguesia, manter qualidade, estilo, preços. Todos possuíam seus próprios instrumentos de trabalho. Uma vez introduzida a mercanização, sua expansão foi rápida apesar da resistência, levando a um aumento da produção em massa. Em 1866 a maior fábrica de calçados tinha 100 operários, em 1909 eram 10 fábricas com mais de 100 operários, sendo 3 com 300 a 350. Em 1920 eram 153 fábricas. O impacto foi violento, e a maioria dos sapateiros foi marginalizada nesse processo, uma vez que as mulheres e crianças passaram a fazer parte da força de trabalho.

A produção fabril de calçados levou a uma progressiva especialização de tarefas. Algumas específicas dos homens, outras que podiam ser feitas também por mulheres e crianças, com ou sem máquina, na fábrica ou em casa. O trabalho em casa era uma complementação que o sapateiro, absorvido pela fábrica, contratava paralelamente para aproveitar seus instrumentos — e aí trabalhava toda a família, inclusive menores de até 6 anos. Nas fábricas, a idade mínima era de 12 anos.

Atuação das empresas

O principal problema das empresas industriais era o recrutamento e a manutenção dos trabalhadores. Dentro do cotidiano das ruas da cidade e devido à herança escravista, era compreensível a dificuldade de adaptação ao sistema fabril. A rotatividade era altíssima.

As empresas têxteis, inicialmente situadas na aréa rural, procuravam envolver as famílias locais em um sistema de fábrica-fazenda, contratando os homens para a produção agrícola e as mulheres e crianças para a fábrica. No caso da fábrica Pau Grande, na Raiz da Serra houve, no final do século XIX, a contratação de trabalhadores no nordeste do País, e de órfãos da Santa Casa de Misericórdia do Rio, pelos quais a empresa passava a se responsabilizar (Stein, Weid & Bastos).

Uma das primeiras políticas de atração e manutenção da mão-de-obra foi a construção de moradias. Na fábrica Pau Grande, a evolução desse sistema chegou à formação, na década de 1920, de uma cidade-vila operária, com toda a infra-estrutura, escola, creche, igreja, loja e clube. Foi-se tornando progressivamente uma comunidade fechada, com controle de entrada e saída, em que a renovação da força de trabalho se fazia dentro da própria comunidade e, eventualmente, nos distritos próximos. O caso da fábrica Bangu foi semelhante, com a diferença de que as casas construídas pela companhia foram somente as primeiras, depois eram os próprios trabalhadores que as construíam em terrenos da fábrica, pelos quais pagavam um aluguel simbólico.

Outro expediente utilizado pelas empresas para manutenção da força de trabalho, era o Fundo de Beneficência, que financiava inicialmente o atendimento médico, remédios e despesas funerárias para os empregados. Depois, passou a financiar creche, escola, atendimento religioso, prêmios por produtividade, etc. Na Bangu, o fundo foi formado a partir de 1895, descontado do salário dos empregados. Na companhia América Fabril, o Fundo de Beneficência foi uma decisão de 1911,sendo deduzido dos lucros retidos da empresa.

Todas essas medidas paternalistas eram comuns às empresas têxteis, tanto na zona rural quanto nas fábricas da cidade. As vilas operárias urbanas não eram tão fechadas quanto as comunidades rurais, mas todos os benefícios financiados pelos Fundos se reproduziam com pequenas variações. O controle do lazer e das relações sociais se dava a partir das empresas — que fundavam clubes, bandas de música e associações de cunho mutualista, como sistemas de formação de mão-de-obra.

As empresas de bondes tinham outro tipo de relações. Os trabalhadores eram recrutados entre as classes populares do Rio, mas uma vez conseguida a licença para conduzir, sobretudo os bondes elétricos, a situação privilegiada fazia com que a rotatividade fosse menor. Além disso, era um trabalho duro, mas com mobilidade e contato social com as populações de diversos bairros. Os cocheiros trocavam muito de uma companhia para outra, mas, quando a Light unificou as linhas, adquiriram maior estabilidade.

As empresas de bondes nunca forneceram moradia aos motorneiros. A maioria morava próximo das garagens ou das linhas a que serviam, em algum tipo de habitação coletiva (casa de cômodos, cortiços), eventualmente em vilas operárias de empresas especializadas em casas para operários (Elia).

A Companhia Jardim Botânico tinha um fundo de Beneficência desde 1894, que dava atendimento médico-hospitalar e até cirúrgico para seus empregados e familiares. Pagava uma pequena pensão para os acidentados de trabalho que ficassem incapacitados, e os doentes tinham o mesmo direito pelo prazo de um mês. O fundo era formado por muitas dos motorneiros e uma dedução de 1% de todos os salários, inclusive da Diretoria.

As jornadas de trabalho dos mortoneiros eram duras — de 12 a 14 horas, chegando a 16 horas por dia e sete dias por semana em 1917. Depois das greves, o Conselho Municipal reduziu a jornada de todos os condutores de transportes para 12 horas. A semana de 7 dias ainda era normal em 1930! No final da década de 1920 quando muitas empresas reduziram as jornadas, e mesmo o número de dias de trabalhados, em função da crise, os mortoneiros e outros condutores de transportes constituíram exceção, chegando mesmo, algumas vezes, a prolongar a jornada.

As empresas de calçados tiveram um processo diferente. As máquinas criavam um sistema que não necessitava de qualificação — as mulheres e crianças podiam substituir os homens qualificados. As oficinas foram sendo progressivamente eliminadas pela nova ordem industrial. Apesar de, ainda em 1920, sobreviverem muitas oficinas, as grandes fábricas já dominavam completamente a indústria de calçados, sendo o Rio de Janeiro, na época, o principal fornecedor de calçados para todo o País.

A semana era de seis dias, e, nos tempos de crise, tinham o fim-de-semana livre. As jornadas iam de oito a onze horas diárias. Em 1917, houve um acordo para o trabalho de oito horas diárias, mas nem sempre era cumprido. Os trabalhadores qualificados, que começavam a ser absorvidos pela fábricas, ganhavam inicialmente por peça — como um sapateiro independente. Com o tempo, o sistema foi sendo modificado e passaram a ter uma função no processo de produção e receber um sálario. E havia, como nas outras indústrias, multas por erro ou insubordinação.

As indústrias de calçados nunca tiveram políticas paternalistas. Havia uma organização empresarial, para troca de experiências e informações, como os empresários têxteis e outros industriais: listas de operários indesejáveis, por exemplo, e atuação conjunta nas greves.

Reação dos trabalhadores

Do ponto de vista dos trabalhadores, vamos seguir o sistema inverso: partir dos que tiveram maior facilidade de conscientização até os que mais sofreram nesse processo.

Os sapateiros, por sua origem corporativa, eram os mais mobilizados — estavam em reação permanente contra a marginalização e a proletarização. O impacto da modernização, por um lado, levou os homens a dividirem trabalho com mulheres e crianças. Por outro lado, o pequeno grupo da oficina se diluía dentro da força de trabalho das fábricas.

Os sapateiros organizaram-se desde cedo, sendo a primeira tentativa, ainda mutualista, em 1875. Em 1898, formava-se a União Auxiliadora dos Artistas Sapateiros, com nova forma de ação: pelas condições e mercado de trabalho, e os sálarios.

Propunha-se a barganhas coletivas e apoio nas greves, pagamentos de fiança nas prisões, seguro-desemprego. Começou a usar-se a greve como forma de luta, e não se aceitava a demissão por greve, lutando-se pela manutenção dos empregos. Tinham uma perspectiva nova, inclusive na idéia de União , mas ainda se referiam a "artistas". Por esta entidade, que durou até 1906, pode-se notar que, mesmo os sapateiros-operários, já proletarizados, tinham uma consciência e uma ação que os distinguia dentro da massa proletária da cidade.

Em 1917, formou-se a Liga dos Operários em Calçados, que chegou a ter entre 2 e 3 mil membros. Usavam novo vocabulário, não eram mais artesães. Tinham o sentimento de que as fábricas haviam-se imposto sobre a tradição artesanal, mas que esta era mais forte, penetrante e difusa do que as fábricas.

Os motorneiros, do ponto de vista da mobilização, estavam no pólo oposto. Sua participação nas greves e movimentos operários foi mais reduzida. Tinham uma associação que dava apoio nas multas e prisões por acidentes, pagando a fiança. Os acidentes eram muito freqüentes desde 1870, e tanto os cocheiros quanto os motorneiros eram responsabilizados pelas respectivas empresas e pela polícia, sendo freqüentemente presos, além de multados.

Mas, a demanda pelo transporte era crescente, e não havia risco de desemprego. Os sálarios eram superiores aos da indústria em geral, e o processo de adaptação foi gradual. Os motorneiros tinham uma posição privilegiada, uma vez conseguida a licença, e seu trabalho se espalhava pela cidade, o que lhes dava extensa rede de comunicação. Qualquer aviso era rapidamente difundido via bondes. Assim sendo, os motorneiros tinham pouca propensão às greves, mas quando alguma questão os levara a radicalizar, suas greves eram bem organizadas, curtas e bem sucedidas. Representavam um instrumento de pressão efetivo, pois paravam a cidade toda. Isto provavelmente também contribuía para sua auto-valorização e fortalecimento de consciência de classe.

Os trabalhadores têxteis foram os que mais dificuldades tiveram para adaptar-se à produção indústrial. O trabalho nas fábricas têxteis era dos mais agressivos — a poeira e o ruído embruteciam os trabalhadores além de provocarem doenças que só foram descobertas mais tarde. Recrutados na massa proletária sem qualificação, resistiam como podiam à mecanização e à disciplina fabril. O resultado era uma altíssima rotatividade e absenteísmo. Ou saíam de seu posto ou faltavam ao trabalho,ou simplesmente iam embora.

Era o setor mais numeroso, mas também o menos mobilizado. O alto nível de concentração nas fábricas significava também isolamento e controle pelas empresas. A União dos Operários em Fábricas de Tecidos tentava dar uma organização aos trabalhadores do setor, mas havia poucos sindicalizados e a participação nos movimentos restringia-se à vanguarda. Os operários que se sindicalizavam eram "listados"pelos empresários e rejeitados por todo o setor.

No caso da fábrica Cruzeiro, da Companhia América Fabril, foi possível detectar as formas de reação operária — quase sempre de resistência à disciplina e ao ritmo fabril, às formas de moldagem ideológica da empresa. Os principais motivos de punição eram o absenteísmo (32,5%) e os comportamentos inadaptados (brincadeiras, erros, descuidos — 17,8%). Além disso a alta rotatividade demonstra o desinteresse dos trabalhadores na manutenção do emprego, apesar das estratégias empresariais. Havia na cidade alternativas de sobrevivência, mesmo marginais, com remuneraçào semelhante à da indústria — sem ônus da disciplina e da perda da liberdade.

As reações da agressividade contra a empresa (15%) ou os companheiros (13%) eram bastante freqüentes. Eram ações isoladas e sem conteúdo consciente, mas que demonstram o clima de tensão vivido por esses trabalhadores em processo de adaptação. Havia também atitudes explícitas contra a ordem — individuais (11,7%) ou coletivas (3,5%) — demonstrando um começo de conscientização, apesar de ainda frágil.

Por outro lado, a decisão da empresa de punir as atitudes de absenteísmo e inadaptação, na década de 1920, sugere que esses comportamentos, apesar de continuarem sendo as reações mais freqüentes (50% dos casos), estavam se tornando menos comuns, permitindo enrijecer o controle com punições radicais como o demissão.

Conclusões da análise

Comparando a evolução dos três setores estudados, percebemos de imediato que o impacto da tecnologia e da modernização atingiu cada um de forma diferente no período. O processo produtivo têxtil não mudou muito sua técnica desde as primeiras fábricas instaladas. No entanto, a origem semi-rural dos trabalhadores dificultou a sua adaptação ao novo sistema e a formação de uma consciência de classe. Foi um processo difícil e doloroso, estando ainda inacabado na década de 1920.

Os sapateiros e outros trabalhadores artesanais foram sendo derrubados pela nova ordem industrial, perdendo sua independência e a qualificação. Foram marginalizados ou proletarizados. Em compensação, sua consciência de classe formou-se desde cedo, tinham grande capacidade de mobilização, facilitada pela concentração dos estabelecimentos na Cidade Velha. Sua fidelidade ou seu ódio não se dirigiam à empresa ou à fábrica, como no caso dos têxteis, mas, respectivamente, à sua classe e ao sistema. Mas, não tinham poder de pressão.

Os cocheiros dos bondes de tração animal tiveram que se ajustar ao sistema elétrico, mas não foi uma adaptação súbita, o ajuste dava prestígio e, sobretudo, suas relações de trabalho não foram afetadas. Não só suas condições de trabalho melhoraram, mas, por sua mobilidade na cidade, rapidamente perceberam sua situação privilegiada e seu poder de barganha. Uma greve dos têxteis ou dos sapateiros, afetava a empresa, que muitas vezes tinha condições de se prevenir através dos estoques — pelo menos os têxteis. Mas, uma greve dos bondes parava a cidade, afetava as outras categorias e os serviços em geral.

A qualificação, que nas fábricas têxteis estava restrita a algumas seções mais especializadas, no caso dos cocheiros dos bondes de burro que passaram a motorneiros dos elétricos generalizou-se, inclusive com a exigência de alfabetização. Com relação aos sapateiros, o processo fabril terminou por desqualificar o trabalho, na medida em que subdividiu as funções e as submeteu à atuação da máquina.

Nesse processo todo, os têxteis, sem dúvida, foram os mais lentos a adquirir consciência de sua condição e de seus direitos e a idéia de unidade de classe, com problemas e vivências semelhantes. A ideologia passada pelo sistema fabril era a da empresa-família, mas com hierarquia e disciplina. Conseguir formar uma consciência de classe com subsistema marginal aberto ao lado foi uma experiência difícil, e os têxteis custaram a conseguir completar o seu processo.

Bibliografia consultada

Abreu, Maurício. *Evolução Urbana do Rio de Janeiro.* Rio de Janeiro: IPLANRIO/Zahar. 1987.

Benchimol, Jaime L. *Pereira Passos, um Haussman Tropical.* Biblioteca Carioca. Rio de Janeiro: Prefeitura da Cidade. 1990.

Carvalho, José Murilo de. *Os Bestializados: O Rio de Janeiro e a República que não foi.* São Paulo: Cia. das Letras. 1987.

Centro Industrial do Brasil. *O Brasil, suas Riquezas Naturais, suas Indústrias.* Rio de Janeiro. 1907.

—— *O Centro Industrial na Conferência Algodoeira.* Rio de janeiro. 1916.

Coaracy, Vivaldo. *Memórias da Cidade do Rio de Janeiro.* 2ª ed. Rio de Janeiro: José Olympio. 1965.

Damazio, Sylvia F. *Retrato Social das Classes Populares do Rio de Janeiro, 1890-1910.* FCRB. 1991. Mimeo, em fase de edição.

Edmundo, Luis. *O Rio de Janeiro do meu Tempo.* Rio de Janeiro: Imprensa Nacional. 1938.

Elia, Francisco Carlos F. *A Questão Habitacional no Rio de Janeiro da Primeira República.* Dissertação de mestrado em História. Niterói: ICHF/UFF. 1984. Mimeo.

Fausto, Boris. *Trabalho Urbano e Conflito Social.* Rio-São Paulo: Difel. 1977.

Giroletti, Domingos. *Fábrica, Convento e Disciplina.* Belo Horizonte: Imprensa Oficial. 1991.

Hardman, Francisco Foot & Leonardi, Vitor. *História da Indústria e do Trabalho no Brasil.* São Paulo: Global. 1982.

João do Rio (Paulo Barreto). *A Alma Encantadora das Ruas.* Rio de Janeiro: Organizações Simões. 1951.

Keremitsis, Eileen. *The Early Industrial Worker in Rio de Janeiro — 1870-1930.* Tese de Doutorado. Columbia Universty, 1982. Mimeo.

Lobo, Eulália Lahmeyer. *História do Rio de Janeiro, da Capital Comercial ao Capital Industrial e Financeiro.* Rio de Janeiro: Ibmec. 1978.

Maram, Sheldon. *Anarquistas, Imigrantes e o Movimento Operário Brasileiro.* Rio de Janeiro: Paz e Terra. 1979.

Morales de Los Rios, Adolfo. "O Rio de Janeiro da Primeira República" in *Revista do Instituto Histórico e Geográfico Brasileiro* (272): 3-200, 1966; (273): 3-116, 1966, (274): 3-86. 1967.

Stein, Stanley J. *Origem e Evolução da Indústria Têxtil no Brasil, 1850-1950.* Rio de Janeiro: Campus. 1979.

Weid, Elisabeth v. d. "The Making of the Industrial Worker in Rio de Janeiro, 1880-1930". Trabalho apresentado no X Congresso Internacional de História Econômica. Leuven. 1990. Mimeo.

—— "Trabalho têxtil rural e urbano no início do século". Trabalho apresentado no VIII Encontro Anual da ANPOCS. Àguas de São Pedro. 1984.

—— & Bastos, Ana Marta R. *O Fio da Meada: Estratégia de Expansão de uma Indústria Têxtil.* Rio de Janeiro: FCRB/CNI. 1986.

José Antonio Segatto
Departamento de Patrimônio Histórico da Eletropaulo

RELAÇÕES E CONFLITOS DE TRABALHO NA LIGHT DE SÃO PAULO

Mito da paz social

Documentos oficiais (públicos e de divulgação) do arquivo histórico da Eletropaulo e depoimentos de muitos antigos funcionários da Light induzem à conclusão de que esta empresa teria permanecido sempre alheia ou distante dos movimentos sociais e políticos. Preocupada com a prosperidade e o bem-estar de seus empregados, remunerando e tratando-os condignamente, a empresa anglo-canadense jamais teria enfrentado problemas nas relações de trabalho, ou tensões e conflitos trabalhistas — como greves, por exemplo.

Pesquisas realizadas em outras fontes (coleção de recortes de jornais e documentos confidenciais do Departamento de Patrimônio Histórico), no entanto, mostram exatamente o contrário. Ou seja, mostram que o relacionamento da Light com seus trabalhadores, ao longo da sua história, foi sempre e fortemente marcado pelas tentativas e mesmo utilização da repressão, controle e manipulação. É o que está presente na realidade dos fatos: repressão aos movimentos reivindicatórios (greves) e organizações (Uniões, Ligas, Sindicatos), controle das entidades (Sociedade Beneficente, Sindicatos) e manipulação (político-eleitoral) etc. Dessa forma, não passa de um mito construído a versão segundo a qual as relações de trabalho na Light ter-se-iam caracterizado pela paz e pela tranqüilidade.

A análise das relações e conflitos de trabalho numa empresa com as características e o porte da Light — grande empresa de capital financeiro, detentora do monopólio dos serviços públicos da região mais desenvolvida do capitalismo no País, de uma metrópole como São Paulo — pode fornecer importantes subsídios para a compreensão da história do movimento operário brasileiro nas primeiras décadas do século XX, já que este tipo de tratamento dispensado às tensões e conflitos trabalhistas não era uma particularidade sua.

Paraíso do capital

O jornal canadense *Globe* (Toronto, 1/3/1902), noticiando, no início do século, o lançamento das ações da Light na Bolsa de Valores de Toronto, faz uma interessante descrição do Brasil. Comenta que "(...) em 1889, após uma revolução sem sangue e pacífica, a República do Brasil começou sua carreira com uma Constituição como a dos Estados Unidos da América". Em seguida, diz que

> "o país é notadamente livre de tendências revolucionárias (...). No Brasil é tão difícil haver qualquer distúrbio da lei e da ordem como em qualquer país mais civilizado da Europa, e o capital está tão seguro e os direitos da propriedade são tão respeitados lá como em qualquer lugar do mundo (...). A Constituição protege expressamente as pessoas, direitos e propriedades estrangeiras e uma orientação política inteligente e honrada para com os estrangeiros que investem nesta República tem sido uma característica marcante de sua administração (...). Tão bem reconhecidas são as oportunidades de lucro nos negócios, assim como as condições de justiça e estabilidade que ali prevalecem, que as companhias formadas na Europa para operar no Brasil ocupam a linha de frente de seus grupos com respeito a crédito e valor dos seus títulos. Essas condições e sanções não são fornecidas somente pela Constituição e pelas leis; elas repousam sobre uma opinião pública inteligente e sadia."

Na verdade, a história parecia dar razão ao jornal canadense: em 15.11.1889 era instaurada a República no Brasil, através da intervenção do Exército. O episódio foi muito bem descrito por um de seus autores, Aristides Lobo: "O povo assistiu àquilo bestializado, atônito, surpreso, sem conhecer o que significava. Muitos acreditavam sinceramente estar vendo uma parada." E, sob a égide do lema "Ordem e Progresso", com uma Constituição de caráter liberal, foi montado o novo regime republicano.

Sob o controle das oligarquias estaduais, principalmente as de São Paulo e Minas Gerais, a recém-instaurada República foi assentada num liberalismo excludente e autoritário. Ao mesmo tempo em que dava garantias e segurança aos negócios e lucros das empresas nacionais e estrangeiras, o liberalismo oligárquico reafirmava a não-intervenção do Estado no mercado e nas relações de trabalho. A regulamentação das relações entre trabalhadores e patrões era vista como prejudicial à livre circulação de mercadorias, mais especificamente à compra e venda da força de trabalho. Em função disso, a legislação trabalhista praticamente inexistia. Paralelamente, os movimentos reivindicatórios eram vistos como perturbadores da ordem e entraves ao progresso — o movimento operário era tratado como "caso de polícia", sujeito a violenta repressão, que ia do fechamento de sindicatos, prisão, expulsão de "estrangeiros" e confinamento de "nacionais", até outras medidas mais drásticas.

O otimismo do jornal canadense, justificado por estas condições favoráveis propiciadas pelo regime republicano, era ainda reforçado pelo fato de a Light, em São Paulo, manter relações bastante estreitas com a oligarquia local, tanto estadual como municipal.

Controle, manipulação e repressão

Se havia condições político-institucionais que justificavam o otimismo da empresa canadense e de seus porta-vozes, a realidade social e seu caráter perverso tinham elementos que o problematizavam.

No Brasil, as condições de vida e trabalho até as primeiras décadas deste século eram extremamente difíceis. A jornada de trabalho, na maioria dos casos, chegava a 12, 14 e até 16 horas por dia, e os trabalhadores não tinham direito a descanso semanal remunerado, a domingos, feriados ou férias anuais. Muitas vezes, nem contratos de trabalho existiam: os operários eram demitidos verbalmente e sem qualquer tipo de indenização; em caso de atraso de pagamento, não contavam com nenhum recurso jurídico. Os empresários não tinham qualquer obrigação em caso de doença do trabalhador, mesmo em se tratando de acidentes de trabalho ou de doenças profissionais. A disciplina e a coerção no interior das empresas eram bastante rigorosas, visando à garantia do máximo de rendimento da mão-de-obra. Os baixos salários e o desemprego forçavam a entrada de mulheres e crianças no mercado de trabalho.

Contra as difíceis condições de vida e de trabalho, os trabalhadores começaram a se organizar e a lutar pela melhoria de sua situação. Através de associações, ligas, uniões, sindicatos, passaram a encaminhar suas lutas e movimentos reivindicativos por aumento de salários e melhores condições de trabalho (diminuição de jornada para oito horas, repouso semanal remunerado, regulamentação do trabalho da mulher e do menor etc.). Sua principal arma de luta passou a ser a greve. Algumas dessas reivindicações foram conquistadas nas primeiras décadas do século, outras só seriam atendidas depois dos anos trinta.

Os empregados da Light não tinham condições de trabalho diferentes dos demais. Por isso, passaram também a fazer reivindicações — tanto pela mudança nas relações de trabalho, como por aumento de salários. E, para conter e obstaculizar as tentativas de organização, a mobilização e os reclamos reivindicativos de seus trabalhadores e para realizar suas articulações políticas, a Light iria utilizar-se de três recursos básicos: o controle, a manipulação e a repressão.

*A) Controle**

Em 1903, foi criada a Sociedade Beneficente dos Empregados da Light — SBEL, objetivando prestar socorros mútuos, ou seja, médicos, jurídicos, auxílio funerário etc. Apesar de certa independência, desde o início a empresa procurou imiscuir-se na vida da SBEL. Não por acaso, seu primeiro presidente foi Edgard de Souza, futuro Superintendente da Light, e, no artigo 11 de seus estatutos, constava a seguinte cláusula:

> "Será expulso imediatamente da Sociedade todo aquele que na sua sede tratar de assuntos políticos, censurar ou criticar qualquer ato da gerência da companhia em que são empregados, ou tomar qualquer deliberação que seja prejudicial à mesma."

---

* Baseio-me aqui no artigo de Luzia M. A. Soares, "Dossiê SBEL". *Revista Memória,* ano IV, n.º 15, p. 48 a 55.

Alguns anos mais tarde, entre 1909 e 1911, a Light passou a interferir de forma mais direta nos assuntos e na direção da SBEL, indicando e nomeando seu Conselho Deliberativo e sua Diretoria. A intervenção da empresa na Sociedade completou-se em 1917, através de modificações estatutárias, submetendo as contas da SBEL à direção da Light. Daí em diante, a Sociedade, que deveria ser dos trabalhadores e por eles gerida, foi colocada sob o controle da Light, que procuraria amoldá-la à sua imagem e semelhança.

B) Manipulação

Em 1907, um importante jornal paulista (*Commercio de São Paulo*, 10, 11, 12, 13 e 14/7) numa série de editoriais, denunciava a Light por intervir nas eleições de São Paulo. As acusações do jornal falavam em manipulação e fraude. Alegavam que a Light "tem procurado intervir nas eleições", alistando seus "centenares de empregados". Dessa forma, a Light estaria se constituindo "em poderoso núcleo eleitoral". Segundo o referido jornal,

> "quem é admitido na Companhia tem que se alistar eleitor, por bem ou por mal, seja estrangeiro ou nacional. Mas, quando ela despede um operário ou quando ele se despede, vai-se o cidadão de mãos limpas. A Light retém-lhe o título, como retém os títulos dos que estão enfermos, dos que morrem, dos que se ausentam (...). Amanhã, para vender um pleito, para eleger os seus apaniguados, para ter prefeitos ou vereadores que lhe façam novas concessões ou que a desonerem de suas obrigações, não tem necessidade de retirar do serviço um só de seus operários. Como lhes extorquiu os títulos, entrega-os a chefes, que os distribuem para indivíduos que não são eleitores. O número de votos, obtidos por esse baixo processo, há de influir na vitória definitiva (...). Essa companhia... dispõe, hoje, com segurança, de mais de mil títulos, que equivalem a mil leitores".

Dizia ainda que a

> "Light, convertida em núcleo eleitoral, tem no Congresso do Estado, nas próprias repartições municipais, quem a auxilie, quem lhe dê apoio, quem a incite a prosseguir na sua intervenção imoral em nossa política. Entre os cúmplices, comparsas da

Companhia... há alguns que se incumbem de alistar eleitores e dividi-los por seções... Em vésperas de eleições, os diretores da Light... comprometem-se a dar a este ou àquele candidato determinado número de votos".

Mas, afirma o diário, não é só nas eleições municipais que intervem a Light — intervem também "em outras eleições de deputados, de senadores, de presidente do Estado". Denuncia que a empresa, na verdade, "pretende eleger vereadores que lhe façam... novas concessões, em detrimento do povo, ou que interpretem, à sua vontade, o contrato que tem com a municipalidade". Assim, "a poderosa empresa, alistando os seus empregados, dando-lhes cédulas fechadas à beira da urna, punindo os que não se submetem, quer influir... sobre o governo do município e sobre a política do Estado". Conclui que "se não reagirmos em São Paulo, nós todos, desde os jornalistas aos operários, a Light amanhã exercerá tremenda influência; há de eleger vereadores, há de escolher prefeitos, há de intervir num pleito a favor deste ou daquele candidato à Câmara dos Deputados ou Senado".

Com um sistema político eleitoral que facilitava a fraude e a manipulação, uma empresa com o poderio econômico do porte da Light encontraria facilidades para intervir na política da cidade e do Estado de São Paulo. Facilidades para alistar seus empregados, utilizar e manipular seus títulos e seus votos como bem entendesse e lhe conviesse.

Aliada às facilidades proporcionadas pelo sistema político-eleitoral, havia as relações de intimidade da Light com a oligarquia dominante local, representada pelo Partido Republicano Paulista (PRP), com o qual seus vínculos eram bastante estreitos, tanto a nível municipal como estadual. Através dessas relações de intimidade e cumplicidade com o Estado e com os dirigentes do PRP, a Light articulava seus interesses e sua intervenção política. Não por acaso o jornal *O Estado de S. Paulo* de 25.6.1908 chegava a afirmar que "Light era um Estado dentro do Município".

Nestas condições e num colégio eleitoral numericamente muito pequeno ou restrito (nas eleições de 14.12.1907, para a Câmara Municipal de São Paulo, o número de votantes foi de pouco mais de 11 mil), a Light com seu poderio econômico e com seus mais de mil alistamentos podia influir decisivamente na eleição de vereadores (na eleição de 1907 houve vários vereadores eleitos com menos de 500 votos, sendo que o mais votado obteve 837 votos e o eleito menos votado teve 313 votos), prefeitos, deputados, senadores e até mesmo governadores. Detendo e controlando cerca de 10% dos eleitores votantes, a Light ficava numa situação política privilegiada para articular seu *lobby* na Câmara Municipal e no Congresso Estadual, na Prefeitura e no Governo do Estado, para garantir e expandir suas concessões e negócios.

Vê-se assim que as denúncias do jornal *Comércio de São Paulo* não eram nem um pouco infundados. E tanto não eram infundadas que no ano seguinte (janeiro de 1908), o superintendente da Light em São Paulo, W. N. Walmsley, em discurso para a diretoria da empresa, congratulava-se com a reeleição de Antonio Prado para a Prefeitura, e a de diversos outros vereadores da confiança da companhia. O mesmo Walmsley, em seu relatório anual (*General Manager's Report*, 1907) para Toronto, fez um relato sobre os resultados eleitorais favoráveis, tanto no âmbito municipal como estadual. Informava que o novo presidente recém-eleito do Estado, Albuquerque Lins, "é um homem bem conhecido da Companhia, e acredita-se que a atitude do novo governo será de manter as justas e agradáveis relações existentes durante a administração passada". Quanto ao município, fala com satisfação da reeleição do prefeito Antonio Prado, "juntamente com um grupo de vereadores, e nas mãos destes cavalheiros os negócios da companhia sempre receberam a mais cordial e honrada consideração". E complementava dizendo ser "natural que estamos interessados nestas questões políticas e podemos muito bem congratularmo-nos, tal qual a população desta comunidade, acerca dos resultados destas eleições".

C) Repressão

Os trabalhadores da Light fundaram, em agosto de 1910, após várias tentativas, a *União Defensora dos Empregados da Light*, que passou a congregar boa parte dos funcionários.

Em meados de novembro, a Light demitiu, sem maiores explicações, o presidente da União Defensora, Victor Papini, e um sócio da entidade, Jaime Pacheco, ambos motorneiros, e com dez anos de serviços, ou seja, desde a instalação da Light no Brasil. Procurando obter a reintegração dos dois funcionários dispensados, motorneiros e condutores resolveram nomear uma comissão para discutir a questão com a Superintendência da Light. Respondendo à solicitação, o Superintendente resolveu estudar o caso e dar uma resposta dentro de alguns dias. Findo o prazo, a empresa manifestou-se negativamente, alegando serem desnecessários os serviços dos dois funcionários demitidos.

Face à resposta da Light, a União Defensora decidiu, no dia 18, declarar em greve o pessoal do tráfego de bondes, agregando à reivindicação a readmissão dos dois funcionários e a revogação dos artigos 4.º e 16.º do regulamento interno da empresa. O fato é que a demissão dos dois funcionários foi apenas a gota d'água para o desencadeamento do movimento paredista.

> "A reivindicação estalou, é certo, fomentada por esse último ato da Companhia, mas a causa que a gerou, alimentou e desenvolveu vem de muito longe: vem da execução de um regulamento humilhante e opressor, vem de uma série de violências exercidas constantemente sobre homens extenuados por um rude trabalho, às vezes, de dezoito horas, que ao cabo de cada mês a companhia recompensa de uma maneira original, pagando-lhes mais em talões de multa que nos 500 réis por hora de labuta" (*O Estado de S. Paulo*, 20.11.1910).

Informada sobre o desencadeamento da greve, na madrugada do dia 19, a Light tomou diversas providências: requisitou a polícia para impedir os piquetes e fazer circular os bondes; readmitiu dezenas de empregados que havia anteriormente na empresa como motorneiros; mobilizou aprendizes de condutores e o pessoal das oficinas aptos a conduzir os bondes, além de reter nas estações durante a noite motorneiros e condutores.

Os grevistas concentraram o movimento todo na estação de bondes da avenida Celso Garcia, no Brás. Com a intervenção policial houve diversos conflitos entre os trabalhadores e a polícia, resultando em prisões, agressões e feridos de parte a parte. Através da repressão policial (prisão dos principais líderes) e da intimidação por parte da Light (ameaça de demissão), a greve tornou-se apenas parcial: "a Light tem diariamente em tráfego 113 bondes e ontem, até as 4 horas da tarde, trafegaram apenas 86 (...). Das 4 horas em diante esse número ficou reduzidíssimo" (*Commercio de São Paulo*, 20.11.1910).

No dia seguinte, porém, o movimento grevista já havia sido abafado e controlado. Os bondes voltaram a circular, acompanhados por policiamento ostensivo. Os motorneiros e condutores retornaram ao trabalho e o tráfego foi normalizado, mas o descontentamento dos empregados da Light, não obstante a derrota do movimento, tenderia a agravar-se.

A União Defensora sofrera um duro golpe. Logo após o término da greve os jornais noticiaram que "a administração da Light tem já em seu poder a lista do Conselho Diretor da União, indicando quais os promotores da greve e que esse pessoal vai ser dispensado" (*Diário Popular*, 21.11.1910).

A greve dos motorneiros e condutores, em novembro de 1910, pelo direito de organização e contra um regulamento interno de trabalho opressivo, constituiu-se na primeira tentativa reivindicatória dos trabalhadores da Light. Apesar de sua curta duração e de não ter sido bem sucedida, ela foi o ponto de partida para a tomada de consciência dos funcionários sobre seus direitos.

Nos anos 1917-29, como conseqüência da Guerra e da crise econômica do período imediatamente anterior (1913-17), que acarretou recessão, queda dos salários e desemprego, as lutas e manifestações operárias no Brasil ganharam intensidade e proporção.

Às mobilizações e ao crescimento dos movimentos reivindicatórios, o regime oligárquico — sobretudo depois de 1919-20 — respondeu com repressão, fechamento de sindicatos, empastelamento de jornais operários, expulsão de estrangeiros e outras medidas, tratando o movimento como "caso de polícia". Foi nesta conjuntura que se desencadeou, em outubro de 1919, a greve dos trabalhadores da Light, que acabaria abarcando outras categorias, ameaçando paralisar a cidade de São Paulo.

No segundo semestre de 1919 os operários da Light começam a organizar a *Liga dos Empregados da Light*, tendo à frente os anarquistas. Seu projeto de estatutos, publicado no jornal *A Plebe* em 10.8.1919, expunha suas pretensões: "o objetivo máximo (da Liga) é a completa emancipação do proletariado" e a "luta por melhorias econômico-sociais dos trabalhadores", devendo servir "unicamente para o trabalho de propaganda e educação dos trabalhadores e sua luta contra desigualdade econômico-social, da ação consciente e solidária de seus associados e dos meios próprios de ação direta, variáveis segundo as circunstâncias de lugar e de momento".

Alguns dias depois, foram realizadas assembléias na sede da *Internacional*, no Largo de São Francisco, para discussão e aprovação dos estatutos. Noticiando o fato, no dia 3/9, o jornal *O Combate* descreve as reuniões:

> "Todos os oradores se externaram em considerações de ordem econômica, profligando energicamente a exploração da empresa canadense e pondo em evidência os processos para conseguir o desmantelamento do baluarte que surgiu para contrapôr-se à sua desmedida ganância; (...) ainda ontem, por exemplo, a Light distribuiu pelos operários numerosas entradas de obséquio, para o circo norte-americano, situado na várzea do Mercado, aconselhando-os a irem divertir ali, em vez de tomarem parte nas reuniões anunciadas para tratar dos interesses da classe (...). O estratagema não surtiu efeito desejado, mas, nem por isso, a Light deixou de ficar furiosa, pois ameaça de perseguições todos aqueles que efetivamente se dedicam à tarefa de organização (...). Aplaudidos freneticamente os discursos proferidos, as assembléias deram início à aprovação dos estatutos os quais deverão por estes dias ser legalizados (...). Antes de terminarem as reuniões, vários operários lembraram ainda a necessidade de intensificar a boicotagem contra a *Antárctica* e de auxiliar a publicação d'*A Plebe* e, no final, foi cantada por um grupo de trabalhadores *A Internacional*, a qual foi ouvida atentamente por todo o auditório."

Organizada a Liga dos Empregados da Light, logo começam os atrigos com a empresa. No final de setembro, numa reunião dos delegados das seções da Light com a direção da entidade, são discutidas as reclamações e protestos contra perseguições a operários associados à Liga. Nas semanas seguintes, a tensão entre a Liga e a Light foi aumentando no sentido do confronto. O estopim, no entanto, viria de fora das relações empregados e empresa.

Em outubro, a polícia passou a prender militantes anarquistas com liderança no movimento operário. No dia 22 foram presos em São Paulo Gigi Damiani e Alexandre Zanelli (redatores de *A Plebe*), Sílvio Antonelli (diretor da Federação Operária) e José Sagai (redator do jornal *Avanti*). Este último foi solto em seguida, por falta de acusações, e os demais deportados. "Foram feitas algumas deportações de indivíduos tidos como libertários e outras vão efetuar-se à medida que se apurarem as responsabilidades dos presos. Para tal fim, foram embarcados anteontem à noite para o Rio, onde aguardam vapor que os leve para o estrangeiro, diversos desses indivíduos e ontem seguiram a bordo do *Mafalda* os deportados Gigi Damiani, Sílvio Antonelli e Alexandre Zanelli, visto que contra estes existem já portarias de expulsão" (*O Estado de S. Paulo*, 24.10.1919).

Solidária com os presos, a Liga dos Empregados da Light convocou uma assembléia para discutir o assunto. Realizada no salão da Sociedade Recreativa Itália Fausta, na rua Florêncio de Abreu, os empregados dos servidores do tráfego, linhas e cabos declaram-se em greve. "Saindo da reunião, os operários, que nenhum memorial entregaram aos seus chefes, dirigiram-se às redações dos jornais da manhã, sinal de protesto contra a prisão dos redatores de *A Plebe*" (*O Estado de S. Paulo*, 24.10.1919).

Informada da greve, a Light providenciou o auxílio da polícia: as estações de bondes de Vila Mariana, Alameda Glete e Avenida Celso Garcia foram tomadas pelas forças de infantaria e cavalaria. Às 4 horas da madrugada alguns empregados tentaram entrar nas garagens (estações), mas foram barrados por piquetes. Somente às 9 horas, a Light conseguiu fazer circular alguns bondes de passageiros nas linhas Avenidas, Barra Funda, Ponte Grande e Higienópolis, dirigidos por fiscais e motorneiros praticantes que furaram a greve e eram escoltados por soldados.

Para substituir os grevistas, a Light deslocou do Rio de Janeiro motorneiros e condutores, visando colocar em funcionamento os bondes. Ao mesmo tempo, estudantes da Escola Politécnica, Faculdade de Direito, Colégio Mackenzie, Escola de Comércio Álvares Penteado e sócios do Clube Paulistano apresentavam-se à Light para substituir os operários grevistas na condução dos bondes. Muitos deles, inclusive, foram utilizados na normalização do tráfego ou no restabelecimento dos trabalhos de ligações e instalações numa manifestação propagandista em defesa da ordem. Apesar de os operários das usinas geradoras e de transformação da Light não terem aderido à greve, Parnaíba foi tomada pela polícia.

Solidarizando-se com os trabalhadores grevistas da Light, a Federação Operária de São Paulo declarou greve geral em todo o Estado. Aderiram à greve os operários da construção da Cia. Telefônica, os trabalhadores da Cia. de Gaz, Cotonifício Crespi, Matarazzo, Pinotti e Gamba, oficinas da São Paulo Railway, das fábricas de chapéus, da construção civil, ferroviários da Bragantina, do Alto da Serra, Jundiaí (pessoal dos armazéns e plataformas), Cia. City de Santos, metalúrgicos e diversas outras categorias ou empresas, tanto na capital como em outros municípios.

Com os operários da Cia. de Gaz em greve, a iluminação da cidade passou a ser feita, precariamente, por bombeiros e escoteiros. Os bombeiros foram utilizados também na fabricação de gás, com funcionários administrativos. O prédio da companhia foi cercado e tomado por tropas.

No dia 23 a polícia apreendeu toda a edição de *A Plebe*, empastelando o jornal e inutilizando suas máquinas, sob alegação de que o periódico anarquista trazia em suas páginas material subversivo. E para reforçar o policiamento, deslocaram-se de Santos para São Paulo tropas de infantaria e de cavalaria. A polícia, conforme informava o jornal *A Gazeta*, "continua efetuando prisões de numerosos indivíduos perigosos, que percorrem as fábricas incitando os operários a se declararem em greve".

Neste mesmo dia, uma comissão de grevistas apresentou uma carta de reivindicações à Light, mas não foram recebidos pelos representantes da empresa. Na carta, afirmavam:

> "A Liga dos Trabalhadores da Light, que arregimenta em seu seio todos os empregados da mesma, é uma sociedade de classe e juridicamente reconhecida; ela foi formada para pôr termo às violências que os chefes dos diversos departamentos estavam praticando, notavelmente B. A. Owens, subgerente do tráfego. Desde que esta Liga se formou, eles redobraram de audácia, já demitindo, já suspendendo inúmeros empregados sem causas, chegando para isso qualquer denúncia improcedente; em vista deste seu proceder resolvemos dirigir-lhes oito memorandos em que pedíamos: melhoramento de salários, oito horas de serviço e a readmissão dos empregados demitidos sem causa e o reconhecimento da Liga. Mas, encontrando-nos sem garantias constitucionais, resolvemos declarar greve pacífica, que manteremos até nos serem dadas, para nessa ocasião nos entender com a Light. Para isso, chega que a polícia não exorbite de suas funções. Ponha ela em liberdade os presos e dê garantias aos refugiados que cessará este estado de coisas e processos, com as formas das leis se tiver por onde. O operário moderno quer ordem e liberdade, não é com processos inquisitoriais que ele se deixará iludir e aterrorizar. Remedeie a polícia, enquanto é tempo, e cessará este estado de coisa."

A Federação Operária, por seu turno, apresentava uma lista com dezesseis itens contendo: liberação dos presos, reconhecimento das associações operárias (com direito de reunião e propaganda), jornada de trabalho de 8 horas, descanso semanal, proibição do trabalho de menores de 14 anos e do trabalho noturno da mulher, abolição das multas, rebaixamento do custo de vida e outras.

Depois de quatro dias, a greve começou a esvaziar-se. Algumas categorias que haviam paralisado o trabalho por 48 horas, em solidariedade aos funcionários da Light, começaram a retornar às empresas. Outros, inclusive os trabalhadores da Light, por pressão da empresa e da polícia, também foram aos poucos voltando aos seus postos. No dia 27, já estava esvaziada e no dia 28 praticamente terminada.

Durante a greve, diversas entidades e instituições de cunho conservador aproveitam a oportunidade para fazer campanha contra o anarquismo e em defesa da ordem vigente. A Liga Nacionalista, em manifesto publicado na imprensa, "aconselha os operários nacionais a não se deixarem arrastar a manifestações de caráter subversivo por elementos estranhos, com grave prejuízo para o nosso país e para as instituições" (*Diário Popular*, 27.10.1919). O Centro Operário Católico Metropolitano, em assembléia geral, aprovava e divulgava a seguinte moção:

> "Os operários católicos hipotecam incondicional apoio a todas as classes conservadoras, na emergência atual, e declaram-se ao lado do governo para a repressão ao anarquismo, protestando contra as Ligas que decretaram a pseudo greve geral de solidariedade com elementos perigosos" (*Correio Paulistano*, 27.10.1919).

Terminada a greve, a Light comunicava à imprensa que "os grevistas, tidos como chefes do movimento, como elementos perniciosos à classe e que continuam a envidar esforços para tentar, em vão, a supremacia do anarquismo, não mais serão readmitidos em serviço" (*A Platéa*, 28.10.1919). Dois dias depois, "comunicou à polícia que não foram readmitidos no serviço cerca de 300 antigos operários, por considerá-los indivíduos perigosos".

Continuidade histórica

Depois da década de trinta, a Light continuaria utilizando-se dos mecanismos de controle, manipulação e repressão. Só que por outros meios, já que muitos passaram a ser função do Estado. Ou seja, com a reordenação do poder, em 1930, o Governo passou a desenvolver uma política no sentido de institucionalizar as relações entre capital e trabalho. Assim, uma das primeiras medidas do governo provisório de Getúlio Vargas foi a criação do Ministério do Trabalho, Indústria e Comércio, com o objetivo de organizar e controlar as relações trabalhistas. O Estado criou um grande número de leis e decretos que regulamentariam as relações entre capital e trabalho (legislação trabalhista), atrelou os sindicatos e criou diversos mecanismos repressivos. Dessa forma, muitos dos meios utilizados por empresas como a Light passaram daí para frente a ser prerrogativa do Estado. Isso não significou que a Light e outras empresas, agora em colaboração e em complementação, deixassem de utilizar aqueles mecanismos repressivos, manipulatórios e de controle das organizações, movimentos, mobilizações ou quaisquer outros meios utilizados pelos trabalhadores contra a opressão e a exploração.

Newton Augusto Cardoso de Oliveira
UFF e Faculdades Gay-Lussac

A ECONOMIA DO SINISTRO: UMA CONTRIBUIÇÃO AO ESTUDO DO TRABALHO, DOS ACIDENTES E DA SEGURIDADE NA INDÚSTRIA TÊXTIL DURANTE O ESTADO NOVO (1937-1945)

É recorrente! 59 anos passaram e as estatísticas indicam: o Brasil está entre os países de maior incidência de acidentes do trabalho no mundo. O quadro de homens, mulheres e até crianças, mutilados ao tentarem ganhar o pão com o suor de seu rosto, já foi "naturalizado".

Impulsionado pelo impacto desta situação hodierna e dada a carência de estudos de caráter histórico sobre essa temática — o acidente do trabalho —, resolvemos debruçar-nos sobre a questão acidentária a partir da indústria têxtil no período do Estado Novo. Contudo, o fio do novelo que procuramos puxar, a partir da análise do acidente, mostrou-se formado de uma trama múltipla.

Para entender a ocorrência do sinistro fabril na indústria têxtil brasileira, fez-se necessário responder, ou ao menos apontar algumas questões prévias.

Qual o comportamento da indústria têxtil, maior ramo industrial brasileiro daquele tempo, em um momento de modificações profundas no processo de acumulação capitalista e reorientação da economia brasileira, no sentido da industrialização de base?

Como se comportaram os trabalhadores diante da supressão quase completa da ação sindical autônoma, ao mesmo tempo em que era implantada a seguridade social estatal e o sindicalismo corporativo?

Que inferências podemos estabelecer a partir de uma conjuntura de repressão política de corte fascista sobre a sociedade e o mundo do trabalho em particular?

Quais as influências adquiridas pelo patronato e pelo Estado num mundo em crise e transformação?

Enfim, qual o significado do acidente do trabalho dentro deste quadro?

Para responder às questões aqui propostas é preciso recuar ao mundo da política internacional do início da década de 1930. É nesta época que se consolidou no mundo ocidental um conservadorismo de novo tipo. Não usava casaca ou "pince-nez", preferia os recentes e modernos métodos de comunicação de massa: o rádio e o cinema. O nome desse novo conservadorismo era *nazi-fascismo.*

O aparecimento deste movimento, no primeiro terço do século XX, está vinculado à crise intestina por que passava o capitalismo, simbolizado pela quebra da Bolsa de Valores de Nova York em 1929[1].

O Brasil, nesta quadra histórica, sentiu de modo importante os impactos da crise, já que a maior parte da economia nacional estava vinculada, direta ou indiretamente, às rendas obtidas pela exportação de café. Com o necrosamento do mercado mundial provocado pela crise, até a consolidação de uma política de substituição de importações, o País viveria momentos difíceis.

Foi dentro deste quadro que aconteceu a chamada "Revolução de 1930", liderada pelo antigo político "carcomido" Getúlio Vargas. Este, a partir de um núcleo central[2], iria empreender a construção de uma alternativa para o Brasil, que, sem romper radicalmente com o passado e tudo o que ele podia representar, modernizaria e colocaria o país em um novo rumo e patamar de desenvolvimento capitalista.

Com efeito, foi nesse cenário político de entrelaçamento de questões nacionais e internacionais que, em 10 de novembro de 1937, Getúlio Vargas encabeçou o Golpe que deu início ao fascismo no Brasil: o Estado Novo[3].

Não se tratou, como era costume na América de línguas latinas, de mais uma ditadura, agora de caráter personalista, aproveitando-se dos ventos fascistizantes da maré internacional. Hoje, em

---

[1] Cf. Klindleberger, Charles P. *La Crisis economica 1929-1933.* Barcelona: Editorial Crítica. 1985.

[2] Gryzspan, Mario & Pandolfi, Dulce C. *Da Revolução de 30 ao Golpe do Estado Novo: a depuração das elites.* Rio de Janeiro: FGV, mimeo.

[3] A esse respeito ver: Lenharo, Alcir. *Nazismo: o Triunfo da Vontade.* São Paulo: Ática. 1989; *A Sacralização da Política.* Campinas: Papirus. 1986; e Vianna, Luiz J. W. *Liberalismo e Sindicato no Brasil.* Rio de Janeiro: Paz e Terra. 1978.

perspectiva, podemos afirmar que o Estado Novo, se não tinha um projeto claro e definido na sua instauração, constituiu-se ao longo de sua vigência num conjunto de práticas que, a partir das reflexões de Barrington Moore, pode ser referenciado como um regime de "fascismo pelo alto"[4].

Neste contexto, é fundamental destacar o impacto no Brasil da Segunda Guerra Mundial. Na indústria têxtil, em particular, os efeitos da Guerra se fariam sentir nas condições e no ritmo da produção, e vincular-se-iam de modo inequívoco à questão acidentária.

A Guerra aceleraria de forma inédita a demanda por produtos têxteis numa estrutura fabril semiparalisada e em grande parte já com sinais de obsolecência[5]. De uma situação estagnada na qual, em 1936, exportava-se 318.745 quilos de tecidos de algodão, já no ano de 1937 as exportações passariam a ser da ordem de 686.687 quilos. No auge da Guerra, elas chegaram em 1943 a 26.045.818 quilos[6].

Uma conseqüência deste estupendo aumento foi o de tornar mais saliente o problema do sinistro fabril, que desde meados dos anos trinta procurava ser equacionado mediante o seu enquadramento no conjunto de leis previdenciárias então em implantação. Vejamos mais de perto qual foi este trajeto.

Como já intuiu um arguto cientista político[7], no caso brasileiro, as leis de seguridade social foram implantadas atendendo a uma demanda do mundo do trabalho, mas informadas por uma estratégia regulacionista e de dominação. Durante o Estado Novo, a norma que enquadrou a questão do acidente foi o Decreto n.º 24.637, de 10 de julho de 1934.

Na indústria têxtil carioca, a aplicação desse decreto deu-se mediante o que estabelecia o seu artigo 40, que permitiu a atuação, no ramo de acidentes do trabalho, dos sindicatos autorizados pelo Ministério do Trabalho. Aproveitando-se desta oportunidade, o po-

---

[4] Moore, Jr., Barrington. *Origens Sociais da Ditadura e da Democracia: Senhores e Camponeses na Construção do Mundo Moderno.* São Paulo: Martins Fontes. 1983.

[5] Baseamo-nos em Stein, Stanley. *Origens e Evolução da Indústria Têxtil no Brasil 1850-1950.* Rio de Janeiro: Campus. 1989.

[6] Idem, p. 194.

[7] Vianna, L. W. Op. cit.

deroso Sindicato das Indústrias de Fiação e Tecelagem (SIFT-RJ), regulamentou o seu órgão segurador, que já atuava desde 1924: a Sociedade Cooperativa de Seguros de Operários em Fábricas de Tecidos (S.C.O.F.T.-RJ).

Isto ocorreu apesar de os ideólogos do governo varguista pretenderem, na época do Estado Novo uma estatização total das iniciativas governamentais em todas as esferas da sociedade, em particular, no âmbito das relações trabalhistas. Contudo, o negócio do seguro era algo muito maior que o enquadramento e a regulação do acidente do trabalho. Nesta atividade econômica, dada a obrigatoriedade do seguro, movimentava-se um volume de capital que transformou a seguridade em um negócio que unia o útil ao agradável.

Útil, porque se protegia o operário, atendendo uma antiga demanda trabalhista, ao mesmo tempo em que se desobrigava o patrão das preocupações com a ocorrência do sinistro no decorrer da labuta diária de seus empregados.

Agradável, na medida em que se descortinou um ramo da atividade seguradora que foi monopolizado pelo capital nacional industrial, em contraste com os demais ramos da mesma, que tinham a predominância do capital estrangeiro e nas quais os empresários nacionais apareciam numa posição subalterna.

Coeva com a implantação da "ideologia da outorga", a implantação de órgãos privados para a execução do Decreto 24.634 apareceu no discurso dos seguradores como dádiva patronal.

> "Não somos dos que patrocinam por sistema a intervenção do Estado, mas [...] junto ao aspecto humanitário do postulado, fez com que as corporações patronais tenham sido mundialmente, as mais dedicadas propulsoras dos institutos de previdência contra acidentes."[8]

Contudo, para chegar a este ponto, a lei de acidentes do trabalho no Brasil tem uma trajetória que merece ser descrita. A primeira manifestação acerca da regulamentação do acidente do trabalho no país foi um projeto apresentado à Câmara dos Deputados por Medeiros de Albuquerque, em 1904. Entretanto, o primeiro docu-

---

[8] *Revista de Seguros*. IRB, n.º 223, jan. 1940.

mento legal que pôs em prática alguma proteção contra o sinistro fabril foi a Lei n.º 3.724 de 15 de maio de 1919.

Esta lei procurou estabelecer uma forma de indenização pela ocorrência do acidente, limitada todavia pela concepção de que a intervenção estatal no âmbito fabril, tem de realizar-se fora dos muros da fábrica.

Ao não questionar as condições de realização do trabalho — campo que, segundo a concepção da época, estava na inviolabilidade da esfera privada — a Lei n.º 3.724, concretamente acabou-se tornando um paliativo para a questão acidentária.

Durante o Estado Novo, um jurista estudioso das implicações legais do acidente do trabalho emitiu um juízo sobre a Lei de 1919, tecendo críticas somente à pouca clareza do texto ao definir o que é *acidente do trabalho.* Visto que este, na forma como foi redigida a Lei, confunde-se com o *acidente no trabalho*[9]. Eram óbices de natureza meramente jurídico-formal, na medida em que em momento algum da crítica indica-se a pouca eficácia do texto legal no sentido do atendimento do acidentado.

A discussão foi trazida para a tecnicalidade jurídica, sendo a crítica montada numa base de inspiração do Direito Positivo. Araújo Castro, o especialista em questão, apesar das críticas, encontrou um grande mérito na lei de 1919. A sua formulação baseada na *teoria do risco profissional.* Este seria o seu ponto alto.

Posto que no debate jurídico sobre os acidentes do trabalho, grassava no mundo a peleja entre a *teoria da culpa,* que inspirada no Direito Romano, resumidamente, diz que cabe ao trabalhador negligente ou imprudente (e aqui esta qualificação fica ao critério da subjetividade de quem julga) arcar com as conseqüências de seu acidente. Assim, antes da Lei n.º 3.724, o trabalhador só tinha direito à indenização quando reunia elementos para provar a culpa do empregador.

Um exemplo disto foi o processo submetido no ano de 1908 à 2.ª Câmara da Corte de Apelação do Distrito Federal. No referido processo, um operário têxtil tinha perdido três dedos da mão ao manusear um batelão. Tudo levava a crer que se tratava de um típico acidente de trabalho. No entanto, o acordão firmado quando do julgamento da ação foi no sentido da não-indenização do infor-

---

[9] Castro, Araújo. *Acidentes do Trabalho.* 1939, p. 29.

tunado, já que o mesmo não tinha como provar a culpa do patrão. Esta foi apenas uma das inúmeras manifestações de radicalidade liberal no período da República Velha, no mundo do trabalho, quando se deparavam patrões e empregados.

Concluímos, por conseguinte, que a Lei de 1919, ao encampar a teoria do risco profissional, foi o modo encontrado pelas classes dominantes de reconhecer a questão social, ao mesmo tempo em que mantinham o mais possível intacta de intromissão estatal a esfera das relações de trabalho.

A saída "por cima" da lei de 1919 já indica uma característica recorrente das classes dominantes nacionais, que procuram implementar a modernização sem rompimento. Isto se torna tanto mais emblemático quando levamos em consideração que o primeiro país a adotar a teoria do risco profissional foi a Alemanha em 1884[10].

A teoria do risco profissional, ainda que significasse um avanço em relação à teoria da culpa era limitada, na medida em que não indagava do papel das condições de trabalho nas causas de ocorrências do sinistro. Ao não realizar este questionamento, ela mostrava a sua face de flexão tática em relação à ideologia liberal, igualando agentes desiguais.

Araújo Castro demonstraria bem isto ao comentar que:

> "A doutrina do risco profissional constitue uma exceção, de antes uma derrogação ao direito comum. Estabelece uma transação entre patrão e operário. A fim de que não haja um pesado encargo para o patrão e possa este garantir sempre à vítima do acidente uma indenização , tornou-se mister adotar essa transação, na qual o operário ganha e perde ao mesmo tempo: ganha porque obtém uma indenização nos casos em que, na ausência de culpa do patrão, a nada teria direito; perde porque consegue menos do que alcançaria se ficasse provada aquela culpa."[11]

A lei de 1919 subsistiu até os dois primeiros anos do governo Vargas. Apesar da Revolução de 1930 ter eleito a questão social como uma de suas bandeiras centrais, e de até ter criado um minis-

---

10 Mereceria um comentário a precocidade da implantação dos direitos sociais na Alemanha. Como isto foge aos modestos objetivos deste trabalho, veja-se: Moore Jr., B. *Injustiça.* São Paulo: Brasiliense, 1987.

11 Castro, A. Op. cit., p. 19-20.

tério específico para tanto apelidado de "o ministério da Revolução", só em 1932 o governo federal começou a atacar a questão dos acidentes de trabalho.

Para tanto foi criada uma comissão presidida por Evaristo de Morais, que baseada em um projeto de lei de Afrânio Peixoto, apresentado à Câmara em 1927 e acoplando um antiprojeto apresentado pelas companhias seguradoras, foi transformado no Decreto n.º 24.637 — a nova lei brasileira de acidentes do trabalho.

Vista a trajetória de criação das duas leis cabe uma comparação sumária. A lei de 1919 foi elaborada numa conjuntura em que o movimento operário-sindical estava em ascensão, no Brasil e no mundo. Já a lei de 1934 não. Ela veio como resultado de uma *Comissão Técnica,* que resgatou uma parcela do debate legislativo sobre a questão dos acidentes e o articulou às demandas da fração burguesa ligada ao negócio do seguro, materializando no seu ponto de chegada em um meio termo neutro.

Essa nova maneira de fazer política social estava visceralmente ligada à expansão do poder executivo que houve sob o governo Vargas, dentro de sua lógica mais geral, que desembocou no "fascismo pelo alto" do Estado Novo. Como indicou um importante estudioso da questão previdenciária no Brasil:

> "A presença do Estado autoritário frente a uma sociedade civil impotente [...] seria a estrutura permanente, própria e específica dos países do capitalismo tardio. As políticas sociais apareceriam como obra e formulação do Executivo."[12]

A criação das leis sobre os acidentes do trabalho no Brasil tem, a partir de 1919 uma dimensão econômica que merece ser ressaltada. Ao criar mecanismos legais para a indenização dos sinistrados, o seguro de acidentes do trabalho transformou-se em mais um mecanismo de capitalização da fração burguesa, que opera este mercado, visto que, com o seguro, o acidente metamorfoseou-se em mercadoria, tornando-se a partir de então parte do circuito capitalista[13].

O seguro institucionalizava o acidente. A partir de então os tra-

---

12 Faleiros, Vicente P. *A Política do Trabalho.* São Paulo: Cortez, p. 23.

13 Idem, p. 57 e ss.

balhadores buscariam auferir a maior indenização possível pelo seu infortúnio. Já os capitalistas, em particular a fração ligada ao negócio dos seguros, buscaria reduzir o valor dos prêmios e apelaria aos industriais e trabalhadores para a adoção de medidas que previnam o acidente.

Ainda que no Estado Novo este apelo tenha ficado para as calendas, ele denotava uma sintonia com as políticas de seguros então implementadas na Europa e nos EUA. Em meio a essa luta apareceram os burocratas do MTIC que iriam envidar esforços para estatizar o mercado de seguros.

No Brasil, o ramo de seguros de acidentes do trabalho surgiu impulsionado pela Lei de 1919. No Rio de Janeiro, a companhia que trata da cobertura aos trabalhadores têxteis existe desde 1924. Trata-se da já citada S.C.O.F.T.-RJ.

O patronato têxtil interessava-se em manter uma companhia seguradora, pois, além do negócio do seguro possibilitar uma via alternativa de acumulação no maior ramo industrial do País, as companhias eram restituídas dos excessos das taxas — restituição esta que, ao final do exercício, era repartida entre a empresa seguradora e a segurada. Representava uma vantagem econômica a partir de uma lei social. É dentro deste quadro que podemos entender a manutenção do seguro de acidentes do trabalho, ao longo do 1.º Governo Vargas, que na feliz expressão de Sonia Draibe promoveu a "estatização dos conflitos".

Apesar de alguns percalços, depois de promulgada a Lei de 1934, a sua regulamentação até estimulou a formação de sociedades cooperativas pelos sindicatos patronais. Além disto, foi instalada a 1.ª Câmara da Comissão Permanente de Tarifas, que reduziu nas suas atividades as taxas dos prêmios para tipos de sinistros, acabando deste modo um problema que existia à época que era o valor do teto dos seguros.

Ao se reduzir o valor do prêmio para atender os reclamos patronais, na prática reduziu-se o valor atribuído ao corpo e à vida dos operários, já que, entre prêmio e risco, deve existir uma dependência rigorosa. Nas condições de funcionamento da indústria têxtil já mencionadas, e com o ritmo produtivo ascendendo, as conseqüências desta medida eram óbvias.

Vencidas as resistências e equacionados os problemas, as cooperativas de seguros de acidentes de trabalho, criadas a partir da iniciativa patronal, corresponderiam, na conjuntura estudada, a uma forma de regulação da disputa intercapitalista. Visando distribuir os custos do sinistro, cumpriam também a função de regulação, dentro do esforço de cooptação dos trabalhadores no contexto do Estado novo.

Além disso, o desenvolvimento da atividade seguradora proporcionou uma aliança entre o capital industrial e o capital financeiro, pois, como indica Faleiros, esta junção acaba. "[...] mediatizando o sistema de indenizações e [provocando] a monetização da perda da capacidade de trabalho."[14]

Se atentarmos para alguns dados do período, veremos a expressão da consolidação das cooperativas de seguros de acidentes do trabalho. No ano de 1940, no Distrito Federal, de um total de 48 instituições que trabalhavam com seguros de acidentes do trabalho, apenas três eram administradas por órgãos de trabalhadores, feita a ressalva de que duas destas eram de operários ligados à atividade portuária, que têm uma relação peculiar com a compra e venda da força de trabalho. O único órgão trabalhista *tout court* era o ligado aos metalúrgicos. Os demais 45 órgãos eram divididos em trinta companhias privadas, seis caixas e nove cooperativas, todas patronais.

Números do *Resumo do Movimento Industrial do Brasil no ano de 1940* indicam o montante dos prêmios recebidos pelas 44 companhias que operavam no setor na ordem de 123.412.289.000 (réis), já abatidos os estornos. O resultado industrial ficou no montante de 31.894.980$000 (réis). Tratava-se de números bastante expressivos.

Vejamos agora as condições e as repercussões do acidente no processo do trabalho propriamente dito. Na conjuntura específica do Estado Novo, com os altos índices de produção da indústria têxtil, seriam maiores as probabilidades de acidente. Contudo, seria exclusivamente o aumento do ritmo de trabalho a variável central ou exclusiva para se entender o aumento do sinistro fabril?

Entretanto, como indica o sociólogo italiano F. Ferraroti[15], o acidente na fábrica tem uma dimensão política. E é justamente esta dimensão que buscamos resgatar ao longo do Estado Novo, na indústria têxtil em particular.

---

[14] Faleiros, Op. cit., p. 74.

[15] Cf. Ferraroti, Franco. *Uma Sociologia Alternativa.* Porto: Afrontamento. 1976.

Já existe um razoável consenso de que o Primeiro Governo Vargas foi marcado por um reforço da ideologia do trabalho no Brasil. Ao mesmo tempo em que se iniciava o processo de substituição de importações de modo decisivo e que se implantavam as indústrias de base, a época Vargas foi marcada por um esforço de nobilitação do trabalho. No Estado Novo até sambas foram modificados sob orientação do DIP (Departamento de Imprensa e Propaganda), para que o bonde de São Januário — linha proletária do Distrito Federal — deixasse de levar mais um "otário" e passasse a levar mais um operário, empolgado, para ir trabalhar.

Esse movimento de idéias reflete a consolidação da divisão organizada do trabalho, o aumento da força produtiva do capital, que, dirigida pela fração industrial da burguesia iria, sob o Estado Novo, impulsionar o confinamento dos operários às operações paralisadas do processo de trabalho, que no seu limite apontam para o embotamento das possibilidades humanas.

Sem embargo, a dominação do capital sobre o trabalho não pode chegar ao limite de aniquilar o termo mais fraco da relação, por maior que seja a degradação. O trabalhador se porta na sua relação com o capital, procurando afirmar-se como individualidade, ainda que esta afirmação seja limitada, em algumas conjunturas, por uma brutal coerção estatal. Por conseguinte, a resistência à exploração na indústria têxtil manifestar-se-ia de formas variadas e no padrão das relações coercitivas a que a conjuntura política estava submetendo o trabalho.

Nesta conjunção de aspectos, a eclosão do acidente pode ser pensada como uma expressão limite de um conflito de subjetividades, e manifestação de não-adesão ao projeto burguês de construção do capitalismo. Até porque o acidente, monetizado e integrado ao circuito capitalista, já tinha sido envolvido pelo "toque de Midas" do capitalismo e se transformado em mercadoria.

A oposição do trabalhador ao capital, num quadro fascista de desorganização da ação sindical autônoma, apareceria no ato da resistência individual, pelo qual o trabalhador procura se auto-reconhecer como sujeito e busca modificar a situação que lhe é impingida. Solitária ou grupal, o importante a destacar é o significado deste ato como manifestação de subjetividade em conflito, e que ele por si só traz embutido o potencial da mudança.

Isto é tanto mais verdadeiro que o patronato e os dirigentes das companhias de seguro, particularmente, iriam, ao término do Estado Novo, liderar um movimento para a prevenção do acidente do trabalho. Será que a única leitura desta atitude está inscrita nos cálculos da racionalidade econômica?!

A dúvida será tanto mais pertinente se levarmos em consideração que no período em tela o Estado iria referendar políticas organizacionais do trabalho que, ao "chão da fábrica", vão procurar impedir a manifestação do conflito, utilizando-se para isto do poder que a organização tem no mando da direção do trabalho. Essas atitudes visavam em última instância impedir, ou dificultar ao máximo, a construção de qualquer solidariedade interclassista na linha de produção.

A afirmativa feita acima fica mais clara se observarmos o que os contemporâneos consideraram um grande avanço: a equiparação, para efeitos do seguro, das tecnopatias aos acidentes. Para a materialização de tal ato foi feita uma normalização detalhadíssima, que acabou restringindo o alcance da equiparação. Moléstias como a pneumonia e a tuberculose só seriam consideradas doenças profissionais se aparecessem logo após um acidente. E mesmo assim se se pudesse estabelecer uma relação clara com um choque, posto que: "[...] um operário recebe um choque no tórax, não escarra sangue, não vai para a cama, retoma seu trabalho após oito dias de repouso e trabalha com boa saúde durante um ano, se no fim desse tempo ele vem a ser atingido de tuberculose, a relação causa e efeito será bem duvidosa."[16]

Ao desconsiderar, no caso da pneumonia e no da tuberculose, os fatores sócio-ambientais incidentes, que propiciam que essas moléstias se manifestem deflagradas pela atividade produtiva, fica a indagação de se a extensa normalização que se seguiu à lei de 1939 não embutia uma ação do Estado voltada para dirimir os conflitos por via técnica, e garantir, ao seu final, a limitação da legislação trabalhista, cuja a suspensão na aplicação dos conceitos da CLT, no período do "esforço de guerra", era o exemplo mais emblemático.

Só nesta clave é possível entender as restrições ao enquadramento da pneumonia e tuberculose como doenças profissionais. Naquele tempo já havia todo um saber médico que relacionava a existência destas doenças a fatores como fadiga, má-alimentação etc... Restrições da mesma ordem iriam limitar o pagamento do seguro ao operário acometido de "afecções nervosas". Os normalizadores aler-

---

[16] Castro, A. Op. cit., p. 125.

tavam os peritos para que tivessem especial atenção de modo a impedir que perturbações mentais advindas do "alcoolismo" ou de "excessos venéreos" sejam interpretadas como tecnopatias e o seguro seja pago.

Ao lado das limitações para o pagamento dos seguros às tecnopatias, os seguradores e seus normalizadores dedicaram especial atenção à chamada *sinistrose*. Esta afecção nervosa em particular não devia ser reconhecida como doença profissional, já que havia o temor que o seu reconhecimento referendasse um instrumento de manifestação do trabalho contra o capital.

Segundo o discurso patronal a *sinistrose* não passava de um trauma inventado. Já que na linha de interpretações das tecnopatias havia uma disjunção entre trauma físico e trauma psicológico, que se encontra na base do caráter restritivo que orienta a interpretação das moléstias profissionais. Nas palavras de Araújo Castro:

> "Considere-se [...] que o acidente consiste apenas em traumatismo localizado, como o esmagamento do pé ou da mão, sem nenhuma repercussão no sistema nervoso."[17]

Todos os elementos apontados concorrem para a resposta da questão central deste trabalho. Qual o significado do acidente?

Marx, ao estudar o processo de trabalho na indústria, ressaltava a atuação *política* da maquinaria que, posta pelo capitalista em ação, leva à realização de uma sofreguidão inesgotável do capital sobre o trabalho. O limite — e o acidente talvez possa ser entendido em conjunturas especiais como este limite — existe porque: na maquinaria se autonomizam o movimento e a atividade operativa do meio de trabalho face ao operário. Torna-se em si e para si um *perpetuum mobile* industrial, que iria produzir ininterruptamente, caso não se chocasse com certas limitações naturais em seus auxiliares humanos, na sua fraqueza corpórea e sua vontade própria."[18]

Nossa proposição é a de que, sob o Estado Novo, a ocorrência do sinistro fabril na indústria têxtil estava vinculada a situações além da fadiga provocada pela atividade laboral. Incorporando-a, nesta ocasião, o acidente junge fadiga e "vontade própria". Certa-

---

[17] Idem, p. 137.

[18] Marx, K. *O Capital*. Livro I, vol. 1, tomo 2, cap. III, p. 28-29.

mente esta é uma proposição polêmica. Portanto, esclarecemos que nosso conceito de "vontade própria" está iluminado pelas reflexões da chamada "teoria marxista da subjetividade"[19], que trabalha com o marxismo numa perspectiva que procura superar o conhecimento das condições contraditórias e objetivas do sistema capitalista. Seu horizonte é o vir-a-ser humano, apreendido mediante a crítica da divisão do trabalho.

A "vontade própria", para afirmar-se, deve ser vista menos como um ato mecânico, e sim como uma ação do trabalhador que sob determinadas condições conjunturais, dá ao seu ato uma base emocional. No Estado Novo, o que se estabeleceu como política do trabalho, e atingiu a indústria têxtil, foi a tensão entre a ilusão criada pela "ideologia da outorga" que cobrava dos trabalhadores a sua contrapartida de colaboração pela "dádiva" das leis do trabalho, e a resistência humana mesmo às condições materiais de realização do trabalho fabril têxtil, durante aquele período.

Sem embargo, se conseguirmos entender a ilusão[20] pelo prisma do imaginário, que é ao nosso entendimento a melhor entrada para a elucidação da idéia de "vontade própria", estaremos superando a oposição entre imaginário e real, e operando na clave que distingue imaginário eficiente e imaginário deficiente. O imaginário, portanto, é ilusão; contudo, para satisfazer um *desejo* pode ser bem sucedido ou não.

Imaginário, desejo, ilusão... Certamente esses termos soam um tanto estranhos em trabalhos de história econômica. Para um melhor entendimento, aclaremos as bases teóricas em que navegamos.

Estamos tratando da convergência metodológica entre Freud e Marx[21]. Os dois pensadores têm pontos de convergência, na medida que, enquanto o primeiro busca encontrar nas motivações do inconsciente o elemento subjetivo da adesão, o segundo busca a origem social desta mesma adesão, isto é, das ideologias. Nas palavras de M. Bertrand: "O valor do discurso reside não no que ele diz, mas no que faz ao dizê-lo."[22]

---

[19] Ibidem.

[20] Doray, Bernard & Silveira, Paulo (orgs.) *Elementos para uma Teoria Marxista da Subjetividade.* São Paulo: Vértice. 1989, p. 11-2.

[21] Idem, p. 27.

[22] Idem, p. 34.

Neste contexto, o acidente, vislumbrado como manifestação de "vontade própria" encontra seu nexo mediante os efeitos que produz ao nível do simbólico, posto que o real é o único acesso ao simbólico, mediante a passagem pelo imaginário. O imaginário como pista de elucidação da "vontade própria" deve ser acompanhado pelas indicações que a alienação provoca a partir do processo de trabalho, sendo, em última instância, esta a detonadora de todo o processo. A alienação em sua dimensão ontológica é resultado de um contínuo empobrecimento do trabalhador e correlata acumulação de capital, ocorrida no processo de trabalho. O empobrecimento se dá não somente do ponto de vista material, mas também e sobretudo do ponto de vista espiritual.

Num mundo em que a realidade aparece coisificada e as relações em geral têm por parâmetro a *troca de coisas*, mediatizada pela mercadoria universal, dinheiro; neste ambiente o acidente emerge pois "[...] sob o regime do capital, o homem não só é separado da natureza, de seu corpo inorgânico, mas das condições que faziam com que a sociabilidade na história aparecesse como uma dimensão da própria natureza."[23] No capitalismo, como a mercadoria força de trabalho, composta de carne, músculos e nervos é fetichizada como as demais mercadorias, vislumbra-se a possibilidade do acidente, já transformado em mercadoria, assumir uma dimensão que transcenda o plano exclusivo de ser provocado pela fadiga ou más condições de trabalho.

Essa transcendência era a manifestação da "vontade própria" na conjuntura fascista do Estado Novo. Uma afirmação-limite da humanidade do trabalho, contra a lógica avassaladora do capital. Ao mesmo tempo em que se manifestava — seja como "vontade própria" ou não — o acidente era capturado pela sua transformação em mercadoria no negócio do seguro, limitando assim o seu potencial de revolta.

Não obstante, alguns parcos exemplos conseguem ser no período em tela a "negação da negação", o avesso do avesso.

No ano de 1941, um artigo publicado na *Revista de Seguros* alertava as pessoas envolvidas no ramo de acidentes de trabalho, para as artimanhas utilizadas por trabalhadores na burla à norma de pagamento de seguros, fato que, se continuado, afetaria a lucrativi-

---

[23] Idem, p. 35.

dade do ramo. O alerta objetivava em particular as liquidações por invalidez permanente, que no ano de 1940 haviam provocado uma sangria nos lucros da ordem de 2.555.440$400 (réis).

Os motivos deste prejuízo, segundo o alerta era a baixa tecnicalidade dos peritos das seguradoras pois: "[...] a perícia médica não raro é influenciada também por esse espírito humanitário — que é um dos traços fundamentais de nossa raça — pelo que os laudos concluem muitas vezes por verdadeiros exageros."[24] O problema em pauta era a equiparação comumente feita entre perda de função e perda anatômica de um órgão, algo que o autor do artigo considerava uma aberração.

Como exemplo citava o caso de um jovem entregador de mercadorias, que após ser atropelado com sua bicicleta, sofreu escoriações de pequena monta, mas uma forte contusão em seu braço direito, porém sem fratura.

> "Submetido ao mais cuidadoso tratamento [...] ficou com o braço em ângulo e com todos os movimentos quase nulos e a mão respectiva sem pressão."[25]

A perícia emitiu sobre o acidentado o laudo de "perda do braço" dada a inutilidade de que fora acometido o membro. Como reforço dizia o perito acerca do sinistrado: "é um infeliz condenado pela fatalidade do destino a suportar *para sempre* a desdita que o vitimou."[26] A esse comentário, acrescentava o autor do artigo: "Puro sentimentalismo de advogado de defesa, a substituir o frio raciocínio da ciência."

Ocorre que, cerca de três meses após o laudo, o jovem invalidado permanente sofreu uma nova queda, o que segundo ele lhe restituiu os movimentos do braço. Diante deste fato, dizia o autor do alerta: "Em tais casos, a justiça para ser coerente, devia obrigar a ex-vítima a restituir à Seguradora a indenização recebida."[27]

Outro significativo episódio de artimanha do trabalho face ao capital, através da manipulação do seguro, foi relatado poucos me-

---

24 Idem, p. 61.

25 *Revista de Seguros*, "Acidente do Trabalho", n.º 240, jun/1941, p. 312.

26 Idem.

27 Idem, p. 313.

ses depois, no mesmo periódico. O tom do alerta passava agora perto do nível da apoplexia. Tratava-se da queda de um carregador, empregado de uma companhia de navegação, que se tornara inválido permamente.

O sinistro ocorreu quando da descarga de um navio, durante a qual o nosso personagem sofreu uma violenta queda. Desde então passou a queixar-se de fortíssimas dores na coluna vertebral. Passemos a palavra ao próprio autor do artigo:

> "Foi-lhe dispensado todo o tratamento médico, passando então a 'vítima' a sentir-se mais aliviada da dor, mas como tivesse dificuldade de se locomover, passou a fazer uso de muletas. O exame médico constatou que se tinha produzido um deslocamento da coluna vertebral. A empresa responsável, não se conformando com o resultado do exame, tão em desproporção com a natureza da queda, requereu novo exame, com assistência de um de nossos médicos mais renomados e esse novo exame confirmou plenamente o resultado do primeiro."[28]

Ao que parecia, a perícia, desta vez, não tinha falhado e a indenização foi paga.

Trabalhador nacional e migrante, nosso personagem infortunado resolveu voltar para o Norte, sua terra natal, provavelmente à bordo de um dos navios da linha ITA.

> "Já a bordo, e quando o navio começava a se afastar do cais e o farsante recebia da terra o adeus dos amigos que, penalizados, se foram despedir do companheiro, aprumou-se atirando as muletas ao mar, soltou uma gargalhada, gritando para os amigos estupefatos: 'Enganei a todos! Eu não tenho nada!' E principiou a andar desembaraçadamente e pular de contente."[29]

O que teria acontecido? Negligência pericial? Erro médico continuado?

> "Mais tarde é que se soube toda a verdade. O farsante tinha sido, na juventude e durante muitos anos, contorcionista de cir-

---

[28] Ibidem.

[29] Ibidem.

cos, advindo daí o progressivo deslocamento da coluna vertebral."[30]

Mais do que o anterior, este é um caso exemplar da utilização de artimanhas pelos trabalhadores para burlar a lógica do capital no Estado Novo. Se o seguro transforma o acidente em mercadoria, e o seu corpo também o é, há nos casos acima uma manifestação explícita de fuga do encapsulamento advindo da fetichização da mercadoria. Na sua ossatura, estes episódios demonstram que mesmo sob as mais adversas condições políticas há manifestação da humanidade do trabalho frente à lógica do capital, subvertendo-se o seu impulso avassalador.

Numa época de repressão, febre do trabalho e industrialização acelerada, nossos personagens foram a personificação de vitórias isoladas do trabalho diante do capital. Eram indícios, sinais, daquilo que chamei o avesso do avesso, inspirado na bela frase de Caetano. A astúcia do trabalho sobrepujando a tecnologia normativa do capital.

Certamente a classe dominante não aceitou passivamente estas vitórias isoladas do trabalho. Com o fim do Estado Novo e a derrota do fascismo, em um novo ambiente nacional magnificamente sintetizado por Alain Touraine como a "redemocratização pela via autoritária", o mundo do trabalho iria se deparar com a implantação do prevencionismo, das CIPA'S e da psicologia do trabalho, instrumentos de busca de adesão do trabalhador à proposta do capital, manifestação índice de tentar superar o conflito de subjetividades.

Mas, isto já é uma outra história...

---

[30] Ibidem.

IV
INVESTIMENTOS ITALIANOS NA AMÉRICA LATINA

Giandomenico Piluso
Fondazione ASSI, Milano

LE BANCHE MISTE ITALIANE IN SUD AMERICA: STRATEGIE MERCATI E ORGANIZZAZIONI (1906-1933)*

Una storia di *joint-ventures*

L'accesso ai circuiti commerciali e finanziari internazionali e l'elevato grado di apertura e complementarità dell'economia italiana si rivelarono condizioni cruciali di quel processo di transformazione degli assetti produttivi che tra otto e novecento condusse alla formazione della prima base industriale del paese[1]. Le partite attive del commercio estero e le rimesse degli emigrati (come altre voci invisibili della bilancia dei pagamenti) consentirono in larga misura di allentare i vincoli esterni all'industrializzazione. Da questo punto di vista il modello dell'industrializzazione italiana elaborato

---

* Il mio primo ringraziamento va a coloro che hanno aiutato la mia ricerca archivistica: in particolare a Francesca Pino Pongolini della Banca Commerciale Italiana, a Pierre de Longuemar della Banque Paribas, a Ubaldo Sassone del Credito Italiano e a tutto il personale dell'Archivio della Banca d'Italia. Desidero quindi ringraziare per commenti e osservazioni: Franco Amatori, Donato Barbone, Giuseppe Berta, Albert Broder, Roberto Cortés-Conde, Flávio A. de Saes, Peter Hertner, Raúl Jacob, Carlos Marichal, Tamás Szmrecsányi e Mira Wilkins. La responsabilità delle tesi qui esposte — come di eventuali errori e impreciosini — rimane naturalmente dell'autore.

1 Per il modello interpretativo della "via italiana" all'industrializzazione cui si fa riferimento si rimanda ai saggi ora raccolti in L. Cafagna, *Dualismo e sviluppo nella storia d'Italia*, Venezia, 1989, p. 281-371, e alla sintesi di F. Bonelli, *Il capitalismo italiano. Linee generali d'interpretazione*, in *Storia d'Italia, Annali I, Dal feudalesimo al capitalismo*, Torino, 1978, p. 1217-33.

da Bonelli e Cafagna ha l'indubbio pregio di riconoscere i fattori che "bilanciarono" le persistenti insufficienze dell'economia italiana dell'età giolittiana, così come le analisi degli apporti degli imprenditori e dei capitali stranieri mostrando quali fossero le capacità di "ricezione" di risorse esterne da parte dell'economia del paese[2]. La progressiva internazionalizzazione dei settori dinamici dell'economia italiana permise tuttavia di trasporre in termini "attivi" la capacità di assorbire e assimilare — in un contesto generale di arretratezza relativa — le risorse finanziare, tecniche e imprenditoriali provenienti dalle aree europee industriali avanzate. In questa prospettiva L'analisi dei tempi e dei modi dell'internazionalizzazione delle banche miste italiane derebbe modo di comprendere non soltanto quale fosse il grado di interdipendenza dei servizi creditizi del paese rispetto alle economie esterne, ma anche in quale misura gli investimenti diretti all'estero abbiano influito sulle strutture organizzative, sui criteri di gestione aziendale, sulla formazione del management e, in generale, sui processi di apprendimento connessi alla crescita di un settore critico per lo sviluppo industriale di un'economia *late joiner* come quella italiana[3].

Nei primi trent'anni del novecento, nonostante la relativa arretratezza economica del paese e l'iniziale dipendenza da modelli operativi stranieri, le maggiori banche miste italiane realizzarono una estesa rete bancaria multinazionale. I primi mercati esteri in cui le banche miste italiane si mossero furono quelli sudamericani: in Argentina e in Brasile gli istituti di credito italiani poterano conquistare ampie quote di mercato sia perché le comunità degli italiani emigrati representavano una clientela con la quale estabilire rapporti privilegiati sia perché — soprattutto a partire dagli anni dieci — aumentarono i flussi commerciali con l'Italia e acquisirono maggiore consistenza gli investimenti diretti di imprese industriali italiane. Le maggiori banche miste italiane avviarono la propria espansione in Sud America non tanto creando filiali o istituti

---

[2] Si veda P. Hertner, *Il capitale tedesco in ltalia dall'Unità alla prima guerra mondiale,* BoIogna, 1984.

[3] Agli effetti dell'internazionalizzazione sulle strutture aziendali interne delle imprese italiane interessate da questo processo accenna anche V. Castronovo, "L'internazionalizzazione dell'industria italiana, una nuova prospettiva", in *L'industria italiana nel mercato mondiale dalla fine dell'800 alla metà dell'900,* Torino, 1993, p. 9-19.

consociati — direttamente dipendenti dalle loro direzioni centrali — quanto piuttosto facendo perno sui rapporti di alleanza che esse intrattenevano con le grandi istituzioni finanziarie europee: si constituirono così istituti a capitale misto (franco-italiano e italo-belga), con sede centrale in Europa e dipendenze in Sud America, secondo un modello organizzativo per certi versi analogo a quello adottato dalle *free-standing companies* britanniche[4].

Dai primi anni del novecento i responsabili della Banca Commerciale Italiana (Comit) e del Credito Italiano (Credit) si impegnarono nell'emulazione dei modelli di investimento diretto *over borders* e di organizzazione delle attività estere di quell'alta banca franco-belga e tedesca nella cui tradizione operativa alcuni di essi si erano formati. L'origine "internazionale" delle due maggiori banche miste italiane avrebbe dettato — con diverse sfumature e secondo originali modalità — lo sviluppo delle loro reti estere almeno fino alla battuta d'arresto verificatasi con la crisi bancaria dei primi anni trenta che portò alla creazione dell'IRI. L'espansione estera dei principali organismi bancari si sarebbe rivelata una "forzatura", seppure in buona misura riuscita, da parte delle banche universali italiane come punte avanzate e dinamiche — aperte ai circuiti finanziari internazionali perché a questi correlate sin dalla loro fase constitutiva — del sistema creditizio italiano. Uno sviluppo dei servizi creditizi che avrebbe accompanato un graduale mutamento dell'offerta dell'economia italiana dai prodotti agroalimentari e tessili verso le produzioni tecnologicamente più complesse della meccanica e della gomma: se da un lato nel primo cinquantennio postunitario l'Italia perse posizioni percentuali nel commercio mondiale (secondo le stime di Paul Bairoch la quota italiana sul totale delle esportazioni europee si contrasse dal 5,1% del 1860 al 4,5% del 1910), dall'altro si assistette a un mutamento della composizione delle esportazioni che presero a interessare sempre meno il settore pimario e sempre più i prodotti del settore secondario e i servizi commercialie finanziari[5].

---

[4] Per la definizione di *free-standing company as a governance structure* cfr. M. Wilkins, "The free-standing company, 1870-1914: an important type of British foreign direct investment". *Economic History Review*, second series, 41 (1988), n. 2, p. 261-4.

[5] Sul commercio estero europeo si veda P. Bairoch, "European Foreign Trade in the XIX Century: The Development of the Value and Volume

L'espansione delle banche miste italiane sui mercati sudamericani si svolse secondo due direttrici di fondo: inserirsi attivamente nel flusso migratorio e in quello degli scambi commerciali da un lato; fornire l'appoggio necessario alle imprese industriali italiane che si impegnavano in investimenti diretti in quelle aree dall'altro. Le strategie di espansione diretta della Comit e del Credit in Sud America furono motivate dall'esigenza di internalizzare alcuni servizi essenziali a coprire quella vasta gamma di lavoro bancario (tesoreria in valuta, cambi, accettazioni sull'estero, ecc.) indispensabile a dare una dimensione completa alle strutture aziendali interne; dall'opportunitá di sviluppare il volume degli affari di banca che offriva la crescita dell'interscambio commerciale e delle operazione dipendenti dai flussi migratori; e dalla necessità di ripartire e rischi degli impieghi attivi mediante una diversificazione degli investimenti su una pluralità di mercati. Internalizzare una parte dei servizi consentiva di ridurre sia i costi di transazione che i conflitti *principal-agent* (passando dal rapporto banca-corrispondente al rapporto banca-consociata). Le modalità specifiche di crescita all'estero adottate dalle maggiori banche miste italiane enfatizzarono la centralità dei *networks* delle alleanze e dei flussi di informazione nelle attività di banca[6].

Sul versante dei vincoli lo sviluppo delle reti estere rientrava nella politica di equilibrio e diversificazione degli investimenti (con la ripartizione dei rischi tra mercato interno e mercati esteri) che avrebbe garantito l'espansione interna. Le operazioni compiute sui mercati esteri da parte delle consociate della Comit e del Credit non erano solo — o lo erano secondariamente (l'eccezione era

---

of Exports (Preliminary Results)". *Journal of European Economic History,* 2 (1973), n. 1. p. 5-36 (per le esportazioni italiane in particolare cfr. la tabella 3, p. 14). Alla fine degli anni venti l'Italia avrebbe esportato in Argentina non solo riso, conserva, olio di oliva, cotonate, seterie, lanerie e marmi, ma anche macchine utensili, macchinari, automobili e pneumatici (importando carni, grassi, pelli, cereali e lane); analogamente in Brasile si sarebbero esportati sia vini, seta tratta e formaggi, sia automobili e macchine (le importazioni riguardavano invece soprattutto il caffè) (cfr. Banca Commerciale Italiana, *Cenni statistici sul movimento economico dell'Italia,* Milano, 1929, p. 340 e 342).

[6] Su questi temi cfr. M. Casson, "Evolution of multinational banks: a theoretical perspective", in *Banks as Multinationals,* a cura di G. Jones, London-New York, 1990, p. 15-7.

constituita dalle filiali di Londra e Parigi) — operazione di *international banking* (operazioni valutarie, classamento di titoli pubblici, ecc.) per cui in genere si manteneva la partecipazione diretta ai sindacati bancari internazionali imperniati sui *networks* tradizionali. Sotto il profilo operativo gli istituti consociati e compartecipati delle banche miste italiane attivi in Sud America erano tendenzialmente polifunzionali senza assumere tuttavia i tratti tipici della banca mista: la raccolta di risorse era assicurata in parte dall'estesa rete territoriale delle dispendenze e in parte dal ricorso ai mercati interbancari europei (e a quelli interni ai gruppi di appartenenza); le attività rendevano questi instituti assimilabili alla banca commerciale (soprattutto per il finanziamento dell'import-export) e alla banca d'affari (per gli appoggi creditizi formiti alle imprese industriali italiane presenti in quei mercati).

La soluzione organizzativa adottata per espandersi sui mercati sudamericani permise agli istituti di credito italiani di affermarsi in cui fino ad allora erano state di gran lunga predominanti le *overseas banks* britanniche e tedesche: gli istituti italiani dovettero individuare vantaggi competitivi specifici-diversi da quelli propri dei *first comers* inglesi e tedeschi appartenenti a sistemi finanziari e industriali avanzati — tali da rendere la loro espansione concretamente possibile in quei mercati[7]. In questa prospettiva, in Sud America le banche miste italiane adottarono di volta in volta strategie collaborative o competitive in base alle caratteristiche specifiche dei diversi mercati creditizi — in particolare queli brasiliano, argentino e uruguayano — in cui seppero inserirsi con successo sottraendo consistenti quote di mercato ai *first comers*.

L'espansione degli investimenti bancari italiani in Sud America passò attraverso due distinte fasi di sviluppo: *a)* nella fase prebellica la Comit e il Credit si mossero mutuando um modello organizzativo incentrato sulla *partnership* con le banche europee alleate, e i mercanti sudamericani costituirono l'area privilegiata della loro espancione all'estere (1906-1914); *b)* nella fase postbellica gli istituti milanesi acquisirono la maggioranza del capitale delle banche comparte-

[7] Cfr. D. Joslin, A *Century of Banking in Latin America*, London, 1963, p. 29-84; G. Jones, *British Multinational Banking 1830-1990*, Cambridge, 1993, p. 24-5; P. Hertner, "German banks abroad before 1914", in *Banks as Multinationals* cit., p. 102-7.

cipate che operavano in Sud America e sovrapposero al modello della partecipazione azionaria in *pool* una vera e propria struttura bancaria multinazionale: in particolare la Comit sviluppò la propria rete estera mediante la creazione di un gruppo bancario multinazionale presente non solo in Sud America, in Francia e in Gran Bretagna (Londra), ma anche negli Stati Uniti (New York, Boston e Philadelphia), nell' Europa danubiano-balcanica (Polonia, Cecoslovacchia, Bulgaria, Romania e Jugoslavia) e nell'area mediterranea e medio-orientale (Tunisia, Turchia, Grecia ed Egitto); il Credit preferì invece consolidare la propria rete multinazionale — una strutura di minori dimensioni — che si estendeva in Gran Bretagna, Francia, Jugoslavia, Turchia e Sud America (1915-1933). I tentativi di penetrazione nei mercati sudamericani — in Brasile e in Argentina — compiuti dal Banco di Roma e dalla Banca Italiana di Sconto nell'immediato primo dopoguerra naufragarono invece incagliandosi subito nella grave crisi di liquidità che in quegli stessi anni interessò questi due istituti[8].

L'ingresso delle banche miste italiane nei mercati sudamericani (1905-1914)

I responsabili delle maggiori banche miste italiane — la Comit e il Credit — iniziarono a considerare l'opportunità di estendere ai mercati esteri una diretta presenza dei propri istituti tra il 1905 e il 1906. Il dibattito che si svolse ai vertici delle banche miste milanesi riguardò sia le aree geografiche di possibile interesse che le soluzioni organizzative da adottare. I consiglieri di amministrazione della Comit e del Credit indicarono, sin dall'inizio, come zone di una eventuale espansione all'estero dei loro istituti — oltre all'Egitto e alla Turchia — l'Argentina e il Brasile[9]. Ai primi del 1906 la Comit inviò in Argentina e in Brasile il direttore centrale Louis Dapples

---

[8] Cfr. A. Confalonieri, *Banca e industria in Italia dalla crisi del 1907 all'agosto 1914,* Milano, 1982, vol. I, p. 393-406. Una prima ricostruzione in G. Piluso, "Le banche miste sui mercati esteri: strategie e modelli di una multinazionalizzazione", in *Giornata di studio in onore di Antonio Confalonieri,* Torino, 1994.

[9] Cfr. A. Confalonieri, *Banca e industria in Italia dalla crisi del 1907* cit., vol. I, p. 305-8.

con l'obiettivo di acquisire informazioni sulle effettive opportunità di sviluppo offerte da quei mercati sotto il profilo dell'incremento delle attività bancarie. Al ritorno di Dapples dal Sud America la Comit assunse il pacchetto azionario di controllo del Banco Commerciale Italiano di São Paulo, un istituto particolarmente attivo con la comunità italiana che era stato fondato sei anni prima da Giuseppe Puglisi Carboni e da un gruppo di imprenditori di origine italiana[10].

I vertici della Comit individuarono così nel Sud America un'area strategica di potenziale sviluppo delle attività bancarie estere dell'istituto. Nel Cono Sur — Brasile, Argentina e Uruguay — si concentravano le comunità di emigrati italiani di insediamento più consolidato e — come aveva notato pochi anni prima Luigi Einaudi — verso quell'area si indirizzavano consistenti flussi non soltanto migratori ma anche commerciali e finanziari: dalla fine dell'ottocento ai mercati sudamericani era rivolta una quota crescente delle esportazioni italiane (il 2,4% nel 1880, il 7,2% nel 1900 e l'11,6% nel 1910) (cfr. la tabella 1)[11].

Oltre ad assorbire consistenti flussi migratori e commerciali, il Brasile e l'Argentina avevano visto formarsi un vero e proprio "subsistema" creditizio etnicamente connotato. Tra la fine dell'ottocento e l'inizio del novecento mercanti e banchieri italiani avevano cos-

---

[10] Cfr. Archivio storico Banca Commerciale Italiana, Milano (AS BCI), Rb, 28 marzo 1907, p. 10-1; A. Confalonieri, *Banca e industria in Italia (1894-1906)*, Bologna, 1980, vol. III, p. 40; M. Marianno, *Sudameris Brasil. 80 anos de trabalho*, São Paulo, 1991, p. 19-21. Louis Dapples, nato a Genova nel 1867, era figlio di un banchiere di origine vodese. A partire dal 1888 Dapples aveva trascorso quindici anni presso la sede di Londra del Crédit Lyonnais, di cui era divenuto in breve vicedirettore; diventato direttore centrale della Comit, dal 1906 trascorse molti anni in Brasile e Argentina alla direzione di Sudameris. Nel 1922 venne chiamato dalla Nestlé per attuarvi una riorganizzazione (cfr. Jean Heer, *Nestlé. Centoventicinque anni dal 1866 al 1991*, Vevey, 1991, p. 128-9). Tra i fondatori del Banco Commerciale Italiano figuravano anche altri imprenditori italiani attivi sulla piazza paulistana: Francisco Matarazzo, Mariano Gatti, Emidio Falchi (Chocolates Falchi) ed Egidio Pinotti Gamba (Grandes Moinhos Gamba) (cfr. J. de Souza Martins, *Conde Matarazzo. O empresário e a empresa*, São Paulo, 1976, p. 32-3).

[11] Cfr. P. Bairoch, "Geographical Structure and Trade Balance of European Foreign Trade from 1800 to 1970", *Journal of European Economic History*, 3 (1974), n. 3, p. 571, table 3, e 573, table 5.

tituito organismi bancari in Brasile e in Argentina con l'obiettivo di assicurarsi le operazioni connesse alle transazioni commerciali con l'Italia e alle attività imprenditoriali promosse da emigrati italiani sui mercati sudamericani. In Argentina, oltre al Banco de Italia y Rio de la Plata di Buenos Aires (1872) promosso da Antonio Devoto e da alcune banche italiane (la Banca di Genova, il Banco di Depositi e Sconti e il Banco Italico), operava il Nuevo Banco Italiano (1887), con filiali a Milano e a Genova. In Brasile vennero via costituiti il Banco Italo-Brasileiro (1891), il Banco Italiano di Campinas (1899), il Banco de Câmbio Italo-Paulista (1899), Banco de Crédito Italiano (1899), il Banco Italo-Popular (1901), la Casa Bancária Italiana (1901) e il Banco Commerciale Italiano di São Paulo (1904)[12].

Tabella 1
Il commercio italiano con l'Argentina e con il Brasile (1909-1931) (in milioni di lire correnti)

	1909-1913*		1918		1925		1931	
	a	b	a	b	a	b	a	b
Totale generale	3.419	2.212	14.102	2.483	26.200	18.274	9.340	7.953
Argentina	129	167	1.493	99	1.370	1.145	564	689
Brasile	47	39	234	44	487	326	231	99
Totale	176	206	1.727	143	1.857	1.471	795	788
%	5,4	9,3	12,2	5,7	7,0	8,0	8,5	9,9

* media annua; a: importazioni; b: esportazioni.
Fonte: Banca Commerciale Italiana, *Cenni statistici sul movimento economico dell'Italia,* Milano, 1919, p. 199-200; Id., *Movimento economico dell'Italia,* Milano, 1929, p. 339; Id., *Movimento economico dell'Italia,* Milano, 1932, p. 523.

Attraverso il Banco Commerciale Italiano, i responsabili della Comit potevano quindi contare sulle concrete opportunità di inserimento su nuovi mercati offerte dalla conoscenza diretta delle economie e dei sistemi creditizi locali e sui legami preferenziali che avrebbero potuto stringere con le numerose colonie degli emigrati italiani presenti in Brasile — "assai numerose ed attive in ogni cam-

[12] Sulle banche "italiane" costituite in Brasile cfr. F. A. de Saes, *Crédito e Bancos no Desenvolvimento da Economia Paulista 1850-1930,* São Paulo, 1986, p. 101-2 e 211-4. Cfr. inoltre L. Einaudi, *Un principe mercante. Studio sulla espansione coloniale italiana,* Torino, 1900.

po di commercio e di industria e in costanti rapporti colla madre patria" —, colonie che costituivano il riferimento sicuro di uno sviluppo estero dell'istituto[13].

Durante il 1906 il Banco Commerciale Italiano mutò la propria denominazione in Banco Commerciale Italo-Brasiliano e portò il capitale sociale da 2.000 a 5.000 contos: in questa occasione la Comit entrò nella compagine proprietaria. Alla direzione Dapples venne affiancato dallo stesso Puglisi, che ben conosceva il mercato paulista, da Edmond Wright e da Davide Canepa (quest'ultimo proveniva dalla direzione centrale di Milano)[14]. Tra il 1906 e il 1910 l'appoggio fornito dalla Comit — la quale prestò le garanzie necessarie per l'apertura di crediti sulle piazze di Parigi, Londra e Amburgo — consentì al Banco Commerciale Italo-Brasiliano di sviluppare la propria attività bancaria e di consolidare nel contempo il capitale sociale mediante una politica di non distribuzione dei dividendi e di contestuale aumento delle riserve: provvedimenti resi necessari dall'instabilità elevata dei sistemi monetari sudamericani.

Dapples dovette anzitutto intervenire energicamente troncando i rapporti con i clienti meno affidabili e risanando senza esitazioni il portafoglio effetti e crediti. La sistemazione delle partite in sofferenza comportò interventi severi verso le società che erano state create "sotto gli auspici della Banca" e che l'istituto aveva sorretto

---

13 AS BCI, Comit, Rb, 28 marzo 1907, p. 10. Sulle comunità italiane in Brasile e in Argentina cfr. E. Scarzanella, *Italiani d'Argentina. Storie di contadini, industriali e missionari italiani in Argentina, 1850-1912*, Venezia, 1983, p. 25-70; D. von Delhaes-Guenther, "La colonizzazione italiana nel quadro dell'emigrazione europea verso il Brasile meridionale (1875-1914)", in *Gli italiani fuori d'Italia*, a cura di B. Bezza, Milano, 1983, p. 453-76; E. Scarzanella, "L'industria argentina e gli immigrati italiani: nascita della borghesia industriale bonaerense", idem, p. 583-633. Per un profilo coevo della presenza italiana in Argentina cfr. G. Parisi, *Storia degli italiani nell'Argentina*, Roma, 1907.

14 Cfr. M. Marianno, *Sudameris* cit., p. 21-3. Agli inizi del 1906, Otto Joel aveva espresso a Max Winterfeldt della Berliner Handels-Gesellschaft l'intenzione della Comit di mettere piede stabilmente in Sud America (cfr. A. Confalonieri, *Banca e industria in Italia (1894-1906)*, Bologna, vol. III, 1980, p. 40). Lo sviluppo della rete del Banco Commerciale, Italo-Brasiliano si accordava con quanto sollecitato alcuni anni prima da F. Ugolotti, *Italia e Italiani in Brasile*, São Paulo, 1897, ripreso in L Einaudi, *Un principe mercante* cit., p. 263-4.

mediante anticipi su azioni e scoperti in conto corrente. Alla fine del 1907 Dapples ridusse sensibilmente lo scoperto concesso sui vari conti (da 6 a 2,5 milioni di contos) facendo ricorso — come gli altri istituti europei — ai crediti che si potevano ottenere in Europa presso le banche amiche (in Brasile d'altronde il risconto era completamente escluso). In questi stessi anni il Banco Commerciale Italo-Brasiliano estese la rete delle proprie agenzie a Rio de Janeiro, Santos, Botucatu, Espirito Santo do Pinhal, São Carlos do Pinhal e Ribeirão Preto[15].

Il processo di espansione delle attività bancarie della Comit e del Credit in Sud America si intensificò tuttavia soprattutto a partire dagli anni 1909-1910 quando la dirigenza degli istituti milanesi comprese quali prospettive di sviluppo potesse offrire l'estensione della compartecipazione a organismi bancari appartenenti a sistemi finanziari forti. Le iniziative di carattere bancario più significative prese all'estero prima della guerra dalla Comit e dal Credit portarono infatti le banche milanesi a partecipare a due importanti istituti di credito — con sede sociale e direzione centrale in Europa e succursali e filiali in Sud America — in *partnership* con quelle che erano le maggiori istituzioni finanziarie franco-belghe d'inizio secolo. La scelta da parte dei responsabili della Comit e del Credit di associarsi a partner francesi e belgi rispondeva d'altro canto a quel principio di graduale sostituzione del capitale tedesco che negli affari bancari italiani avrebbe portato in breve tempo a ridimensionare drasticamente il peso degli azionisti tedeschi e austriaci già prima del 1914[16].

Tra il 1909 e il 1910, in accordo con le stime di Louis Dapples, i vertici della Comit avevano infatti considerato opportuno potenziare il Banco Commerciale Italo-Brasiliano secondo un "programma proporzionato alle crescenti esigenze del paese" — la cui economia attraversava l'intenso sviluppo — che tenesse conto delle

---

15 Si veda quanto scrisse Dapples a Cesare Mangili, vicepresidente della Comit, alla fine del 1907 in AS BCI, Carte Otto Joel, cart. 10, fasc. "Mangili Cesare. Corrispondenza con diversi. Dapples Louis", lettera di Dapples a Mangili del 26 dicembre 1907. Sull'espansione delle filiali cfr. M. Marianno, *Sudameris* cit., p. 22-3.

16 Sul rapido declino della presenza del capitale tedesco e austriaco nella compagine proprietaria della Comit cfr. P. Hertner, *Il capitale tedesco in Italia* cit., p. 177-83.

buone relazioni che l'istituto aveva stabilito con le imprese francesi presenti in Brasile[17]. Quest'ultima considerazione aveva suggerito di associare i partner della Banque de Paris et des Pays Bas (Paribas) all'organizzazione bancaria sviluppata dalla Comit in Brasile. Nel 1906, Paribas aveva d'altro canto inviato in Sud America un alto funzionario, Paul Rengnet, il quale si era convinto che le prospettive di sviluppo delle economie sudamericane rendessero concretamente possibile l'ingresso di nuovi soggetti su mercati marginali, come quello argentino, che l'anno precedente avevano dato alle banche europee discreti dividendi (mediamente superiori al 9%). Nel 1907 il direttore generale di Paribas Joseph Henri Thors aveva compiuto a sua volta un lungo viaggio in Sud America: due anni dopo il consiglio di amministrazione di Paribas aveva costituito un apposito comitato incaricato di porre le basi per la creazione di una banca consociata in Brasile[18].

Tramite il direttore dello stesso Banco Commerciale Italo-Brasiliano furono così avviate trattative con Paribas — che era a sua volta rappresentata nel consiglio di amministrazione della Comit da Edouard Noetzlin, Albert Turrettini e Joseph Henri Thors —, proponendo di liquidare l'istituto italo-brasiliano (le cui attività furono complessivamente valutate in 10 milioni di franchi) e di costituire quindi un nuovo organismo con sede a Parigi: la Banque Française et Italienne pour l'Amérique du Sud (Sudameris). La scelta della sede parigina doveva servire a porre la direzione della banca in diretto contatto con una delle principali piazze finanziarie in-

---

17 Sulla marcata accelerazione della crescita economica brasiliana negli anni 1903-1913 — dovuto ai mutamenti strutturali consentiti dalla realizzazione delle infrastrutture (porti e ferrovie), dall'importazione di beni strumentali e dall'aumento del prezzo del caffè dopo il 1909 — cfr. W. Cano, *Raízes da Concentração Industrial em São Paulo,* São Paulo, 1990, p. 140-56. Sul ruolo dei capitali stranieri nell'industrializzazione brasiliana cfr. S. Topik, "Capital estrangeiro e o Estado no sistema bancário brasileiro, 1889-1930". *Revista Brasileira de Mercado de Capitais,* 5 (1979), n. 15, p. 395-421; e, infine, F. A. de Saes & T. Szmrecsányi, *The Role of Foreign Banks in the Early Industrialization of São Paulo 1880-1930,* 1993, mimeo, p. 1-8.

18 Cfr. Archives historiques Banque Paribas, Paris (AH BP), conteneur 252, dossier 27, "Argentine", P. Rengnet, *Rapport sur la fondation d'une banque en Argetine,* 17 giugno 1906; e idem, Paribas, Cda, 30 aprile 1907 e 9 novembre 1909.

ternazionali, una piazza finanziaria particolarmente importante sia per gli istituti di credito che per i titoli pubblici italiani. Alla costituzione nel maggio 1910, il capitale sociale di 25 milioni di franchi di Sudameris venne sottoscritto per metà dalla Comit e dai suoi "amici Italiani e Brasiliani" (la Banca Zaccaria Pisa, la casa bancaria privata Marsaglia, gli eredi Balduino e il gruppo di azionisti italo-brasiliani capeggiato da Giuseppe Puglisi Carboni) e per metà da Paribas e dal suo gruppo (Société Générale, Ernest Cassel, Kuhn Loeb and Co. e Warburg and Co.)[19].

Alla vigilia della prima guerra mondiale i sistemi finanziari sudamericani erano ancora caratterizzati da una consistente presenza su quei mercati degli istituti di credito stranieri: secondo una stima del Department of Commerce statunitense nel 1913 le banche straniere raccoglievano il 40% dei depositi complessivi del mercato brasiliano, il 33% di quello uruguayano e il 28% di quelli argentino e cileno. La relativa debolezza delle banche sudamericane lasciava ampi margini di intervento da parte degli istituti finanziari europei e statunitensi. Le banche d'oltremare britanniche e tedesche si erano specializzate nelle operazioni di finanziamento dei commerci internazionali (la London and River Plate Bank sosteneva l'esportazione di carne argentina), di collocamento delle emissioni di titoli pubblici, delle società di pubblici servizi costituite in Sud America (ferrovie, gas, elettricità) e delle filiali locali delle imprese industriali europee (come le tedesche Siemens e AEG che erano appoggiate dalla Deutsche Überseeische Bank e dalla Deutsch-Südamerikanische Bank)[20].

---

19 Cfr. A. Confalonieri, *Banca e industria in Italia dalla crisi del 1907* cit., vol. I, p. 399-403; M. Marianno, *Sudameris* cit., p. 29-30. Sui rapporti di Paribas con Ernest Cassel, i Warburg e la Kuhn & Loeb cfr. E. Bussière, *Paribas 1872-1992. L'Europe et le monde,* Antwerp, 1992, p. 45-9. Sulle relazioni tra i Warburg e la Kuhn & Loeb cfr. R. Chernow, *I Warburg,* Milano, 1993, p. 152-84.

20 Si vedano le stime riportate in W. Lough, *Banking Opportunities in South America,* Department of Commerce, Special Agents Series, 106, Washington D.C., 1915, p. 66, e riprese in C. Marichal, *El nacimiento de la banca mexicana en el contexto latinoamericamo: problemas de periodización,* in *Banca y poder en México (1800-1925),* a cura di L. Ludlow & C. Marichal, México-Barcelona-Buenos Aires, 1986, p. 256-7. Si rimanda inoltre alle osservazioni di D. J. Joslin, *A Century of Banking in Latin America* cit., p. 96-112.

L'ingresso della Comit nei mercati brasiliani con l'acquisizione del controllo del Banco Commerciale Italo-Brasiliano che era stato costituito sei anni prima proprio in considerazione delle opportunità offerte dalle attività economiche degli emigrati italiani si collocò in una fase di intenso sviluppo del sistema bancario brasiliano. Nel decennio precedente la prima guerra mondiale alle banche straniere attive in Brasile dagli anni sessanta e ottanta dell'ottocento — la London and Brazilian Bank (1862), la British Bank of South America (1863), la Brasilianische Bank für Deutschland (1888), la London and River Plate Bank (1891) e la Banque Française du Brésil (1897) — si affiancarono infatti altri istituti europei: la Banque Belge des Prêts Fonciers (1900), il Banco Alliança (1906), il Banco Español del Rio de la Plata (1907), la Deutsch-Südamerikanische Bank (1912) e la Deutsche Überseeische Bank (1912)[21].

Inserendosi dinamicamente nella fase di marcata accelerazione della crescita industriale dello Stato di São Paulo, Sudameris si affermò nel sistema bancario paulista soppiantando in pochi anni le *overseas banks* britanniche (la London and Brazilian Bank, la British Bank of South America e la London and River Plate Bank) e rivaleggiando con successo con la Brasilianische Bank für Deutschland sia nella raccolta di depositi che nell'impiego dei capitali. Nel 1910-1911 la rete paulista di Sudameris — che corrispondeva a quella creata dal Banco Commerciale Italo-Brasiliano e a quella dell'assorbito Banco Suizo-Americano — deteneva una quota di mercato del 17,2% per la raccolta di depositi (oltre 2,1 milioni di sterline) e dell'11,4% per gli impieghi (oltre 1,2 milioni di sterline): Sudameris era la prima banca straniera attiva nella raccolta dei depositi, seconda solo al brasiliano Banco do Comércio e Indústria de São Paulo (36,6%); in termini di impieghi Sudameris veniva invece dopo la Brasilianische Bank für Deutschland (15,7%)[22].

Il rapido sviluppo di Sudameris — dovuto in larga misura al sostegno degli istituti europei partecipanti — dovette tuttavia fare

---

21 Cfr. F. A. de Saes, *Créditos e Bancos* cit., p. 95-107; M. B. Levy, "The Banking System and Foreign Capital in Brazil", in *International Banking 1870-1914*, a cura di R. Cameron & V. I. Bovykin, New York-Oxford, 1991, p. 356 e 364-5.

22 Si vedano F. A. de Saes, *Créditos e Bancos* cit., p. 220; F. A. de Saes & T. Szmrecsányi, *The Role of Foreign Banks in the Early Industrialization of São Paulo* cit., p. 5 e tabella 3.

presto i conti con le esplicite riserve che i responsabili di Paribas espressero sulla politica di investimento perseguita dal direttore Dapples e dalle varie succursali brasiliane. La direzione sudamericana dovette inoltre affermare insistentemente l'opportunità che l'istituto partecipasse ai consorzi bancari di collocamento dei titoli pubblici argentini e brasiliani. Malgrado le resistenze opposte da Paribas, tra il 1912 e il 1916 Sudameris riuscì a estendere la propria attività di mediazione ai titoli del debito pubblico dei governi centrali e federali (nonché di quelli delle province) degli stati sudamericani: Sudameris si inserì nella mediazione dei titoli pubblici argentini e brasiliani, sia direttamente attraverso la partecipazione ai sindacati di collocamento delle emissioni, che indirettamente nei casi in cui le filiali brasiliane e argentine servirono più che altro da tramite per conto di Paribas[23].

Sudameris si distinse tuttavia soprattutto nell'apertura di crediti — non solo commerciali ma anche a medio termine mediante il continuo rinnovo degli sconti (secondo una prassi seguita anche dalle banche miste italiane) — alle imprese industriali brasiliane, attive in genere nel settore cotoniero, costituite e dirette da emigrati italiani. Le direzioni locali di Sudameris concessero così ampie linee di credito al gruppo Mechanica-Tecidos de Juta dei Siciliano (presente nel comitato di sorveglianza della direzione di São Paulo), al Cotonificio Crespi e alle Industrias Reunidas Fábricas Matarazzo. Nonostante il diverso orientamento dei responsabili delle succursali brasiliane, la sede centrale di Parigi cercò di limitare la concentrazione dei rischi che derivava dalla concessione di crediti a un numero limitato di imprese industriali. In questo senso la sede centrale di Parigi volle ricordare alla succursale di São Paulo che Sudameris doveva mantenere livelli di liquidità che si accordassero con il carattere di banca di deposito assunto dall'istituto, soprattutto in considerazione dell'impossibilità di effettuare risconti in quei sistemi e della conseguente importanza che in aree moneta-

---

[23] Cfr. A. Confalonieri, *Banca e industria in Italia dalla crisi del 1907* cit., vol. I, p. 401-2; e AH BP, conteneur 368, dossier 9, "Sudameris J. Kulp", lettera di Kulp al presidente del 26 maggio 1913. A questo proposito cfr. inoltre *ibidem*, conteneur 637, Paribas, "Procès-Verbaux du Conseil. Minutes", Cdam (Cda minutes), 30 marzo 1915, 25 gennaio 1916 e 28 novembre 1916.

riamente instabili i mezzi di cassa avevano nella gestione di eventuali crisi di fiducia[24].

Tra il 1910 e il 1911 anche il Credit si mosse in vista di una espansione bancaria in Sud America, appoggiandosi — come avevano fatto i colleghi della Comit — su prestigiosi partner europei e sulle loro estese reti di alleanze finanziarie. A differenza della Comit, tuttavia, non fu il Credit a prendere l'iniziativa: anzi l'istituto mantenne per qualche anno un ruolo sostanzialmente poco attivo, per così dire defilato, rispetto agli alleati belgi che avviarono l'iniziativa rivolgendosi all'istituto milanese.

Ai primi del 1911 — sollecitato dalla Société Générale de Belgique e dalla Banque de l'Union Anversoise — il Credit acquisì infatti una partecipazione di minoranza nella Banque Brésilienne Italo-Belge, un istituto con un capitale sociale di 20 milioni di franchi e con sede ad Anversa. L'istituto — nel cui consiglio di amministrazione il Credit ottenne due membri su dodici — avviò subito una rapida espansione in Sud America, aprendo via la direzione di São Paulo in Brasile nel 1911, la succursale uruguayana di Montevideo nel 1912, l'agenzia di Rio de Janeiro e la succursale argentina di Buenos Aires nel 1913[25].

La rapida espansione territoriale e aziendale delle banche doveva quindi tenere il passo con la capacità di dotare l'istituto del personale direttivo e di quello esecutivo che avrebbe concretamente avuto il

---

24 Cfr. AH BP, conteneur 368, dossier 9, "Sudameris J. Kulp", lettera di Kulp e Crétènier da Parigi a L. Toeplitz a São Paulo dell'11 gennaio 1915. La concessione di crediti ai gruppi Siciliano, Crespi e Matarazzo non comportò tuttavia per Sudameris l'assunzione di impegni esclusivi ni riguardi di un ristretto numero di imprese: "nous avons toujours eu à regretter les gros engagements, témoins: Brazil Railway, affaire Guiulé [gomma?], affaire Crespi, etc." *(ibidem)*. Sui rapporti tra la Brazil Railway e Paribas cfr. F. A. de Saes, *Os Investimentos Franceses no Brasil: o caso da Brazil Railway Company (1900-1930)*, p. 23-42.

25 Nel 1914 la Banque Brésilienne Italo-Belgue avrebbe mutato ragione sociale in Banque Italo-Belge (cfr. A. Confalonieri, *Banca e industria in Italia dalla crisi del 1907* cit., vol. I, p. 311-2; G. Piluso, *Le banche miste sui mercati esteri* cit.). Per una recente panoramica dell'evoluzione delle grandi banche belghe per il periodo considerato cfr. G. Kurgan-Van Hentenryk, "Finance and Financiers in Belgium, 1880-1940", in *Finance and Financiers in European History, 1880-1960*, a cura di Y. Cassis, Cambridge, 1992, p. 317-35.

compito di seguire il lavoro della direzione e delle filiali. Nel consiglio di amministrazione di Sudameris vennero nominati esponenti della Comit (Cesare Mangili, Luigi Della Torre, Otto Joel, Federico Weil, Luigi Marsaglia e Giuseppe Balduino) e amministratori di spicco di Paribas (Edouard Noetzlin, Jacques Frédéric Kulp, Joseph Henri Thors e Albert Turrettini), alcuni dei quali erano contemporaneamente presenti anche nel consiglio dell'istituto milanese (Noetzlin, Thors e Turrettini).

La direzione di Sudameris venne affidata all'ex direttore centrale della Comit Louis Dapples, a cui in questo modo vennero così riconosciuti i buoni risultati conseguiti alla direzione del Banco Commerciale Italo-Brasiliano. Negli uffici centrali di Parigi assunsero la direzione Jacques F. Kulp e Paul Créténier (consiglieri di nomina Paribas) che avevano maturato esperienze dei mercati latino-americani (il primo nel consiglio del Banco Nacional de Mexico e il secondo in quello della Peruvian Corporation). Le succursali e le filiali sudamericane venivano invece dirette da direttori la cui autonomia operativa formalmente si limitava alla conduzione degli affari ordinari (quelli che impegnavano somme superiora a un milione di franchi necessitavano invece dell'assenso esplicito della sede centrale di Parigi).

I rapporti tra la direzione centrale di Parigi e la rete periférica delle succursali e delle filiali sudamericane non furono tuttavia sempre facili e rispecchiarono in parte i diversi criteri di impostazione delle attività bancarie che dividevano le principali componenti della compagine proprietaria. Da un lato si collocavano i direttori periferici — spesso appoggiati dagli azionisti di minoranza italo-brasiliani — che sostenevano l'opportunità di un maggiore impegno di Sudameris nel financiamento — non soltanto ordinario — delle imprese che costituivano il nocciolo della clientela; dall'altro stavano i rappresentanti di Paribas che propendevano invece per lo svolgimento delle sole attività ordinarie di banca, che fossero preferibilmente *self-liquidating:* l'accettazione di carta commerciale e la concessione di anticipazioni su caffè, zucchero e altre merci di esportazione e di importazione.

Nonostante i limiti imposti da Paribas, l'organizzazione di Sudameris doveva d'altronde tenere conto dell'impostazione generale che si doveva dare a una banca che lavorava in mercati così distanti dall'Europa. Sudameris non era una banca assimilabile agli altri istituti stranieri presenti in Sud America: marcata era innanzitutto la distinzione tra le dipendenze sudamericane (filiali e succursali) e la sede europea. In Brasile Sudameris doveva essere considerata come una banca diretta autonomamente dalla direzione di São Paulo, alla stregua delle altre banche locali: una tale autonomia di gestione era dovuta al fatto che gli amministratori europei (compresi Kulp e Créténier) non conoscevano a fondo i mercati sudamericani. Una tale organizzazione — osservava Louis Dapples — aveva dato a Sudameris *"une très grande élasticité et une promptitude de décision"* che le altre banche europee attive in Sud America non sempre possedevano in egual misura[26].

La direzione dell'importante filiale di São Paulo e della sede centrale di Parigi venne assegnata fino alla metà degli anni trenta a un alto funzionario proveniente dalla direzione centrale della Comit. L'affidabilità del direttore di una filiale tanto lontana dall'Europa in anni in cui i tempi di comunicazione e quelli dei transporti erano ancora molto dilatati doveva essere garantita da una selezione rigorosa da parte degli organismi centrali di controllo, una selezione che garantisse pienamente l'affidabilità e la capacità della direzione sudamericana. I processi di apprendimento e di selezione venivano in tale modo trasferiti dai *networks* informali precedenti alle strutture bancarie multinazionali che li avevano internalizzati[27]. Nel caso di Sudameris i direttori delle filiali sudamericane venivano in genere selezionati e preparati durante un periodo di formazione presso le direzioni centrali europee di Paribas e della Comit. Alla sede parigina di Sudameris il personale della direzione e delle ispezioni era reclutato soprattutto in Francia (specialmente tra i diplomati dell'Ecole des Hautes Etudes Commerciales), i funcionari erano ammessi per concorso e venivano quindi preparati al lavoro d'ufficio direttamente sul campo negli uffici parigini della direzione di rue Halévy. I funcionari italiani erano invece maggioritari in Sud America sia perché, a differenza dei loro colleghi francesi, erano più disponibili a compiere l'intera carriera professionale in Brasile o in Argentina, sia perché la clientela d'oltremare di Sudameris era per la maggior parte di origine italiana ed era quindi evidente

---

26 AH BP, conteneur 368, dossier 9, "L. Dapples", lettera di Dapples da São Paulo a Créténier e Kulp a Parigi del 5 dicembre 1912.

27 Osservazioni utili si trovano in M. Casson, "Evolution of multinational banks" cit., p. 19-20.

l'opportunità che i quadri direttivi delle filiali in contatto con il pubblico fossero italiani[28].

La direzione effettiva della Banque Brésilienne Italo-Belge venne invece affidata a un belga, Hector Carlier, con il quale Federico Ettore Balzarotti — l'amministratore delegato del Credit — mantenne costantemente contatti epistolari e personali. L'amministatore delegato della Banque Italo-Belge, Carlier, dirigeva l'istituto dalla direzione di Parigi, compiendo periodicamente viaggi di ispezione e di controllo nelle succursali e nelle filiali sudamericane. Nonostante le ripetute richieste di Carlier di avere funzionari italiani da inviare in Sud America e da assegnare alla clientela italiana, la direzione centrale del Credit si dimostrò piuttosto restia a privarsi di elementi qualificati in una fase in cui ancora non aveva completamente risolto il problema del personale direttivo in Italia. La selezione del personale direttivo avveniva sulla base di procedure informali nelle direzioni europee degli istituti partecipanti, senza ricorrere a forme concorsuali di reclutamento come faceva invece Sudameris: una procedura non apprezzata da Carlier e Balzarotti, i quali ritenevano che un metodo così formalizzato non potesse dare adeguate garanzie sulla affidabilità e sulla professionalità dei funzionari[29].

La politica di espansione in Sud America della Comit e del Credit si concretò secondo differenti strategie di sviluppo: se i responsabili della Comit presero l'iniziativa rilevando una banca preesistente ed estendendo quindi la partecipazione ai partner di Paribas, quelli del Credit presero invece parte alla creazione di un organismo bancario *ex novo* limitandosi, almeno inizialmente, ad accodarsi ai

---

28 Cfr. AH BP, conteneur 252, dossier 28, "Sudameris. Divers", lettera di Kulp alla Direction des Affaires Politiques et Commerciales-Amérique del Ministère des Affaires Etrangères del 28 gennaio 1928. Adottando la prassi di formare negli uffici europei i direttori da inviare nelle dipendenze sudamericane Sudameris seguiva la consuetudine delle maggiori *overseas banks* britanniche: era questo un modo per risolvere i conflitti *pricipal-agent* che potevano insorgere tra la direzione centrale e le direzioni periferiche in termini di politica di impiego e di modalità gestionali (in proposito si veda G. Jones, *British Multinational Banking* cit., p. 163-73).

29 Cfr. Archivio storico Credito Italiano, Milano (AS CI), Credit, Cda, 19 aprile 1911, 27 maggio e 22 novembre 1915 e la corrispondenza tra Balzarotti e Carlier in ibidem, "Banque Italo-Belge", cart. 8.

partner belgi. Sudameris e la Banque Italo-Belge si configurarono come istituti scarsamente specializzati sotto il profilo geografico sull'esempio delle altre *overseas banks* europee: sia Sudameris che la Banque Italo-Belge tesero quasi subito a espandere la loro presenza ai mercati sudamericani in cui potevano contare sulle comunità di emigrati italiani e su consistenti flussi commerciali con l'Italia, con la Francia e con il Belgio (Brasile, Argentina, Uruguay e Cile). Il ruolo degli uffici europei di Parigi e di Anversa era invece particolare e si incentrava soprattutto nella definizione delle strategie di investimento a medio e lungo termine, nel coordinamento e nel controllo delle dipendenze sudamericane, nello svolgimento di operazioni in divisa e nel finanziamento dei commerci esteri delle piazze europee.

Nei primi passi verso la creazione di una rete bancaria sui mercati sudamericani sia la Comit che il Credit adottarono la soluzione organizzativa sperimentata da Paribas: una struttura di alleanze incentrata sulla compartecipazione azionaria e gestionale e finalizzata alla ripartizione dei rischi e alla condivisione delle conoscenze e delle opportunità dei mercati, soprattutto di quelle opportunità offerte dalle colonie degli emigrati italiani e dalle imprese commerciali francesi e belghe presenti in Sud America[30].

Lo sviluppo delle reti bancarie italiane in Sud America (1915-1922)

Alla fine della prima guerra mondiale anche le altre banche miste italiane tentarono di estendere la rete delle filiali e delle consociate

---

[30] Sin dall'inizio della loro attività Sudameris e la Banque Italo-Belge non seguirono quello che era il modello di organizzazione adottato dalle *overseas banks* britanniche — a lungo sostenuto dalla Bank of England —, un modello incentrato sulla specializzazione geografica e sulla distinzione tra attività *over borders*, e attività all'interno dei confini nazionali: le prime eccezioni emersero negli anni venti quando la Lloyds Bank e la Barclays Bank crearono una propria rete estera. Una prima e parziale diversificazione geografica si ebbe solo negli anni venti e trenta (cfr. G. Jones, *British Multinational Banking* cit., p. 138-57 e 205-9). La condivisione del controllo azionario con uno o più partner rispondeva piuttosto alla soluzione adottata anche da Paribas nell'espansione dell'istituto in America Latina (cfr. E. Bussière, *Paribas* cit., p. 56-7).

ai mercati del Sud America. Nel corso del 1918 la Banca Italiana di Sconto cercò, sebbene senza successo, di acquisire una partecipazione nel Banco Commerciale Italiano di Buenos Aires. Tra il 1919 e il 1920 la Bis procedette quindi alla creazioni di proprie filiali in Brasile (São Paulo, Santos e Rio de Janeiro). Il crollo in borsa della Bis nel dicembre 1921 mise tuttavia fine ai tentativi di ingresso della terza banca mista italiana sul mercato bancario brasiliano[31].

La compartecipazione nella Banque Italo-Belge rimase anche dopo il conflitto il maggiore impegno di carattere bancario preso all'estero dal Credit, che rafforzò anzi la propria posizione azionaria acquisendo il pacchetto di maggioranza relativa dell'istituto (cfr. la tabella 2).

Tabella 2
Ripartizione del capitale azionario della Banque Italo-Belge (1919)*

	Numero azioni	%
Credit	8.900	8,9
Banque de l'Union Anversoise	5.921	5,9
Banque Belge pour l'Etranger	3.800	3,8
Société Générale de Belgique	3.000	3,0
Bunge et Cie	2.000	2,0
Ernest Solvay	1.166	1,1
Anglo-South American Bank	1.000	1,0
Banque Générale de Belge	500	0,5
Banque d'Outre Mer	500	0,5
Banque Centrale d'Anvers	500	0,5
Société Mutuelle Mobilière et Immobilière	500	0,5

* sono indicati solo gli azionisti con più di 500 titoli.
Fonte: AS CI, "Banque Italo-Belge", cart. 8, Banque Italo-Belge, *Rapports*, 26 novembre 1919.

Superata la crisi che colpì le maggiori economie sudamericane negli anni 1913-1914, alla fine della guerra la Banque Italo-Belge registrava un incremento di tutte le principali voci di attività: si evidenziarono un aumento del volume delle operazioni, un maggiore lavoro presso tutte le succursali sudamericane e un ampliamento della clientela. Nel 1920 la Banque Italo-Belge conquistò così il quinto posto in un sistema bancario importante come quello dello Stato di São Paulo nella raccolta di depositi (con una quota pari al 6% del

[31] Si veda A. M. Falchero, *La Banca italiana di sconto 1914-1921. Sette anni di guerra*, Milano, 1990, p. 159-65.

totale) e arrivò a occupare il terzo posto per capitale in quello uruguayano, a pari livello con la Royal Bank of Canada. Durante gli anni venti le succursali e le filiali sudamericane della banca si impegnarono principalmente nelle operazioni di financiamento delle esportazioni e delle importazioni tra Italia, Belgio e Sud America (in particolare per il finanziamento delle esportazioni di zucchero la Banque Italo-Belge strinse raporti privilegiati con i gruppi Tornquist e Portails)[32].

Il lavoro delle succursali sudamericane della Banque Italo-Belge (lavoro di carattere essencialmente ordinario) verteva inoltre sullo sconto di carta commerciale e di crediti documentari, come nel caso del cotonificio Crespi, e nel finanziamento delle campagne di raccolta e di esportazione del caffè e dello zucchero: un interessamento che si concentrava quindi sulle principali voci dell'economia brasiliana, comprendendo sia il finanziamento all'esportazione dei beni primari che il sostegno finanziario a breve termine di imprese del principale settore industriale del paese[33].

La Banque Italo-Belge seguiva con attenzione anche quelle imprese industriali italiane che si avviavano a essere presenti sui mercati sudamericani, imprese ritenute da Carlier "tout à fait désirables au point de vue des relations de la Banque". Il direttore della *gerencia* di Buenos Aires Antonio Parenti — un alto funzionario particolarmente stimato da Carlier e dai suoi colleghi franco-belgi — entrò così nei consigli di amministrazione della filiale argentina della Pirefli, della Compañia Italo-Argentina de Electricidad e della Compañia General de Fósforos[34].

---

32 Cfr. AS CI, "Banque Italo-Belge", cart. 8, Banque Italo-Belge, *Rapports*, 26 novembre 1919 e le lettere di Carlier a Balzarotti del 10 e 15 ottobre 1918. L'esportazione di caffè, sia negli Stati Uniti che in Europa, continuava in massima parte a essere finanziata tramite Londra (cfr. D. Joslin, A *Century of Banking in Latin America* cit., p. 160). Sulle attività finanziare del gruppo guidato da Ernest Tornquist cfr. D. J. Guy, "Dependency, the Credit Market, and Argentine Industrialization, 1860-1940". *Business History Review*, vol. 58 (1984), n. 4, p. 545-8.

33 Sul lavoro bancario di carrattere commerciale in relazione all'esportazione di zucchero e caffè cfr. AS CI, "Banque Italo-Belge", cart. 8, lettera di Carlier a Balzarotti del 20 agosto 1918.

34 Cfr. ibidem, lettera di Parenti a Balzarotti del 15 ottobre 1917 e lettera di Calier a Balzarotti del 1° Iuglio 1918. "Sull'espansione all'estero della Pirelli — oltre alle brevi notc", in Alberto Pirelli, *La Pirelli. Vila di unu*

Nel 1917 la filiale argentina della Pirelli & C. si appoggiò alla Banque Italo-Belge per evitare di incorrere nel rischio del cambio in una fase di marcate turbolenze monetarie nel momento in cui si apprestava a raccogliere il denaro necessario a finanziare la costruzione dello stabilimento che aveva deciso di impiantare in Argentina per produrre cavi e conduttori elettrici da commercializzare direttamente sui mercati sudamericani (lo stabilimento che sarebbe entrato in funzione nel 1924). Parenti quale direttore della Banque Italo-Belge venne nominato sindaco della filiale argentina della Pirelli nella prospettiva non tanto di rendere preferenziali i legami con una banca legata al Credit — istituto che era d'altro canto il tradizionale alleato finanziario della Pirelli in Italia —, quanto piuttosto di esercitare un prudenziale controllo e fornire assistenza finanziaria nel momento in cui l'impresa milanese si apprestava a trasformare la propria succursale argentina in società anonima[35].

L'espansione della rete delle succursali della Banque Italo-Belge venne concepita come la naturale prosecuzione della politica di estensione della presenza dell'istituto sulle maggiori piazze sudamericane — sempre con un particolare riguardo verso le colonie di italiani. Nei primi anni venti la Banque Italo-Belge completò la propria rete di succursali sudamericane, ativando a estendere la presenza dell'istituto in Brasile (São Paulo, Rio de Janeiro, Santos e Campinas), in Argentina (Buenos Aires) e in Uruguay (Montevideo). Il progetto di installare una succursale in Cile a Valparaiso non andò invece in porto e la banca dovette accontentarsi, come in passato, di un semplice corrispondente: segno evidente che in un momento

---

azienda industriale, Milano, 1946, p. 64-5 (Brasile e Argentina) — si vedano D. Bigazzi, "La Pirelli e la Fiat nel mercato mondiale", in *Storia della società italiana. L'Italia di Giolitti,* vol. XX, Milano, 1981, p. 126-43; B. Bezza, "L'attività multinazionale della Pirelli (1883-1914)". *Società e Storia,* 10 (1987), n. 35, p. 53-80; id., "L'intervento del capitale italiano nell'industria elettrica argentina (1910-1920)", in *Energia e sviluppo. L'industria elettrica italiana e la Società Edison,* a cura di B. Bezza, Torino, 1986, p. 319-49; e, da ultimo, D. Barbone, "L'internazionalizzazione come condizione di sopravvivenza: il caso Pirelli", in *L'internazionalizzazione dell'industria italiana* cit, p. 90-4.

35 Cfr. AS CI, "Banque Italo-Belge", cart. 8, lettera di Parenti a Balzarotti del 15 ottobre 1917.

di crisi i non bassi costi di installazione non sempre potevano essere affrontati e che le conoscenze dei mercati (monetari e finanziari) e degli operatori locali che erano necessarie non sempre potevano essere acquisite in tempi utili per avere a breve ritorni economici accettabili[36].

L'espansione della rete delle succursali dovette d'altronde fare i conti con la penuria estrema di personale direttivo italiano, personale che nonostante le reiterale richieste avanzate da Carlier e Parenti a Balzarotti la direzione milanese del Credit continuò in questi anni a centellinare. Nell'esposizione dei risultati di un viaggio fatto in Cile nella primavera del 1918 per valutare la concreta possibilità di aprirvi una succursale, Antonio Parenti osservava sì che "manca[va] a Valparaiso una banca italiana e detta mancanza [era] assai sentita dagl'italiani di colà che nelle altre banche non po[teva]no naturalmente trovare il trattamento desiderato", ma in quel critico momento il Credit dal canto suo non poteva assolutamente distogliere funzionari dalla direzione centrale per estendere in Sud America la presenza della Banque Italo-Belge, pur sapendo che la clientela italiana preferiva essere seguita da direttori italiani, e il lavoro di banca di un direttore — o di un alto funzionario — non poteva essere svolto da semplici impiegati soprattutto quando si era deciso di "lavorare solo con una clientela scelta"[37].

Benché fosse minoritaria la presenza di personale italiano nella direzione delle succursali e filiali sudamericane della Banque Italo-Belge, la preparazione e la competenza dei direttori inviati dal Credit erano piuttosto apprezzate dai loro colleghi francesi e belgi, tanto che nel giugno 1918 Carlier poteva scrivere a Balzarotti:

> *"Je vous signale l'excellent esprit que j'ai constaté chez tous nos gens en Amérique du Sud. Je dois dire qu'Italiens et Belges font toujours très bon ménage et que chez nous il ne peut être question de rivalité entre nationalités. Vous remarquez que ce sont les Belges qui réclament*

---

36 Cfr. ibidem, lettera di Carlier a Balzarotti del 26 giugno 1918 e lettera di Parenti a Balzarotti del luglio 1918.

37 Ibidem, lettera di Parenti a Balzarotti del luglio 1918. Secondo le stime di Parenti la colonia di immigrati italiani in Cile — tra le 6.000 e le 7.000 unità — sarebbe stata una clientela senza dubbio di un certo interesse: in Cile le imprese costituite da italiani erano infatti le prime per numero e le seconde per capitale tra quelle straniere (ibidem).

des Italiens à côté d'eux pour la clientèle et vis et versa. Je n'en dirai pas autant de la Française et Italienne [Sudameris]"[38].

Nei primi anni venti dal canto suo la Comit attuò una politica di diretta espansione all'estero individuando due grandi aree di interesse: il Sud America e l'Europa centro-orientale e balcanica. Nell'attuazione di una strategia di diversificazione geografica durante gli anni venti la Comit sovrappose due distinti modelli organizzativi delle attività bancarie all'estero.

Alcuni vincoli di carattere generale — il venir meno del sistema dei cambi fissi garantiti dal *gold standard*, l'incipiente nazionalismo e protezionismo economico, i correlati mutamenti nelle forme di organizzazione e nelle stesse strategie delle grandi banche internazionali e alcune iniziali opportunità di espansione nell'area danubiano-balcanica — convinsero i responsabili della Comit ad adottare un modello organizzativo che si riteneva meglio rispondente a garantire l'espansione diretta dell'istituto su nuovi mercati. La Comit si impegnò così nella costituzione di una estesa rete europea ed extra-europea di banche affiliate e associate dando vita a un vero e proprio gruppo multinazionale presente in Sud America, Stati Uniti (New York, Philadelphia e Boston), Francia (Sudameris e Comit-France), Gran Bretagna (Londra), Svizzera (cantoni di lingua italiana), Polonia, Cecoslovacchia, Ungheria, Romania, Bulgaria, Jugoslavia, Grecia, Turchia, Egitto e Tunisia (cfr. la tabella 3).

Il Credit in parte rafforzò la rete estera, soprattutto in Francia e in Tunisia, e in parte dovette provvedere a riorganizzare la rete estera che era stata creata dalla Banca Italiana di Sconto quando assunse il controllo della Banca Nazionale di Credito, l'istituto di nuova creazione a cui venne attribuita la liquidazione della Banca Italiana di Sconto (cfr. la tabella 4)[39].

---

[38] *Ibidem*, lettera di Carlier a Balzarotti da Parigi del 19 giugno 1918. Hector Carlier aggiungeva poi in quella lettera: "Je m'excuse de vous avoir entretenu si longuement de ces questions mais, vous savez mieux que moi, cher Monsieur Balzarotti, que le facteur le plus important de réussite dans notre métier ce sont les hommes!" *(ibidem)*.

[39] Cfr. A. Confalonieri, "Considerazioni sull'esperienza del Credito Italiano 1914-1933", in *Il Credito Italiano e la fondazione dell'IRI*, Milano, 1990, p. 60-1.

Tabella 3
Banche associate e banche affiliate della Comit (1932)

	sede	a	b
a) banche associate:			
Sudameris	Parigi	30	1910
Bank Handlowy w Warsawie	Varsavia	17	(1927)
Banco Italiano, Lima	Lima	8	(1919)
Banca della Svizzera Italiana	Lugano	4	(1909)
b) banche affiliate:			
Bicitrust New York	New York	1	1924
Bicitrust Boston	Boston	-	1929
Bicitrust Philadelphia	Philadelphia	1	1929
Bancomit Corporation	New York	-	1928
Comit-France	Parigi	10	1918
Romcomit	Bucarest	8	1920
Bulcomit	Sofia	3	1919
Banca Ungaro Italiana	Budapest	20	1920
Banco Italiano Guayaquil	Guayaquil	1	(1923)
Hrvatska Banka	Zagabria	1	(1928)
Comit-Hellas	Atene	3	1928
Banca Commerciale per l'Egitto	Alessandria	9	1924

a: filiali, succursali e agenzie; b: anno di costituzione.
Fonte: AS BCI, *Mattioli*, cart. 3, e *The Bankers'Almanac and Year Book for 1932-1933*, London, 1933.

Tabella 4
Banche consociate del gruppo Credit (1932)

	sede	a	b
Banque Italo-Belge	Anversa	7	1911
Banca Dalmata di Sconto	Zara	2	1919
Banca Unione di Credito	Lugano	1	1919
Banque Italo-Française de Crédit	Paris	4	
Banco Italo-Egiziano	Cairo	8	
Italian Bank for China	Shangai	2	1920*

a: filiali, succursali e agenzie; b: anno di costituzione.
* costituita come Sino-Italian Bank mutò ragione sociale nel 1924.
Fonte: The Bankers'Almanac and Year Book for 1932-1933, London, 1933.

La prima guerra mondiale costituì una cesura sotto il profilo sia delle condizioni ambientali generali — il venir meno di un sistema di cambi fissi e la restrizione dei commerci internazionali — che dei vantaggi comparati che le banche italiane avevano nei mercati sudamericani in ragione della contrazione delle emigrazioni verso quell'area e della conseguente diminuzione delle rimesse degli emigrati.

La crisi dei mercati sudamericani (1923-1933)

Durante la prima guerra mondiale Sudameris — superato un momento di difficoltà nel 1915 — aveva collocato quote consistenti di titoli del debito pubblico italiano sia attraverso la sede di Parigi che mediante le filiali sudamericane. L'estensione della rete delle filiali sudamericane richiese ben presto un potenziamento dei mezzi propri della banca, così che nel 1919 il capitale sociale di Sudameris venne raddoppiato da 25 a 50 milioni di franchi: in questa occasione la Comit acquisì la maggioranza assoluta delle azioni rilevando la quota azionaria della Société Générale, tanto che Sudameris — secondo le parole dei responsabili della Comit — nel 1922 poteva "in parte considerarsi quasi un prolungamento dell'azione nostra oltre gli oceani"[40].

Nonostante la buona prova complessivamente data dalle banche affiliate di nuova costituzione (Bulgaria, Romania e Francia), tra il 1918 e il 1925 la Comit confermò nel Sud America l'area in cui concenntrare le partecipazioni bancarie estere di rilievo strategico. Nel corso del 1919 la Comit, "sempre nel concetto di collaborare allo sviluppo della influenza italiana in altre plaghe", prese parte a un aumento di capitale del Banco Italiano di Lima, un istituto che lavorava con buoni risultati, "fornendo anche personale direttivo alla sua gestione"[41]. Come negli anni prebellici Sudameris rimase affidata a un direttore proveniente dagli uffici milanesi della Comit — Giuseppe Zuccoli — che negli anni dieci aveva preso il posto di direttore della rete delle succursali e filiali sudamericane che era stato di Louis Dapples (il quale sarebbe passato all'inizio degli anni venti alla riorganizzazione della Nestlé). Giuseppe Zuccoli avrebbe diretto Sudameris dalla sede centrale di Parigi, anziché dalla direzione locale di São Paulo come aveva fatto Dapples: la scelta di Zuccoli di dirigere l'istituto dagli uffici parigini avrebbe avuto conseguenze sul grado di formalizzazione della struttura organizzativa di Sudameris.

Nell'immediato primo dopoguerra Sudameris estese la propria rete di succursali e di filiali in Brasile, Argentina, Cile, Colombia e

---

40 AS BCI, Comit, Rb, 23 marzo 1922, p. 16.

41 Idem, Comit, Rb, 30 marzo 1920, p. 15.

Uruguay, portando il loro numero da 21 a 31 tra il 1920 e il 1925 (cfr. le tabelle 6 e 7). Il ruolo di Sudameris nei sistemi bancari sudamericani si confermò nel corso degli anni venti non soltanto rispetto alle altre banche europee ma anche nei confronti delle banche brasiliane, argentine e uruguayane. Nel 1920 Sudameris deteneva la quota in assoluto più consistente del mercato paulista nella raccolta di depositi con il 22,8%, mentre negli impieghi era seconda solo al Banco do Comércio e Indústria de São Paulo con il 14,9%. Nel 1928 la posizione di Sudameris venne confermata in termini di *ranking* rispetto alle altre banche straniere sia nella raccolta di depositi con una quota ridotta del 7,5% che negli impieghi con il 8,3%; l'istituto perse invece posizioni nei confronti delle banche brasiliane cha andavano allora rafforzando la loro posizione (Banco do Brasil, Banco do Estado de São Paulo e Banco de Comércio e Indústria)[42].

Tabella 5
Ripartizione del capitale azionario di Sudameris (I1919)

	numero azioni	%
Paribas	9.175	18,35
Société Générale	6.175	12,35
Ernest Cassel	2.000	4,00
Kuhn, Loeb and Co.	2.000	4,00
Warburg and Co.	1.000	2,00
altri azionisti	1.450	2,90
"gruppo francese"	21.800	43,60
Comit	22.310	44,62
Comit(consiglieri)	850	1,70
"gruppo brasiliano"	1.840	3,68
"gruppo italiano"	25.000	50,00
consiglieri Sudameris	3.200*	6,40

* di cui 1.500 in mano a Edouard Noetzlin.
Fonte: AH BP, conteneur 252, dossier 28, nota del 30 settembre 1919.

42 Cfr. F. A. de Saes & T. Szmrecsányi, *The Role of Foreign Banks in the Early Industrialization of São Paulo* cit., tabelle 4 e 5. Sul rafforzamento della posizione delle banche brasiliane cfr. S. Topik, "Capital estrangeiro", cit., p. 408-16; G. Triner, "Os bancos brasileiros na economia: 1906-1918". *Estudos econômicos*, 21 (1991), n. 3, p. 435-73.

Tabella 6
La formazione della rete delle dipendenze di Sudwneris in Sud America (1920-1927)

	Brasile			Argentina	Cile	Colombia	Uruguay	totale
	a	b	c	c	a	a	a	
1920	6	13	19	2	-	-	-	21
1921	7	13	20	2	1	-	-	23
1922	7	15	22	2	1	-	-	25
1923	7	15	22	2	2	-	-	24
1924	7	15	22	2	2	1	1	28
1925	8	16	24	3	2	1	1	31
1926	8	16	24	3	2	1	1	31
1927	8	16	24	3	2	1	1	31

a: succursali; b: agenzie; c: succursali + agenzie.

Tabella 7
Distribuzione del personale presso le dipendenze di Sudameris (1920-1927)*

	1920	1921	1922	1923	1924	1925	1926	1927
Brasile	657	714	683	749	820	880	912	853
Argentina	311	272	284	279	289	291	292	273
Cile	—	—	33	35	43	121	112	101
Colombia					36	40	41	51
Uruguay					—	—	30	31
Parigi	368	440	406	479	566	606	622	532
totale	1336	1426	1406	1542	1754	1938	2009	1841

* non sono comprese le direzioni delle succursali.

In Uruguay Sudameris aveva installato la propria succursale di Montevideo nel 1924: tra il 1931 e il 1938 la rete uruguayana di Sudameris — seconda tra le banche straniere per capitale — fece progressi in termini sia di raccolta di depositi (passando dal settimo al quinto posto), che nel volume complessivo degli sconti e delle anticipazioni (salendo dal quarto al secondo posto). In Uruguay Sudameris veniva dopo la Bank of London and South America con il 19% contro il 50% del capitale complessivo degli istituti stranieri; mentre nella raccolta di depositi Sudameris deteneva una quota del 7% del settore rappresentato dalle banche straniere che operavano in Uruguay contro il 57% della Bank of London and South America, il 12% della National City Bank di New York, il 10% della Royal Bank of Canada e 1,8% della Deutsche Überseeische Bank[43].

[43] Cfr. R. Jacob, *Los bancos estranjeros (1911-1938)*, Montevideo, Ciedur-Serie Investigaciones 105, 1993, p. 24-6, e id., *La banca en Uruguay:*

Durante gli anni venti — malgrado i discreti risultati complessivi — Sudameris si dibatté tra le continue crisi dei mercati in cui era interessata e la crescente concorrenza delle altre banche straniere, una concorrenza che limitava il volume degli affari e soprattutto i margini di profitto conseguibili sulle piazze sudamericane. L'acuirsi della concorrenza tra le banche straniere presenti in Argentina era tuttavia stato avvertito — e lamentato nella corrispondenza con i referenti europei — sin dal 1917 anche da Antonio Parenti, il direttore della *gerencia* di Buenos Aires della Banque Italo-Belge. Nell'ottobre 1917, riferendosi implicitamente alla crescente concorrenza tra istituti di credito stranieri, Parenti scrisse a Balzarotti che "gli affari [era]no ridotti alla minima espressione, le Banche [era]no aumentate e il denaro vi si trova[va] paralizzato [...] Tutte le Banche assedia[va]no le buone Ditte offrendo denari a condizioni irrisorie"[44].

Dell'inasprimento della concorrenza tra le banche europee e tra le stesse affiliazioni bancarie italiane non mancò di dare notizia, nella primavera del 1918, anche l'amministratore delegato della Banque Italo-Belge Carlier a Balzarotti. A São Paulo tra la Banque Italo-Belge e Sudameris — si lamentò Carlier — c'era ormai *"une guerre au couteau"*, in contrasto con lo spirito di collaborazione che regolava i rapporti tra i due istituti su altre piazze, poiché Sudameris continuava a offrire i propri servizi e il proprio credito alle Industrias Reunidas Fábricas Matarazzo, uno dei maggiori gruppi industriali attivi in Brasile, con cui l'istituto diretto da Carlier era da tempo in rapporti d'affari, mettendo in serie difficoltà la Banque Italo-Belge *"vis-à-vis de la colonie italienne"*[45].

---

algunos indicadores (1921-1938), Montevideo, Ciedur-Investigaciones 79, 1992, p. 10. In Uruguay la direzione di Sudameris si mosse nella prospettiva di investire parte delle proprie riserve (30.000 pesos) nella Sociedad Uruguaya de Combustibles, che avrebbe dovuto realizzare la prima raffineria petrolifera nazionale: nel 1931 la fondazione di un ente statale (l'Ancap) avrebbe fatto naufragare questo progetto. Tra i direttori locali figuravano sia rappresentanti delle amministrazioni pubbliche che esponenti di imprese statunitensi (come Blas Vidal della Hallgarten & Co. e del Guaranty Trust di New York) (cfr. R. Jacob, *Los bancos estranjeros* cit., p. 25-6).

44 AS CI, "Banque Italo-Belge", cart. 8, lettera di Parenti a Balzarotti da Buenos Aires del 15 ottobre 1917.

45 Ibidem, lettera di Carlier a Balzarotti dell'8 maggio 1918. La Banque Italo-Belge aveva inizialmente fissato i seguenti limiti nei riguardi delle

L'inasprirsi della concorrenza sulle piazze sudamericane venne lamentato anche dall'amministratore delegato della Comit Giuseppe Toeplitz nel maggio 1921 in una lettera a Vincenzo Frontini e Settimio Sampò — direttori di Sudameris rispettivamente a São Paulo e a Buenos Aires — con cui anticipava loro una visita di Osvaldo Riso, funzionario del Banco di Roma, che aveva in programma un viaggio in Brasile e in Argentina per organizzarvi alcune filiali dell'istituto romano. Le filiali brasiliane e argentine del Banco di Roma non sarebbero tuttavia mai state istituite, sia per le gravi difficoltà interne incontrate dalla banca romana che per l'eccentricità dei mercati sudamericani rispetto alle aree di espansione all'estero individuate negli anni precedenti dall'istituto (la Spagna, il Mediterraneo e il Levante)[46].

L'accrescersi della spinta alla concorrenza tra le banche straniere presenti in Sud America nel corso degli anni venti dovette condizionare la politica di Sudameris e della Banque Italo-Belge. Sudameris, sotto la direzione di Giuseppe Zuccoli, dimostrò di essere in grado di reagire all'aumento dei soggetti in competizione e alla riduzione dei margini di profitto mantenendo la propria posizione rispetto alle altre banche straniere; lo sviluppo della Banque Italo-Belge risentì invece della politica di prudenza nell'espansione della rete territoriale perseguita negli anni venti accusando un secco ripiegamento nelle relative quote di mercato occupate (in termini sia percentuali che assoluti): sull'importante piazza paulista tra il 1920 e il 1928 la quota dei depositi raccolti dalla Banque Italo-Belge si contrasse dal 6% (oltre 3,3 milioni di sterline) all'1% (poco più di 1

Industrias Reunidas Matarazzo: 2.000 contos per i crediti di accettazione, da 50.000 a 70.000 sterline per i crediti a valere sull'estero e 2.000 contos per le facilità di cassa. Tali cifre — ricordava Carlier a Balzarotti — erano senz'altro considerevoli e tuttavia *"il faut passer par là"*, poiché i rapporti con i Matarazzo erano necessari per preservare lo *standing* della banca agli occhi della colonia italiana di São Paulo *(ibidem)*: il gruppo Matarazzo, nella prospettiva di alleggerire le singole esposizioni debitorie, intratteneva contemporaneamente rapporti con la Banque Italo-Belge, con Sudameris e con la Bank of London and South America (cfr. J. de Souza Martins, *Conde Matarazzo* cit., p. 29).

46 Per le lettere di Toeplitz ai direttori sudamericani di Sudameris cfr. AS BCI, Copialettere Toeplitz (CpT), lettere di Toeplitz a Frontini e a Sampò del 14 maggio 1921. Cfr. inoltre L. De Rosa. *Storia del Banco di Roma*, Roma, 1983, vol. III, p. 229 e sgg.

milione di sterline); analogamente, tra il 1931 e il 1938, in Uruguay l'istituto diretto da Hector Carlier passò dal terzo al sesto posto nel *ranking* delle banche straniere definito sulla base del capitale[47].

Secondo le stime riportate in una relazione interna del febbraio 1928, tra il 1920 e il 1927 le filiali di Sudameris — come quelle della Banque Italo-Belge — ridussero sensibilmente gli importi complessivamente raccolti sulle piazze sudamericane. In linea con l'andamento generale, la quota di Sudameris sul totale dei depositi raccolti dagli istituti di credito stranieri operanti in Sud America si contrasse dal 9,17% del 1920 al 7,6% del 1927 (nello stesso periodo la quota della Banque Italo-Belge scese dal 6,86 al 4,11%): dalla terza posizione di inizio decennio, nel corso degli anni venti Sudameris aveva dovuto subire un vistoso arretramento fino a collocarsi alla settima posizione del 1927 (cfr. la tabella 8).

Tabella 8
Variazione dei depositi delle maggiori banche straniere operanti in Sud America (1920-1927) (in milioni di pesos carta)

Banca	1920	%	1927	%
Deutsche Überseeische Bank	54.692	6,09	74.251	9,61
Anglo South American Bank	149.738	16,68	78.151	10,12
British Bank of South America	97.955	10,91	58.428	7,56
Banco Frances del Rio de la Plata	57.515	6,40	67.132	8,69
Sudameris	82.299 *	9,17	58.727	7,60
Banco Germanico	31.895	3,55	35.444	4,59
Banque Italo-Belge	61.608	6,86	31.802	4,11
London and River Plate Bank	190.510 **	21,23	—	—
London and Brazilian Bank	31.588 **	3,52	—	—
Bank of London and South America	—	—	190.291	24,64
First National Bank of Boston	55.808	6,21	92.273	11,94
National City Bank	65.711	7,32	65.985	8,54
Royal Bank of Canada	17.954	2,00	19.699	2,55
depositi complessivi	897.273		772.183	

* sono compresi anche i depositi in titoli del Tesoro francese e in titoli del Tesoro italiano.
** nel 1923 i depositi della London and River Plate Bank e la London and Brazilian Bank confluiscono nella Bank of London and South America.
Fonte: AS BCI, Segreteria Toeplitz, cart. 63, fasc. 2, lettera di Zuccoli a Toeplitz, Parigi, 20 febbraio 1928, allegato "Note", tabella "Comparaison des dépôts des grandes banques".

---

47 Cfr. F. A. de Saes & T. Szmrecsányi, *The Role of Foreign Banks in the Early Industrialization of São Paulo* cit., p. 8, tabelle 4-5; Raúl Jacob, *Los bancos estranjeros* cit., p. 26.

L'indebolimento della posizione di Sudameris nella raccolta dei depositi era il segno della riduzione non solo della capacità di crescita della rete delle dipendenze dell'istituto ma soprattutto di una attenuazione dei legami con i connazionali emigrati in Sud America. In questi anni si registrò un calo del numero degli italiani che emigrarono in Argentina e Brasile, sia in percentuale che in termini assoluti: si dovette perciò delineare un graduale allentamento dell'efficacia che potevano avere i canali privilegiati con le comunità nell'indirizzare le scelte delle generazioni che non erano nate in Italia o che erano da tempo lontane dall'Italia.

La crescita della rete delle succursali e delle filiali e il dinamismo operativo della dirigenza europea e sudamericana consentirono tuttavia a Sudameris di conservare una parte consistente delle quote di mercato acquisite nei primi quindici anni di attività. La formalizzazione delle funzioni e dei poteri delle direzioni locali e la definizione di procedure di controllo e di comunicazione tra gli organismi direttivi locali e la sede centrale negli anni venti e trenta permise a Sudameris di reggere alla concorrenza bancaria crescente e alla progressiva chiusura dei mercati sudamericani.

Nel corso degli anni venti si precisarono sia l'assetto organizzativo complessivo di Sudameris che i poteri delle filiali sudamericane rispetto alla sede parigina. Dopo l'istituzione di viaggi di ispezione periodici e la messa a punto di metodi di controllo negli anni prebellici, nella seconda metà degli anni venti con un "regolamento interno" si definirono le competenze delle filiali in base alle aree geografiche. Nel 1928 un *Réglement interieur des directions regionales et locales* stabiliva che le varie direzioni regionali (São Paulo, Rio de Janeiro, Curitiba, Pernambuco, Porto Alegre, Buenos Aires, Santiago, Montevideo e Bogotá) avessero ampi poteri decisionali e il controllo delle direzioni delle succursali e agenzie (direzioni locali) sudamericane. Negli anni trenta il decentramento attuato nel 1928 con la creazione delle direzioni regionali — per esigenze essenzialmente di controllo — subì una parziale revisione: la sorveglianza e il controllo delle succursali e filiali brasiliane venne affidato alla direzione di São Paulo, il cui comitato di direzione (nominato dalla direzione centrale di Parigi) assunse estesi poteri nei riguardi di tutte le direzioni regionali brasiliane[48].

---

48 Cfr. AH BP, conteneur 591, dossier 3, "Divers", *Réglement interieur des directions regionales & locales*, aprile 1928.

La preminenza della Comit nella compagine proprietaria di Sudameris venne confermata quando nel 1928 si effettuò un nuovo raddoppio del capitale sociale — portato da 50 a 100 milioni di franchi — consentendo in questo modo a Zuccoli di dotare l'istituto di quei mezzi che si riteneva fossero necessari ad assorbire la crescita dei rischi di cambio che il deterioramento delle monete deboli dell'area sudamericana comportava per gli istituti europei attivi in quei mercati creditizi.

Ciononostante alla fine degli anni venti Sudameris si trovò al centro di una polemica che ripropose la diversa posizione della Comit e di Paribas rispetto alla politica di espansione di Sudameris. L'espansione di Sudameris, sia in Francia che in Sud America, incontrò infatti più volte la resistenza esplicita di Paribas. Nel 1928 il direttore generale di Paribas, Horace Finaly, si oppose infatti alla creazione di una succursale a Le Havre e di un'agenzia di città alle Halles a Parigi. Finaly fece opposizione passiva anche quando l'amministratore delegato di Sudameris Zuccoli propose di assumere una partecipazione nel Banco de Rio Grande do Sul. Opponendosi ai progetti di espansione diretta e indireta di Sudameris, Horace Finaly mirava di fatto a fare delle riunioni di comitato di Paribas la sede decisionale effettiva dell'istituto diretto da Zuccoli, e ora controllato per oltre la metà del capitale azionario dalla Comit, attenuandone nel contempo la marcata spinta alla crescita sia in Sud America che in Francia (dove nel 1919 la Comit aveva costituito una propria banca affiliata, Comit-France, che aveva assunto la rappresentanza dell'istituto milanese su tutto il territorio francese con l'eccezione di Parigi).

Nonostante i contrasti con Horace Finaly di Paribas, Sudameris rimase la sede privilegiata per raccogliere informazioni e per avere contatti diretti e personali con i maggiori esponenti della comunità finanziaria internazionale. Non solo Zuccoli poteva mantenere i contatti con Paribas, ma a Parigi aveva incontri e scambi di idee e di informazioni sui mercati internazionali — informazioni che volgeva poi a Toeplitz e alla direzione centrale della Comit — con i grandi banchieri d'affari europei e statunitensi: da André e René Meyer della Lazard Frères a Felix Somary della Blankart di Zurigo e Weill della Lazard di New York[49].

---

[49] Cfr. AS BCI, Segreteria Toeplitz (ST), cart. 63, fasc. 2, lettera, "strettamente confidenziale", di Zuccoli a Toeplitz del 24 febbraio 1928 e

Nei primi anni trenta Sudameris era la maggiore banca estera associata del gruppo multinazionale creato dalla Comit (l'istituto milanese deteneva il 61% del capitale) sia per il volume degli affari che per l'ampio raggio d'azione. Sudameris aveva aperto oltre trenta dipendenze tra succursali, filiali e agenzie, arrivando a essere presente in Brasile, Argentina, Cile, Colombia e Uruguay. La Comit era inoltre presente in Perù attraverso il Banco Italiano di Lima, di cui aveva il controllo azionario e a cui forniva buona parte del personale direttivo. La Comit aveva assunto il controllo azionario del Banco Italiano di Lima nel corso del 1919 (di cui negli anni trenta deteneva il 34% del capitale): il Banco Italiano era il maggiore istituto di credito del Perù, estendendo la propria attività al 50% del lavoro bancario ordinario del paese, e aveva concentrato il suo lavoro sui crediti agricoli. La Comit era infine presente in Ecuador attraverso il modesto Banco Italiano di Guayaquil di cui aveva assunto il controllo a partire dal 1923[50].

Nel quadro del gruppo bancario multinazionale costituito dalla Comit negli anni venti nei loro rapporti con la capogruppo le filiali, le affíliate e le associate si dividevano in *datrici* e *prenditrici* di fondi. La sede di Parigi di Sudameris aveva in genere fornito fondi alla Comit, mentre le succursali e le filiali sudamericane di Sudameris avevano ricevuto fondi, così come le banche consociate del gruppo che operavano nei Balcani, nell'Europa centro-orientale e nel Levante[51].

Nei primi anni trenta il personale direttivo di Sudameris — a differenza della dirigenza della Banque Italo-Belge — era in prevalenza italiano. Le varie filiali sudamericane erano state riunite in gruppi per aree regionali e dipendevano dalla sede centrale di Parigi dove invece il personale era soprattutto francese. A causa della distanza le filiali sudamericane erano tuttavia dotate di una relativa autonomia, mentre alla sede centrale — che svolgeva anche funzioni di tesoreria in divisa per l'intera rete — spettava il compi-

---

e *ibidem,* cart. 73, fasc. 1. Per una prima ricostruzione dei contrasti e delle divergenze di vedute tra Zuccoli e Finaly si veda G. Piluso, *Le banche miste sui mercati esteri* cit.

50 Cfr. AS BCI, *Carte Mattioli,* cart. 3, "Fasciolo II, Parte IIa", *L'Estero,* p. 76-8, 108-12 ,113-4.

51 Cfr. *ibidem,* "Fasciolo I, Parte Ia", *L'Italia,* p. 3-4.

to di tracciare le direttive generali e di effettuare i controlli periodici sulla gestione ordinaria, per la quale le filiali avevano in dotazione un capitale di entità variabile in valuta locale.

Nel 1934 la direzione generale di Parigi avrebbe inviato in Brasile Guido Colombo per verificare la necessita di effettuare eventuali modificazioni nella struttura amministrativa delle locali succursali di Sudameris. Oltre all'apertura proposta dal direttore di São Paulo, Arturo Apollinari, di nuove agenzie nelle regioni dell'interno che da poco si dedicavano alla coltivazione del caffè, Colombo propose a Raffaele Mattioli, il nuovo amministratore delegato della Comit, di concentrare nella direzione paulistana le funzioni di controllo e analisi dei rischi dell'intera rete brasiliana. Dopo la creazione di un comitato di direzione a São Paulo proposta da Colombo, la struttura locale di Sudameris avviò una serie di analisi settoriali e previsionali sull'economia brasiliana[52].

L'insieme delle partecipazioni bancarie estere concretava, in ultima analisi, la struttura organizzativa della rete bancaria multinazionale della Comit, tanto che la situazione patrimoniale e finanziaria dei diversi istituti poteva avere riflessi quasi immediati sulla stessa capogruppo.

> Come Comit — si osservava infatti in un interessante studio approntato dai tecnici dell'IRI nell'ottobre 1933 —, salvo circostanze straordinarie, non potrebbe lasciare in difficoltà una banca del suo gruppo senza gravissimo danno per il suo proprio credito, così un offuscamento del credito a prestigio di Comit si tradurrebbe in un pericolo per le banche dipendenti, molte delle quali portano il nome di Comit in forma appena alterata[53].

Nei difficili primi anni trenta evitare l'offuscamento dello *standing* di un organismo così importante come Sudameris divenne l'obiettivo della politica di elevata liquidità perseguita dagli uomini della Comit presenti nelle strutture dell'istituto franco-italiano, sia in Europa che in Sud America. L'alto grado di instabilità economica — e anche politica — dei paesi sudamericani in cui Sudameris operava indusse la dirigenza della banca da un lato a sviluppare la

---

[52] Cfr. M. Marianno, *Sudameris* cit., p. 53-5.

[53] AS BCI, *Carte Mattioli*, cart. 3, "Fascicolo II, Parte IIa", *L'Estero*, p. 136.

propria presenza sul mercato delle accettazioni di Parigi (un mercato il cui sviluppo era favorito dalla Banque de France) e dall'altro a preferire una politica di attesa e a mantenere una "grandissima liquidità" che faceva perno sugli accantonamenti e sulle riserve costituite prima della svalutazione delle dotazioni in divisa locale delle filiali extraeuropee[54].

Se si escludono le filiali di Londra e di New York — la cui creazione rispose a ragioni di ordine organizzativo e funzionale di completamento dei servizi di banca (tesoreria in valuta per tutto il gruppo Comit) —, l'espansione all'estero delle maggiori banche misse italiane si sviluppò in due distinte fasi e secondo due diverse strategie: la prima guerra mondiale costituì la cesura non solo in termini temporali, ma anche in termini di mutamento delle strategie di espansione e delle strutture organizzative adottate dalla Comit e dal Credit.

Le banche consociate e comparttecipate della Comit e del Credit in Sud America (Brasile, Argentina, Uruguay, Cile, Perù e Ecuador) erano rivolte soprattutto ad acquisire il lavoro bancario offerto dalle colonie italiane e a sostenere il commercio estero e le imprese italiane attive su quei mercati. La precoce internazionalizzazione delle punte avanzate del sistema bancario di un paese *late joiner* come era l'Italia degli anni dieci venne perseguita dalla Comit e dal Credit attraverso l'adesione a un sistema flessibile di alleanze con le maggiori istituzioni finanziarie franco-belghe.

I falliti tentativi postbellici della Banca Italiana di Sconto e del Banco di Roma di espandersi in Brasile e in Argentina non potevano andare a buon fine *anche* a causa del loro mancato inserimento in una rete internazionale di alleanze finanziarie forti che compensassero le loro debolezze organizzative. Il contrasto tra i casi di successo della Comit e del Credit e i fallimenti della Banca Italiana di Sconto e del Banco di Roma dimostrava che per riuscire era necessario soddisfare due condizioni generali: *a)* creare strutture organizzative relativamente efficienti che rendessero possibile coordinare le attività delle direzioni europee (che l'assenza dei risconto rendeva imprescindibili) e *b)* inserirsi attivamente in una

[54] La politica di attesa e liquidità seguita tra il 1931 e il 1934 consentì a Sudameris di conservare una discreta situazione patromoniale in anni di incertezza e deterioramento del quadro economico generale. Cfr. AS BCI, Comit, Rb, 28 febbraio 1932, p. 23-4 e 25 marzo 1933, p. 16-7.

rete di alleanze i cui partner forti assicurassero l'accesso diretto alle maggiori piazze finanziarie europee (Parigi e Londra) e consentissero la partecipazione a quelle operazioni — come il collocamento delle emissioni di titoli pubblici — che avrebbero dato modo di elevare lo *standing* e la reputazione degli istituti agli occhi della clientela delle dipendenze periferiche.

Le banche miste italiane si inserirono sui mercati bancari sudamericani — fino allora dominati dalle *overseas banks* britanniche e tedesche — in una fase di crescita economica e di aumento dei soggetti creditizi concorrenti. Nella prima fase di sviluppo della rete estera delle grandi banche miste italiane rimanevano quelle condizioni permissive (l'assenza di restrizioni legislative all'entrata, l'apertura dei mercati internazionali e la relativa debolezza dei sistemi bancari locali) che avevano consentito l'affermazione delle banche britanniche e tedesche negli anni sessanta e ottanta dell'ottocento.

Le banche italiane avevano tuttavia in Sud America alcuni vantaggi competitivi rispetto ai maggiori concorrenti europei: l'Italia non era un paese esportatore di capitali né aveva un livello di investimenti diretti all'estero pari a quello della Gran Bretagna, della Francia o della Germania; l'Italia aveva però un discreto interscambio commerciale con il Sud America e soprattutto le numerose colonie di emigrati italiani, i quali in genere preferivano avere rapporti d'affari con istituiti diretti da propri connazionali, costituivano un sicuro mercato in fase di crescita (imprese, cambi, rimesse e titoli di stato).

Gli istituti di credito consociati sudamericani delle banche italiane risposero alla duplice esigenza di diversificazione dei rischi di impiego e di sviluppo delle attività creditizie così come veniva richiesto a istituti che intendevano avere una dimensione operativa internazionale e non soltanto nazionale. La validità organizzativa di un sistema qual era quello messo a punto dalla Comit — e che aveva nei mercati sudamericani la parte più consistente delle attività di banca all'estero — permise all'istituto milanese di ottenere "un'oculata discriminazione e ripartizione di investimenti e di rischi ed un proficuo diretto sfruttamento di vantaggiose possibilità nel mutevole ritmo dello svolgimento dei rapporti economici e finanziari fra i diversi Paesi"[55].

---

[55] AS BCI, Comit, Rb, 29 marzo 1930, p. 13-4.

Le maggiori banche miste italiane si rivolsero ai mercati sudamericani negli anni dieci e venti nella prospettiva di conseguire tre obiettivi: assumere in proprio i servizi bancari connessi alle transazioni commerciali internazionali internalizzando la rete dei corrispondenti esteri, acquisire una dimensione operativa di livello internazionale mediante l'affermazione in quei mercati che costituivano una sorta di estensione del mercato interno, diversificare la politica di impiego così da ripartire i rischi correlati agli investimenti in base alle opportunità offerte dalla pluralità dei mercati resi accessibili dalla progressiva integrazione economica mondiale.

Nonostante il notevole ritardo, la Comit e il Credit riuscirono così a conquistare quote significative di mercato realizzando una struttura organizzativa che ben si prestava a valorizzare quelle attività di raccolta e impiego dei capitali sui mercati esteri locali. Sudameris e la Banque Italo-Belge non soltanto svolgevano ordinarie operazioni in valuta e di finanziamento del commercio estero, ma concedevano crediti di esercizio alle imprese operanti nei settori manifatturieri in crescita (tessile e meccanica), appoggiavano le imprese italiane presenti su quei mercati e si impegnavano in attività bancarie trascurate dalle banche d'oltremare tedesche e britanniche, come la raccolta di depositi tra la clientela locale attraverso una fitta rete di filiali presenti nei principali centri commerciali, agricoli e industriali *(retail banking).* Sudameris, in particolare, si affermò con successo in Brasile, Argentina e Uruguay negli anni dieci e venti, sottraendo cospicue quote di mercato alle banche straniere che vi operavano da alcuni decenni: solo la crisi delle economie sudamericane, l'adozione di politiche protezionistiche e, soprattutto, l'affermazione di soggetti bancari nazionali — parallelamente al rafforzamento degli istituti centrali (il Banco do Brasil e il Banco Central in Argentina) e all'istituzione di forme di controllo dei flussi valutari — ridimensionarono in parte il ruolo di Sudameris e della Banque Italo-Belge durante gli anni trenta[56].

---

56 Sulla caduta dei prezzi del caffè soprattutto dopo il crollo della *Defesa* nell'ottobre 1929, e dello zucchero — le voci principali di una struttura economica come quella brasiliana dipendente dai settori agroesportatori — cfr. le notazioni di C. Furtado, *La formazione economica del Brasile,* Torino, 1970, p. 229-48 ; T. Szmrecsányi, "Growth and Crisis of the Brazilian Sugar Industry, 1914-39", *Rivista di storia economica,* n.s. 5

Durante gli anni trenta si ridusse il peso relativo della componente estera delle banche miste italiane — mentre istituti di credito come la Banca Nazionale del Lavoro iniziarono proprio in quegli anni a uscire dai confini nazionali[57] — in relazione sia al mutato quadro degli scambi internazionali che al processo di risanamento e di riforma del sistema bancario interno. Nel corso del decennio si ridusse via quella spinta all'internazionalizzazione delle strutture societarie delle maggiori banche italiane che aveva invece caratterizzato gli anni dieci e venti: in questi decenni si erano tuttavia in buon grado accummulate quelle risorse immateriali — conoscenza dei mercati e dei sistemi monetari e finanziari, consolidate relazioni con gli operatori economici di quei mercati e una rete di alleanze di riferimento — che nel secondo dopoguerra avrebbero consentito agli istituti di credito italiani di reinserirsi nei circuiti internazionali.

Quale effetto di ritorno dell'internazionalizzazione delle maggiori banche miste italiane — la Comit e il Credit — si ebbe una graduale acquisizione di capacità di crescita diretta sui mercati esteri, attraverso strutture che erano in larga parte dipendenti e controllate dalle direzioni centrali. L'inserimento dei banchieri italiani nei *networks* finanziari internazionali che doveva assicurare credito e informazioni negli anni venti si trasformò nell'attivazione di

---

(1988), n. 2, p. 193-219. Sulla crisi dell'industria cotoniera brasiliana cfr. S. H. Haber, "Business Enterprise and the Great Depression in Brazil: A Study of Profits and Losses in Textile Manufacturing", *Business History Review*, vol. 66 (1992), n. 2, p. 335-63. Sull'evoluzione dei sistemi bancari sudamericani in rapporto alle banche europee si vedano le notazioni contenute in D. Joslin, A *Century of Banking in Latin America* cit., p. 226 e 230; G. Jones, *British Multinational Banking* cit., p. 191-3; per il sistema monetario brasiliano si veda C. M. Peláez & W. Suzigan, *História monetária do Brasil: análise da politica, comportamento e instituições monetárias*, Rio de Janeiro, 1976, p. 239-77. La riforma bancaria e monetaria nei paesi sudamericani seguì spesso le missioni di Otto Niemeyer, il quale non poté non notare: *"the dependence of the Argentine upon export trade in pimary commodities; the rigid way in which, under the existing monetary system, the supply of currency is linked to the trade balance; and the evil effects of the way in which foreign loans have been employed in ways not calculated to expand Argentine exports so as to cover their service"* (*Argentine Banking Reform*, in *Economist*, 13 maggio 1933, p. 16-7).

57 Cfr. V. Castronovo, *Storia di una banca. La Banca Nazionale del Lavoro e lo sviluppo economico italiano 1913-1983*, Torino, 1982, p. 189-95.

strutture organizzative direttamente collegate agli organi direttivi centrali degli istituti, così da fornire un accesso alle risorse e alle informazioni che non fosse più mediato esclusivamente da una base informale e personale. L'internalizzazione dei servizi non fece cadere la componente personale e fiduciaria come elemento che consentiva di avere uno "sguardo" diretto sulle operazioni di banca di portata internazionale trasformando le opportunità offerte dalle alleanze in affari concreti.

L'elemento personale e fiduciario implicito nelle modalità di funzionamento e regolazione dei *networks* — *"le facteur le plus important de réussite dans notre métier ce sont les hommes"* come scrisse Carlier a Balzarotti — venne anzi valorizzato da un'accresciuta capacità di intervento derivante dalla rete di dipendenze estere la cui rilevanza si esprimeva concretamente nella formazione dei sindacati bancari internazionali e nello svolgimento delle relative operazioni di collocamento. Dalla dimensione personale tipica della *haute banque* europea gli istituti italiani poterono passare alla dimensione, organizzativamente più complessa, dell'impresa bancaria multinazionale: una configurazione operativa e organizzativa che tendeva a enfatizzare le funzioni gerarchiche delle organizzazioni formali rispetto a quelle dei complessi reticoli personali, familiari ed etnico-religiosi.

Le maggiori banche miste italiane si mossero sui mercati esteri nella fase di sostanziale apertura degli scambi internazionali, quando i riferimenti monetari erano ancora quelli rassicuranti del sistema di cambi fissi del *gold standard.* Negli anni venti le banche miste italiane riuscirono in un primo tempo a realizzare una estesa rete bancaria multinazionale; i dirigenti della Comit e del Credit dovettero quindi attuare un progressivo raccoglimento nella prospettiva di salvaguardare le esperienze organizzative e gestionali, i contatti pesonali e gli spazi di mercato che erano stati acquisiti nei due decenni precedenti. Nel secondo dopoguerra il ritorno dell'economia italiana — e dell'economia mondiale — alla crescita degli scambi con l'estero avrebbe segnato il rilancio delle strategie di espansione oltre il mercato interno.

Bruno Bezza
Libero Istituto Universitario C. Cattaneo, Castellanza

L'ESPRIT D'ENTREPRISE ITALIEN, LE MARCHÉ SUD-AMÉRICAIN ET LES INITIATIVES INDUSTRIELLES: LE CAS DE LA SOCIÉTÉ PIRELLI (1900-1920)

Ces dernières années, plusieurs études ont été faites sur le rôle joué par l'émigration italienne en Amérique Latine et en Argentine, notamment. Un aspect important, bien qu'insuffisamment traité, est le rôle que les Italiens ont joué à l'étranger dans la formation des entreprises locales. Sous plusieurs aspects, l'Argentine represente le principal pays où des mécanismes de croissance de forces d'entreprise d'origine italienne et, en même temps, c'est le pays où l'exportation italienne a constitué, pendant certaines périodes, une partie importante du commerce extérieur. En outre, l'Argentine et, en une moindre mesure le Brésil, ont été de 1900 à 1930 les lieux préférés des entreprises italiennes qui y ont fait des investissements directs.

Pour brosser un tableau assez fidèle à l'intérieur duquel on pourra saisir les causes et les comportements des sujets économiques, nous commencerons par analyser les problèmes que provoqua l'émigration italienne en Argentine, puis les comportements qui découlèrent en Italie du fait de considérer ce pays du point de vue aussi de l'économie.

L'Argentine en tant qu'appendice du marché italien

L'importance de l'émigration italienne en Argentine et les conditions générales dans lesquelles celle-ci eut lieu entrainèrent la formation de communautés fortement liées à des modèles de vie et de consommation caractéristiques du lieu de provenance. Tant il est vrai que les principaux produits exportés de l'Italie vers l'Argentine pendant tout le XIXe siècle et une grande partie du XXe furent des denrées alimentaires, des boissons et des tissus. La présence d'une forte communauté italienne a fini par produire un bon nombre de *self made men* qui constituaient l'ossature de l'organisation des commerces entre l'Argentine et l'Italie.

Une grande partie des *self made men* sont à l'origine de simples ouvriers ou de petits artisans provenant du triangle industriel italien. Il y a ceux qui se sont essayé dans plusieurs métiers et peut-être aussi dans d'autres pays d'immigration (Grèce, Tunisie et Brésil). Un cas singulier est celui d'Antonio Tomba, un important industriel vinicole. Avant de s'établir à Mendoza, il avait été, tour à tour, boulanger, épicier, briquetier et vivandier à la suite des entreprises qui construisaient le chemin de fer du Pacifique. Les laboratoires et les ateliers avec lesquels la plupart a commencé sont très modestes: un hangar, quelques machines-outils et des plus simples et un nombre réduit d'ouvriers souvent dotés d'une formation tout à fait insuffisante.

Les *curricula vitae* de ces entrepreneurs révèlent qu'au cours des derniers vingt ans du XIXe siècle, l'augmentation de la taille industrielle des initiatives dépend presque toujours de la capacité d'épargne des émigrants qui, compte tenu du bas niveau technologique, leur a permis d'accumuler les capitaux initiaux réduits nécessaires à devenir des entrepreneurs industriels.

A notre avis, les deux éléments les plus caractéristiques sont les suivants: *a)* l'appel des parents restés en Italie pour remplacer la main-d'oeuvre à des prix réduits; *b)* la constitution de sociétés quasi exclusivement avec des conationaux.

L'entrée de nouveaux associés, dans ces entreprises industrielles de taille limitée, s'accompagnait presque toujours de l'apport de nouveaux capitaux qui n'étaient pas disponibles autrement. La taille modeste des ateliers et des magasins souvent ne permettait pas de recourir à l'emprunt bancaire. Ou bien elle entraînait l'exigence de faire entrer les compétences manquantes dans l'entreprise.

Cette solidarité ethnique et familiale, qui résolvait en partie le problème des fonds, des compétences et de la main-d'oeuvre qualifiée dans un milieu à développement retardé qui n'était pas hostile, constitue le trait dominant de l'influence italienne en Argentine et dans l'état du Rio Grande do Sul au Brésil. D'autre part, les barrières à l'entrée dans la constitution de petites entreprises industrielles en Argentine étaient beaucoup plus faibles qu'en Italie où, à la même période, le milieu compétitif ressentait déjà de la concurrence des autres pays européens, et où les contraintes technologiques et de dimension de l'entreprise ne cessaient de s'accroitre.

Faire fortune en Amérique latine (autrement dit, en Argentine et au sud du Brésil) était l'objectif de nombreux artisans et ouvriers expulsés du marché du travail en Italie, notamment de la Ligurie, Piémont, Lombardie et Vénétie, qui constituaient une part importante de ce courant migratoire. Nous pourrions décrire sommairement les comportements des entrepreneurs italiens en Argentine et les caractéristiques des entreprises qu'ils dirigent de la façon suivante:

1) absence de spécialisation, taille réduite, propriété familiale avec des parents directement concernés dans le processus de production;

2) productions qui se rattachent entre elles ou non, déterminées par le manque de spécialisation productive et par leur faible contenu technologique;

3) co-présence d'activités de production et d'importation (souvent l'activité de production dépend du commerce: réparations, montage, adaptations et modifications);

4) marché restreint, limité tout au plus aux communautés italiennes (plus particulièrement de produits alimentaires et de boissons);

5) importation de l'Italie de machines et de matières premières;

6) emploi de main-d'oeuvre quasi exclusivement d'origine italienne.

Une nouvelle génération à cheval des deux siècles

Au début du XXe siècle, nous assistons à un processus de concentration des petites entreprises italiennes. Une concentration qui servait à augmenter la dimension de l'entreprise pour faire face à la concurrence et mieux exploiter les opportunités du crédit. A côté d'attitudes encore imprégnées du caractère individuel de l'entreprise, on commence à voir, dans les principaux secteurs de l'économie argentine, la diffusion des sociétés anonymes. En outre, au cours des dernières années du siècle dernier, l'émigration entre dans une nouvelle phase: celle des "colonisateurs industriels". Ils sont déjà présents dans l'industrie manufacturière italienne et ouvrent des succursales de leurs entreprises en Argentine, unissant ainsi à l'exportation de produits italiens la fabrication sur place des mêmes produits. Les raisons de cette expansion, bien que limitée, sont dues essentiellement au développement du marché sud-américain qui a lieu ces mêmes années et aux mesures protectionnistes que le gouvernement argentin adopte pour privilégier les entreprises locales.

La participation du capital marchand à des initiatives industrielles devient évidente avec la diffusion des sociétés anonymes, notamment celles par actions. Ce sont, en effet, les commerçants Devoto, Stoppani et Profumo qui participent en 1889 à la constitution, à côté des petits producteurs du secteur, à la Compañía General de Fósforos. En 1904, des commerçants cotonniers s'associeront à l'industriel lainier Barolo pour donner naissance à la Compañía Algodonera Nacional, première fabrique de filés de coton en Argentine.

Mais, par rapport à des pays qui ont une longue tradition coloniale, les initiatives commerciales permanentes et non à caractère temporaire et purement spéculatives sont rares. La Società per l'Esportazione de Dell'Acqua a son siège à Milan, mais doit bien vite se transformer en une société de droit argentin pour éviter le protectionnisme de ce pays. A la Sociedad Arrocera y Almidonera Argentina dont le siège est à Gênes, elle aussi italienne, s'ajouteront Frigorifico Argentino, Compañía Nacional de Tejidos e Compañía Nacional de Fósforos.

Toutefois, il convient de préciser que les Italiens sont exclus des secteurs oú se constitue le plus grand nombre de sociétés par actions, à savoir, des secteurs où le processus de concentration est naturellement plus accentué: sucre, bière et viandes. Dans ces secteurs, c'est la présence anglaise qui, traditionnellement, domine aux côtés des anciennes familles argentines d'origine espagnole et ici les barrières à l'entrée sont encore plus fortes que dans d'autres secteurs, vu la nécessité de plus de capitaux, de connaissances techniques spécifiques et de dimensions de production plus grandes.

L'intervention du capital italien dans l'industrie électrique argentine (1910-1920)

Au début de la deuxième décennie du XXe siècle eut lieu le cas le plus important, et peut-être le plus singulier, de financement à l'étranger par des industries italiennes, dans le secteur électrique argentin. L'initiative de Pirelli, de Franco Tosi, de Tecnomasio Italiano Brown-Boveri et des partenaires suisses, visant à la constitution et au financement de la Compañía Italo-Argentina de Electricidad de Buenos Aires, constitua un cas très important dans toute l'histoire des investissements italiens à l'étranger, aussi bien pour les motifs qui induirent à cette opération que pour le milieu qui la promouvait. Si, pour certaines entreprises italiennes, le financement de sociétés à l'étranger pouvait rentrer dans une logique d'expansion sur les marchés internationaux et ouvrir ainsi d'importants débouchés sur les redoutables places étrangères — c'est le cas de Pirelli et de Tosi — et si pour d'autres, une opération semblable servait à répondre à des stratégies de grande envergure organisées par leur partenaire à l'étranger — c'est le cas du rapport complexe entre Tecnomasio Italiano Brown-Boveri de Milan et Brown-Boveri de Baden — il n'en reste pas moins que, pour d'autres groupes qui y participèrent, l'opération avait un caractère plus spéculatif à proprement parler: tels Cinzano, Dellachà, Melzi d'Eril, Clerici et autres.

Le milieu commercial, industriel et spéculatif de Buenos Aires joua un rôle de premier plan dans toute l'histoire. Dans cette ville, la communauté italienne pouvait compter sur d'importants appuis au Banco de Italia y Rio de la Plata et disposait sur le marché argentin de certains hommes d'affaires de premier plan (les ingénieurs Mauro Herlitzka, Giovanni Carosio, Vittorio Valdani et Pietro Vaccari), qui lui donnaient un avantage indéniable en termes de facteurs managériaux et techniques. L'ingénieur Mauro Herlitzka était né à Trieste et avait fait ses études au Polytechnique de Turin. En 1898, il émigra en Argentine où il occupa le poste de directeur général de la Compañía Alemana Transatlántica de Electricidad (Cate) de Buenos Aires. Pendant la période comprise entre 1900 et 1910 il entretint des liens étroits avec les sociétés Franco Tosi et Pirelli, des entreprises qui étaient devenues, durant cette même période, les principaux fournisseurs de la Cate. En 1910, Herlitzka se retira de la direction Cate pour diriger personnellement et gérer "avec des capitaux en majorité propres, un groupe d'entreprises électriques situées dans différentes villes de la République argentine, groupe qui forme aujourd'hui, dans la branche de l'industrie électrique argentine, un ensemble d'affaires très important".

Pietro Vaccari, figure singulière de courtier et de *manager* italo-américain, au début du siècle avait réussi à devenir un des principaux hommes d'affaires dans le secteur de l'achat et vente de combustibles; en outre, il gérait toutes les activités de la Compañía Nacional de Tejidos et de la Compañía General de Fósforos; avec d'autres il avait fondé une société pour l'industrie et l'exportation italo-américaine et, enfin, il occupait quelques charges honorifiques — celle de consul du Paraguay en Italie et celle de consul italien à Buenos Aires qui lui avaient été attribuées compte tenu de son influence dans le milieu d'affaires de l'Amérique latine.

L'ingénieur Vittorio Valdani avait été nommé en 1902 directeur de l'Etablissement Pirelli de Villanueva y Geltrú, en Espagne. En 1907 il avait démissionné par suite de quelques contrastes internes sur la gestion de l'établissement. Il fut alors envoyé par Pirelli à diriger la filiale de Buenos Aires qui venait d'être ouverte. Quelques années après, il quitta définitivement l'entreprise milanaise et la direction de la filiale argentine pour devenir gérant de la Compañía General de Fósforos.

L'ingénieur Giovanni Carosio avait fondé, au début du siècle, la Compañía Industrial de Electricidad del Rio de la Plata et la Compañía de Electricidad de la Provincia de Buenos Aires, cette dernière avec des capitaux anglais. Dans les deux compagnies il avait la charge de *general manager.* Suite à la fusion et à l'absorption qui avaient eu lieu entre 1900 et 1907, Carosio s'était retiré des activités directes de gestion des sociétés électriques.

Des trois entreprises italiennes interessées à l'opération complexe d'investissement dans le secteur électrique à Buenos Aires, la Pirelli joua indéniablement le rôle le plus important. L'entreprise avait commencé dès 1881 la fabrication de fils et câbles électriques dont une partie importante était destinée à l'exportation et, en 1895, elle était en mesure de fabriquer des câbles électriques souterrains s'étant assuré, au début de la décennie, d'importants brevets. Dans les premières années de sa vie, les exportations de Pirelli étaient modestes, mais à la fin du siècle elles atteignirent 30% de la production totale, les principaux pays de destination étant Espagne, Portugal (40%), Etats-Unis (15%), Grande-Bretagne (17%), France (7%), Russie, Australie et Orient (8%). En 1906, afin de faire face de façon rationnelle aux nouvelles exigences dues à l'imposant développement de la motorisation et du secteur électrique, l'entreprise décida de construire un nouvel établissement dans la banlieue de Milan (Greco-Bicocca). Dans la première décennie du nouveau siècle, Pirelli mit en oeuvre une politique de pénétration massive sur le marché espagnol, où elle avait déjà obtenu d'importants accords gouvernementaux pour les câbles télégraphiques posés entre l'Espagne et les Baléares, d'une part, et l'Espagne et le Maroc, d'autre part. Dans le secteur électrique, la politique de pénétration se fondait sur l'achat de participations de minorité dans des sociétés électriques régionales (Catalana de Gas y Electricidad S.A., Barcelona) qui souvent étaient subordonnées ou à des marchés de fourniture ou à des rapports d'affaires avec d'autres sociétés (Franco Tosi, Riva, Monneret, Tecnomasio Italiano Brown-Boveri). Or, cela ne pouvait avoir lieu sans l'accord ou du moins le consentement tacite de trois grands groupes européens avec lesquels l'entreprise maintenait des rapports de sous-traitance: Brown-Boveri de Baden, Oerlikon de Zurich et Thomson-Houston de la Méditerranée de Paris.

Au début de la première décennie du siècle, la firme Pirelli se trouva à devoir élargir son marché et regarda tout particulièrement au marché de Buenos Aires où, en 1910, elle ouvrit une filiale commerciale. La nature de la production — câbles et conducteurs électriques — exigeait l'accord avec d'autres fabricants de matériel électromécanique (dynamos, turbines, etc.) afin de bloquer les fournitures aux sociétés électriques d'exploitation et de cerner, dans les pays encore peu industrialisés, les groupes financiers disponibles à s'accorder avec les fournisseurs pour la constitution d'entreprises de production d'énergie électrique. Il en découla une lutte acharnée avec les concurrents étrangers, notamment avec les entreprises allemandes, fortes d'une solide tradition en Argentine.

Brown-Boveri fut constituée comme société en commandite en décembre 1890 par Charles Eugene Lancelot Brown et Walter Boveri, auxquels se joignit en février de l'année suivante, en tant qu'associé accomandité, Fritz Funk qui allait ensuite s'assumer la responsabilité commerciale de l'entreprise. L'activité entrepreneuriale, au sens étroit du terme, commença vers la fin de 1891 avec vingt-cinq employés et une centaine d'ouvriers à Baden. Son activité consistait dans la fabrication de machines et appareillages électriques de tous genres dont notamment générateurs, moteurs et transformateurs à courant alternatif, tableaux et appareils pour la transformation de l'énergie. Par la suite, vu le nombre réduit d'entreprises d'installation qui s'occupaient d'énergie électrique destinée à l'éclairage et à l'industrie, l'activité de l'entreprise s'étendit à la conception et à la mise en oeuvre de réseaux privés et d'appareills destines aux habitations et à l'industrie.

Le grand développement de l'activité productive et la nécessité d'importants apports de capitaux amena Brown-Boveri à constituer, le 20 septembre 1895 à Baden, une société de financement pour les entreprises électriques à l'instar d'AEG, de Siemens & Halske et de Schuckert.

Néanmoins, au début, Brown-Boveri se heurta à maintes difficultés pour convaincre les milieux bancaires suisses à participer au projet de constitution d'une société financière, bien que le capital initial prévu ne s'élevât qu'à trois millions de francs: aucune des grandes banques de Zurich, de Bâle et de Genève n'accepta de participer à l'opération et ce n'est que la S.A. Leu & Co., l'une des banques suisses les plus anciennes, et la Banque de Baden qui répondirent affirmativement, souscrivant respectivement 200.000 et 50.000 francs. Aussi Brown-Boveri fut-elle obligée de faire appel à des capitaux étrangers.

La constitution eut lieu à Baden le 20 novembre 1895 avec la dénomination sociale de "Motor AG. für elektrische Unternehmungen". La présidence alla à Walter Boveri, la direction technique fut confiée à l'ingénieur Agostino Nizzola et la direction administrative au commerçant allemand August Dotzheimer.

Par la suite, Motor, avec l'aide de Brown-Boveri, conçut et construisit des installations hydroélectriques en Suisse et en Italie à proximité du massif des Alpes, constituant une société d'exploitation. Parallèlement, profitant de la situation conjoncturelle des premières années du siècle, elle acheta d'importantes participations dans des sociétés mécaniques, électromécaniques et électrochimiques en Italie, France et Suisse. Néanmoins, si Brown-Boveri était en mesure d'avoir une évolution favorable sur le marché européen grâce aux projets d'avant-garde et à l'obtention d'importants brevets concernant l'utilisation du courant à haute tension, la Motor, elle n'avait pas autant de mobilité dans un secteur où la concurrence des groupes industriels majeurs, appuyés par les grandes banques allemandes et suisso-allemandes, était prépondérante. Les opérations conduites jusqu'alors par Motor avec l'aide de Brown-Boveri s'étaient désormais consolidées et apparaissaient comme de pures et simples intermédiations financières. Or, Motor commençait à souffrir du manque d'opportunités de projets et d'investissements.

L'intervention italienne

Au cours des quinze premières années du siècle, les exportations de matériel électrique de l'Italie vers l'Argentine s'étaient consolidées au point qu'elles représentaient une part non-négligeable du marché. Les trois grandes entreprises intéressées — Marelli, Pirelli et Tosi — étaient présentes sur le marché de Buenos Aires avec leurs propres filiales ou leurs représentants: Alfredo Gessaroli, directeur de la filiale de Buenos Aires de Pirelli et Giovanni Carosio, entrepreneur et *manager* de nombreuses compagnies d'électricité, pour Franco Tosi.

Durant ces années, la place de Buenos Aires était théâtre de manoeuvres complexes, ainsi que le témoigne cette lettre qu'Alberto Pirelli écrivit à Mauro Herlitzka le 9 novembre 1911:

> "Ces jours-ci la participation d'un groupe italien à la constitution d'une société argentine dont vous aurez peut-être vu l'annonce et qui a été promue par Monsieur Carosio s'est concrétisée. Il y a quelque temps nous fûmes approchés par certains amis qui nous demandèrent si nous acceptions d'entrer nous aussi dans cette société, laquelle allait être fondée avec un caractère et un nom italien grâce aussi à la participation de forts éléments italiens à Buenos Aires. Après avoir examiné la question, nous avons fini par accepter avec Messieurs Tosi et Vaccari, bien que l'entreprise ne se présentât pas sous la forme que nous aurions préféré et que nous avions espéré pouvoir donner à une combinaison italo-argentine lorsque nous en avions parlé avec vous, il y a de cela un an. Nous aurions préféré encore la constitution ici en Italie d'un Syndicat à large base et qui aurait pu prendre des participations dans plusieurs groupes et plusieurs entreprises, plutôt que prendre part à la constitution d'une seule entreprise, fût-elle destinée à avoir un champ d'action assez vaste. Mais puisqu'un groupe s'était constitué qui avait un caractère italien sympathique et que nous subîmes plusieurs pressions par de bons amis, nous avons fini par accepter et nous espérons avoir bien fait tant pour l'entreprise elle-même que pour l'importance des commandes qui pourraient en découler."

D'une autre lettre d'Alberto Pirelli à Valdani il ressort que les intentions des sociétés Pirelli et Tosi n'étaient pas claires du tout et que l'attitude générale ressentait de leur inexpérience aussi bien sur le marché argentin qu'à propos des futurs développements des opérations financiares complexes:

> "Il est peut-être étrange qu'après avoir hésité ici sur la participation à d'autres entreprises dont nous connaissions les évolutions et les précédents, on se soit décidé à présent à participer à une affaire qui est toute faite sur la base de la confiance en Monsieur Carosio. De toute façon, nous étions déjá prêts à faire quelque chose avant et puisque cette fois-ci les Tosi ont accepté, nous avons vu volontiers que l'on pouvait faire ce premier pas. On ne sait pas encore si la Brown-Boveri participera ensuite elle aussi, mais, avec ou sans elle, l'affaire semble conclue et Vaccari a télégraphié à Carosio pour l'informer que notre groupe avait participé avec 400.000 pesos, mais que nous demandions — puisqu'il avait été question d'une participation d'un groupe européen d'un million de pesos que l'on réservât une émission de 600.000 pesos pour une éventuelle combinaison de notre société avec la Brown-Boveri ou autres."

Comme on peut le voir, le tableau était plein d'incertitudes et de décisions contradictoires: d'abord on prend contact avec Herlitzka, puis on l'abandonne pour accepter la proposition Carosio (semble-t-il, de ce qui ressort de la documentation, en vertu de la simple rivalité entre les deux); puis on veut partager le risque avec d'autres partenaires et c'est alors qu'entre en scène la société Tosi; enfin, on veut la participation de Motor, pour pouvoir décharger sur elle la plus grande part de l'investissement.

En 1910, l'ingénieur Herlitzka s'était retiré de Cate. Nous ne savons pas ce qui poussait Pirelli à refuser la proposition d'Herlitzka et à accepter celle de Carosio, Vaccari et autres. Il est vrai pourtant que ces derniers jouissaient de l'appui du Banco de Italia y Rio de la Plata (établissement fondé par le Credito Italiano et la Banca Lombarda di Depositi e Conti Correnti) et, le 24 août 1911, Carosio, le partenaire financier local, envoyait à Vaccari, consul italien à Bogotá et titulaire de sociétés d'exportation en Amérique latine, la dépêche suivante:

> "Etant donné que depuis quelque temps la nouvelle Compagnie anglaise n'achète pas de nouvelles centrales et étant don-

> né qu'elle offre en vente quelques-unes des existentes avec un bénéfice brut actuel non inférieur à 15 pour cent, j'ai cru avantageux former une nouvelle Compagnie qui pourra se développer parallèlement à la Cep (Compañía de Electricidad de la Provincia de Buenos Aires) anglaise en d'excellentes conditions."

Par la suite, plus exactement le 7 septembre, eut lieu à Milan une rencontre entre Alberto Pirelli, Gianfranco Tosi et Pietro Vaccari. Ce dernier expliqua que la Cep anglaise avait des problèmes de liquidité et n'était pas en mesure d'absorber d'autres centrales électriques. Il assura Pirelli et Tosi qu'"au cas où ceux-ci participeraient financièrement à la constitution de la nouvelle société (...) les commandes de la Province (Cep) aussi pourront plus facilement à l'avenir" être adressées aux entreprises italiennes. Vaccari mit l'accent sur ses excellents rapports avec la Cep, démontrés par le fait que la Compañía Industrial (une société d'import-export sise à Buenos Aires et à Milan) qu'il dirigeait aurait continué à être fournisseur de la Cep. L'ingénieur Carosio, lui, était associé en affaires de Vaccari dans la Compañía Industrial de Electricidad del Rio de la Plata, dont il était administrateur délégué et détenait également la charge d'administrateur délégué de la Cep.

Enfin, en novembre 1911, la société Motor de Baden entra dans l'affaire par l'intermédiaire d'Agostino Nizzola, son représentant le plus important. C'est ainsi que commencèrent les manoeuvres pour la formation du conseil d'administration.

La Pirelli prétendit que le groupe européen (Tosi, Motor, Pirelli même) eût un représentant en commun et que, parmi les commissaires aux comptes, figurât Alfredo Gessaroli. Toute l'opération aurait été axée sur les marchés de fourniture en exclusivité qui auraient été signés dans quelques mois par la nouvelle société électrique de Buenos Aires, la Compañía Italo-Argentina de Electricidad, avec la Compañía Industrial de Electricidad del Rio de la Plata, Pirelli, Tosi et Motor.

En 1912, la Compañía Italo-Argentina obtenait la première concession de la Municipalité de Buenos Aires.

> "Le groupe suisse — écrivait Vaccari à Pirelli — est prêt à répondre en mesure suffisante ou avec un agrandissement de son cercle, à tous nos besoins (...). Nous craignons à raison qu'en obtenant des crédits uniquement du consortium suisse les fa-

bricants italiens (...) ne perdent sous peu la prépondérance ou la proportion équitable d'influence eue jusqu'à présent (...). Nous n'avons pas à nous plaindre jusqu'á présent de nos amis suisses, mais il est évident que derrière l'argent il y aura inévitablement du matériel, des machines et des idées; toutefois, tant qu'il est temps, nous demandons un examen sérieux du problème."

La proposition des Italo-Argentins était de fonder une banque italienne pour les entreprises d'électricité, dont la tâche était de financer l'Italo-Argentina pendant les premières années. Dans les jours qui suivirent, une rencontre eut lieu avec le groupe suisse et l'idée prenait corps d'une société financière italo-suisse qui contrôlât l'entreprise de Buenos Aires et se chargea de ses besoins financiers. Au bout de trois mois à peine, la Columbus Société Anonyme d'Entreprises Electriques était constituée, son siège étant à Glaris (Suisse).

L'objectif de ces rapports enchevêtrés était, comme nous l'avons déjà dit, de conclure des marchés de fourniture: pour Pirelli, câbles et conducteurs, pour Tosi, chaudières, et brûleurs et alternateurs pour Brown-Boveri. Avant la création de la société Columbus, les rapports entre la Pirelli et la société argentine étaient régis par deux conventions signées au début de 1913, prévues pour une durée de dix ans. Il s'agissait en somme de marchés de fourniture en exclusivité pour ce qui concernait câbles, conducteurs électriques et leurs accessoires, fils et cordes de cuivre nu et articles de caoutchouc en général. Pirelli bénéficiait de l'option de fourniture pour ces produits et, en outre, la Compañía Italo-Argentina s'engageait pour elle-même, pour les entreprises qui s'y rattachaient et pour tous ceux qui lui fourniraient des installations. Pour ces mêmes produits, une convention était signée entre Pirelli et la Compañía Industrial de Electricidad, qui engageait cette dernière à donner sa préférence à Pirelli si le matériel acheté était ensuite revendu à la Compañía Italo-Argentina. Toutes deux auraient bénéficié d'une majoration du prix de 5 pour cent.

La constitution de la société financière Columbus imposait la révision de toute l'organisation des rapports de fourniture. Un intermédiaire était créé dans le but de gérer les flux d'argent pour les investissements ordinaires et extraordinaires, venant de la puissante Brown-Boveri. Tout au long de l'année 1913 et dans les premiers mois de 1914 on essaya de trouver un accord en vue de concilier les différents intérêts: d'une part, Columbus s'engageait, à son nom et à celui des sociétés où son influence était predominante, à faire en sorte que les commandes de câbles et de conducteurs électriques isolés, de matériaux isolants et produits en caoutchouc en général fussent dirigées vers Pirelli. A son tour, celle-ci s'engageait elle-même ainsi que ses filiales à ne pas entreprendre d'initiatives concurrentes de celles de Columbus. Suite à cet accord, un autre fut signé entre Pirelli et Brown Boveri. Dérogeant aux accords intervenus avec Columbus, au cas où Brown-Boveri aurait commencé la production ou acheté des participations de majorité dans des firmes productrices de câbles et de conducteurs électriques isolés, la société financière aurait dú repartir les commandes à raison de 60 pour cent à Pirelli et 40 pour cent à Brown-Boveri. Des contrats analogues furent signés entre Franco Tosi et Brown-Boveri de Baden.

En juillet 1914, Columbus informait Pirelli ainsi que la Compañía Italo-Argentina que la Brown-Boveri avait acheté la majorité des actions de Rheinische Draht & Kabelwerke GmbH de Köln-Riehl et que, par conséquent, il fallait mettre en oeuvre la dérogation prévue dans la convention. Mais les événements se compliquèrent outre mesure. Le début de la première guerre mondiale empêcha de fait Columbus d'utiliser la production de câbles souterrains suisse-allemands en remplacement de ceux Pirelli.

Dès 1914, Pirelli avait passé ses participations dans Columbus à Pirelli Produkte de Zurich qui, jusqu'à la constitution de la Compagnie Internationale Pirelli, allait rester la seule dépositaire des participations à l'étranger de l'entreprise italienne. Cependant, avec l'intervention massive entre 1923 et 1925 des banques suisses dans le refinancement de la société Motor-Columbus, l'entreprise milanaise se trouva partiellement mise à l'écart, bien qu'Alberto Pirelli continuât d'en être le Vice-Président, en tant que représentant de Pirelli Holding S.A.

Assez vite, la contrepartie bancaire fit sentir son poids et, en 1928, la Société Suisse-Américaine d'Electricité fut fondée à Zurich dans le but d'élargir le cadre financier des initiatives de Motor Columbus en Amérique du Sud. Celle-ci céda à la nouvelle société une partie des actions des compagnies sud-américaines en échange d'actions de la série B de la Société Suisse. La principale participation de la nouvelle société fut constituée par la Compañía Italo-Argentina.

A partir des années 20, le panorama argentin changea profondément de physionomie: la grande antagoniste de la Compañía

Italo-Argentina de Electricidad, la vieille Compañía Alemana Transatlántica de Electricidad, se transforma en Compañía Hispano-Americana de Electricidad, AEG ayant vendu ses actions à un syndicat bancaire espagnol et belge et laissant ainsi la compagnie graviter dans l'orbite de la Sofina. Ce n'est qu'en 1936 que la Chade aurait été achetée par la Compañía Argentina de Electricidad, revenant, du moins formellement, sous le contrôle du capital argentin. Au contraire, la Cia continua d'obtenir d'importantes concessions municipales: en 1926, pour l'extension du service électrique à Avellaneda; en 1928, à Lomas de Zamora et à Quilmes. A la fin des années 20, le réseau électrique de la compagnie était de 3.721 kilomètres et la Cia était désormais devenue la compagnie électrique argentine la plus importante.

V
ESTUDOS DE CASO DE EMPRESAS BRASILEIRAS E ESTRANGEIRAS

Carlos Gabriel Guimarães
Departamento de História, UFF

O BANCO MAUÁ & CIA. (1854-1878): UM BANCO NO BRASIL DO SÉCULO XIX

A organização da estrutura financeira de um país — os ativos, mercados e instituições — está intimamente ligada à organização do Estado Nacional e ao desenvolvimento das forças produtivas. Em outras palavras, "a estrutura financeira destaca-se pela extrema sensibilidade às manipulações de caráter jurídico-político"[1].

Durante a primeira metade do século XIX, a estrutura financeira e do crédito no Brasil era bastante limitada, em virtude da própria conjuntura política e econômica brasileira. A construção do Estado Nacional brasileiro, e os problemas de ordem econômica e política ligados a ela, fizeram com que as instituições financeiras e os ativos financeiros criados satisfizessem os gastos públicos. Somente dessa maneira podemos compreender porque o Banco do Brasil (o primeiro, criado em 1808 e liquidado em 1829), os títulos da dívida externa e os empréstimos no exterior foram instrumentos com que o Estado contou para fazer face às despesas com as guerras da Independência e as indenizações pagas a Portugal[2].

No início do período regencial, pouca coisa mudou. Mas, com o restabelecimento das exportações do Nordeste e a ascensão do café do Vale do Paraíba, no final da década de 1830, surgiram os bancos comerciais. Essas instituições financeiras privadas, embora proibidas pelo Estado de emitirem papel-moeda, o que cabia ao Tesouro, passaram a emitir vales. Tais ativos financeiros, que eram

---

[1] Levy, Maria-Barbara. *História da Bolsa de Valores do Rio de Janeiro.* Rio de Janeiro: IBMEC. 1977, p. 47.

[2] Idem, p. 48.

papéis comerciais, que rendiam juros e com data de expiração fixa, constituíram-se num importante mecanismo de crédito para atender a demanda de numerário exigido pela atividade comercial[3].

A vitória do *regresso conservador*, ao final da década de 1840, significou não só a vitória dos comerciantes e dos grandes proprietários de terras e de escravos do Sudeste, como também a centralização política do Império, em torno do Rio de Janeiro. A "nova Metrópole", ao defender os interesses da *casa*[4], iria estender seus domínios sobre o sistema financeiro o que significava maior controle sobre o crédito e sobre as instituições. Não foi à toa que os conservadores, tais como Eusébio de Queiroz, o Visconde de Itaboraí, o Marquês de Paraná e outros, que estiveram à frente das principais decisões de caráter político e econômico na década de 1840/1850, defenderam o metalismo e o controle das emissões contra o papelismo e as descentralizações[5].

Como expressão dessa vitória conservadora figuram medidas institucionais como a Reforma Monetária e o padrão-ouro de 1846, o fim do Tráfico Negreiro, a criação do Código Comercial e a Lei de Terras, ambos surgidos em 1850. Embora se reconheça que algumas dessas medidas possibilitaram uma "modernização" na economia, como por exemplo, o incremento da atividade urbana, com o surgimento de sociedades anônimas e sociedades comanditas nos setores secundário e terciário da economia[6], elas significaram a vitória dos proprietários de terras e de escravos, da agricultura de exportação, que através de uma "modernização" dentro da ordem, possibilitou a inserção do Brasil na ordem capitalista mundial.

Foi, portanto, dentro dessa conjuntura que surgiu o Banco Mauá,

---

3 Levy, Maria-Barbara. *História dos Bancos Comerciais no Brasil.* Rio de Janeiro: IBMEC. 1972, p. 18-9.

4 A respeito da vitória do regresso e a consolidação do Império ver: Matos, Ilmar Rohloff de. *O Tempo Saquarema.* São Paulo: Hucitec. 1987; Carvalho, José Murilo de. *A Construção da Ordem.* Rio de Janeiro: Campus. 1980.

5 Cameron, Rondo. "Metrópole e Hinterlândia na História das Finanças", *Revista Brasileira de Economia.* Vol. 26, n.º 3. Jul/set 1972.

6 Levy, Maria Barbara. *A Indústria do Rio de Janeiro através de suas Sociedades Anônimas (esboço de história empresarial).* Tese para o concurso de Prof. Titular de História Econômica Geral e Desenvolvimento Econômico da FEA/UFRJ. Rio de Janeiro. 1988.

Mac Gregor & Cia., depois Banco Mauá & Cia. Essa instituição financeira, num período de transformação e consolidação da *ordem imperial*, levanta as seguintes questões: qual foi a intenção de Mauá em criar um banco, e que tipo de banco era o banco Mauá? Qual foi o significado dessa instituição privada num momento de centralização política? Tais questões serão respondidas neste trabalho, que se constitui no estudo preliminar de uma futura tese de doutorado.

A fundação do Banco do Brasil de Mauá

Com o fim do tráfico negreiro e a criação do Código Comercial, a estrutura financeira e o crédito no Brasil se modificaram. A grande disponibilidade de capital e a possibilidade de organizar estabelecimentos de crédito, geraram um surto econômico e financeiro sem precedentes. Aproveitando-se desse momento, Mauá — um respeitado comerciante do Rio de Janeiro, com negócios também no setor manufatureiro, como a fundição de Ponta da Areia — fundou seu primeiro estabelecimento bancário, o Banco do Comércio e Indústria do Brasil, conhecido como o Banco do Brasil de Mauá, em 1851. Conforme consta na sua *Autobiografia*, sua intenção era de

> "(...) reunir os capitais, que se viram repentinamente deslocados do ilícito comércio, e fazê-los convergir a um centro donde pudessem ir alimentar as forças produtivas do País, foi o pensamento dominante que me surgiu na mente ao ter a certeza de que aquele fato era irrevogável"[7].

Essa iniciativa de Mauá contou com a participação de importantes comerciantes e financistas, como Darrigue Faro, futuro Barão do Rio Bonito, J. M. Pereira da Silva e Pimenta Bueno[8]. Pelo projeto original, o Banco teria um capital inicial de 10 mil contos, e ficaria autorizado a emitir letras que não ultrapassassem 50% do seu capital. Entretanto, o decreto do Governo que autorizou o Banco a funcionar modificou o projeto original. O Banco do Brasil, um ban-

---

[7] Mauá, Visconde. *Autobiografia*. Rio de Janeiro: Zélio Valverde. 1943, p. 120.

[8] Ibidem.

co de depósitos e descontos, com o capital autorizado de 10 mil contos, poderia emitir vales ou letras a prazo de cinco dias, cuja soma nunca excederia a um terço do fundo efetivo[9].

Esse Banco do Brasil, o segundo, teve dois anos de vida, durante os quais, com o Banco Comercial do Rio de Janeiro, constituiu um dos principais bancos da praça do Rio de Janeiro, com seus vales sendo considerados verdadeiro papel-moeda, em virtude da carência deste. A concorrência entre esses dois bancos foi, para muitos, a principal causa para a fusão deles, gerando o terceiro Banco do Brasil[10].

Entretanto, a fusão dos dois bancos, e a formação de um grande banco emissor, responsável pelo crédito, e sob controle do governo imperial, já vinha sendo arquitetada. No seu relatório apresentado em 1853 à Assembléia Legislativa, o ministro da Fazenda Joaquim José Rodrigues Torres, o Visconde de Itaboraí, partidário da corrente metalista, chamava atenção para a necessidade de um novo banco de emissão. Segundo o ministro,

> "a riqueza pública, e, com ella, a somma de transacções tem crescido; o espírito industrial começa a desenvolver-se de uma maneira bem acentuada, e, por fim, a insuficiência do papel moeda é attestada pela presença de 16:000:000$ ou 20:000:000 metálicos, com que se acha augmentada a massa do meio circulante. (...). Parece chegado o prazo de crear-se um banco de emissão, que não só auxilie o governo no resgate do papel-moeda, mas, ainda, o progressivo aumento do crédito e da riqueza nacional (...)"[11].

Transformado em lei[12], o projeto foi rapidamente executado. O novo Banco do Brasil era um banco de depósito, desconto e de emissão. Seu capital foi fixado em 30 mil contos, podendo ser au-

---

[9] Carreira, Liberato de Castro. *História Financeira e Orçamentária do Império do Brasil.* Rio de Janeiro: Fundação Casa de Rui Barbosa. 1980, p. 327 (a primeira edição deste livro é de 1889).

[10] Andrada, Antonio Carlos R. de. *Bancos Emissionistas no Brasil.* Rio de Janeiro: Leite Ribeiro. 1923, p. 42.

[11] Brasil: Ministério da Fazenda. *Relatórios.* 1853.

[12] Lei n.º 683, de 5/7/1853.

mentado por deliberação da Assembléia Geral de Acionistas, e mediante *aprovação* do Governo. O presidente do Banco era nomeado também pelo Governo, e suas notas, conversíveis à vista em ouro ou papel, constituíram-se em moeda legal. O limite da emissão ficou fixado no dobro do fundo do capital, salvo autorização dada pelo Governo.

A nova orientação do Banco do Brasil, que correspondeu ao controle do meio circulante e do crédito, fez com que Mauá e outros acionistas deixassem o banco, e organizassem dois novos bancos: o Banco Mauá, Mac Gregor & Cia. e o Banco Rural e Hipotecário.

A fundação do Banco Mauá, Mac Gregor & Cia.

Não concordando com a fusão bancária, nem aceitando o monopólio de emissão dado ao Banco do Brasil, Mauá organizou a Sociedade Bancária Mauá, Mac Gregor & Cia. em julho de 1854. De acordo com seu contrato social[13], os sócios-gerentes solidariamente responsáveis por todos os seus bens para com terceiros eram: "nesta Corte, o Barão de Mauá, Alexandre Donald Mac Gregor e João Ignácio Tavares; em Londres, os mesmos e mais um indivíduo escolhido pela Administração". Este último seria José Reynall de Castro, "grande amigo de Mauá, e responsável pelos negócios na Inglaterra"[14].

A ligação de Mauá com o capital inglês vinha desde o início de sua "prodigiosa" carreira. Ainda moço, chegando ao Rio de Janeiro, vindo do Rio Grande do Sul, Mauá foi trabalhar na firma de Pereira de Almeida, comerciante português ligado à venda de tecidos, e com ligações com os ingleses. Ao falir em 1828, essa firma foi anexada pelo seu principal credor, à firma inglesa Carruthers &

---

[13] O contrato social foi firmado em 31/7/1854, e reduzido a escritura pública de 12/8/1854, Liv. 213, fols. 87 do Livro de registro do tabelião Fialho, antigo cartório do 3.º ofício.

[14] José Reynall de Castro era filho de D. Miguel Caetano de Castro, físico-mor de D. João VI. A respeito dos sócios de Mauá ver: Marchant, Anyda. "A new portrait of Mauá the banker: a man of business in nineteenth century Brazil", *Hispanic American Historical Review.* Vol. XXX, nov. 1950, n.º 4, p. 413.

Irmãos, com sede no Rio de Janeiro e filiais em Portugal[15]. Para seu principal biógrafo, foi com Richard Carruther, comerciante inglês ligado ao setor de importação e exportação, que Mauá aprendeu o valor do crédito para negócios mais amplos em uma praça comercial em que a circulação monetária era reduzida[16].

No início da década de 1840, Mauá, que já era sócio da firma Carruthers, empreendeu sua primeira viagem à Inglaterra. Nessa viagem, Mauá estabeleceu seus primeiros empreendimentos com seus sócios ingleses. Apoiado pelo seu "antigo" patrão Richard Carruther, nome de peso no sistema financeiro inglês, na City, Mauá fundou em Manchester a firma Carruthers, De Castro & Company. Seus sócios eram o próprio Carruther e José Henrique Reynall de Castro. A partir desse momento estava formada a conexão inglesa de Mauá[17].

Outra importante característica dessa instituição financeira de Mauá foi sua forma de organização. Ela era uma sociedade comandita por ações, que, segundo o próprio Mauá, foi a fórmula encontrada para fazer "funcionar a nova sociedade fora do arbítrio governativo (a) que estavam sujeitas as sociedades anônimas, existindo no Código — o Código Comercial — a disposição exorbitante de poderem ser dissolvidas administrativamente sem a intervenção dos votos dos acionistas, o que, tratando-se do emprego do capital, parecia-me uma anomalia (...)"[18].

Aproveitando-se do silêncio da lei na qual nada constava acerca da sociedade comandita por ações, e face ao não-impedimento por parte das autoridades, o Banco Mauá passou a funcionar e, em dois dias, todas as ações foram subscritas. De um total de 6 mil contos, 5 mil contos eram do fundo de comandita[19]. Como o projeto de Mauá

---

15 Besouchet, Lidia. *Mauá e seu Tempo.* Rio de Janeiro: Nova Fronteira. 1978, p. 26.

16 Faria, Alberto. *Mauá. Irineu Evangelista de Souza, Barão e Visconde de Mauá 1813-1889.* Rio de Janeiro: Paulo Ponguetti & Cia. 1926.

17 Marchant, Anyda. Op. cit., p. 413.

18 Mauá. Op. Cit., p. 232.

19 Na lista de subscrição constavam 182 sócios comanditários, com vários nomes de peso tais como Militão Máximo de Souza (Barão de Andaraí), José Antonio de Figueiredo (pai do Conde de Figueiras), o Marquês do Paraná, e outros. Ver a lista completa em Mauá. Op. cit., p. 233, nota 197.

estava baseado na subscrição de ações — ou seja, na preferência de compra de ações que representam aumento de capital — em 23.12.1854, na Assembléia Geral dos Acionistas, reorganizou-se o banco na forma de uma sociedade comandita simples.

O Banco Mauá, além de ser um banco comercial, de depósito e desconto, concorrendo com o Banco do Brasil, atuou também no setor produtivo e de transportes, através de sociedades anônimas por ele organizadas. Aproveitando-se do decreto do governo de 1852, que permitia a organização de estradas de ferro, e com a garantia de juros dadas pelo Estado a tais empreendimentos, o Banco Mauá, com seu aporte financeiro externo, organizou, por exemplo, a E. F. Mauá, que ligava a praia de Estrela até Raiz da Serra, em Petrópolis, região de fornecimento de alimentos para o Rio de Janeiro; organizou em conjunto com a N. M. Rothchild and Sons a San Paulo Railway, que ligaria o porto de Santos até Jundiaí. No setor de transformação, o Banco era acionista da Cia. Anônima Luz Steárica de Produtos Químicos, que fabricava sabão e velas; da fundição de Ponta da Areia; e organizou a Cia. de Iluminação a Gaz do Rio de Janeiro.

O ano de 1857 consolidou o prestígio e poder do Banco Mauá. Em virtude do crescimento das atividades comerciais e manufatureiras, o governo autorizou o Banco do Brasil a emitir o triplo dos fundos disponíveis. Tal permissão possibilitou a manutenção dos investimentos diretos na produção, às custas da inflação[20]. O receio conservador de que a emissão e as práticas econômicas pudessem gerar uma crise econômica, e com isso a situação fugir do seu controle, já se fazia sentir. José de Alencar, em artigo no *Correio Mercantil*, alertava para o perigo que as especulações e o jogo de ações na praça do Rio de Janeiro poderiam gerar para a ordem imperial, propondo uma maior intervenção do Governo[21].

Com a morte do Marquês do Paraná, assumiu a presidência do Conselho do Estado o conservador Marquês de Olinda, que nomeou Bernardo de Souza Franco para ministro da Fazenda. Grande amigo de Mauá, Souza Franco promoveu uma reforma bancária e monetária em 1857, que acabou com o monopólio do Banco do

---

20 Levy, Maria-B. Op. cit., p. 83

21 Alencar, José de. "Ao Correr da Pena". *Correio Mercantil*. Rio de Janeiro. 21/1/1855, *in* Levy, M. Op. cit., p. 83.

Brasil, e reconheceu o direito de emissão a diversos bancos, entre eles o Banco Mauá[22]. Essa política do ministro da Fazenda vinha de encontro às idéias de Mauá, de que somente a proliferação de bancos emissores facilitaria o crédito a longo prazo, canalizando os recursos ociosos para o setor produtivo.

No entanto, essa política emissionista coincidiu com a crise mundial de 1857. A notícia da retomada das exportações russas de cereais, que eclodiu em Nova York com uma espetacular queda dos preços, repercutiu em cadeia pela Europa Ocidental atingindo bancos e bolsas. Esse abalo nos preços das *commodities* interrompeu uma alta geral provocada pela descoberta de ouro da Califórnia e da Austrália no início da década.

No Brasil, os credores ingleses passaram a pressionar, exigindo que os débitos fossem saldados imediatamente. Como o Brasil tinha adotado o padrão-ouro, com a reforma de 1846, isso significou uma saída líquida de moeda, "já que a conversibilidade do papel-moeda funcionava para os credores como uma garantia para os momentos de crise"[23].

Abandonado pelo Banco do Brasil, cujo presidente Torres Homem divergia de sua política emissionista, Souza Franco apelou ao Banco Mauá para que o auxiliasse. Mediante um cronograma de saques junto à sua filial em Londres, a crise foi superada, e o câmbio restabelecido.

A atuação do Banco Mauá fez com que a Assembléia, controlada pelos conservadores, passasse a acusar o ministro da Fazenda de estar privilegiando o Banco Mauá, e de promover a agiotagem e a especulação. Fragilizado, Souza Franco foi substituído por Torres Homem, que apresentou um projeto de lei, "no qual repetia os postulados do padrão-ouro e insistia no retorno do monopólio de emissão ao Banco do Brasil"[24]. A partir desse momento, começou um período de dificuldades para a atividade bancária e outras formas de associação.

---

22 Lobo, Eulália M. Lahmeyer. *História do Rio de Janeiro (do capital comercial ao capital industrial e financeiro)*. Rio de Janeiro: IBMEC. 1978, p. 214.

23 Levy, Maria-B. Op. cit., p. 59.

24 Idem, p. 85.

A Lei dos Entraves e o Banco Mauá & Cia.

Aprovado o projeto em 1860, a lei resultante ficou conhecida como a "Lei dos Entraves"[25]. Entre os pontos principais desta lei, destaca-se o maior rigor para a constituição de sociedades anônimas, que, além de dependerem da autorização do Governo, passaram a depender também do Conselho de Estado. No tocante à atividade bancária, nenhum banco independente poderia emitir, enquanto não se mostrasse capaz de reembolsar os vales em ouro, o que implicava declaração de falência. Apenas o Banco do Brasil e os seus bancos independentes tiveram essa autorização[26].

Como resultado dessa política de estabilização econômica ortodoxa, de restrição das emissões e do crédito, o mercado financeiro se retraiu, firmas faliram, inibindo com isso o "espírito de associação de capitais"[27]. Essa política restritiva veio de encontro aos interesses dos grupos agrário-exportadores, que não eram favoráveis à instabilidade econômica gerada por políticas que beneficiassem os interesses mercantis urbanos.

Dentro dessa conjuntura, surgiram os primeiros bancos britânicos no Brasil. A nova legislação, que exigiu lastro-ouro para emissões, concorreu para os interesses ingleses em operar num mercado em que a conversibilidade da moeda garantisse seus interesses.

A presença dos bancos ingleses — como, por exemplo, o London and Brazilian Bank Limited — no mercado brasileiro, trazendo com eles uma inovação na área bancária, o *cheque,* significou uma ameaça para os bancos brasileiros. Essa inovação, "uma nova ordem de pagamento que oferecia a comodidade de nele se poder inscrever a quantia exata do pagamento, independentemente de troco, e de constituir, uma vez pago pelo banco, um recibo de quitação, exigia, entretanto, um grau de confiança muito maior do que a nota do banco"[28], que só os grandes bancos tinham.

A junção de fatores, como política restritiva e concorrência desigual dos bancos ingleses, contribuiu para a eclosão da crise de

---

25 Lei n.º 1.083, de 22/8/1860.

26 Levy, Maria-B. Op. cit., p. 85.

27 Expressão utilizada por Maria-B. Levy, no livro citado.

28 Idem, p. 89.

1864, conhecida como a crise do Souto, em virtude da falência da Casa Bancária Antonio José Alves Souto & Cia.

Essa crise repercutiu no Banco Mauá, Mac Gregor & Cia. Desde o início da década de 1860, a aplicação de uma política restritiva do crédito, e o poder do Banco do Brasil, já eram vistos com temor por Mauá e seus sócios[29]. Nesse momento, percebe-se uma discordância entre Mauá e seus sócios na Inglaterra, principalmente com relação à cautela nos negócios. Nesse período, o Banco Mauá contava com filiais em Porto Alegre, Pelotas, Santos, Campinas, Belém, Buenos Aires e Montevidéu. A filial deste último, além de banco emissor, era um dos principais credores do Uruguai.

Ao regressar de sua viagem à Europa, Mauá reorganizou o banco, cujas reservas de 6 mil contos tinham sido absorvidas pela conjuntura da crise. Aproveitando-se do que constava no contrato social, no tocante à liquidação da firma e do prazo de expiração da sociedade, Mauá resolveu concentrar todos os seus estabelecimentos bancários e empresas existentes numa só empresa, inclusive seus bens pessoais. Essa empresa era o Banco Mauá & Cia.

Passando a funcionar a partir de 1866, a situação não era nada favorável ao novo estabelecimento bancário de Mauá. Desde 1864, as operações financeiras passaram a gravitar em torno do Banco do Brasil, que era credor do Banco Mauá, e dos bancos ingleses. Para fugir desse aprisionamento financeiro, Mauá tentou a fusão de seu banco com o London Brazilian Bank, para dar origem ao London Brazilian Mauá Bank, o que no entanto deixou de ocorrer[30].

Com a eclosão da Guerra do Paraguai, o governo passou a emitir moeda face às despesas de guerra. Essa política, se por um lado significou o abandono da política contencionista e das pretensões da conversabilidade preconizado pelo padrão-ouro — o Banco do Brasil deixou de ser emissor —, pelo outro significou que "o Governo se tornasse o principal agente do crédito interno, através do mecanismo inflação e compra; ao mesmo tempo que aumentava impostos, recolhia ouro através de recursos sistemáticos de lançamento de títulos públicos"[31].

---

29 Copiador de cartas no ano de 1861, in Mechant, Anyda. Op. cit., p. 40-2.

30 Besouchet, Lidia. Op. cit., p. 137.

31 Levy, Maria-B. Op. cit., p. 82.

Essa drenagem periódica do dinheiro, em virtude do atrelamento da moeda ao ouro e à sazonabilidade da agricultura de exportação, estava dando origem a uma crise comercial. A situação do Banco Mauá se complicou na década de 1870. Além dos problemas ligados ao fechamento da filial do Uruguai, que era o principal banco emissor e credor do governo daquele país, amargando com isso um enorme prejuízo, e dos problemas com o grupo Rothchild, ligados à San Paulo Railway, o banco caiu com a crise de 1875. Essa crise estava ligada ao empréstimo que o governo contraiu em Londres no valor de 5 milhões de libras a 5% emitido com deságio de 3½%, dos quais utilizara 1,1 milhão, pretendendo sacar o restante 3,9 milhões de libras em abril.

Como garantia para o empréstimo, "os bancos deveriam reunir os fundos indispensáveis em moeda nacional para comprar os saques sobre Londres. Paralelamente, os depósitos dos bancos ascendiam a 65 mil contos, e o encaixe total desses estabelecimentos não chegava a 5 mil. Após uma ampla política de empréstimos, os bancos ficaram com uma margem de apenas 7,3%"[32]. Diante de tal fato, os bancos credores pressionaram os devedores. Estes começaram a falir, levando junto os credores. Nessa nova onda de falências estava o Banco Mauá.

Considerações finais

Retornando às perguntas formuladas na introdução, podemos dizer que o Banco Mauá não só se constituiu num banco comercial, como também num de investimento. Foi justamente essa última característica do banco que lhe trouxe problemas. Como banco de investimento, o Banco Mauá teria que contar com uma ampla política de créditos, o que contrariava os setores que estavam por trás da formação do Estado Imperial.

O Banco Mauá também representou uma forma de atuação do capital financeiro no Brasil. Sua falência, no plano simbólico, significou o esgotamento desse modelo, com o surgimento do capitalismo monopolista a partir da década de 1870.

---

[32] Idem, p. 97.

Raúl Jacob
CIEDUR, Montevideo

URUGUAY: GENESIS Y DESARROLLO DE UN GRUPO ECONOMICO FINANCIERO: EL BANCO FRANCÉS SUPERVIELLE (1887-1941)

El Banco Francés Supervielle fue fundado en 1887 por Luis Bernardo Supervielle. La casa matriz la radicó em Montevideo, abriendo además una filial en Buenos Aires.

Poco es lo que sabemos sobre las razones de esta elección. Quizás estuvo determinada por la vigencia en Uruguay del patrón oro y las consecuentes facilidades para el libre ingreso y egreso de capitales. Cierto misterio rodea a la figura — casi legendaria — de Supervielle. En 1885 integró la Comisión Fiscal de la Liga Industrial, gremial empresarial fundada em 1879 para difundir el ideal proteccionista y que logró reunir a algunos artesanos e industriales[1]. Este hecho sugiere su vinculación a ese núcleo económico, en buena medida constituido por inmigrantes, especialmente italianos y españoles. Pero cuando la institución financiera ya era una pujante realidad, Reginal Lloyd lo definió como "un opulento propietario de nacionalidad francesa"[2].

Artesano o financista, Supervielle comenzó a operar como banquero simultáneamente en Montevideo y Buenos Aires, con un capital suscrito de quince millones de francos[3]. Desconocemos el origen del mismo, así como si el uso del franco como medida de valor era en homenaje al titular de la empresa, o se trataba de una inversión francesa en el Río de la Plata. (Una de las modalidades

---

1 *El Telégrafo Marítimo,* 1.º de junio de 1885.

2 Reginald Lloyd. *Impresiones de la República O. del Uruguay en el Siglo XX*. Londres: Lloyds Greater Britain Publishing Co. Ltd. 1912, p. 333.

3 Ibidem.

de expansión de la banca francesa fue la participación como "corresponsal" en el desarrollo de otras instituciones).

El fundador falleció en 1901. Los negocios continuaron bajo la dirección de su hijo, Luis J. Supervielle, y la razón social se transformó en Supervielle y Cía. Los socios solidarios eran Martina M. de Supervielle, Luis. J. Supervielle y Bernardo Etchehoun. En 1909, para conseguir aumentar el capital, sin necesidad de transformarla en sociedad anónima, se amplió el número de participantes de la firma con familiares: Esteban Baron — al que se le sumó Mariana Munyo de Supervielle como socios solidarios; y Agueda Supervielle de Berthélemy, Blanca Supervielle y Julio Luis Supervielle como socios comanditarios[4].

A partir de ese momento el "Banco Francés" publicitó su imagen de "empresa familiar":

> "Precisamente — se escribió en 1913 en el suplemento que conmemoró el cincuentenario del diario *El Siglo* — lo que destaca esta institución y constituye el secreto de su solidez es que está en poder de una sola familia, lo que le asegura la inalterabilidad de los propósitos que animaron al jefe de esta casa, al fundar el establecimiento de su nombre."[5]

Años después, en 1925, en *El Libro del Centenario del Uruguay* se destacaba que era en el Río de la Plata, y tal vez en América del Sur,

> "la única institución de crédito sujeta al régimen de sociedad colectiva, régimen en el que como se sabe, los bienes de las personas que forman la razón social están afectados solidariamente al cumplimiento de las obligaciones por aquella contraídas."[6]

Su inserción en ambas márgenes del Plata, y sus relaciones con bancos europeos, le permitió consolidarse y expandirse. La casa matriz de Montevideo y la filial de Buenos Aires estaban unidas por una línea telegráfica de su propiedad, lo que facilitaba las tran-

---

[4] *El Siglo 1863-Cincuentenario-1913*, p. 14.

[5] Ibidem.

[6] *El Libro del Centenario del Uruguay.* Op. Cit. Mvo. Agencia Capurro. 1925, p. 418-9.

sacciones, ya que servía para trasmitir diariamente las cotizaciones de valores bursátiles y productos de exportación. Entre 1921 y 1935, era el cuarto banco privado en importancia en el País por su capital. En 1935, ocupó el sexto lugar (el séptimo en el sistema financiero nacional, si se incluye al estatal BROU) en la captación de depósitos y en la concesión de créditos.

El protagonismo de este grupo económico* en buena medida fue obra de Luis J. Supervielle (diputado por Tacuarembó en 1920, directivo de la Federación Rural durante un período, primer presidente del Frigorífico Nacional). Pero contó con dos auxiliares de importancia.

Uno de ellos fue Juan M. Gorlero, incorporado en 1893 al personal de la sucursal de Buenos Aires. Desde 1907 y hasta 1929, año en que se jubiló gerente de la casa matriz en Montevideo, Gorlero fue el apoderado general del banco. Luego de su desvinculación de la firma Supervielle y Cía, fue director del Banco de la República (1932-33)[7].

El otro fue Jorge West Gorlero, quien ingresó al banco en 1889, ocupando posteriormente la Gerencia. Entre 1906 y 1921, West se desempeño como gerente del BROU, del que fue presidente en 1934. Fue miembro del directorio del Banco de Crédito (1923-34) y presidente del Banco Popular del Uruguay. Estuvo además vinculado a la industria láctea y dirigió la empresa que construyó el ferrocarril de Treinta y Tres a Río Branco[8].

Interesa subrayar el papel de ambos gerentes en otras instituciones financieras, ya que, sin descuidar el rol que pudo cumplir el Francés como "escuela de banqueros", la desvinculación del banco no lo fue de otras empresas de las que ellos junto con Supervielle eran directivos.

---

* La categoría "grupo económico" está utilizada sin sofisticación alguna: se trata de un capital que controla un banco importante, y que está diversificado en un conjunto de empresas, con las que mantiene algún tipo de vínculo. Precisar más este concepto implicaría conocer archivos a los que no se pudo acceder.

7 Arturo Scarone. *Uruguayos contemporáneos.* Montevideo. 1938, p. 231-2.

8 Idem, p. 531-2.

El Banco Francés como institución financiera

El Banco Francés Supervielle y Cía se caracterizó por ofrecer una amplia gama de servicios bancarios, los asumidos por la banca comercial privada, tanto la nacional como la extranjera. Una de sus singularidades era principalmente esa: se trataba de un banco "nacional" conectado al mundo, por lo que sus clientes podían contar con todas las ventajas ofertadas por las sucursales de las instituciones extranjeras. De ahí que su propietario utilizara el magnetismo que en los turbulentos años de crisis económicas y desarreglos financieros podía concitar la apelación al origen francés de su fundador o del capital originario, que sugería el respaldo, la protección o simplemente la adhesión de y a una de las grandes potencias mundiales.

El banco recibía dinero en depósito en cuenta corriente, a la vista y a plazo fijo. También admitía dinero en caja de ahorros (hasta diez mil pesos em 1913)[9]. Compraba y vendía giros a noventa días, a la vista y por telégrafo. Expedía cartas de crédito, letras de cambio y transferencias por cable sobre cualquier plaza de América y Europa, como era la norma de las instituciones especializadas en negocios con el exterior que servían a importadores y exportadores.

Descontaba documentos de comercio y cobraba letras y pagarés por cuenta de terceros. Colocaba capitales en hipoteca, en el país y en el exterior, lo que da la pauta de un fenómeno todavía sin evaluar en su magnitud: las inversiones uruguayas en el extranjero. Recibía valores en custodia y tenía instalado en una parte de su local un servicio de cofre-fort. Se encargaba de comprar y vender títulos y valores cotizables en las plazas comerciales, y del cobro de cupones y dividendos.

De tal forma canalizaba la emigración de capitales al exterior. Así, en 1915, publicitaba en la prensa de Montevideo las bondades del "Empréstito Nacional Francés 5%": 5,73% nego de ganancia, sin contar la prima por cambio y el beneficio eventual del reembolso a la par[10].

De desearlo, un ciudadano uruguayo podía participar en la

---

9 *El Siglo...* Op. Cit., p. 4 y 5.

10 *El Siglo.* 1.º de diciembre de 1915, p. 5.

financiación del esfuerzo bélico francés, haciendo caso omiso a la posición neutral de la cancillería de su país. Eso, siempre que no se inclinara por la "opción nacional", adquiriendo títulos de deuda uruguayos, lo que también podía hacer por intermedio del banco.

El Francés Supervielle también incluyó entre sus negocios los seguros, aunque contrariamente a lo que podía esperarse, fue agente de una empresa británica: La Unión Comercial.

La sección Administración de Propiedades

Al igual que otras instituciones creó una sección especializada en la administración de propiedades, uno de los buenos negocios de la plaza, si se considera que el censo de población y vivienda de 1908 reveló que la población inquilina era el 67,79% del total de la de Montevideo, y el 63,79% de las casas ocupadas en la capital eran alquiladas. En 1930 el censo municipal constató la duplicación en el número de habitantes metropolitanos[11].

Los servicios ofrecidos a los propietarios les permitía desentenderse de sus fincas[12]. El banco administraba las casas, cobraba los alquileres, se encargaba de las inspecciones, custodiaba los títulos de propiedad, tramitaba los seguros y el pago de impuestos municipales y nacionales.

Aceptaba poderes y se hacía cargo de asuntos judiciales y de tramitar sucesiones y expedientes ante las oficinas públicas. Además cobraba hipotecas, vales e intereses, sueldos y pensiones por cuenta de terceros. En la temporada de verano asumía la administración de chalets y casas amobladas, destinadas a ser alquiladas a turistas, especialmente a los argentinos.

A comienzos de la década del cuarenta, la administración de casas para alquilar era uno de los frutos más apetecibles del Banco: se decía que producía ganancias que iban desde los ciento setenta mil pesos a los cuatrocientos mil pesos (equivalía al 6% o al 13% del capital neto de la institución en 1939)[13]. — Por *capital neto* denomi-

---

[11] Alvarez Lenzi, Arana, Bocchiardo. *El Montevideo de la expansión (1868-1915).* Montevideo: EBO. 1986, p. 58 y 59.

[12] *Almanaque-Guía El Siglo.* Año 1932, p. IX (Aviso).

[13] *Diario de Sesiones de la Cámara de Representantes* (DSCR). Tomo 465, 27 y 28 de diciembre de 1945, p. 13-7.

namos al capital integrado. Lo distinguimos del *capital* (capital integrado más fondos de reserva y de previsión).

El banco participaba directamente o como intermediario en el negocio de la venda de solares a plazo, generalmente a diez años. *El Día*, en junio de 1914, refiriéndose al proyecto de contribución inmobiliaria en Montevideo, atribuyó al Banco Francés la tenencia de tres mil boletas de pago, más las que correspondían a la firma Supervielle y Cía[14]. Si bien ellas no tenían porque ser exclusivamente de terrenos sin edificar, pueden dar una vaga idea de la dimensión que en ese entonces ya había adquirido la "Sección Administración de Propiedades" del banco fundador de los barrios "Dr. A. Cabral" en la intersección de las arterias Gral. Flores e Industrias (1908) y "Capurro" en las inmediaciones de la Bahía (1911)[15].

Siguiendo el ejemplo de sus competidores, expandió sus actividades en dirección al este, promocionando el remate de solares en el balneario "mejor emplazado del mundo": Punta del Este[16]. La "Sección Administración de Propiedades" era complementada por la de "Remates", que vendía o remataba toda clase de bienes inmobiliarios, tasando fincas y tierras, y fraccionando terrenos.

La Sección Rural

El enlace de la ganadería y la banca que produjo la irrupción del frigorífico determinó la creación de una sección rural especializada. Fue también estimulada por la inversión de los Supervielle en la producción agropecuaria, que de esta forma lograba integrarse y completar su ciclo (producción-comercialización).

La Sección Rural del Banco Francés Supervielle y Cía. fue organizada en cuatro sub-secciones, atendiendo a la especificidad de los negocios: 1) Operaciones en general. 2) Barraca. 3) Tablada. 4) Ferias.

---

[14] José Rilla. *La mala cara del reformismo.* Montevideo: CLAEH. Serie Investigaciones n.º 41. 1990, p. 110 y 111.

[15] Alfredo Castellanos. *Historia del desarrollo edilicio y urbanístico de Montevideo (1829-1914).* Montevideo: Junta Departamental de Montevideo. 1971, p. 248-50.

[16] *Revista de la Sección Rural del Banco Francés Supervielle y Cía.* N.º 13, 1 de enero de 1929, p. 16.

La primera de ellas atendía el cobro de arrendamientos; la inspección, recibo y entrega de campos; el fraccionamiento de tierras para ser colonizadas; la compra, venta y remate de campos y haciendas; la tasación y liquidación de estancias y ganado; la administración general de campos y chacras[17].

Este último renglón adquirió importancia: en julio de 1926 el banco publicitó la administración de 168.000 hectáreas. En dicienbre de 1932 había ascendido a 240.417 hectáreas entre estancias y chacras, de las que algo más del 12% eran explotadas bajo su dirección[18].

En 1926 el Francés inauguró su "barraca" en Montevideo, y tiempos después, otra en Salto. Recibía en consignación lana, cereales, etc., adelantando el ochenta por ciento del valor de la producción. Ofrecía en venta bolsas de arpillera, etc. Se encargaba de adquirir para sus clientes y depositarlos a la espera de completar las cargas en los vagones de ferrocarril, todo tipo de insumo para el agro, desde postes y alambre hasta sarnífugos, sin excluir los artículos de almacén[19].

La repartición de ventas en la Tablada recibía en consignación ganado para ser comercializado con destino al abasto y a los frigoríficos cercanos a Montevideo, adelantando fondos sobre los mismos. Una vez vendidos, las liquidaciones se podían hacer efectivas en el día.

La organización de ferias ganaderas fue la última gran apuesta de la Sección Rural del Banco. Las exposiciones — ferias ganaderas — la primera de que se tiene noticia se realizó en 1879 en Salto —, que cristalizaron en la década del noventa del siglo XIX, reflejan cambios en la transacción de ganado en pie, al irrumpir formas capitalistas que al poner en contacto directo a cabañeros, invernadores y criadores, van desplazando progresivamente al tradicional tropero[20].

---

17 *Revista de la Federación Rural*. N.º 12, julio de 1927 (Aviso).

18 *Revista de la Sección Rural...* Op. cit., n.º 10, 15 de diciembre de 1932, s/p.

19 Idem, n.º 6, 15 de agosto de 1928, p. 13; n.º 7, 30 de setiembre de 1928, p. 12; n.º 23, 1 de junio de 1929, p. 4; n.º 40, 15 de febrero de 1930, p. 4.

20 J. P. Barrán & Benjamín Nahum. *Historia rural del Uruguay moderno*. Tomo 3. Montevideo: EBO. 1973, p. 223 y siguientes. María Inés Moraes. *Bella Unión: de la estancia tradicional a la agricultura moderna (1853-195\65)*. Montevideo: CINVE-CALNU. 1990, p. 48.

Su profisión puede dar la pauta de la rentabilidad del negocio. El Banco se encargó de difundir algunas cifras, reservándose las más íntimas, es decir las de las ganancias.

En el primer semestre de 1930, la "Sección Italo Supparo —Anexa a la Sección Rural del Banco Francés Supervielle y Cía." facturó por concepto de liquidaciones, tambos, ventas particulares y locales ferias una suma aproximada al capital neto del banco, que era de $1:700.000. Las ventas en los seis locales de la institución constituía el 57% del total. Un año después, ya sin Supparo, que había renunciado, la Sección Rural superó en ventas al capital neto del Banco, que había crecido a 2:350.000 pesos (al 31 de diciembre de 1931). Lo aportado por los ocho locales ferias propios, más cuatro de sociedades rurales que utilizaron sus servicios llegó al 54% de ese total[21].

Inversiones en la región

Los Supervielle directamente, o por medio del banco de su propiedad, invirtieron en otros países. Cuesta huir de la tentación de hablar de inversiones "en el exterior", ya que ello supondría partir de la base que el origen de su capital era nacional. Pero, nacional o nacionalizado, una de sus fuentes de acumulación era el Uruguay. Por supuesto que este tema exige cierto cuidado o cautela, ya que una institución financiera permite la canalización del bien que intermedia, el dinero, que puede ser originario de diversos países, personas e instituciones. Al fin de cuantas, el buscarlo y aplicarlo, es una de las tradicionales funciones de bancos y banqueros. El Banco Francés se encargó de difundir, precisamente, una imagen en la que se resaltaba su papel de inversor, aunque acotado a la región, sin nombrar otros países, lo cual también resulta llamativo si se atiende la francofilia de su fundador

> "se ha preocupado también de fundar poderosas compañías industriales y de crédito en el Río de la Plata y hasta en el Brasil, llevando a todas partes su espíritu de empresa y de progreso"[22].

---

[21] *Revista de la Sección Rural.* N.º 50, 15 de julio de 1930, s/p; n.º 74, 15 de julio de 1931, p. 5.

[22] *El Siglo 1863 — Cincuentenario...* Op. cit., p. 5.

¿Motivo de orgullo, señuelo publicitario para inversionistas del exterior, idea de solidez? Difícil resulta encontrar la explicación de esta auto-propaganda.

De acuerdo a la información de la institución, en Buenos Aires, en el año 1911 se constituyó con los auspicios del Banco, el Crédit Foncier de Buenos Aires, con un capital en acciones de 6:250.000 francos y 18:000.000 de la misma moneda en obligaciones. La filial de Buenos Aires participó también del aumento de capital de las sociedades La Vascongada y Bilz[23].

En Brasil, tenía intereses en el Banco Pelotense del Estado de Río Grande (con representación en el Río de la Plata) y en el Crédito Territorial de Río Grande. En 1909 inició la fundación de la "Compañía Telefónica Riograndense" de Porto Alegre[24]. Otra semblanza de la institución la reconoció como "principal accionista" de esta empresa[25].

Años después, en *El Libro del Centenario del Uruguay,* se informó que había implantado em Porto Alegre y Río Grande la automatización de los teléfonos, aunque habló genéricamente de que "algunos de sus socios participan en importantes empresas", citando, además de la Telefónica, fábricas de vidrio en Porto Alegre y Río de Janeiro[26].

Además de estas inversiones, existieron otras, no difundidas por el banco. Una de ellas fue el saladero de la Sociedad Anónima Industrial y Pastoril, fundado cerca de Livramento en 1907. Lo presidió Luis J. Supervielle. El saladero fue uno de los tantos creados en Brasil por uruguayos que buscaban huir de la legislación proteccionista que dificultaba el ingreso del tasajo a ese mercado. En 1918 fue vendido a la empresa estadounidense Wilson para ser transformado en frigorífico[27].

Lo contradictorio de la información no permite deslindar nítidamente las inversiones del banco de las de sus propietarios.

---

23 Ibidem.

24 Ibidem.

25 Carlos Maeso. *El Uruguay a través de un siglo.* Montevideo: Tipografía Moderna. 1910, p. 369.

26 Idem, p. 418 y 419.

27 Aníbal Barrios Pintos. *Rivera — Una historia diferente.* Tomo 2. Montevideo: MEC. 1990, p. 177.

Inversiones en Uruguay: bancos

Los Supervielle — quizás resulte más acertado hablar del grupo familiar que del banco — tenían intereses en otras instituciones financieras.

Luis J. Supervielle presidió la comisión liquidadora del Banco de Préstamos Inmobiliarios en el período 1923-1926. Había sido fundado en 1907 con el objeto de conceder créditos sobre bienes inmobiliarios, garantidos con hipotecas, y de facilitar la adquisición de bienes raíces. A comienzos de la década del diez gestionó un empréstito con capitalistas franceses para extender sus operaciones[28].

El arquitecto de la institución — Ing. Juan P. Fabini — y uno de sus directores — Remigio Castellanos — fueron compañeros de Supervielle en el directorio de la empresa "Salus". Desconocemos el grado de vinculación de Supervielle con su competidor[29].

En 1937 el Banco Francés Supervielle y Cía. era accionista del Banco Italiano del Uruguay, fundado en 1887 y reorganizado en los años veinte, después de sortear una crisis que lo obligó a solicitar la moratoria[30].

Inversiones en Uruguay: tierras

El total de tierras que poseían los Supervielle es difícil de evaluar, por lo que nos limitaremos a citar algunos ejemplos.

Uno de los establecimientos más prestigiosos fue la Estancia La Franco-Platense, fundada en 1904 con la razón social E. Benausse y Cía. A partir de 1910, en que su capital aumentó a medio millón de pesos, fue dirigida por un directorio que presidió Supervielle, secundado como secretario por Félix Bernausse. Luis J. Supervielle fue, en sus comienzos, el único miembro del grupo en él. En 1913 La Franco Platense comprendía veinte mil hectáreas ubicadas en el departamento de Lavalleja — de las que mil se dedicaban a la agri-

---

[28] Lloyd. Op. cit., p. 336.

[29] Raúl Jacob. *Banca, Estado y Poder Económico, Directorio 1915-1940.* Montevideo: CIEDUR. Serie Investigaciones n.º 81, 1991.

[30] *Diario Oficial.* 21 de diciembre de 1937, p. 3.146 c.

cultura — y una dotación de veintisiete mil cabezas de ganado de diverso tipo.

Presumiblemente, le sucedió la Cabaña La Franco-Platense de Luis J. Supervielle, situada en San Jacinto, departamento de Canelones, y administrada por Eduardo Hughes. Cuando éste en 1929 fue designado representante de los municipios en el primer directorio del Frigorífico Nacional — que presidió Supervielle — La Cabaña pasó a ser administrada por la Sección Rural del Banco, junto con otros establecimientos agropecuarios de la familia[31].

En 1913 la Sucesión Supervielle figuró en la nómina de productores rurales del departamento de San José, con 3.694 hectáreas situadas en la sexta sección judicial. En 1932, el que fue incluido en una lista de hacendados de ese departamento, fue Luis J. Supervielle con tierras en Libertad[32].

En 1929 Luis J. Supervielle presidió la S.A. Estancia del Ombú, que explotaba 16.000 hectáreas en el departamento de Río Negro. Integraban su directorio entre otros, Benausse y el abogado del Banco Francés, el Dr. Horacio Abadie Santos[33].

En 1938 se formó la S.A. Rural Argentino Uruguaya, con un capital autorizado de dos millones de pesos. Era presidida por Supervielle, y aparecían otros miembros del grupo[34]. Además, Luis J. Supervielle fue propietario de la Estancia San Antonio, en el departamento de Salto.

Por su parte Mariana Munyo de Supervielle explotaba la Estancia Agueda (cinco mil hectáreas en el departamento de San José) y la Estancia y Cabaña Tupambaé, en el departamento de Cerro Largo[35].

En algún momento, estos establecimientos — más el Anita — pasaron a girar en la órbita de la sección especializada del Banco, que centralizó su administración.

---

31 Lloyd. Op. cit., p. 245; *El Siglo 1863 — Cincuentenario...*, p. 71; *Revista de la Sección Rural...*, n.º 15, 1.º de febrero de 1929, p. 13; *La Mañana*, 12 de setiembre de 1928, p. 12.

32 *Boletín de la Oficina Nacional del Trabajo*, n.º 3, 15 de julio de 1913, p. 134; *Almanaque-Guía El Siglo*, año 1932.

33 *Diario Oficial*. 9 de noviembre de 1929, p. 1.379-81 c.

34 *Diario Oficial*. 15 de diciembre de 1938, p. 2.853 c.

35 *La Mañana*. 9 de enero de 1930, p. 11.

Inversiones en Uruguay: comercio

En 1925 Luis J. Supervielle presidió la S.A. Compañía Zona Franca de Colonia. La fundación de esta empresa coincidió con la colocación de la piedra fundamental de las obras e instalaciones que albergarían a este enclave, creado por una ley de 1923, que facultó al Poder Ejecutivo a contratar, previa licitación, la explotación de la zona franca por un término no mayor de treinta años.

El vicepresidente de la compañía fue Pedro Cosio — director-gerente del Banco Popular del Uruguay, y el secretario Domingo Baqué, propietario de canteras en Colonia y vocal del Banco de la República Oriental del Uruguay (1924-32). Entre los accionistas se encontraban los ganaderos Dominto Bordaberry y Arturo Wilson, el empresario de la construcción Adolfo Shaw, los corredores de bolsa de Pedro Saenz y Víctor Paullier.

Las expectativas que despertó la zona franca comenzaron a diluirse en 1931, al asumir el Estado su explotación, aunque reservando a los particulares el arrendamiento de algunos servicios.

La compañía subsistió, y en 1942, junto con la empresa de transportes ONDA, y Rodolfo Mezzera Alvarez (accionista del Banco Mercantil del Río de la Plata y vinculado a empresas de navegación), constituyó Mirador Limitada con la finalidad de construir y explotar un hotel en la ciudad de Colonia. En tal sentido sus estatutos habían sido lo suficientemente bien redactados como para contemplar numerosas actividades; podía gestionar y celebrar contratos y concesiones para la construcción, explotación y administración de puertos, tranvías, ferrocarriles, depósitos, zonas francas, fábricas, establecimientos comerciales e industriales, etc.[36].

Inversiones en Uruguay: teléfonos

En 1922 nació La Internacional Empresa Telefónica S.A. con la finalidad de adquirir a Juan Ganzo Fernández las empresas tele-

---

[36] Eduardo Acevedo. *Anales históricos del Uruguay*. Tomo VI. Montevideo: Barreiro y Ramos. 1936, p. 314 y 315; *Diario Oficial*. 3 de agosto de 1925, p. 743-5; Caetano-Jacob. *El nacimiento del terrismo*. Tomo 1. Montevideo: EBO. 1989, p. 114 y 115; *Diario Oficial*. 7 de febrero de 1942, p. 854 c; *Revista del Banco Popular del Uruguay*. N.° 5, mayo de 1925, p. 3.

fónicas que servían a las ciudades de Artigas y Rivera. El capital social era de cien mil pesos, dividido en doscientas acciones de quinientos pesos, de las que ciento sesenta se entregaban a Ganzo Fernández por la compra del activo y pasivo de su propiedad. En los estatutos se establecía la duración del primer directorio — hasta 1927 — y se lo facultaba para emitir obligaciones. Lo presidía Luis J. Supervielle y actuaba en la vicepresidencia Juan M. Gorlero, gerente y apoderado del Banco Francés.

Teniendo el grupo una empresa telefónica en el fronterizo estado de Río Grande del Sur, su estrategia parece haber sido intentar conectar las líneas de ambas y crear una sociedad binacional para después expandir sus operaciones, razón por la cual se reservaban el derecho de emitir obligaciones para captar capital.

En 1938 fue autorizada a aumentar su capital a un millón de pesos. Esto no deja de llamar la atención, ya que en octubre de 1931 Uruguay había estatizado sus servicios telefónicos, lo que afectó los intereses de los Supervielle recién en 1945, en que vendieron a Usinas y Teléfonos del Estado — UTE, la red telefónica de La Internacional, que servía a Rivera, Artigas, Treinta y Tres, Cerro Largo y Tacuarembó.

Según se sugirió en el Parlamento, la venta no resultó un mal negocio en sí, ya que del millón de capital con el que la empresa figuraba en Uruguay, habría utilizado setecientos mil pesos para automatizar los teléfonos del estado brasileño de Santa Catarina, que explotaba en régimen de monopolio. Entre sus propietarios seguían figurando Ganzo Fernández, Supervielle y la familia Supervielle[37].

Inversiones en Uruguay: transportes y turismo

Luis J. Supervielle presidió la Compañía Nacional de Lanchajes y Remolques S.A. en 1932, cuando se reformaron sus estatutos. El momento era de dificultades para las empresas que prestaban servicios a la navegación en el puerto de Montevideo, ya que a las

---

[37] *Diario Oficial.* 14 de setiembre de 1923, p. 1.898-900 c; idem, 7 de noviembre de 1938, p. 1.290 c; *50 Aniversario del teléfono automático en el Uruguay.* Montevideo: ANTEL. 1983, p. 12; DSCR Tomo 465, 27 y 28 de diciembre de 1945, p. 222 y 227 (denuncias del diputado Ferrer Serra).

consecuencias de la crisis económica mundial le debieron sumar la amenaza del Estado que pretendía estatizar los servicios portuarios en todo el país. Ocupaba la vicepresidencia Joaquín Secco Illa — presidente del Banco de Cobranzas, Locaciones y Anticipos. Entre los accionistas figuraron el Dr. Jacinto D. Durán — integrante del Comité de Dirección del Crédit Foncier de l'Uruguay —Antonio F. Braga — vicepresidente del Banco de Cobranzas y director del Comercial — y numerosos corredores de bolsa y cambistas: Nicolich, De Simoni, Forcella, etc.[38].

En 1927, Juan M. Gorlero, como apoderado de Luis J. Supervielle, participó de la asamblea constitutiva de Aeroposta Uruguaya, junto al abogado Octavio Morató, Juan Domingo Lanza y Julio Mailhos y representantes de capitales internacionales: Compañía Argentina Comercial e Inmobiliaria y "Societé Franco-Sudaméricaine de Travaux Publics". Eran los tiempos en que la Aeropostale — antecesora de la Air France — luchaba para unir por vía aérea Francia con América del Sur para establecer un servicio regular de correo. Esta inquietud empresarial, en momentos que la aviación era todavía una aventura de pioneros — recién en aquel año uniría Lindbergh Nueva York con París por el Atlántico —, demuestra una actitud abierta hacia el futuro.

Los Supervielle seguirían apostando en la aviación. Con algunos de sus aliados — Ing. José Serrato, Dr. Federico Fleurquin, etc. decidieron apoyar la Compañía Aeronáutica Uruguaya S.A. — CAUSA, a la que en 1937 se le había concedido autorización para explotar la línea Montevideo-Buenos Aires, lo que haría con hidroaviones de orígen alemán. Luis J. Supervielle presidió en 1942 el directorio de CAUSA, mientras que Serrato y Fleurquin pasaron a ocupar los cargos de vocales. Fracasó un intento por asociarse con las Primeras Líneas Uruguayas de Navegación Aérea — PLUNA, fundada por los hermanos Alberto y Jorge Márquez Vaeza en 1936 para establecer una línea comercial entre Montevideo, Salto y Rivera. Ambas empresas se beneficiaron del apoyo estatal, com lo cual lograron transferir parte del riesgo a la sociedad[39].

---

[38] *Diario Oficial.* 14 de octubre de 1932, p. 396 c.

[39] Idem, 5 de enero de 1928, p. 127-30 c; *CAUSA — Memoria Balance General al 31 de diciembre de 1942*, p. 3; Alberto Marquez Vaeza. *Memoria de aeroplanos.* Montevideo, segunda edición, 1989, p. 228 y 229.

El Banco tenía también una colateral especializada en viajes y pasajes, establecida en Uruguay en 1917, que funcionaba en Montevideo, Buenos Aires, Río de Janeiro y París con la denominación de "Exprinter".

Inversiones en Uruguay: medios de comunicación

En 1915, en momentos en que el conservadurismo y el batllismo estaban enfrentados políticamente, una sociedad anónima (*La Prensa*) adquirió la empresa editora de los diarios *El Siglo, La Razón* y *El Telégrafo.* El primero de ellos precisamente se vangloriaba de su condición de vocero de los sectores conservadores.

El directorio de esta sociedad estaba presidido por el Dr. Manuel Quintela — uno de los propulsores de la Federación Rural, que nacería pocas semanas después — y contaba con la colaboración de Luis J. Supervielle en la vicepresidencia. El secretario era Juan Capurro y los vocales Vicente F. Costa — que militaría en el riverismo y la Federación Rural — y el Ing. Juan P. Fabini — batllista y hombre de la Salus, al igual que Supervielle.

Por su parte Capurro y Fabini eran socios en la agencia de publicidad que adoptaría el nombre del primero. En 1928 los tres órganos de prensa fueron adquiridos por el sosismo, sector político perteneciente al Partido Colorado.

Esta inversión de Supervielle debe verse no sólo en función de las posibilidades publicitarias que ofrecía la prensa, sino también en la necesidad de incidir sobre el Estado, dada la discreta presencia del grupo en el sistema político (fue diputado en el año 1920) y en las gremiales empresariales (fue directivo de la Federación Rural en 1925)[40].

Al respecto parece haber toda una evolución, que quizás pueda, en mucho, ser paradigmática: del órgano de prensa se pasó a la acción directa. Pero finalmente se optó por la vía que resultó en la

---

[40] *El Libro del Centenario...*, p. 418 y 419; *Búsqueda*, 6 de octubre de 1988, p. 13. *El Siglo*, 24 de noviembre de 1915, p. 3; *Diario Oficial*, 16 de julio de 1928, p. 326-8 c; Campodónico, Cures, Da Cunha, Ezcurra, Ferrando Lacuesta. *Gremiales empresariales — 1915-1945. Seis estudios.* Montevideo: Facultad de Humanidades y Ciencias, Departamento de Historia del Uruguay. 1988.

práctica más efectiva, la alianza económica con "influyentes" con trayectoria política (Fabini, Fleurquin, Serrato) y la utilización de un abogado (Abadie Santos) relacionado con el sistema político. Cuando este último falleció fue sustituido en sus funciones jurídicas por un profesional de la familia.

Inversiones en Uruguay: inmobiliarias y financieras

Integrantes del Banco — con Luis J. Supervielle como presidente — fundaron en 1936 El Porvenir S.A., con la finalidad — vaga en su generalidad — de operar en negocios inmobiliarios, industriales y ganaderos.

Pero la que adquirió notoriedad — por su vinculación con la desaparición del Banco Francés — fue la S.A. Crédito Inmobiliario Financiero, o CIFSA, creada en 1938 por miembros del grupo y al igual que la anterior presidida por Luis J. Supervielle. Nació con un capital autorizado de tres millones de pesos. Según el balance de la CIFSA, al 31 de marzo de 1941 era propietaria de doscientas hectáreas en el balneario Punta del Este y había invertido en bonos de la Asunción Port Concession Corporation por un valor cercano al medio millón de dólares[41].

Este tipo de empresas, que podían ser utilizadas como *holdings*, servían para evadir capitales al exterior o radicarlos en el País. En tal sentido debe recordarse que, a partir de 1931, el Estado — por intermedio del Banco de la República Oriental del Uruguay — asumió el control de la comercialización de moneda extranjera y la fijación administrativa del tipo de cambio.

La inserción regional del grupo ofrecía más beneficios que desventajas, ya que le permitía operar en por lo menos tres plazas financieras: Argentina, Brasil y Uruguay.

Inversiones en Uruguay: industria

El Banco Francés Supervielle y Cía. fue promocionado como una auténtica *banque d'affaires*. Estas instituciones — literalmente "ban-

---

[41] *Diario Oficial*, 12 de noviembre de 1936, p. 143 c; idem, 14 de enero de 1939, p. 321 c; *Concordato del Banco Francés Supervielle y Cía.* Montevideo. 1942, p. 68-73.

co de negocios" — según Kindleberger hacían préstamos a largo plazo a la industria, de cuyas empresas eran frecuentemente copropietarias, "en contraste con la banca comercial, o, la privada en forma de sociedad anónima, que, al menos en teoría, sólo prestaba a corto plazo"[42]. Las características de la participación del Francés en la actividad fabril no es demasiado explícita en sus reseñas, lo que en parte puede deberse a la falta de concisión de la información proporcionada a los periodistas que las radactaron. Así en la inserta en la obra de Carlos Maeso, *El Uruguay a través de un siglo,* se dice: "ha intervenido en la fundación y reorganización de las compañías Salus y Materiales de Construcción". Y en *El Libro del Centenario del Uruguay* consta que "ha facilitado el establecimiento de importantes empresas industriales", citando a la Compañía de Materiales de Construcción[43].

La consideración de este aspecto, que involucra al sistema financiero y a la función de banca de inversión que pudieron cumplir sus integrantes, es de suyo complicada si no se cuenta con la fuente básica para cualquier estudio que intente abordar sus relaciones con la industria: los archivos de las empresas. También juegan las características de la formación económica uruguaya, sintetizadas en una interrogante ¿cuando aparecen industriales en los directorios de un banco es porque este invirtió en industrias o porque canalizó capital del sector industrial? Por otra parte no se puede soslayar el papel de los grupos económicos, una de cuyas características más salientes es la necesidad de diversificar sus inversiones, y para los cuales el poder contar con un banco lo es también con la oportunidad de acceder a nuevos capitales[44].

En el caso que nos ocupa, resulta difícil discriminar en ocasiones si se trata de inversiones del Banco o de su director más notorio, Luis J. Supervielle. Pero lo que sí tenemos claro es que el Francés, como *banque d'affaires* fue muy peculiar, ya que fue propiedad de una familia que se transformó en grupo económico gracias a su banco.

---

42 Charles P. Kindleberger. *Historia financiera de Europa.* Barcelona: Crítica-Grijalbo. 1988, p. 636.

43 Maeso. Op. cit., p. 369, y *El Libro del Centenario...,* p. 418 y 419.

44 Véase Stolovich, Rodríguez, Bértola. *El poder económico en el Uruguay actual.* Montevideo: CUI. 1987.

Supervielle, o el Banco, se habrían vinculado a la compañía Salus en 1902. La empresa había sido creada unos años antes para explotar una fuente de agua mineral situada cerca de la ciudad de Minas. La incorporación de o de los Supervielle significó de hecho una alianza con otra familia, los Fabini, que también tendrían un marcado protagonismo económico[45].

Recién en 1907, la Salus se transformó en sociedad anónima. La presidió Luis J. Supervielle e integró su primer directorio Jorge West, que se había desempeñado al frente de la gerencia del Banco Francés[46].

Con el transcurso del tiempo la Salus creció y amplió sus actividades. En 1912 compró una competidora, Acqua Vera y Canteras del Verdún[47]. En los años treinta se fusionó con la S.A. Weimar, duplicando su capital a dos millones de pesos, lo que le permitió instalar una fábrica de cerveza. Además construyó un hotel y montó sobre una extensión de dos mil hectáreas una agroindustria para abastecerse de madera, cebada y frutales[48].

En 1942, después de la desaparición del Banco Francés, la seguía presidiendo Supervielle. Jorge West continuó vinculado a ella en la década del treinta. Otro Supervielle — Bernardo — fue su abogado por esos años. Por otra parte, una asamblea de accionistas en julio de 1935, se realizó en el local del Banco Francés Supervielle y Cía.[49].

El capital — que en 1942 el Poder Ejecutivo autorizó a ampliar a tres millones de pesos — reflejó un alto grado de concentración: en 1935 quince accionistas representaron con 2.963 acciones el sesenta por ciento de las integradas; en 1936, veintiocho accionistas totalizaron más del setenta y seis por ciento del capital social[50].

La estrategia de intentar integrar las distintas etapas de pro-

---

45 *Minas: la Suiza del Uruguay.* N.º 1, octubre de 1936, p. 37-9.

46 *Nuevos estatutos de la Compañía Salus.* Montevideo: El Siglo — La Razón, El Telégrafo. 1917.

47 Alcides Beretta, en Beretta et al. *La industrialización del Uruguay 1870-1925 — Cinco perspectivas históricas.* Montevideo: Fundación de Cultura Universitária. 1978, p. 159.

48 *Minas... y Nuestra Tierra — Los Departamentos: n.º 5 — Lavalleja.* Montevideo: Editorial Nuestra Tierra. 1970, p. 30 y 31.

49 *Diario Oficial,* 28 de setiembre de 1935, p. 2.831 c.

50 Ibidem, y *Diario Oficial,* 7 de marzo de 1936, p. 1.640 c.

ducción llevó a miembros de la Salus a invertir en una fábrica de vidrios para abastecerse de botellas: la S.A. Vidriería y Cristalería Nacional. En 1913 la presidió Luis J. Supervielle. Juan M. Gorlero — gerente del Banco Francés — fue su vicepresidente. Estuvieron en su directorio otros hombres de la Salus: Santiago Fabini (secretario), Jorge West (vocal); Manuel Lessa, Juan H. Cóppola, Enrique Fabini (suplentes)[51]. La fábrica era provista de materia prima por una arenera que Supervielle explotaba en las márgenes del río Santa Lucía.

En 1931 Agustín D. Gorlero, como secretario, y Jorge Supervielle, como suplente, participaron de la constitución de la "Fábrica Nacional de Vidrios S.A.". Ocupó la presidencia Federico Fleurquin, y fue vicepresidente el Ing. José Serrato[52]. Ambos estarían en el futuro asociados a los Supervielle en otras empresas.

La Salus utilizó los servicios de los talleres gráficos de la editora de *El Siglo, La Razón* y *El Telégrafo,* administrada por una compañía de la que Supervielle y el Ing. Juan Fabino fueron directores.

Otro rubro que canalizó inversiones de los Supervielle fue el de materiales para la construcción. Esto también fue parte de su lógica empresarial, si se considera que el Banco Francés vendía solares y fundaba barrios residenciales.

En 1931 Luis J. Supervielle presidió la "Compañía de Materiales de Construcción". Su abogado fue el del Banco, el Dr. Horacio Abadie Santos[53]. Había sido fundada en 1906, y entre sus propulsores también figuraron algunos hombres de la Salus: Remigio Castellanos, que fue su secretario y Santiago Fabini, su administrador. El Ing. Juan Monteverde — socio de Juan P. Fabini en una empresa de construcción — en 1913 ejerció la vicepresidencia.

Aparentemente surgió por la fusión de varios establecimientos existentes: la arenera de Supervielle, la cantera de mármol de Burgueño en el departamento de Maldonado, una cantera de granito de La Paz, etc.

Construyó en Montevideo una fábrica de ladrillos sílico-calcáreos que fue abastecida por la arenera de Supervielle. La empresa logró en los años siguientes una situación próspera debido al desarrollo

---

[51] *Cincuentenario El Siglo...,* p. 28.

[52] *Diario Oficial,* 9 de diciembre de 1931, p. 2.367 c.

[53] Idem, 8 de julio de 1931, p. 216 y 217 c.

de la industria de la construcción, a la que proveyó de ladrillos, mármoles, granitos, pedregullo, adoquines, carbonato de cal, etc.[54].

Pero el paso más transcendente en este campo fue la fundación en 1937 de la Compañía Nacional de Cementos S.A. con un capital autorizado de dos millones y medio de pesos. Nació en el estudio jurídico de los doctores Supervielle (Bernardo) y Laurenti. Fue su presidente Luis Julio Supervielle, y su vicepresidente el Ing. José Serrato. Entre los vocales estuvo Juan M. Gorlero, y como suplente Daniel Supervielle[55]. Aunque las acciones eran al portador, el núcleo fundador respondía al grupo Supervielle y sus aliados.

La planta industrial se instaló cerca de la localidad de Pan de Azúcar, y fue la segunda en el País (la primera era propiedad de capitales radicados en Estados Unidos). Quizá esta presencia extranjera fue un factor importante en la decisión del grupo, ya que la ley fundacional de ANCAP reservó en 1931 una parte del mercado para ser abastecida por el Estado. Suponemos que una eventual estatización — amenaza algo alejada de la orientación del gobierno del presidente Terra — debió haber sido pesada, así como la desigual suerte que podía correr el capital privado nacional frente al extranjero. De todos modos la ley no le confirió al Estado la exclusividad, y Supervielle se adelantó a éste para romper el monopolio de fabricación existente. Eran los tiempos en los que se emprendía la construcción de la represe hidroeléctrica de Rincón del Bonete.

Inversiones en Uruguay: empresas de capital extranjero

Las conexiones internacionales del Banco Francés de hecho proporcionaban a sus propietarios una excelente oportunidad: la de ser intermediarios de inversionistas extranjeros. Ese papel parece haber sido cumplido por Luis J. Supervielle. (En 1922 regresó de Europa después de sondear las posibilidades de que el capital francés apoyase una planta frigorífica.)[56] Al final de cuentas, una

---

[54] *Cincuentenario El Siglo...*, p. 89; *El Libro del Centenario...*, op. cit., p. 772-5 y Beretta, op. cit., p. 175 y 176.

[55] *Diario Oficial*, 22 de noviembre de 1937, p. 1.983 c.

[56] *Revista de la Federación Rural.* N.º 119, diciembre de 1928, p. 453-9.

de las especialidades de los banqueros es hallar los capitales en los lugares en que se encuentran disponibles. Si bien las inversiones francesas no eran importantes en Uruguay, comparadas com las británicas o con las norteamericanas, los Supervielle — agentes de una compañía de seguros británica y directivos de una empresa de aviación que usaba aparatos alemanes — mostraron tener la suficiente ductilidad como para que el origen de la familia no fuese un lastre en sus decisiones económicas.

Por otra parte, en las empresas industriales de las que participaron, intentaron dejar espacio para los capitalistas de cualquier nacionalidad: así la asamblea de la Salus, realizada en noviembre de 1935, solicitó autorización para emitir obligaciones por valor de un millón de pesos y las acciones de la fábrica de cemento eran al portador. Otras cotizaron sus acciones en la Bolsa. De todas formas, el capital que se pudo conseguir por esta vía y su procedencia, es difícil de estimar.

No encontramos a Supervielle en los directorios de empresas extranjeras radicadas en el País y, por lo tanto, ignoramos si sirvió de enlace para alguna inversión directa. Quizás la Aeroposta Uruguaya estaba llamada — al igual que su homónima argentina que dirigió en 1929 Saint-Exupéry — a ser subsidiaria de la Latecoére, luego Aeropostale, que competía con los alemanes por el transporte aéreo del correo sudamericano a Europa. No figuraba en una lista de sociedades anónimas extranjeras existentes en Uruguay a fines de 1931. La nómina había sido elaborada por la oficina estatal encargada de fiscalizarlas.

En cambio sí se había incluido a la Compañía Franco-Uruguaya de Obras Públicas, con un capital de un millón cien mil pesos, presidida en 1930 por Juan M. Gorlero, vinculado al grupo[57]. También el otro exgerente, Jorge West, ese año encabezó el directorio de una británica, la Empresa Constructora Uruguaya[58]. Por esa fecha, Supervielle se encontraba moralmente imposibilitado de aparecer, ya que ocupaba la presidencia del Frigorífico Nacional, en la que el Estado tenía representación.

57 *La Mañana*, 4 de octubre de 1932, p. 7 y *Diario Oficial*, 11 de diciembre de 1930, p. 2.755 c a 2.757 c.

58 *Diario Oficial*, 28 de enero de 1931, p. 690 c a 692 c.

Del "Banco Francés Supervielle y Cía." al "Banco de Montevideo"

Hacia 1930 los balances publicados por el Banco permitían avizorar ciertas nebolosas[59]. Entre 1921 y 1930 el capital se había mantenido incambiado en un millón setecientos mil pesos (al 31 de diciembre). Se podría pensar, que la política de la institución había sido la de incrementar sus reservas. Sin embargo, éstas disminuyeron en unos pocos miles de pesos: en 1921 existían seiscientos cincuenta mil pesos en reservas, más doscientos seis mil quinientos ochenta y tres pesos con cuarenta centésimos bajo la denominación de "Reserva especial"; en 1930 las reservas alcanzaban los ochocientos cincuenta mil pesos, seis mil pesos menos que la suma de las existentes nueve años antes.

En el transcurso de 1931, el capital se elevó a dos millones trescientos cincuenta mil pesos (crecimiento 38%) y las reservas aumentaron a novecientos diez mil pesos (crecimiento 7%). Este salto admite dos explicaciones. La primera, que se trató de un moderado proceso de capitalización. La segunda, que el Banco tenía su capital en moneda extranjera y corrigió las cifras, computando la desvalorización de la unidad uruguaya (a mediados de 1937 el capital era de tres millones de pesos).

Si se toman las cantidades publicitadas al finalizar los años 1921 y 1930, se percibe disminución en los depósitos del Francés en el Banco de la República; en los valores descontados; en el dinero captado en régimen de cuenta corriente; en los valores y títulos de renta. En cambio, aumentaron los préstamos en cuenta corriente; los montos de los corresponsales en el exterior y las cuentas en moneda extranjera; los valores depositados; y las cuentas en caja de ahorro y plazo fijo.

Esto permite inferir algunos cambios. Por ejemplo, el aumento de los depósitos en caja de ahorros y plazo fijo en detrimento de las cuentas corrientes permitía aumentar, de desearse, la duración de los préstamos. Los depósitos y préstamos en moneda extranjera y cuenta con corresponsales en el exterior, que en parte suponen

[59] Los balances fueron publicados en el *Boletín del Ministerio de Hacienda* y en el *Diario Oficial.*

transacciones realizadas por el banco fuera del país, se habían multiplicado casi por diez.

Pero lo que realmente llama la atención es la aparición en 1930 de un rubro "deudores en gestión" por una suma cercana a los siete millones de pesos. ¿Se trataba de inversiones en empresas, de terrenos vendidos a plazo, de ambas cosas? Probablemente se trate de negocios en tierras.

El 4 de noviembre de 1940 se iniciaron los procedimientos del concordato del Banco Francés Supervielle y Cía. El Dr. Juan J. Carbajal Victorica, en representación del acreedor Nidera Argentina S.A., entendió que una de las causas del desastre fue

> "la posibilidad permitida por nuestra legislación, de que un Banco de depósitos fuera al mismo tiempo Banco de negocios y fundador de empresas de riesgo económico"[60].

En el activo del Banco habían aparecido las acciones de Crédito Inmobiliario Financiero S.A. — CIFSA, de propiedad del grupo, en pago de una deuda de un millón cien mil pesos de Luis J. Supervielle con la institución de la que era copropietario. CIFSA además había emitido obligaciones por un millón ochocientos mil pesos, que se encontraban en manos de muchos ahorristas[61]. CIFSA era propietaria de tierras en Punta del Este y de valores de una sociedad extranjera.

En la ocasión se desentrañaron algunos aspectos de cómo funcionaba el Banco con las empresas en las que los Supervielle tenían intereses. A octubre de 1941 la Compañía de Materiales de Construcción tenía vales, redescontados en el Banco de la República Oriental del Uruguay, por trescientos treinta y cinco mil pesos; y la Zona Franca de Colonia por cien mil pesos[62].

El Banco fue suplantado en su local y actividades por otro, que debía liquidarlo si el concordato era homologado[63]. En la Cámara de Representantes, el diputado Francisco Gilmet denunció en 1945 que el gobierno de facto (habla del que instauró el golpe de 1942) había dejado sin efecto la sentencia de la justicia

---

[60] *Concordato...* Op. cit., p. 51.

[61] Ibidem.

[62] Idem, p. 57.

[63] Idem, p. 83.

"y permitía ir al concordato que el Juez, en cuya jurisdicción radicaba el expediente, había negado por no reunirse las condiciones indispensables. Se confió la liquidación del Banco Francés al Banco de Montevideo, presidido por el señor Serrato"[64].

Era la época de la campaña del herrerismo contra las "implicancias" y el gobierno de Juan José de Amézaga, uno de cuyos blancos fue el ex-Ministro de Relaciones Exteriores, Ing. José Serrato (1943-45) vinculado a empresas de Supervielle.

El Poder Ejecutivo concedió la personería jurídica al Banco de Montevideo en noviembre de 1941. Representaban a los acreedores el Ing. José Serrato (que lo presidió) y el Dr. José Irureta Goyena (hijo), que fue vocal: y al Banco Francés Supervielle y Cía. el Dr. Bernardo Supervielle, que ingresó como vocal en el primer directorio de la nueva institución. Pero aparecieron otros intereses económicos: Julio Mailhos S.C. y Bunge y Born, representado por su directivo Juan Gyselynk, que pasó a ser vocal del Banco de Montevideo. El Banco se reservó un activo papel en las transacciones rurales, (Art. 3.º de los Estatutos)[65].

Años después, en el Parlamento, se habló de que se le había "regalado" la cartera de administración de propiedades del Francés — que el "Banco de Cobranzas" pretendió adquirir en un cuarto millón de pesos — y de una "venta" al consorcio internacional Bemberg[66].

Conclusiones

La caída del Banco Francés Supervielle y Cía., o su transmutación; la expropiación o venta de la empresa telefónica, etc., parecían vislumbrar la disminución del peso o el comienzo del ocaso del grupo Supervielle en Uruguay. Hacia 1950, Bernardo Supervielle continuó en el directorio del Banco de Montevideo, Julio Enrique Supervielle en el de Exprinter, Agustín D. Gorlero en la Fábrica Nacional de

---

64 DSCR, Tomo 465, 27 y 28 de diciembre de 1945, p. 17.

65 *Diario Oficial*, 29 de diciembre de 1941, p. 2.835 c.

66 DSCR, Tomo 465, ibidem.

Vidrios S.A., Luis Supervielle y Agustín Gorlero en el de la Compañía de Materiales de Construcción S.A., Luis Supervielle en la Compañía Aeronáutica Uruguaya S.A. En cambio ninguno de sus habituales representantes estaban en los cargos claves en los directorios de la Compañía Salus, de la Compañía Nacional de Cemento S.A., en la de Lanchajes y Remolques[67].

Quizás todo el *affaire* del Banco Francés deba vincularse a algún episodio de la internacionalización del grupo económico, que continuó teniendo intereses en otras partes del mundo. En la sentencia del Juzgado Letrado de Primera Instancia en lo Civil de Cuarto Turno (21 de mayo de 1942), después de subrayarse que, en última instancia, el concordato no era decidido por los acreedores reales y efectivos sino por el propio deudor, se señalo que el capital estaba disperso "en diversas empresas y negocios muchos de los cuales por radicarse fuera del país están al abrigo de todo contralor eficaz"[68].

Resulta sugestivo constatar que en Argentina, en 1941, se inscribió el Banco Supervielle como de nacionalidad francesa, con un capital aportado por la Casa Matriz en un 51% y por fuentes nacionales en el 49% restante. (Según otro testimonio en 1945 ingresó a Argentina la institución bancaria francesa Supervielle Société Générale.)[69]

¿La disminución de su presencia en el país fue el principio de su fin, o marcó la decisión de migrar en búsqueda de nuevos horizontes? Por lo pronto a fines de la década del ochenta el "Grupo Supervielle" sobrevivia manteniendo vinculaciones con el sistema bancario (Banco de Montevideo, Exprinter Casa Bancaria), con el sector servicios (Exprinter Turismo), con el agro y con el exterior (Exprinter International Corporation)[70].

Visto específicamente como institución financiera, se puede afirmar que el "Banco Francés Supervielle y Cía." cumplió funciones de "banco de negocios", facilitando el surgimiento y desarrollo de

---

[67] *Registro General de Firmas.* Montevideo: Florensa y Lafon. 1950.

[68] *Concordato...*, p. 10.

[69] Eduardo Basualdo. *La Estructura de Propiedad del Capital Extranjero en la Argentina — 1974.* Buenos Aires: Centro de Economía Transnacional. 1984, p. 65; y *Las Empresas Transnacionales en Argentina.* CEPAL. Documento de Trabajo n.º 16. 1985, p. 130.

[70] Luis Stolovich, Juan Manuel Rodríguez, Luis Bértola. *El Poder Económico en el Uruguay Actual.* Montevideo: CUI. 1987, p. 384.

empresas. Pero su gestión no se puede desligar de su "propiedad". Por lo tanto, corresponde hablar de una familia que diversificó sus inversiones utilizando un banco de su pertenencia y que se constituyó un grupo económico de origen financiero.

Délia Beatriz Espina

O PAPEL DAS EMPRESAS MULTINACIONAIS NA INDUSTRIALIZAÇÃO PERIFÉRICA: UM ESTUDO DA TRAJETÓRIA DA IBM (INTERNATIONAL BUSINESS MACHINES) NO BRASIL*

É objetivo central deste trabalho fazer uma análise empírica da trajetória de uma empresa norte-americana — a IBM — no Brasil, abrangendo desde a entrada e o crescimento da subsidiária até o presente[1] e focalizando, mais especialmente, o impacto que a empresa produziu, e produz, no desenvolvimento industrial e tecnológico brasileiro.

A expansão da IBM do seu país de origem, os Estados Unidos, ao Brasil, é um fato histórico relevante que envolve não só a história da empresa, mas também a história dos dois países. Acreditamos, contudo, que a relação empresa matriz-subsidiária brasileira é parte de um fenômeno mais abrangente: o desenvolvimento da *cultura da IBM* que, a partir dos Estados Unidos, se propaga pelo mundo inteiro, através de suas subsidiárias. A compreensão desse fenômeno mais geral, que denominamos cultura da IBM, pode ajudar-nos a dimensionar em toda sua profundidade o impacto que a empresa produziu e produz no desenvolvimento industrial e tecnológico do Brasil.

---

* Este trabalho é um resumo do Relatório Parcial apresentado ao CNPq, resultado da pesquisa em andamento que está sendo financiada por essa Instituição, através de uma bolsa Recém-Doutor. A pesquisa está sendo patrocinada pelo DPCT — Instituto de Geociências (UNICAMP) sob responsabilidade do Prof. Dr. Tamás Szmrecsányi.

1 Atualmente a subsidiária brasileira, como o resto da organização, enfrenta uma profunda crise que provocou a remodelação da estrutura interna da empresa.

Para facilitar o estudo da trajetória da IBM, no Brasil, a análise foi subdividida em dois períodos: 1.º) desde a chegada da empresa ao Brasil, em 1917, até fins da década de 1960, e 2.º) desde 1970 até o presente.

O trabalho que estamos apresentando refere-se ao primeiro período da história da empresa, precedido de uma caracterização da IBM em sua totalidade.

O surgimento da IBM

A CTR (Computing Tabulating Recording Company), rebatizada IBM em 1924, surge nos Estados Unidos em 1911, a partir da consolidação de três empresas: Computing Scale Company, International Time Recording Company, The Tabulating Machine Company. Estas empresas eram, por sua vez, o resultado da fusão de diversas companhias que fabricavam máquinas de precisão. Seus produtos variavam desde balanças comerciais, cortadoras de frios, relógios de ponto, moedoras de café, até máquinas tabuladoras e perfuradoras de cartões.

A emergência da CTR, a partir da fusão de empresas que produziam bens e serviços diversos, responde a uma forma típica de consolidação, a *combinação horizontal*, que visava a constituição de uma única grande empresa industrial ou "holding company". A consolidação da CTR, em 1911, insere-se no momento histórico exato em que a formação dos grandes "trusts" surge e se generaliza nos Estados Unidos, desde fins do século XIX até o término da Primeira Guerra Mundial.

Num cenário que brindava grandes desafios e oportunidades, as empresas americanas responderam de forma verdadeiramente revolucionária às mudanças do meio, assistindo-se, no período que precede a Primeira Guerra, à rápida emergência de umas e à mortalidade de outras, do que resultou o nascimento das *gigantes*, destinadas a sobreviver e crescer até o presente.

A prematura *vocação expansiva* das empresas predecessoras da CTR, o *caráter inovador* dos produtos que comercializava, a adoção de uma *organização administrativa científica* permitem caracterizá-la como sendo um caso típico da constituição da *grande empresa industrial americana.*

Bem antes da consolidação, em 1911, as empresas predecessoras da CTR já tinham mostrado sua vocação expansiva, não só a partir da venda de seus produtos, mas também da realização de investimentos produtivos fora dos Estados Unidos. Desde fins do século XIX, a maioria das empresas que constituíram a CTR tinha-se expandido pela Europa e o Canadá, criando fortes vínculos comerciais que facilitariam a rápida expansão geográfica da CTR, a partir de sua constituição em 1911.

Além da vocação pioneira para a expansão geográfica, as três empresas que formaram a CTR destacavam-se pelo caráter inovador dos produtos que comercializavam. Em todas elas estava presente o inventor do produto ou *machinery maker.* O caráter inovador dos produtos iniciais da CTR é outro elemento que nos permite caracterizá-la como sendo um caso típico da constituição da empresa industrial norte-americana. A Tabulating Machine Company foi a que aportou a maior força inovadora. Ao fundir-se à CTR, converteu-se na responsável pela rápida expansão que inicia a empresa, a partir de 1911. Se alguém representou o *empresário-inventor de máquinas* foi a figura de Herman Hollerith, fundador da Tabulating Machine Company. Engenheiro e estatístico, formado na School of Mines de Columbia College, Hollerith trabalhou no censo norte-americano de 1880, interessando-se pelos problemas de processamento de dados demográficos.

Durante os anos de 1885 e 1887, Hollerith fez as primeiras experiências para codificar as informações, utilizando máquinas tabuladoras e perfuradoras de cartões. Em 1889, conseguiu patenteá-las, obtendo um grande triunfo ao ser contratado pelo US Census Bureau, para realizar o recenseamento de 1890. A partir do censo de 1890, o impacto produzido pelas máquinas tabuladoras de Hollerith introduziu a empresa no caminho revolucionário das inovações tecnológicas.

A complexidade dos produtos que a CTR produzia, o volume que alcançara a produção e a comercialização, a partir da consolidação, em 1911, iriam exigir a transformação revolucionária da estrutura administrativa da empresa, superando a presença do empresário pioneiro que era, simultaneamente, proprietário, inventor e administrador, para alcançar a estrutura moderna de gerenciamento.

O nível de complexidade que adquiriam as empresas que surgiam por combinação horizontal, como a CTR, tanto da produção como da comercialização e distribuição, em um mercado em rápido processo de oligopolização, requeria uma planificação capaz de combinar decisões de curto e de longo prazo. A percepção da empresa, como sendo um todo orgânico, e o conhecimento do mercado em que atuava, eram imprescindíveis para assegurar o controle e o crescimento a longo prazo. A administração da empresa, a partir de um acordo entre as firmas conglomeradas, tinha se tornado completamente ineficiente para enfrentar os novos desafios econômicos.

Os homens capacitados para tomar e implementar as decisões, nas novas empresas, eram aqueles que possuíam o poder real ou efetivo, e não simplesmente o poder legal de alocar os recursos disponíveis, em função dos objetivos gerais da empresa. O *Gerente Geral* era esse homem[2].

Em 1914, Thomas John Watson assume o cargo de Gerente Geral da CTR, levando à empresa a enorme experiência que tinha adquirido na National Cash Register, ao lado de John Henry Patterson, administrador na NCR e seu grande mestre. Na NCR, Watson tinha participado da revolução que experimentaram as novas empresas americanas, desde começos do século, em relação à comercialização e distribuição da produção. Patterson, como administrador da NCR, tinha elevado a empresa, desde início do século, a líder do mercado americano.

Posteriormente, como administrador da CTR, Thomas Watson implementou todas as técnicas administrativas e de vendas que aprendera com Patterson, iniciando a reestruturação revolucionária da empresa, seguindo a linha de produtos e de funções (*Staff and Line Structure*).

A primitiva centralização administrativa da CTR foi modificada por Thomas Watson, a partir de 1949. Naquele ano, Watson criou a World Trade Corporation, iniciando um processo de descentralização da organização. Subsidiária da IBM doméstica, com operação independente, a WTC centralizava a administração das empresas que atuavam fora dos Estados Unidos. Em 1970, a WTC alcançou uma receita de 2,5 bilhões de dólares, igualando a receita da IBM-Estados Unidos, confirmando as previsões de Watson, sobre a potencialidade de seu crescimento.

---

[2] Chandler Jr., Alfred D. *Strategy and Structure: Chapters in the History of American Industrial Enterprise.* The MIT Press. 1969.

IBM — Brasil

Em 1917 a CTR chegava ao Brasil. Naquele ano a empresa já se encontrava, nos Estados Unidos, entre as líderes do ramo, com um capital superior a 24,4 milhões de dólares.

O crescimento experimentado pela Computing Tabulating Recording Company, nos Estados Unidos, a partir de 1914; a posição que alcançara, em 1917, no mercado doméstico, e sua interação com as firmas correntes são os principais fatores que impulsionaram a expansão geográfica da empresa. O contexto internacional favorecia essa expansão. O período correspondente à Primeira Guerra Mundial caracterizou-se pelo estreitamento de vínculos comerciais e financeiros dos Estados Unidos com os países da América do Sul. Terminada a Guerra, a atividade comercial internacional acelerou-se, favorecendo a entrada das empresas norte-americanas nos países sul-americanos. A profunda transformação experimentada pelo Brasil durante as décadas de 1910 e 1920, converteu o País em ponto de atração para a expansão das atividades da CTR.

Desde fins do século XIX, a inserção da economia exportadora cafeeira na economia mundial impulsionava o desenvolvimento integrado do Brasil, promovendo o surgimento de uma indústria doméstica incipiente. Esse processo foi acompanhado por importantes mudanças demográficas. A crescente necessidade de mão-de-obra, conseqüência da expansão econômica, favorecia a entrada de imigrantes europeus. O aumento da população e o impulso industrial do começo do século incentivavam a urbanização. Durante a década de 1920, a renda real cresceu 7,3% ao ano, favorecendo a constituição de um importante mercado consumidor.

Nesse contexto de profundas transformações sócio-econômicas o governo brasileiro preparava, desde meados da década de 1910, a realização de um censo demográfico e agrícola.

A conjuntura nacional e internacional era especialmente propícia aos planos pessoais de Valentim F. Bouças. Economista, de origem brasileira, hábil negociador, consegue convencer Thomas J. Watson a abrir uma representação da CTR no Brasil.

Em 1917, sob o comando de Bouças, a CTR iniciava suas operações no País, depois de assinar um contrato com a Diretoria de Estatística Comercial Brasileira, para a realização do censo de 1920. Desde 1917 começaram a chegar ao Brasil as modernas máquinas

Hollerith. Em 1920, foram introduzidas as impressoras, que serviram para agilizar e aperfeiçoar a contagem dos dados do censo.

Em 1922, as máquinas Hollerith foram expostas ao público, pela primeira vez, na Exposição do Centenário da Independência. A partir de então, com o nome de Serviços Hollerith, a CTR estendia suas atividades a importantes órgãos públicos e privados da indústria e do comércio brasileiros[3].

Em 28 de março de 1923 os Serviços Hollerith assinaram um contrato com a Diretoria de Contabilidade do Ministério da Fazenda e iniciaram suas atividades no Tesouro Nacional. Em 31 de dezembro de 1923 os Serviços Hollerith assinaram contrato com a Alfândega para executar trabalhos em todos os pontos do território nacional onde ela existia. Todos os trabalhos aduaneiros foram divididos em grupos, que estavam subordinados a uma direção central, a Diretoria da Receita Pública, com sede no Rio de Janeiro.

Os Serviços Hollerith Brasil estendiam, também, suas atividades na esfera privada. Ficaram registrados, no livro de Valentim F. Bouças, os serviços prestados pela empresa aos estabelecimentos comerciais "A Capital", destinados ao controle do estoque, análise de vendas, com apuração dos lucros para cada mercadoria. Em 1924 a empresa assinou contratos com a Light and Power Co.; com a Companhia Paulista de Estradas de Ferro; com o Loide Brasileiro; com o Instituto Brasileiro do Café e com o Banco do Brasil.

O prestígio dos Serviços Hollerith cresceu ao longo da década de 1920, ficando seu sucesso registrado em distintas publicações e jornais da época. O "Jornal do Commércio", de 18 de outubro de 1924, fez um elogioso histórico da empresa. Artigos de igual teor foram publicados no "Correio do Povo", de Porto Alegre, de 2 de novembro de 1924; e no jornal da Capital Federal "A Noite", de 30 de dezembro de 1924. Nesse mesmo vespertino, em sua edição de 14 de fevereiro de 1925, foi publicada uma notícia sobre o desfalque de ouro descoberto pelos Serviços Hollerith, na Alfândega de Santos. A "Gazeta de Notícias", de 15 do mesmo mês de 1924, fazia referência ao mesmo assunto. O mesmo jornal, em 21 de janeiro de 1926, publicou um artigo, sob o título "Os importantes Serviços Hollerith".

---

[3] Bouças, Valentim F. *Serviços Hollerith*. Rio de Janeiro: Papelaria Atlântica. 1927.

Em 31 de dezembro de 1924 a empresa era autorizada por Decreto n.º 16.757, do Presidente Arthur Bernardes a atuar no Brasil, sob o nome de International Business Machines Co. of Delaware. Valentim F. Bouças era designado Gerente Geral da empresa, com sede no Rio de Janeiro. É interessante notar que no mesmo ano de 1924, em que a IBM recebera autorização do Governo brasileiro para atuar no Brasil, também a recebera a Burroughs.

Desde sua instalação, em 1917, foi estratégia primordial da IBM lograr uma decisiva inserção no mercado, onde já atuavam concorrentes internacionais, e obter o controle financeiro da empresa. Desde fins da década de 1920, ao tempo que a empresa expandia-se geograficamente, iniciava um rápido crescimento através da diversificação dos produtos que comercializava.

O período de luta pela recuperação da economia nacional, que seguiu à Grande Depressão, entre 1929-33, não afetou a expansão da empresa. Em 1931 abriu uma sucursal em São Paulo; em 1933, inaugurou sucursais em Porto Alegre, Belo Horizonte, Salvador, Recife e Niterói. Naquele mesmo ano, iniciou a montagem e depois a fabricação de relógios industriais.

O acelerado crescimento da IBM do Brasil nesse período a fez merecedora de um lugar de destaque em relação às demais subsidiárias. Em 25 de janeiro de 1933, Valentim F. Bouças recebeu, nos Estados Unidos, o "Watson International Trophy", das mãos de Watson, como prêmio por ter atingido a máxima quota de vendas da IBM, desse ano.

Em 1934 a IBM começou a comercializar, no Brasil, as então revolucionárias máquinas alfabéticas de processamento de dados. Em 1935, passaram a ser fabricados, no país, os cartões de perfuração.

A complexidade das máquinas comercializadas pela IBM, já nessa época, exigiam um considerável conhecimento técnico para sua manutenção. Em 1935, a empresa organizou o primeiro curso regular para Representantes de Serviços Técnicos, iniciando, no Brasil, sua tradicional política de formação e aperfeiçoamento de seus técnicos.

O processo de crescente atividade manufatureira da IBM, e a especial conjuntura econômica nacional e internacional criada pela Crise Mundial de 1929, impulsionaram a instalação da fábrica, em 1939, no bairro de Benfica, no Rio de Janeiro.

O colapso sofrido pelo comércio internacional, a partir de 1929, produziu um declínio médio das importações mundiais de 65%, entre 1929 e 1932. Nesse período, as importações brasileiras experimentaram um declínio de 75%, sendo os produtos importados dos Estados Unidos os mais afetados.

As drásticas medidas econômicas tomadas pelo governo brasileiro, para enfrentar a crise, aprofundaram as dificuldades para importar. Por exemplo, em 19 de setembro de 1931, o Brasil suspendeu o pagamento dos serviços da dívida externa; entre 1929 e 1932 decretou a elevação geral das tarifas alfandegárias (acima de 10%); a taxa de câmbio foi depreciada em 54%, em 1931, e em 108%, em 1939, em relação aos valores de 1928-29, o que provocou um forte aumento nos preços relativos das importações.

Todas essas medidas de política monetária e fiscal que restringiam as importações afetaram as subsidiárias de empresas estrangeiras. Contudo, foram as medidas de controle cambial as que maior impacto produziram sobre elas. O controle cambial colocava as empresas importadoras em grandes dificuldades para trocar mil-réis pelos dólares necessários para pagar a matriz. Além de criar dificuldades para importar, a política cambial favorecia a acumulação de fundos, em moeda nacional, nas empresas subsidiárias. Esse fato, no caso específico da IBM, que contava com um mercado em crescente expansão para seus produtos, deve ter sido um forte incentivo, para o início das atividades industriais da empresa no País.

A abertura da fábrica, em 1939, foi um acontecimento relevante para a IBM. Thomas J. Watson viajou ao Rio de Janeiro para estar presente à inauguração. No entanto, é importante destacar que, antes de 1939, a IBM já tinha aberto fábricas de cartões para perfuração em diversos países, e que possuía fábricas de equipamentos diversos no Canadá e na Europa, onde tinha implementado uma política de instalação de fábricas nas principais capitais: Vincennes, perto de Paris (1922), Berlim (1927), Estocolmo (1932), Amsterdã (1932), Milão (1936). No mesmo ano da abertura da fábrica, em Benfica, a IBM instalou uma fábrica de cartões em Yokohama, Japão. Esses dados desmentem a informação, generalizada nas publicações da IBM — Brasil, que considera a fábrica brasileira de Benfica como sendo a primeira aberta pela IBM, fora dos Estados Unidos.

A fábrica destinada à manutenção, recondicionamento e montagem de equipamentos de tabulação e fabricação de relógios era uma construção de três andares. A estrutura da fábrica planejada no Brasil foi alvo de críticas, no momento da inauguração, por parte de Thomas J. Watson. Em sua opinião, a construção plana ajustar-se-ia melhor às necessidades do trabalho fabril, agilizando a comunicação e, com isso, aumentando a eficiência no trabalho.

Quando abriu a fábrica, em 1939, a empresa tinha abandonado a venda de máquinas moedoras de café, cortadoras de carne e queijo e balanças. A fabricação desses produtos tinha sido desativada, nos Estados Unidos. Manteve-se ativa a comercialização de relógios e relógios industriais, chegando a produzir-se, na fábrica do Rio de Janeiro, até 1958, relógios nacionais. Naquele ano, a divisão de montagem de relógios foi vendida à DIMEP.

Em 1943 foi inaugurado o relógio da Central do Brasil, no Rio de Janeiro, produzido na fábrica de Benfica. O relógio de grande porte, com ponteiros que medem nove metros, e com quatro faces comandadas por um relógio mestre, converteu-se, na época de sua instalação, em ponto de atração pública.

Em 1949, com a criação da IBM World Trade, subsidiária da IBM doméstica, produziu-se uma importante reestruturação da empresa no Brasil. Thomas J. Watson retirou, nesse ano, a representação de Valentim F. Bouças e a IBM World Trade assumiu o completo controle da subsidiária brasileira.

Em 27 de maio de 1960 a empresa foi rebatizada como IBM do Brasil — Indústria, Máquinas e Serviços Ltda., subsidiária da World Trade Corporation. Dois anos mais tarde, comemorava dois milhões de horas de trabalho sem acidentes.

A principal produção da IBM, na fábrica de Benfica, até a abertura da fábrica de Sumaré, em 1971, eram os cartões de perfuração e a fabricação de máquinas. Na década de 1940, os cartões para perfuração eram fabricados também na fábrica de Bom Retiro, em São Paulo. Os cartões, cortados e impressos segundo as necessidades do cliente, eram exportados para outros países da América Latina, como Uruguai, Paraguai e Chile.

A fabricação de máquinas, na fábrica de Benfica, contava com duas subdivisões: DP (*Data Processing*), que produzia máquinas processadoras de dados, perfuradoras e verificadoras, e OP *(Office Product)*, que produzia máquinas de escrever. Existia outra subdivisão, UR (*United Record*), encarregada do recondicionamento de máquinas, principalmente de máquinas de contabilidade, calculadoras de grande porte e classificadoras.

Em 1956 a fábrica iniciou a fabricação de máquinas de escrever, modelo A, de barras de tipos; em 1960, lançou o modelo C, de barras de tipos; em 1967 passou a produzir máquinas de escrever modelo 72, de esfera de tipos. A despeito da diversidade de modelos introduzidos na fabricação de máquinas de escrever, a grande importância que adquiriu a fábrica deveu-se à influência decisiva que obteve no mercado brasileiro de processamento de dados. A fábrica produziu grande variedade de máquinas de registro unitário, as predecessoras dos computadores, abrindo caminho para o ingresso de novas tecnologias no País. É importante destacar que quase todos os engenheiros e técnicos que trabalhavam em Benfica eram brasileiros. Através deles a empresa abria um caminho para a transferência de novas tecnologias ao Brasil. Ao longo das décadas de 1940, 50 e 60 o processo de fabricação nacional de peças foi ascendente com crescente participação de fornecedores privados, sendo esta outra via de transferência de tecnologia.

Em 1951, começou a ser fabricada a classificadora eletrônica de cartões, modelo 082. Desde 1955, a IBM iniciou um programa de exportação dessas classificadoras para 11 países da América do Sul e América Central. Em 1958 iniciou-se a fabricação de perfuradoras 024/026 e verificadoras 056. Em 1959, a empresa importou o primeiro Computador Eletrônico, IBM 650.

Sob o governo do Presidente Juscelino Kubitscheck de Oliveira as empresas multinacionais encontraram espaço propício para crescer. Nessa conjuntura, a IBM acelerou a importação de computadores, até que, em 1961, a fábrica de Benfica esteve em condições de montar os primeiros computadores da linha 1401. A despeito de a IBM entrar com atraso na fabricação, em relação a seus concorrentes, o processo de penetração no mercado brasileiro foi rápido. Durante os tumultuosos primeiros anos da década de 1960, a despeito da instabilidade política do País, a empresa elaborou planos para expandir sua produção e dar início às exportações.

Em 1959, instalou o primeiro computador no setor privado, adquirido pela Anderson Clayton, um RAMAC-IBM 305. Esse computador obedecia a programas que executava através de cartões perfurados ou de gravações nos discos magnéticos, que guardavam até cinco milhões de caracteres, podendo se estender até 20 milhões.

Em 1960, um RAMAC IBM-305 era instalado na Volskwagen do Brasil, sendo a primeira instalação de um sistema de grande porte na indústria automobilística. Naquele mesmo ano, um RAMAC 305 foi utilizado para apurar e analisar votos em eleições de âmbito nacional.

Sob o governo João Goulart, no início dos anos sessenta, foi formada uma comissão pelo ministro Santiago Dantas, com a finalidade de implantar sistemas automatizados para controle do Imposto de Renda. Dois anos mais tarde, o modelo 1401 era utilizado com esse fim. O mesmo modelo foi instalado, em 1962, no IBGE e na Prefeitura de São Paulo, inaugurando o Centro de Computação Eletrônica da Prefeitura. Naquele mesmo ano, a Secretaria de Finanças do Estado da Guanabara inaugurou o Serviço Mecanográfico, instalando dois sistemas 1401.

A Pfizer do Brasil, em São Paulo, instalou um computador 1401, em 1963, centralizando a contabilidade estatística de vendas e o controle de matéria-prima de estoque, em oito filiais. Naquele mesmo ano o equipamento IBM foi adquirido pela Petrobrás, no Rio Grande do Sul, para a construção da Refinaria Alberto Pasqualini. Na década seguinte, a crise mundial de petróleo obrigaria a Petrobrás a acelerar as pesquisas e prospecções na busca desse produto. Com essa finalidade a Petrobrás instalou um computador IBM Sistema/360 modelo 65.

A IBM doméstica tinha lançado o Sistema/360 no mercado mundial em 1964. O projeto custou 5 bilhões de dólares e revolucionou o mercado mundial de computadores, tornando obsoletos os próprios produtos IBM. Da fábrica de Poughkeepsie, onde o Sistema foi montado, o produto foi lançado no mercado com a máxima cobertura mundial. O cenário de apresentação do Sistema/360 envolveu, simultaneamente, 62 cidades, nos Estados Unidos, e 14 países estrangeiros. Até aquele momento nenhuma outra empresa do setor da eletrônica tinha colocado no mercado, de uma só vez, seis modelos de computadores totalmente novos, com um sistema de programação de altíssima complexibilidade. O Sistema/360 foi a maior "família" de computadores do mercado que usou o mesmo software e periférico nos equipamentos.

Sob o impacto causado pelo Sistema/360 a IBM emergiu, definitivamente, como uma corporação internacional, elevando-se à categoria de colosso da informática, permanecendo como líder mundial até finalizar a década de 1980.

Em 1965, a IBM do Brasil anunciava o seu novo sistema IBM/360, assinando sete contratos de instalação. Nesse ano introduziu, também, o IBM 1130, assinando cinco contratos de instalação com instituições educacionais. Em 1966, o primeiro Sistema/360 modelo 20 foi instalado na Bayer do Brasil.

Em 1965, foi instalada na Lion S.A. o primeiro IBM 6400, máquina de contabilidade com características magnéticas. Com anterioridade, em 1964, a Volkswagen do Brasil tinha adicionado a seu RAMAC 306 um IBM 1401, instalado na fábrica de São Bernardo do Campo, para realizar faturamento e controle de estoque de produção.

O maior contrato do Bureau de Serviços da IBM do Brasil foi assinado, em 1966, com o Instituto Brasileiro de Reforma Agrária, para realizar o recenseamento da propriedade rural e o cálculo do imposto territorial rural, em todo o País. Naquele mesmo ano, a empresa exportou um IBM 1401 para o Chile, para ser utilizado nos Jogos Olímpicos de Inverno, e introduzia, no Banco Nacional, o Plano Padrão de Contas Correntes IBM. O Banco de Minas Gerais, em 1966, também instalava um computador IBM.

Ao longo da década de 1960, a IBM do Brasil praticou uma estratégia bem sucedida de penetração no setor universitário. Com tal objetivo realizou importantes investimentos nesse setor. Em 1966, financiou a criação do Rio Data Centro, um dos principais centros de pesquisa em software, localizado na Pontifícia Universidade Católica do Rio de Janeiro (PUC-RJ). Também data deste período a doação de um equipamento científico à Universidade de São Paulo (USP). Por representarem pólos de congregação do meio acadêmico de todo o País, a PUC e a USP transformaram-se em importantes instrumentos de marketing da IBM. Sob sua inspiração, outras universidades adquiriram máquinas da empresa.

Essa estratégia foi acompanhada de uma política de promoção de cursos, e de financiamento de programas de pós-graduação e organização de palestras, reunindo cientistas renomados. Em 1962 a IBM ofereceu um Curso de Computadores Digitais no Rio de Janeiro, para treze engenheiros, professores da Universidade do Rio Grande do Sul. Em 1965, com o ITA (Instituto Tecnológico da Aeronáutica), promoveu uma conferência do Dr. J. D. Huskey, Professor de Matemática e Engenharia Elétrica da Universidade da Califórnia, Berkeley. Naquele mesmo ano, a empresa participou do VII Congresso de Ensino Técnico Comercial e do Seminário Pan-Americano de Febre Aftosa; promoveu um Seminário de Marketing Científico e de Universidades e apresentou palestras na televisão paulista, no programa "A TV Explica Computadores".

O quadro se altera na década de 1970, em boa medida, "por falta de visão administrativa ou ressentimento contra a política de reserva de mercado"[4]. Ao substituir palestras de cientistas famosos e financiamentos de programas de pós-graduação pela presença de vendedores, a empresa perdia espaço nas universidades, que passaram a substituir seus sistemas por equipamentos de fabricantes concorrentes. As Universidades de Pernambuco (UFPE) e Campinas (UNICAMP) trocaram IBM por Vax. A PUC escolheu Control Data e as de São Paulo (USP) e do Rio Grande do Sul (UFRGS) passaram a utilizar Burroughs.

A partir de 1964, atendendo às diretrizes do Governo Militar que fomentava as exportações, a IBM acelerou seu programa de exportação já iniciado desde fins da década de 1950. Em 1964, a empresa exportou Perfuradoras e Verificadoras 024, 026 e 056 para a América Latina, África e Oriente Médio. Em 1965, as exportações da IBM do Brasil atingiram a marca de 1 milhão e 800 mil dólares. Ao comemorar cinqüenta anos de atividades no País, as exportações excediam os nove milhões de dólares, sendo exportados 94% do total da produção.

Desde a abertura da fábrica de Benfica, ao longo das décadas de 1940, 50 e 60 o crescimento da empresa foi acompanhado de sua expansão territorial. Em 1949 abriu a filial em Fortaleza; em 1953 em Curitiba; e em 1963 em Brasília, onde já funcionava desde 1960 um escritório.

---

[4] Paula, Jana de. "Uma Senhora de Talento", in *Info*, março. 1987.

VI
O ESTADO
E AS EMPRESAS DE SERVIÇOS PÚBLICOS

Albert Broder
Université de Paris XII, Institut Jean Baptiste Say

UN ASPECT DES RELATIONS ÉTAT-TECHNOLOGIE-INDUSTRIE: LA COMPAGNIE GÉNÉRALE D'ÉLECTRICITÉ ET LE DÉVELOPPEMENT DE L'ÉLECTRICITÉ EN FRANCE, 1898-1946*

La connaissance que l'on a de l'industrie française est, jusqu'ici, à la fois incomplète et controversée. Hors du pays, l'image la plus répandue est issue des analyses anglo-saxonnes, particulièrement celle de David Landes à laquelle ont abondé nombre d'historiens français, tel Lévy-Leboyer, soucieux de ne pas apparaître éloigné des canons de la mode. Il en résulte une impression plus qu'une réalité.

Un pays qui se situe depuis le dix-huitième siècle entre le second et le quatrième rang mondial n'est que rarement analysé comme l'un des modèles industriels à l'instar (chronologiquement) du Royaume Uni, des États-Unis, de l'Allemagne et — de nos jours — du Japon. Nation de petits entrepreneurs frileux, de banquiers prudents, de paysans et d'industriels protectionnistes chapeautés par un État omniprésent et omni-dirigeant, telle est l'image qui ressort d'une littérature spécialisée hypnotisée par le modèle victorien, et qui néglige trop souvent le dirigisme de l'État allemand ou les protectionnismes américain et germanique, à la fois plus précoces et plus rigoureux que le français. La responsabilité en incombe certainement à l'historiographie française; souvent insuffisante en la matière. Rares sont les bonnes histoires d'entreprise[1] et il n'existe

* Cette étude est issue de *Alsthom Alcatel, Histoire de la CGE 1898-1992.* Paris: Larousse. 1992. (La période 1950-1992 a été rédigée par Mlle. F. Gambrelle. Il s'agit d'un ouvrage général. La rédaction académique de la période 1898-1850 est en cours de publication et comportera l'appareil scientifique habituel.)

[1] La meilleure à ce jour est la thése de A. Baudant sur Pont-à-Mousson.

pas de biographie de grands "capitaines" d'industrie tel Azaria, Citröen Cavalier ou Schneider[2], ou des pères de la grande banque moderne: Henri Germain ou Horace Finaly.

Cette communication se situe à l'intersection d'une triple interrogation issue des faits précédents. Compte tenu du retard technologique français au regard de l'Allemagne et des États Unis à la fin du XIXe siècle, de la cartellisation des industries de pointe au niveau international et de l'intervention étatique, systématiquement jugée négative par un courant dominant de l'historiographie contemporaine, comment s'explique le succès d'une entreprise — la Compagnie Générale d'Électricité — née dans des conditions modestes et difficiles à la fin du XIXe siècle, et parvenue, un siècle plus tard, au premier rang mondial dans ses secteurs d'activité.

La loi, l'État et l'électricité en France: 1881-1946

Comme toute généralisation, l'image d'un État omniprésent est totalement erronée dans la domaine du développement des services publics français, et singulièrement de l'électricité. Il en va de la réglementation comme de la législation douanière. Les deux sont rétroactifs en ce qu'ils disciplinent des actions déjà réalisées: *la technique précède toujours la réglementation, car on ne peut réglementer que ce qui existe.*

Le temps de l'incertitude: 1881-1914

Au départ, les services de l'État ignorent totalement l'électricité et laissent la responsabilité aux administrations locales. Phénomène urbain, l'électrification relève, comme l'adduction d'eau et la distribution de gaz de deux règles simples:

(a) La permission de voirie, ou droit d'établir le réseau sur la voie

---

Dans un registre inférieur mais fort honorable citons le travail de P. Fridenson sur Renault (nécessiterait un approfondissement, mais bien écrit); de J. P. Daviet sur la Société Générale d'Entreprises (gros travail, utile, mais de lecture difficile). Ces titres ne constituant qu'un échantillon.

[2] Respectivement fondateurs de la Compagnie Générale d'Électricité, de Citröen Automobiles, de Pont-à-Mousson et du Creusot.

publique. Elle dépend des municipalités (voirie urbaine), des départements (Conseils Généraux et Préfets) pour l'électrification rurale. Seule l'interconnexion inter-régionale fera intervenir l'État bien après la première guerre mondiale. Cette "permission", une fois accordée, est un *droit acquis* que le bénéficiaire peut utiliser ou négocier.

(b) La concession: normalement dépend des municipalités (y compris du plus petit village). Elle accorde un *droit exclusif de canalisation.* Les concessions accordées varient entre 18 et 50 ans, à l'issue de quoi l'ensemble des installations revient à la municipalité (sauf renouvellement).

Mais, *la jurisprudence laisse l'utilisateur libre de son choix.* Autrement dit, dans une ville équipée au gaz, la permission de voirie n'est pas exclusive. La concession ne peut concerner que l'éclairage public (ou le transport de voyageurs). On peut accorder une concession d'électricité qui désservira les usagers en concurrence avec la gaz. Mais on ne pourra installer un éclairage public électrique.

Il en va de même des installations. La construction d'une centrale thermique ne dépend que du pouvoir municipal qui accorde la concession. L'action des pouvoirs publics se limite à l'*enquête "Commodo et incommodo"* vérifiant que les règles (légères) de sécurité de l'environnement sont respectées. Ainsi, la première centrale génératrice de la *Société Normande d'Électricité,* maison-mère de la CGE, est elle installée dans une église désaffectée dont le clocher sert opportunément de pylône de départ des lignes. La même absence de réglementation se rencontre dans l'octroi de l'exploitation des chutes d'eau. Les concessions sont municipales et s'y ajoute l'exigence de l'accord des propriétaires des berges.

Cette situation pose de graves problèmes juridiques aux sociétés d'électricité. En effet, les décisions de la Cour de Cassation et du Conseil d'État renforcent les droits des concessionnaires tant de gaz que des tramways hippomobiles. Un certain nombre de décisions de justice aboutissent à obliger les compagnies d'électricité à démonter leurs installations de distribution et à verser (parfois la municipalité elle-même y est contrainte) des indemnités au plaignant. Il s'ensuit un freinage du développement de l'électricité et, très souvent, le développement d'installations individuelles électrogènes d'usines, de bureaux, de magasins (auto-producteurs) limitant d'autant les capacités d'extension du marché.

Les interventions de l'État avant 1918

Les pouvoirs publics s'intéressent avant tout à la réglementation technique des réseaux. Le décret "historique" est celui du 15 mai 1888 et concerne l'installation des "conducteurs" servant au transport de l'électricité. Purement technique il ne se rapporte qu'aux conditions de nature et d'installation des fils. Il est complété et remplacé par une loi beaucoup plus précise et technique du 25 Juin 1895 créant entre autres un "Comité Technique de l'Électricité", premier organe officiel de réglementation dans le secteur. La *grande loi* est celle du 15 Juin 1906 dont les *principales dispositions sont toujours en vigueur.* Elle relève essentiellement du domaine reglementaire et ne concerne pas la nature des entreprises.

A la veille de la Grande Guerre, la France ne dispose pas d'un instrument juridique permettant d'organiser et de rationaliser sa production d'énergie électrique. Compte tenu du poids de l'étroit juridisme des corps chargés de dire le droit (Cour de Cassation, Conseil d'État) et des importants pouvoirs dévolus aux municipalités, dont il faut rappeler le grand nombre (36 mille) et l'absence de coopération institutionnelle[3], *il n'est pas possible d'envisager la mise en place d'unités de production à la taille des États Unis, de l'Allemagne voire même de la Suisse.* On ne peut négliger ce facteur dans les difficultés et le retard de mise en place d'une industrie électrotechnique adaptée à la montée en puissance des installations au début du XXe Siècle.

L'entre-deux-guerres et la nationalisation: 1919-1946

Les exigences de la Guerre ont totalement modifié le point de vue du gouvernement. La perte temporaire du bassin houiller du nord et des centrales thermiques de cette région ont eu pour consé-

---

[3] Le Canton n'est qu'une circonscription électorale sans existence administrative. Les "syndicats mixtes" n'apparaissent que dans les années 1920 pour l'électrification rurale, les adductions d'eau. Avant 1914, les rares ententes entre municipalités urbaines concernent les transports publics. Et encore de façon très limitée comme le fait ressortir l'histoire du Métro de Paris, conçu dans le refus total de prise en compte de l'agglomération.

quence un énorme effort dans le domaine de l'hydroélectricité dont les capacités se situent dans la moitié sud du Pays. Il en est résulté une succession d'actes législatifs essentiels pour comprendre les transformations de l'industrie française:

1. *La loi du 16 Octobre 1919* transfère à l'État la *totale propriété* de toutes les sources d'énergie issue de l'eau: chutes, courants (fleuves), marées. L'État en cède la concession à des entreprises privées par décret pour une durée de trente ans (estimation de l'amortissement des installations) à la suite de quoi l'ensemble est repris par l'État. (Les installations supérieures à 100 mille kW ne peuvent être concédées que par une loi.)

2. *La loi du 11 Juillet 1922* réserve à l'État la constitution des réseaux et l'interconnexion. Comme pour les installations la concession peut en être faite à des collectifs de producteurs-distributeurs. Ainsi se constitue un corpus légal qui se compare *mutatis mutandis* à la législation sur les chemins de fer.

Si les municipalités gardent le pouvoir sur les réseaux locaux, l'État a pris en main la totalité de l'organisation au niveau national. On peut comparer cela avec le système mis en place à la même époque par les britanniques sous le nom de *grid*. En effet, la totalité des installations hydroélectriques sont désormais dépendantes d'une décision gouvernementale. Officiellement les centrales thermiques lui échappent. En réalité, par le travers de la loi de 1922, le contrôle s'exerce indirectement, car les grands ensembles thermiques modernes ne peuvent s'implanter que dans trois zones: le Nord Pas de Calais, la Lorraine (dans ces deux cas houillères et hauts-fourneaux) et la Région Parisienne. Dans les deux premiers cas, la puissance susceptible d'être installée dépasse largement les besoins régionaux; la rentabilité dépend de la possibilité de vendre du courant à Paris. Donc, de l'interconnexion qui est aux mains du Gouvernement. Il en va de même des grandes unités prévues autour de Paris, dont la planification est prévue en coordination avec l'arrivée de fluide des centrales hydrauliques du Massif Central (dès avant 1914 La Truyère, puis Eguzon) puis des Alpes.

Mais il faut noter un point largement passé sous silence dans le travaux récents. Par le mécanisme des concessions à terme fixé, l'État met en place l'appareil de nationalisation de l'électricité puisque les installations lui reviennent à l'échéance. D'une part les centrales hydrauliques (les sites ne sont pas renouvelables) d'autre part les réseaux d'interconnexion lui donnent la haute main (là aussi à terme) sur l'ensemble thermique qu'il n'est pas intéressant d'étatiser pour trois raisons (entre autres):

a) l'obsolescence rapide de ce type d'installation exige un amortissement accéléré. La "reprise" par la puissance publique freinerait les investissements nécéssaires;

b) mis à part la Région parisienne, ces installations sont souvent complémentaires d'un approvisionnement hydraulique dans les grandes villes (Lyon, Marseille) et nombre de concessions sont susceptibles de revenir aux municipalités. Se pose aussi le problème du lien organique entre les sociétés d'électricité de certaines villes et les tramways urbains; lesquels bénéficient de tarifs préférentiels;

c) il ne peut être envisagé d'étatiser les grands ensembles de centrales des houillères, d'autant plus que les charbonnages seront nationalisés. Un autre problème se présente concernant les centrales thermiques des sociétés métallurgiques et hydrauliques de l'électrochimie et électrométallurgie. Ces dernières seront nationalisées, mais recevront le courant nécessaire à des conditions particulières.

En 1945, le paysage électrique, issu du système qui vient d'être décrit est particulièrement complexe. Plus de 20 mille concessions dont certaines concernent des communes de moins de 500 abonnés. Des régies municipales souvent issues des régies du gaz[4] au nombre de 250 mais qui couvrent 5% de la population[5]. A côté on compte 200 sociétés de production, une centaine de transport et 1.150 chargées de la distribution[6].

Dans la réalité pratique on a affaire à des regroupements financiers que le langage approximatif de l'époque qualifie de *Trusts de l'Électricité.* Il s'agit de groupes financiers fédérant des sociétés surtout de distribution (aspect le plus rentable financièrement) dont

---

[4] Dans certains cas (Tourcoing, grande ville industrielle du Nord de la France), la municipalité qui tire d'importants revenus de la régie municipale du gaz, s'oppose à l'électricité qui exige d'importants investissements sans garantir la croissance des revenus. Le maire ne cède que sous la pression des commerçants et limite longtemps la distribution d'électricité aux rues du centre.

[5] Picard, Beltran, Bungener. *Histoire de l'EDF.* Paris. 1985, p. 11.

[6] Idem.

les plus importants sont l'Union d'Électricité, fondée en 1919 par la banquier Petsche, auquel succède un haut fonctionnaire "passé" au privé, Ernest Mercier. Alliant de réelles compétences à des liens privilégiés dans l'administration, Mercier contrôle le premier marché français: la Région parisienne et promeut l'interconnexion nationale.

Le second *trust:* l'*Énergie Industrielle,* fondé par un notaire Lyonnais, Pierre Marie Durand, domine le Sud-Est à partir de Lyon, et principalement l'hydro-électricité. En fait, ces *trusts* fédèrent les nombreuses sociétés qu'ils contrôlent généralement par des minorités de blocage; utilisant, comme les chemins de fer au siècle dernier, l'emprunt obligataire comme moyen privilégié de financement. Cette structure permet une entente entre les groupes, afin de réaliser des interconnexions régionales puis nationale, telle l'Union pour l'Industrie de l'Électricité, fondée en 1931, et au sein de laquelle se retrouvent les *trusts* mais aussi les grands industriels producteurs/consommateurs (électrochimie, métallurgie) et les constructeurs de matériel électrotechnique. Ainsi se trouve, presque empiriquement, réalisée avec un tiers de siècle de décalage, une structure qui avait permis l'essor précoce de l'industrie électrique en Allemagne et aux États Unis.

En même temps, cette unification qui rationalise les matériels utilisés, mais aussi la production, les normes et partant le contrôle de l'État justifie l'interventionnisme public croissant. Ce dernier est facilité par la communauté de formation et de carrière des responsables techniques des sociétés et des ministères, pratiquement tous issus de la voie: École Polytechnique — École des Ponts-et-Chaussées (dits X-Ponts). Il en résulte le décret-loi de 1938, dit "Programme des 3 milliards", d'aménagement hydroélectrique et d'achèvement de l'interconnexion à haute tension. Programme voulu par l'État mais devant être mis en oeuvre par un groupement national des entreprises privées (*Groupement pour l'Électricité*), chargé d'émettre en commun les emprunts nécéssaires et de réaliser les travaux. En fait, il s'agit de l'ancêtre des Groupements d'Intérêts Économiques qui joueront un rôle essentiel dans l'investissement industriel privé en France entre 1950 et 1980. Ce programme ne fut pas mis en application du fait de la Guerre, mais il sert de support aux projets de nationalisation.

Il n'y a pas de véritable opposition à la nationalisation de l'électricité, dont les structures et le personnel technique supérieur se trouvent en mesure de passer naturellement du statut privé à celui d'établissement public. Le principal problème nous intéressant ici réside dans le mode d'indemnisation du capital-actions. Ce dernier est échangé contre des bons amortissables. La valeur des actifs résultera d'une estimation en Bourse pour les sociétés cotées ou d'une estimation contradictoire[7]. Une "Caisse de l'Énergie" est créée pour réaliser l'amortissement des bons par une dotation de 1% du chiffre d'affaires de l'EDF. Entre temps les bons peuvent être négociés en Bourse[8].

La Compagnie Générale d'Électricité (Alsthom Alcatel): naissance d'une grande entreprise dans le contexte juridique et économique français: 1898-1946

La situation juridique présentée dans la première partie peut être illustrée, pour les difficultés qu'elle comporte au regard des nécessités de l'industrie, par les exemples des principales agglomérations françaises. Lesquelles normalement eussent dû fournir le marché privilégié de l'électricité dans ses deux premières décennies. En 1900, la France ne comportait que quatre concentrations urbaines dépassant 400 mille habitants.

L'agglomération lilloise, conurbation d'une vingtaine de municipalités, comporte plusieurs sociétés de distribution dont une régie municipale. Lyon et Marseille, atteignant tout juste 500 mille habitants sont partagées en deux sociétés. A Lyon, l'une d'entre elles distribue du courant continu, l'autre va vendre du courant alternatif. A Marseille, les deux compagnies distribuent du fluide de période différente. Enfin, Paris est partagé entre huit compagnies (secteurs), dont les caractéristiques techniques sont presque totalement incompatibles. Ceci pour la Ville même (2 millions d'habi-

---

[7] Certaines ne seront conclues qu'en 1951, soit cinq ans après le vote de la loi.

[8] Cette somme, égale à celle que l'EDF réserve à ses oeuvres sociales sera à l'origine d'une perte de valeur des bons. En effet, la politique de bas coût de l'électricité poursuivie jusqu'en 1974 résultera en une croissance très lente de l'indemnisation. La situation s'inverse avec la crise pétrolière. Mais à ce moment la CGE s'est depuis longtemps séparé e de ses titres indemnitaires...

tants), les communes de banlieue relevant de la concession municipale locale[9].

La brièveté des concession parisiennes (18 ans) interdisent des travaux importants. L'unification dans la Ville proprement dite se fera en 1914 par un consortium associant les détenteurs de concessions de secteurs: la Compagnie Parisienne de Distribution d'Électricité. Les conséquences en étaient encore visibles récemment[10]. De même faut il attendre 1920 pour qu'un décret unifie le type d'alimentation des chemins de fer électrifiés[11].

Face donc à la puissance originelle des groupes américains ou, plus logiquement comparables, aux consortiums allemands associant industriels, municipalités et pouvoirs des États (Berliner Elektrizitäts, RWE...) les industriels français, déjà handicapés par la profonde crise de l'économie nationale et la stagnation urbaine ne disposent pas de l'appui nécessaire à la mise en place d'un outil industriel concurrentiel.

Il s'ensuit aussi de graves difficultés pour faire admettre sur le marché international les innovations techniques françaises. L'insuffisance de la législation française sur les brevets, l'absence de soutien à l'égal des grands groupes étrangers font que ces brevets sont repris et utilisés par d'autres, tel celui de Gaulard sur le courant alternatif et le montage en parallèle des transformateurs[12].

De même dans le secteur des turbines, l'étroitesse du marché par l'absence de grands équipements handicape les constructeurs de turbines à vapeur. C'est ainsi que RATEAU ne s'impose que lentement et que la CEM (Compagnie Électromécanique) utilise dès

---

9 Tempéré par le fait que plusieurs municipalités voisines accordent la concession à une société de distribution: Est-Lumière, Ouest-Lumière, Nord-Est-Lumière...

10 Le monopole d'éclairage de la Compagnie du gaz explique que la disparition de ce type d'éclairage public ne se fera à Paris qu'au début des années 1960. De même faudra t'il attendre 1960 pour voir disparaître à Paris la distribution de courant continu.

11 En 1500 volts continu.

12 Les expériences de Gaulard ont eu lieu à Turin (22/9/1884) et la première expérimentation pratique à Tours le 18 Janvier 1886. Mais, son manque de moyens retarde le dépôt des brevets et il est devancé par Stanley (Westinghouse) et Zypernowski (Ganz). De ce fait les industriels français doivent acquérir les droits sur le procédé Zypernowski. Schneider s'entendra sur ce fait avec Ganz (Broder, 1986).

1883 les brevets Brown-Boveri puis Parsons. Dans ces cas (comme dans celui de Westinghouse France) l'impossibilité d'exporter que comportent les accords de cession des brevets interdit d'atteindre des conditions de production et de prix permettant de rattraper le retard industriel sur l'Allemagne et les Etats Unis. C'est sans doute le raisonnement des banques qui apportent leur soutien financier aux entreprises. Ainsi Rothschild, qui a financé la Compagnie Générale d'électricité de Creil, n'intervient pas lorsque cette dernière passe entre les mains de l'allemand Schuckert peu avant que ce dernier ne fusionne avec Siemens.

C'est dans ce contexte qu'apparaît la CGE. Au départ, il y a une petite société d'électricité produisant et distribuant le courant dans la ville de Rouen: La Normande d'Électricité[13]. Son jeune directeur Paul Azaria[14] se rend rapidement compte de l'impossibilité de développer l'affaire. Le soutien de la municipalité de Rouen ne peut rien contre la compagnie du gaz qui fournit l'éclairage public. Ajoutons que l'absence d'une législation adéquate explique le peu d'intérêt à s'éntendre en banlieue. Les industriels sont autoproducteurs pour les plus importants, et le très faible niveau de rémunération des populations ouvrières ne permet pas d'entrevoir la rentabilité financière d'installations coûteuses. Un autre élément technique intervient, car la faiblesse de la consommation ne permet pas d'installer des turbo-alternateurs puissants et économiques.

La création de la CGE correspond à une réponse complexe à la situation à la fois économique et légale de l'électricité en France. D'une part, la reprise très forte de l'économie française[15] crée les conditions tardives, mais réelles, d'un marché d'autant plus dynamique que le retard à combler est important. De l'autre, la domina-

---

[13] Sa concession se limite à la ville elle même — d'où son marché limité, car elle ne dispose pas des tramways et encore moins des importantes industries toutes situées dans le vallées hors des limités municipales, et qui sont souvent des autoproducteurs.

[14] De son vrai nom Boutros Azarian c'est un jeune ingénieur de l'Ecole Centrale de Paris, orphelin d'une famille arménienne du Caire. Du fait d'un rang de sortie médiocre et de sa totale absence de "relations" il a accepté ce poste dont il dirait lui même, qu'en l'état, il s'agissait d'une situation difficile et sans grand avenir.

[15] Broder. *Histoire économique de la France au XIXe siècle*. Gap-Paris: Ophrys. 1993.

tion du marché existant par les groupes industriels américains et allemands impose des contraintes particulières à tout nouveau venu — la Thomson Houston, filiale de la General Electric contrôlant à elle seule 60% des producteurs d'électricité et disposant d'un accord de partage sur le marché français avec AEG. A quoi s'ajoutent les liens entre l'Alsacienne de Belfort et Siemens, ou la forte implantation du groupe belge Empain (ACEC) tant à Paris que dans le Nord, que contrôle le constructeur électrique Jeumont. Tout nouvel intervenant sur le marché électrotechnique français doit donc impérativement disposer de liens directs avec des concessionnaires de production distribution.

D'où la structure originelle de la CGE. La Normande d'électricité, avec la concession de Rouen, apporte un "savoir faire" et une connaissance des arcanes de la décision administrative. Ses actionnaires disposent en outre d'actifs industriels modestes mais participant au secteur: tréfilerie de cuivre et manufacture d'ampoules électriques. L'intérêt de l'affaire réside dans la participation suisse. En effet, dès le début, et semble t'il grâce à l'entregent d'Azaria, on trouve Walter Boveri (de Brown-Boveri) et la banque Commerciale de Bâle qui est un des supports du groupe BBC. Il s'agit pour les helvétes, qui disposent d'importantes unités de production en France (en particulier la CEM), de s'ouvrir un marché dont nous avons noté le bouclage. Le lien visible se faisant par la filiale française de la banque bâloise: la Banque Suisse et Française, devenue en 1917 le CCF en raison du climat nationaliste du moment. Les autres participants financiers (Société Nancéienne et Société Générale) ne jouant qu'un rôle secondaire, tout comme l'Omnium Lyonnais, qui semble surtout à l'affût de plus-values financières.

Dans les limites de cette communication l'intérêt sera marqué sur quelques aspects particuliers de l'entreprise. Le retard technique et l'absence de moyens financiers sont des handicaps majeurs. En outre, se lancer dans la production de matériel électrotechnique est suicidaire. La CGE ne dispose pas de brevets. Produire est donc risqué, car la clientèle veut l'assurance d'unités de production aux pannes limitées et à l'entretien garanti. C'est aussi concurrencer la CEM qui dépend de Brown-Boveri et plus encore les "grands" européens. Il y a risque de faire naître une opposition à laquelle la société n'est pas à même de résister. D'où une stratégie à orientation multiple:

1) acquérir des concessions d'électricité afin de se constituer un

"portefeuille" de producteurs-distributeurs et donc d'exister sur le marché;

2) prendre le contrôle d'entreprises de matériel électrique dans des secteurs non mécaniques afin de devenir un opérateur sur le marché sans affronter la concurrence des grands groupes;

3) pénétrer le domaine des techniques avancées en s'associant à des sociétés connues, mais de taille moyenne.

Dans le premier cas on citera (à titre d'exemple) outre Rouen les prises de concessions électriques de Nantes, Bordeaux, Marseille (en concurrence), Nancy, et plus modestement Angers, Brest et surtout Meaux, petite concession mais stratégiquement située en cas d'interconnexion entre Paris et la Lorraine. Du second poste on retiendra surtout l'investissement dans le câble, les accumulateurs (Tudor), les isolants électriques (porcelaine, électro-céramiques) ainsi que la SGEE entreprise de travaux publics chargée de réaliser les réseaux tant sur les concessions CGE que pour des tiers. Enfin, dans le troisième domaine, c'est l'association avec la société suisse Sprecher et Schuh dont la technique est mondialement renommée. Association qui permettra plus tard l'implantation de la CGE outremer (l'entente étant encore en vigueur à la fin des années 1960 entre autres au Brésil et en Espagne).

Il est intéressant de noter que cette politique se fait *en l'absence totale d'intervention des pouvoirs publics.* Contrairement à la pratique allemande ou espagnole, la puissance publique se désintéresse des conditions de mise en place des infrastructures au point de se trouver dans une situation difficile lorsqu'il lui faudra recenser et organiser les moyens lors de la guerre de 1914. On en voit l'illustration lors des négociations entre la CGE et Siemens à propos des concessions en Catalogne. Le Ministère des Affaires Étrangères croit que le Président de la CGE, le futur Président de la République Paul Doumer, négocie pour un contrôle français alors qu'en fait il cède à l'entreprise allemande tout les contrats électrotechniques[16].

Cette politique n'empêche pas la CGE d'être en situation de constante fragilité. Le très faible soutien des banques (le Crédit Lyonnais analyse négativement ses bilans et la Société Générale se contente de placer les obligations) et l'absence d'une politique cohé-

[16] Broder. *Le rôle des intérêts étrangers dans la croissance économique de l'Espagne 1768-1923.* Paris: Lille. 1982.

rente à laquelle se rattacher font que l'entreprise est forcée à de constants arbitrages au sein de son groupe.

Ainsi doit elle abandonner trois de ses principaux fleurons — Bordeaux, Nantes et Rouen — simplement par ce que leur essor passe par l'électrification des tramways. Or dans tous les cas l'investissement dépasse les moyens de la CGE. On peut également se poser la question du rôle du groupe dominant, la Thomson Houston qui dispose en France d'un quasi monopole dans la construction des motrices avec le brevet américain Sprague, et contrôle les principaux réseaux de tramways hors Paris[17].

A la veille de la Première Guerre Mondiale, la CGE est une entreprise de taille modeste, faiblement implantée et surtout dont les moyens techniques et financiers sont très limités. Ses liens suisses se sont distendus, dans la mesure ou Brown Boveri semble avoir été déçu du faible marché que représente la CGE pour ses installations électriques de puissance. Le groupe helvétique s'est renforcé par le biais de la CEM et paraît préférer une politique de fournisseur indépendant. On peut également s'interroger sur la liaison entre ce changement de stratégie et la lutte qu'a dû mener la société suisse pour briser la tentative de prise de contrôle par AEG.

L'absence d'une politique cohérente de l'État est également sensible sur l'ensemble de la filière électrotechnique. A aucun moment n'envisage t'on une norme française. La tendance est au courant à 50 périodes, mais dans certaines concessions on trouvera du 25 périodes jusqu'aux années 1930. Lorsque les chemins-de-fer envisagent leur électrification, la plus complète liberté est laissée aux responsables. A aucun moment il n'est envisagé de coordination, voire de norme. Certains réseaux vont installer des systèmes différents sur les divers tronçons qu'ils équipent. Il en résulte l'absence d'une politique cohérente d'investissement industriel, le 1500 volts de tension au caténaire (maximum admissible pour les moteurs de traction avant 1914) n'étant rendu obligatoire qu'en 1920. On comprend dès lors l'accord discret signé entre Siemens et Schneider pour la création d'une société d'électrification des chemins-de-fer

---

17 Le métro de Paris, construit à partir de 1898 (première ligne ouverte en 1900) est un cofinancement Belge (Empain) et Lyonnais. Toutes les motrices sont à moteur Sprague et le resteront lors des différentes modernisations jusqu'au delà de la Seconde Guerre Mondiale.

au sein de laquelle la firme allemande, solidement appuyée sur l'harmonisation des locomotives mises au point sous l'égide de l'état-major germanique, était destinée à fournir tout le matériel électrique[18]. Cet exemple illustre cependant le problème d'une entreprise "jeune" comme la CGE.

Dans une structure où n'existe aucune orientation étatique et encore moins de politique d'ensemble ne serait-ce qu'au niveau régional, l'espace est laissé libre à des structures cartellisées internationales. Les deux autres modèles "dominants" — l'américain, dans lequel une structure financière chapeaute les branches industrielles et de production/distribution fournissant aux premières la clientèle des seconds; l'allemand, où les groupes électrotechniques sont directement parties prenantes aux ensembles régionaux de service public fournissent la base d'un dévellppement relativement cohérent de l'appareil industriel et de sa normalisation. Ce n'est certes pas la garantie du succès. Mais certains échecs allemands tel Bergman qui ne bénéficient pas de cette dualité sont indicatifs des faiblesses que représente l'abstention (libérale ou myope?) des autorités françaises.

La CGE et la politique de l'État 1914-1940

L'absence de politique et d'orientation de l'État révéla l'ampleur de ses faiblesses au moment de la Guerre. L'insuffisance de la production d'électricité, et surtout le retard pris dans les grands équipements ne constitue qu'un aspect. D'autant plus que la neutralité des États Unis et de la Suisse ont préservé la capacité de fonctionnement et le plus des brevets. Mais, dans certains secteurs — comme celui des céramiques électriques ou de l'électricité automobile (et aéronautique) — on s'est trouvé à la limite de la paralysie[19].

Pour la CGE la situation est contrastée. Ses distributions d'électricité, toutes thermiques, souffrent du blocage des tarifs alors que le prix du charbon s'envole. Mis à part Marseille, qui bénéficie d'un

---

[18] La guerre rendra caduc cet accord, qui ne sera jamais appliqué.

[19] En particulier dans les secteurs des accumulateurs, des bougies pour moteur à explosion, secteur dominé par l'allemand Bosch, et celui des charbons pour l'électricité dont le principal producteur en France est la filiale du groupe Austro-Hongrois Hardmuth.

lignite à bas prix, toutes les sociétés sont en difficulté. Les pertes sont telles que le capital de plusieurs d'entre elles est réduit de moitié. Quand à celui de la concession d'Amiens, proche du front, il est totalement perdu et la CGE doit même lui faire remise de ses dettes tout comme pour Nancy. Ces difficultés, auxquelles l'État refuse d'apporter une compensation ne sont cependant pas graves. En effet, la CGE bénéficie largement des besoins accrus nés de la durée du conflit. Important transformateur de cuivre, elle devient l'un des grands fournisseurs de munitions, et l'État l'aide à construire d'importantes usines à Bourdeaux et Orléans.

Pour ce faire, elle bénéficie d'importants crédits suisses garantis par la banque de France au titre des industries de guerre. En outre, ses installations de matériel électrique deviennent précieuses dès lors que la concurrence allemande est momentanèment absente et que les contraintes des cartels sont abolies avec l'aval des autorités. C'est ainsi que se développent les fabrications d'ampoules électriques et surtout les ateliers de Lyon, en partie hérités des accords suisses, spécialisés dans le câble, bénéficient de la politique accélérée de construction de centrales hydroélectriques. L'extension rapide et vitale des lignes à haute tension bénéficie largement à la CGE.

Sur le plan financier, aux crédits largement accordés, s'ajoute le maintien de la pratique, classique dans l'industrie française, de l'amortissement annuel des travaux neufs. Même si le retour à la paix oblige à une difficile reconversion; la société a su se renforcer. En 1919 elle dispose de moyens industriels puissants et modernisés. Son assise financière ne pose plus guère de problèmes.

En réalité, les moyens sont nettement supérieurs, car après un long conflit avec les banques et les milieux dirigeants de l'industrie, l'État a renoncé a imposer les bénéfices de guerre et a abandonné, dans des conditions très favorables aux entreprises, ses créances sur les investissements qu'il avait suscité pour l'armement. Dans ce contexte la CGE n'est d'ailleurs pas le grand bénéficiaire. On ne peut la comparer au succès d'André Citröen et des usines du quai de Javel à Paris. Au contraire, la difficile reconversion des établissements de Bordeaux, la Rochelle et, dans une moindre mesure, Orléans ont tellement marqué les dirigeants du groupe qu'ils exigeront des garanties extraordinaires lorsq'en 1938, devant la menace germanique renouvelée, l'État demandera à la CGE de se rééquiper en unités de production de munitions.

La CGE de l'entre deux guerres: cartels internationaux et politique de l'État

C'est au cours de cette période que s'établit la structure définitive de la CGE. La politique du groupe comporte un certain nombre de choix précis sans que l'on puisse faire la différence entre décisions stratégiques et adaptation à des réalités sur lesquelles l'entreprise n'a pas de prise directe.

Il est certain que l'échec des tentatives d'autonomie de la Thomson française par rapport à la General Electric, les manoeuvres du groupe américain dans les coulisses de la Commission des Réparations[20] et le rétablissement de ses liens étroits avec l'industrie allemande ont amené la CGE à abandonner ses velléités d'expansion hors des frontières. Le peu de soutien que la Thomson française obtient du Gouvernement dans ses tentatives polonaises pousse à la prudence. Il en résulte l'abandon des projets communs avec Thomson en Italie (E. Clerici, Adda), mais aussi le retrait complet de Catalogne en 1923 face à l'entente germano-américaine derrière la Barcelona Traction[21]. De même, malgré son expansion pendant la guerre la CGE doit se plier aux injonctions de l'IGEC qui, en accord avec les allemands, reconstitue le cartel des lampes. En 1921 à la suite de la "visite" Paris d'un dirigeant de la GE, Woodward[22], la CGE joint son activité à celle de la Thomson dans la "Compagnie des lampes" où elle ne dispose que de 25% des parts[23].

Par contre, la CGE reprendra directement au groupe américain son secteur d'isolants électriques: "les Porcelaines de Lesquin", ce qui renforce sa position dans le secteur des équipements de lignes.

---

20 Broder, loc. cit., en particulier le rôle tout à fait clair d'Owen B. Young afin d'empêcher que les brevets électriques allemands entrent dans le cadre des réparations, au contraire des brevets chimiques. Or la GE a des liens étroits avec AEG (tout comme Westinghouse avec Siemens).

21 Broder. Op. cit. infra note 17.

22 Phoebus à Genève.

23 Au départ le capital est 50-50. Mais la CGE doit céder la moitié de sa part, soit 25%, à l'IGEC qui envisage de la rétrocéder au néerlandais Philips au cas où ce dernier préféretait entrer dans la Compagnie des lampes. Philips préférant, comme le cartel l'y autorise, produire ses propres ampoules en France, l'IGEC détient la majorité absolue via son contrôle sur Thomson et les 25% cédés par la CGE.

Cette rectification entraîne le retrait du domaine "grand public" et l'accroissement du potentiel dans celui des grands travaux.

Le redéploiement sur l'industrie découle de la prise en compte d'un certain nombre de paramètres. La CGE ne dispose pas des moyens nécéssaires à la poursuite d'une double politique industrielle et de producteur d'énergie. Le marché financier français est certes capable d'alimenter les investissements, mais l'organisation du "pouvoir industriel" n'est pas favorable à la constitution d'une structure type AEG ou General Electric. En outre, la CGE souffre, depuis son origine, d'une faiblesse dans ses liaisons avec la haute bureaucratie ou "l'établissement économique". L'origine "centralienne" des ingénieurs dirigeants est un handicap dans la structure très hiérarchisée des "pouvoirs" en France. Ceux-ci, au sommet de la bureaucratie, est généralement polytechnicienne (X Mines et surtout dans l'électricité X Ponts)[24] lorsqu'il s'agit des ministères techniques, "Sciences-Po"-Inspection des Finances pour les ministères économiques. Ce n'est qu'à la fin des années 1930 que la situation évolue à la CGE avec la disparition de l'équipe fondatrice autour d'Azaria. A contrario c'est aussi l'indication que l'entreprise est désormais admise dans "la cour des grands".

Or, la politique de l'État est désormais à la fois cohérente et exigeante. Sans négliger le thermique, l'accent et l'aide sont orientés vers l'hydraulique pour des raisons économiques: la France manque de charbon et l'importation grève une balance des paiements désormais déficitaire alors que l'énergie hydraulique est abondante mais mal exploitée. Les raisons en sont également stratégiques: le charbon se trouve près des frontières menacées (Nord, Lorraine) alors que les ressources hydrauliques sont dans des zones "sures" et protégées par le relief. Jusqu'à la fin des années 1930 les sites de barrages sont hors de portée de l'aviation allemande.

Se lancer dans la course aux concessions nécessite d'importants moyens financiers, et des réseaux de relations dont la CGE est mal pourvue. Par contre la société dispose depuis la Guerre d'un outil industriel performant avec de fortes capacités d'expansion. Le choix est important, car, dans le secteur du matériel électrotechnique, les concurrents ont fortement accru leur capacité de production en

[24] On retrouve cet exclusivisme dans la hiérarchie de l'EDF jusqu'à nos jours.

bénéficiant, jusqu'en 1920, de la politique énergétique liée à la Guerre et de l'absence de concurrence étrangère. Au contraire, dans les années qui suivent la concurrence allemande réapparaît sous la forme d'un *dumping* industriel que facilitent l'effondrement du mark et le statut ambigu de la Sarre.

Jouer sur les deux tableaux de la concession et de l'équipement risquait de mécontenter les puissants groupes de service public en formation et de favoriser les concurrents au niveau des commandes. Alors que ces derniers se renforcent en particulier des Ateliers Électriques de France, l'Alsacienne de Construction Mécanique, est libérée de l'emprise Siemens et de la CEM, qui à absorbé la filiale française de Westinghouse.

Il s'ensuit une réorganisation du secteur électricité et une redéfinition de ses priorités. Isolée, la concession d'Amiens est cédée. Par contre la position de Nancy est renforcée par l'acquisition de l'exploitation sur cinq départements se situant entre la grande zone productrice de la sidérurgie lorraine (thermique) et celle hydraulique rapprochant la centrale suisse d'Olten et le projet de Kembs sur le canal d'Alsace. La cession de la concession de Meaux au Nord-Est parisien se fait par échange de capital. Ce qui permet à la CGE c'entrer au conseil de cette structure stratégique du premier marché national. Les résultats sont éloquents puisque les filiales industrielles (Delle, Câbles de Lyon, Isolants, CGEE) réalisent la ligne à 100 mille V Olten-Epinal, puis Vincey-Briey (120 mille V) l'ensemble constituant la première phase de l'interconnexion Est-Paris.

La politique d'interconnexion dont il a été fait mention dans la première partie de cette étude et le bon résultat de ce premier "essai", démontrent le bien fondé de la stratégie de l'équipe d'Azaria. Elle est donc poursuivie par la création de trois *holdings* financiers: en 1926, l'*Union Houillère et Électrique*, et, auparavant, la *Société Provinciale d'Électricité*, mais surtout ainsi que par le rachat d'un des anciens "secteurs" de la ville de Paris: la *Continentale Edison*[25] et sa participation dans une autre société disposant d'une puissante assise parisienne: la *Société Parisienne de l'Air Comprimé.*

Avec ces sociétés financières, et tout particulièrement les deux

[25] A l'origine il s'agit d'une des deux sociétés créées par Edison en 1881 à Paris et destinées à constituer la base de ses opérations en Europe. Après le rapprochement Edison-Rathenau la société a perdu sa fonction

premières, la CGE dispose d'un instrument à la fois souple et discret pour assurer le financement et l'acquisition de participations dans le monde touffu juridiquement des concessions d'électricité. C'est particulièrement net pour l'UHE, créée en commun avec la société houillère d'Ostricourt qui ouvre le CGE le monde des sociétés minières du Nord, donc une des bases de l'électrification thermique dans la seconde région industrielle de France. D'autant qu'Ostricourt dispose, à la suite des dommages de guerre versés par l'État d'un portefeuille chimique et électrique (Énergie Électrique du Nord de la France) et est actionnaire du puissant holding financier "l'Union des Mines"[26]. Lequel devient en 1930 le troisième actionnaire d'UHE derrière Ostricourt et la CGE, cadenassant ainsi au lendemain de son introduction en Bourse (1929) le contrôle des participations électriques.

C'est sous cette structure discrète que la CGE et ses associés peuvent réaliser des opérations sur différentes sociétés d'électricité sans y apparaître en nom propre, la Provinciale d'Électricité devenant un sous-holding de l'UHE. La finalité principale de ces opérations se trouve dans la création en 1928 d'une troisième société financière: *La Financière Lorraine d'Électricité,* totalement contrôlée par la CGE. Cette dernière est créée aux fins de permettre le rachat de certaines activités (industrielles mais aussi concessions locales) de la Compagnie Générale Électrique de Nancy. Outre des moyens industriels accrus, la financière lorraine permet d'étendre le domaine régional de la CGE, en fédérant de petites concessions autour d'un *leader* "régional" et d'en faciliter le financement sur le marché local (Bourse de Nancy).

Tout comme le bras financier de la CGE à Paris: Electro-Crédit[27]. Il s'agit d'assurer le financement plus difficile des entreprises industrielles et d'améliorer le bilan de la maison-mère en remplaçant des participations industrielles immobiles par des actions de sociétés financières que l'on peut plus aisément négocier. En outre, les sociétés financières permettent des ajustements fiscaux plus favorables que pour les sociétés anonymes traditionnelles.

---

industrielle et est devenue essentiellement un des opérateurs parisiens. Lors de la création de la Compagnie Française Thomson Houston, la Général Électric s'est désengagée de la Continentale Edison.

26 Aujourd'hui intégré au groupe Suez.

27 Qui avec la crise absorbera la FLE en 1933.

Ces transformations aboutissent à donner à la CGE une apparence tout à fait nouvelle. La société fait figure de *holding* industriel et financier gérant, pour l'essentiel, des participations. Même si, au bilan, demeurent encore quelques entreprises industrielles administrées directement. Ce qui permet aux filiales industrielles de participer directement aux appels d'offre concernant les grands équipements électriques: centrales, barrages, lignes à haute tension et plus encore à l'électrification rurale dont la branche travaux publics de la CGE: la CGEE sera un des principaux bénéficiaires. Cette souplesse permet de se présenter au même titre que l'Alsacienne, la CEM, Jeumont ou Schneider tout en bénéficiant de l'avantage relatif de la présence des sociétés financières dans nombre de conseils des sociétés lançant les appels d'offres.

Plus nettement encore, lorsqu'avec la crise on arrivera à un accord d'auto-limitation (sic) de la concurrence allemande et à un partage du marché du gros matériel[28] (génératrices et gros transformateurs), la répartition officielle des parts de marché est la suivante: Alsthom, 4,78%; Jeumont 0 (?) Schneider-Westinghouse (SW), 4,89%; CEM, 30,03%; *Savoisienne (CGE), 44,3%;* AEG, 0,92%; Siemens, 15,06%.

Le résultat est d'autant plus remarquable qu'Alsthom résulte de la fusion des branches gros matériel de l'Alsacienne de Constructions Mécaniques et de la Thomson française et que SW traduit le retour en France du second groupe américain, lequel avait cédé ses usines à la CEM en 1919 et revient associé au premier groupe français de grosse mécanique.

La stratégie d'expansion du groupe ne se limite pas au domaine de l'électricité, mais touche les secteurs externes où il acquiert une position de *leader* national (accumulateurs, tréfilerie et métallurgie

[28] Cet accord, qui laisse aux allemands plus d'un sixième du marché français limite les exportations françaises dans la "zone préférentielle" allemande: (Allemagne, Autriche, Hongrie; Dantzig et Finlande) à un total dérisoire de 25 millions de F (1 million de $). En outre, sous réserve de l'accord du suédois ASEA, la zone préférentielle allemande sera étendue aux pays riverains de la Baltique: Danemark, Norvège, Suède, Pologne et les trois états "baltes". Autant dire que la France accepte officiellement d'être exclue du marché de l'Europe du Nord et centrale contre une quasi-protection de son marché national. Au demeurant, elle n'y était présente qu'indirectement par l'intermédiaire des intérêts Schneider dans l'industrie électrotechnique tchèque et quelques participations modestes en Pologne.

du cuivre, porcelaines et isolants en verre), ou même une place parmi les premiers mondiaux (piles de puissance). Ainsi se rapproche-t'il de l'ambition exprimée par Azaria dès 1898: "construire une AEG française".

Ce qui intéresse ici c'est de confronter la politique du groupe aux réalités juridiques et politiques du secteur. Ceci afin de comprendre les caractères particuliers du développement de l'électricité en France. Mais aussi de pouvoir définir des rapports de force qui ne sont pas simplement financiers ou techniques.

Au travers de l'évolution de la CGE comparée à Thomson puis aux grands groupes de production-distribution, la nature du patronat français apparaît beaucoup plus subtile que ne l'ont fait ressortir certains historiens récents. La réussite de la CGE au début des années 1930 ne se mesure pas simplement à sa puissance industrielle et financière.

Désormais, l'un des grands de l'industrie avec un chiffre d'affaires dépassant 1,3 milliard de francs dès 1930 (52 millions de dollars de la même année), si elle ne dispose pas des liens avec la haute banque, ni même avec les grandes banques de dépôt, les modifications de son conseil sont significatives. Dès 1924 y apparaissent Ernest Mercier et Peyerimhoff de Fontenelles. Le premier, en passe de devenir le grand maître de l'électricité thermique et l'un des principaux inspirateurs de l'interconnexion nationale est le modèle presque caricatural du haut fonctionnaire technocrate "passé" au privé; aspirant à la gestion économique et politique du pays dont la France de la Ve République est représentative. Le second appartient au milieu de la grande industrie traditionnelle des barons du charbon et de l'acier. Le fait qu'il ait épousé la fille d'Azaria est signe de l'intégration de la CGE dans le monde fermé des grands de l'industrie[29]. L'importance nationale du groupe sera confirmée en 1937 avec l'entrée au conseil d'un des représentants les plus éminents de la technocratie polytechnicienne: Raoul Dautry avec le titre d'Administrateur Délégué (n.º 2 du groupe) ainsi que du conseiller d'État Georges Hua.

[29] Fait d'autant plus caractéristique qu'Azaria, comme indiqué, est un émigré sans famille et que son diplôme de l'École Centrale n'est pas de ceux qui, comme Polytechnique ou l'Inspection des Finances ouvrent les portes de la haute bourgeoisie parisienne.

Il demeure que la politique de la CGE, compte tenu de sa faiblesse à l'origine, pose un certain nombre de problèmes. Il est clair que, comme la plupart des très grandes entreprises, le succès est dû pour une bonne part au génie d'un homme: Paul Azaria. Pour rester sur le continent européen et l'électricité, il est de l'espèce des E. Rathenau, Berliner, Schuckert, D. Dockers. Comme les trois premiers c'est un ingénieur doué de qualités financières, lui permettant, avec une équipe réduite et soudée, de faire les choix financiers nécéssaires en toute connaissance de cause industrielle.

Mais les choix dans le domaine délimité par cette communication ne peuvent se réduire à ce point. Lequel, au demeurant, fait partie de l'analyse de l'ouvrage principal. Dans quelle mesure l'importance des engagements de la banque suisse et singulièrement genevoise dans l'hydro électricité et l'électrométallurgie des Alpes Françaises n'a t'elle pas amené la CGE à éviter l'engagement dans un secteur où elle manquait de moyens et mal connu de ses techniciens? Au départ, en effet, ce secteur se développe dans la conjonction énergie-chimie / métallurgie à laquelle même la Thomson française évite de s'associer directement.

Dans le domaine thermique, l'entreprise a su se rendre compte assez rapidement que ses moyens ne lui permettaient pas de poursuivre à la fois une politique de concessions coûteuse du fait de l'absence de législation permettant des réseaux régionaux et la mise en place d'une base industrielle. Certes la constitution d'ensembles régionaux est possible, mais par accord entre concessionnaires: soit en créant une société commune, comme la CPDE à Paris (cas exceptionnel), soit en fédérant des distributeurs autour d'un producteur. Cette dernière situation, rare avant 1914, sera mise en application par la CGE au début des années 1920 en Lorraine sud-Champagne.

Mais, à ce moment, le choix industriel préférentiel est fait, les sources internes du groupe l'attestent. D'où la politique des sociétés *holdings* permettant d'intégrer les grands ensembles en formation et de se développer en symbiose avec eux. Évolution d'autant plus logique que les relations entre l'électricité et la puissance publique ont été profondément modifiées par la Guerre. La perte des sources houillères pendant le conflit et la nécessité de disposer d'une énergie nationale ont fait comprendre aux autorités politiques l'importance de l'hydroélectricité. Mais, en outre, la structure du rapport de l'offre et de la demande et l'impossibilité de stocker cette énergie, éclairent le pouvoir politique sur l'urgence de la mise en place d'un système de transport à haute tension et d'une interconnexion à l'échelle nationale.

Il s'en est suivi un triple mouvement: une législation favorable au transport et au regroupement; en particulier par l'extension de la normalisation des tensions et des matériels. Un profond renouvellement des dirigeants des entreprises d'électricité avec l'entrée en force des technocrates issus de la haute fonction publique. Reproduisant à un demi siècle de distance le schéma des chemins de fer.

La question se pose de l'élément moteur de ce changement. S'agit il de la part des entreprises d'un "appel" aux compétences et aux relations de corps des agents de l'État? Ou, comme a tendance à le faire l'historiographie de l'EDF, de la prise de conscience, par ces derniers, de la nécessite de "prendre les rênes" pour la réalisation d'un projet d'importance nationale. Présentation flatteuse pour la technocratie et qui correspond à la haute opinion qu'elle a de ses capacités et de son dévouement à l'intérêt national[30].

Sans doute, les deux mouvements sont apparus simultanément. Il reste que les résultats sont remarquables, avec une interconnexion nationale achevée dès 1936. Avec en contrepartie une véritable colonisation des états majors d'entreprises par les hauts fonctionnaires issus de Polytechnique ou de l'Inspection des Finances. Ce qui crée, au delà des conflits d'intérêt une synergie entre l'État et les groupes en formation, non exempte de tensions (par exemple sur l'indice charbon servant de base au prix du kwh). Les lois sur la houille blanche et le transport à haute tension donnent à l'État les moyens d'imposer rationalisation et régulation. On peut en déduire qu'elles résultent, et résulteront chaque fois plus d'une collaboration entre les deux forces. Les cadres de l'une (État) étant susceptibles de devenir les dirigeants de l'autre qui furent souvent, antérieurement, des agents de l'État.

C'est dans ce contexte que se forment les grands groupes. Celui du Nord, peu à peu dominé par une entente entre sociétés houillères (l'union des Mines) et les intérêts du groupe belge Empain[31], le

---

30 C'est l'idéologie véhiculée lors de la crise par le groupe X — Crise entre autres.

31 Juridiquement belge, ce groupe dispose d'intérêts puissants en France et souvent hors d'Europe en conjonction avec des intérêts français

groupe méditerranéen issu de l'entente entre l'Énergie Électrique du Littoral Méditerranéen (Thomson, Marseillaise de Crédit, Péchiney), et les deux ensembles fédérateurs du "nord" (Mercier) et du "sud-est" (Durand). On saisit dès lors la logique de la CGE. Participer par une présence au pouvoir du plus grand nombre d'entreprises et se créer des liens avec la technocratie en formation. Mais réserver les moyens humains, techniques et financiers du Groupe à l'affirmation industrielle.

Ainsi l'entreprise était-elle, au niveau du Groupe, moins sensible à ce qui fut le problème le plus aigu de la période: la fixation par l'État du prix de cession de l'électricité. Cette politique et la diversification constante de la CGE expliquent également qu'elle fut, parmi les grandes sociétés cotées en Bourse, l'une des moins affectées par la crise des années trente à l'opposé d'Alsthom[32] et de Thomson.

Le programme de "relance" envisagé dès 1936 et décidé en 1938 (le programme dit des 3 milliards) oblige les sociétés de production à s'unir dans un cartel de financement — l'UNIE — et prévoit de grands travaux hydroélectriques sous un statut de société mixte État-Privé, tel qu'il a été réalise pour le barrage de Kembs en Alsace ou la Compagnie nationale du Rhône[33]. La CGE s'y trouve dans une position favorable: faiblement impliquée du fait de la structure de ses participations, elle est au contraire un des destinataires

---

(Égypte). L'analyse de sa politique et le poids de ses entreprises française dans ses affaires, indiquent qu'il ne peut être considéré comme "étranger" au même titre que les filiales des groupes allemands ou américains.

[32] Cette dernière, fusion récente, a approché la faillite en raison surtout d'importants investissements en vue de l'électrification des chemins de fer. Or la crise arrêt brutalement tous les investissements du secteur. A la Bourse, Alsthom perd 90% de sa valeur. L'action CGE perd néanmoins 66% de sa valeur boursière entre 1929 (maximum) et 1935. Mais entre temps avait eu lieu une forte augmentation du capital, fort critiquée par la presse spécialisée.

[33] Qui du fait de son statut mais aussi de l'intervention à l'Assemblée nationale de son administrateur Édouard Herriot ne sera pas nationalisée. Elle a réalisé depuis 1945 les plus grands équipements hydroélectriques sur le Rhône. Ce sont ces équipements, dont le premier envisagé dès 1936 fut Génissiat, qui expliquent la décision de l'État d'installer à Pierrelate les grands équipements de chimie nucléaire.

privilégiés des commandes qui doivent, en principe, découler des investissements prévus.

De la Guerre aux nationalisations

Un aspect intéressant de la politique du Groupe réside dans sa réaction aux demandes des autorités lorsqu'en 1938 ces dernières se décident à accélérer l'effort de préparation à la Guerre. S'agissant d'un secteur non directement lié à l'électricité nous n'y faisons qu'une allusion rapide. Les demandes de l'État portent esentiellement sur l'activité métallurgique du cuivre. Il s'agit d'obtenir de la CGE, forte de son expérience de 1914-18, la mise en place d'une production en masse de douilles (balles, obus) et rubans d'alimentation d'armes automatiques.

Ce à quoi l'entreprise ne peut qu'acquiescer. Mais, se remémorant la difficile reconversion des ateliers d'Orléans et Bordeaux en 1918-19[34], elle obtient du gouvernement des garanties extrêmement précises. Non seulement au sujet de la reconversion au retour à la paix; mais au cas où "la guerre n'aurait pas lieu ou serait retardée" une modulation des prix en fonction des quantités. Ainsi se trouve, en principe, préservé l'investissement. Cette politique prudente[35] est le fait de la nouvelle équipe dirigeante dont les relations avec les pouvoirs traditionnels de l'État et de l'Industrie sont beaucoup plus étroits que du temps d'Azaria (parti en 1937).

La Guerre n'apporte pas de modification profonde à la structure de la compagnie. Ses installations échappent aux destructions tant en 1940 qu'en 1944, sauf, dans ce dernier cas d'une destruction partielle des usines de Lyon (Delle) par les allemands en retraite. Les usines de la zone occupée sont mises sous contrôle en-

---

[34] La société a, comme beaucoup d'autres, avait connu de brutales difficultés à l'hiver 1918 en raison de l'annulation brutale des commandes. Il est cependant évident que l'état des finances publiques justifiait largement cette mesure prise sans préavis.

[35] La correspondance interne montre que les responsables sont fort inquiets du conflit à venir car ils sont très conscients de l'affaiblissement de la capacité de production de biens d'équipement en France du fait de l'absence d'investissements au cours des années 1930. Alors qu'ils ont la prescience que cette guerre sera avant tout une guerre de matériels.

nemi, qui oblige à produire en fonction de ses besoins; allant jusq'à installer des cadres allemands (de chez Siemens en particulier) afin de contrôler l'application des normes germaniques. Par contre, les usines du sud-est produisant le gros matériel électrique, mais aussi les réseaux électriques, fonctionnent à peu près normalement. Une double dégradation apparaît progressivement dans la production (manque de charbon, de matières, premières, de métaux) et dans les recettes du secteur distribution en raison du blocage des tarifs. Mais dans l'ensemble la période est financièrement favorable au groupe. D'une part, en raison des efforts poursuivis dans l'électrification hydraulique; de l'autre, grâce à un financement aisé sur le marché où l'épargne offerte est abondante jusqu'en 1943.

A l'inverse, la production devient très difficile dès 1943, touchée par la disparition des matières-premières et l'usure rapide des équipements qui ne peuvent être remplacés. A la libération du territoire, la CGE se trouve dans une situation paradoxale avec une trésorerie très à l'aise (mais que fragilise l'inflation), des perspectives de commandes extrêmement favorables, mais un outil industriel en attente d'une rénovation urgente.

Les années 1944 à 1946 vont voir les responsables se concentrer sur quatre problèmes principaux:

— L'avenir de la métallurgie des non-ferreux. Avertis par leus liens avec la Suisse neutre, les dirigeants de la CGE comme ceux de Péchiney[36], sont inquiets d'une surproduction mondiale de non-ferreux due à l'essor des production des États Unis, du Canada et du Chili. D'où la mise en commun d'une partie essentielle de leurs productions avec la création de la société CEGEDUR. Ce qui a également pour avantage de "libérer" le bilan de la CGE des problèmes que posent en permanence les fortes fluctuations de cours du cuivre.

— Le développement des branches téléphone et radio. Domaine très complexe que nous ne faisons qu'évoquer. Si la CGE persiste avec sa filiale téléphonique (CIT devenue SIT), décevante en raison de l'absence e d'une politique nationale du téléphone jusqu'en

---

[36] Dès les années 1920 il y a eu échange de capital entre les deux groupes. Le Président de Péchiney siège au conseil de la CGE et vice-versa. La CGE dispose d'environ 1,3% du capital de Péchiney.

1974[37], les liens tissés avec Paribas autour de la CSF dans le secteur hertzien n'aboutiront pas[38].

— La remise à niveau de l'outil industriel. Elle dépend de la possibilité d'acquérir les machines et dans quelques cas (piles de puissance) des brevets aux États Unis. Mais surtout de la politique industrielle telle que la définira la planification.

— *Enfin et au premier plan l'avenir de la branche production distribution.* La décision échappe aux responsables de la CGE dans la mesure où les négociations ont lieu entre les responsables des grands groupes et le Ministère de la Production Industrielle, à la tête duquel le Général De Gaulle a nommé l'ancien syndicaliste de la CPDE et responsable communiste Marcel Paul.

Une fois la nationalisation votée et le mode d'indemnisation défini — bons de l'énergie portant 3% d'intérêt et amortissables au moyen de la mise à disposition de 1% du chiffre d'affaires annuel d'EDF — deux problèmes se posent à la CGE:

— Qu'en sera-t'il des participations stratégiques mais faibles: 0,4% de la CPDE, 1% de l'Union d'Électricité. Question secondaire au vu des montants impliqués, et de la disparition des raisons de participer aux groupes. Désormais les marchés seront passés par EDF.

— *Mais surtout l'avenir des Holdings au sein desquels la CGE a une position dominante.* En particulier l'UHE (L'Union Houillère et Électrique) devenue à la suite des années 1930 l'instrument des participations et le lien avec l'Union des Mines par Ostricourt D'autant que le domaine houiller des maisons-mères de ces sociétés est nationalisé de son côté.

Dans un premier temps, Ostricourt va se dissoudre au moyen de trois opérations financières se clôturant le 17 Octobre 1950. A ce moment, les actions Ostricourt ont été échangées contre des actions nouvelles créées par UHE, et distribuées aux actionnaires Ostricourt. Ainsi, ceux-ci deviennent personnellement actionnaires d'UHE. Ce qui renforce le poids du portefeuille groupé de la CGE. D'autant plus que UHE, étant elle même actionnaire d'Ostricourt

---

37 Il s'agit néanmoins des fondements de la branche ALCATEL qui a en outre absorbé ITT Europe.

38 La CSF sera absorbée par Thomson, dont elle est aujourd'hui le pôle électronique: aéronautique, radars, missiles.

par le système des participations croisées, reçoit 120 mille de ses propres actions en échange des 40 mille Ostricourt qu'elle possède et les annule immédiatement.

Une deuxième phase se réalise avec une "rectification" de participations au sein des *holdings* CGE. UHE cède à Electro Crédit l'essentiel de son portefeuille de "nationalisées" indemnisables en bons négociables en Bourse, contre des participations industrielles détenues par Electro Crédit (Parisienne de l'Air Comprimé, CGEM...); mais en même temps acquiert des actions des anciennes filiales de distribution de la CGE (Nantaise, Marseille) afin d'accroître ses droits à indemnisation. Une opération d'échange avec la Lyonnaise des eaux (ancien groupe Petsche-Mercier) est conduite avec la même finalité.

Lorsque, en 1951, l'indemnisation par la Caisse de l'Énergie touche à sa fin, l'UHE dispose d'un important portefeuille de bons négociables mais n'a plus de finalité économique. La CGE dispose à ce moment de trois *holdings* (Electro Crédit, CGEM et UHE) dont les deux derniers n'ont pas de raison d'être conjointement. La CGEM qui gérait la branche métallurgie ayant cédé à CEGEDUR ses exploitations. Une fusion est donc opérée par échange de trois actions UHE contre deux CGEM, simplifiant l'organogramme de la CGE tout en accroissant son poids au sein de cette dernière société financière.

Au terme de cette dernière opération, la CGE apparaît comme un puissant *holding* industriel à dominante électrotechnique. Elle se trouve à l'époque au second rang national derrière Thomson et occupe des positions dominantes dans le secteur de l'équipement des centrales, des transformateurs, des lignes à haute tension. Elle occupe aussi une position de force dans le secteur des piles, des isolants et se prépare à l'extension du téléphone. Rétrospectivement les archives de l'entreprise démontrent que tel était, dès 1898, un des buts des fondateurs. Pari risqué, compte tenu des rapports de force sur le marché français.

L'autre volet, le service public a relativement tourné court et la CGE n'a jamais pu disposer du poids de AEG ou de la General Électric dans leurs pays respectifs. L'explication s'en trouve dans l'absence de réglementation nationale du secteur avant 1914. Situation sans doute surprenante pour l'étranger habitué à voir une France colbertiste réglementant tout. Mais la Troisième République à la "belle époque" est peu réglementaire et se méfie du pouvoir central. Anatole France n'écrit t'il pas qu'on *"lui pardonnait de mal gouverner parce qu'elle gouvernait peu"*.

Lorsqu'au lendemain de la Guerre commence à se rationaliser le réseau sous l'influence d'une réglementation d'État, la CGE a choisi sa voie. On doit y voir la conséquence des investissements de guerre, mais à notre avis plus encore de la faiblesse de ses liens organiques avec l'établissement industrial-bureaucratique caractéristique des allées du pouvoir. Garder un moyen d'intervention, de participation; mais apparaître de plus en plus comme un équipementier et non un concurrent sur le champ des luttes pour le contrôle des réseaux, telle est la politique des responsables animés par Azaria.

La nationalisation n'est dans ce cas qu'une forme d'achèvement d'une évolution qui eut sans doute abouti à la fusion des affaires CGE au sein de consortiums nationaux dans un cadre plus "libéral". Elle permet à la société de mieux se recentrer sur ses activités privilégiées. Mais aussi, en faisant d'EDF le client unique de la profession elle permet une rationalisation du matériel favorable à l'abaissement des coûts. Ce qui améliore la compétitivité internationale de l'industrie française. Ce dont la CGE de par son positionnement sur le parché est un des principaux bénéficiaires.

Au cours de son quasi centenaire, la CGE n'a jamais été une entreprise dépendante du pouvoir politique. Même si, à partir des années 1950, elle a choisi nombre de ses dirigeants parmi le personnel technico-politique de niveau national. Ceci mis à part les quelques années de nationalisation entre 1982 et 1987. De cette indépendance pas toujours désirée mais toujours assumée, issue des origines même de la société, il n'est pas possible d'extrapoler des conclusions sur le rôle de l'État dans le développement industriel. Modestement peut on affirmer que l'exemple de la CGE est indicateur de l'importance primordiale des hommes sur les institutions, les structures ou les traditions. Un prolongement de l'étude jusqu'aux années 1980 confirmerait cette opinion au travers de la "gestion" par la CGE de ses interventions dans l'électricité nucléaire.

Ricardo Maranhão
IFCH, UNICAMP

ESTADO E CAPITAL PRIVADO NA ELETRIFICAÇÃO DE SÃO PAULO

Desde 1899, o processo de eletrificação da região mais rica e desenvolvida do Brasil, o eixo Rio-São Paulo, esteve sob o comando e o monopólio do "Grupo Light". Capitaneado pela *holding* Brazilian Traction, Light & Power, o grupo tinha capital anglo-americano-canadense e sede em Toronto, Canadá. Ao longo de sua existência, a "Light", como era popularmente conhecida, enraizou-se solidamente como conjunto de empresas privadas de serviços urbanos, controlando não só o fornecimento de energia elétrica como o de iluminação pública, gás, transportes e telefones das duas maiores capitais brasileiras e de inúmeros municípios de seus arredores.

Ora, desde a década de 1930, houve pressões políticas no sentido de ampliar a participação do Estado nos serviços públicos brasileiros; embora até o final da Segunda Guerra Mundial eles tivessem continuado privados e na sua maioria estrangeiros, o pós-guerra assistiu a um crescente movimento estatizante no setor energético, tanto no plano da propaganda política como no de ações concretas como a criação, pelo Poder Federal, da Companhia Hidrelétrica do São Francisco; e pelos poderes de alguns estados, de empresas elétricas como a Centrais Elétricas de Minas Gerais, a Companhia Estadual de Energia Elétrica do Rio Grande do Sul ou, em São Paulo, a Companhia Hidrelétrica do Rio Pardo, entre outras.

No segundo governo Vargas (1951-1954), os movimentos nacionalistas cresceram muito em apoio popular e de massas. O discurso de defesa intransigente dos interesses nacionais e de combate radical à exploração estrangeira tornou-se quase hegemônico entre as lideranças populares e os políticos populistas. A retórica governamental deixaria as multinacionais em geral e o grupo Light de Toronto, monopolista do setor elétrico, em situação particularmente difícil. Entretanto, isso não levaria necessariamente à tomada de medidas efetivas contra as empresas de serviços públicos. Estas, como a Light, teriam que passar a década de 1950 mergulhadas num árduo combate político-ideológico contra nacionalistas e estatizantes. Mas, a multinacional canadense conseguiria uma série de acordos excelentes para sua sobrevivência, e no governo de Juscelino Kubitschek (1955-1960) seria capaz de obter um pacto de cooperação com o poder federal extremamente benéfico.

Um novo momento do capital

O grupo Light, capitaneado pela *holding* Brazilian Traction, Light & Power, estava solidamente enraizado no Brasil desde 1899, como conjunto de empresas de serviços urbanos com sólido controle monopólico sobre transportes, iluminação, energia elétrica, telefone e gás em todo o eixo Rio-São Paulo, centro econômico do País. Mas, as dificuldades políticas que passou a viver no início dos anos cinqüenta têm relação também com o novo momento estratégico vivido pelo capitalismo mundial a partir do pós-Segunda Guerra.

Nesta nova fase, *algumas grandes empresas* de serviços públicos que atuavam em escala mundial entraram de fato em relativo declínio, abrindo espaço para os Estados se ocuparem crescentemente desses serviços. Tal foi o caso de uma das maiores *holdings* norte-americanas de eletricidade e transportes, a American & Foreign Power, Amforp, de propriedade da Bond & Share. Entre 1947 e 1950 ela teve sudidiárias expropriadas na China, na Colômbia e na Argentina, nacionalizadas na Índia, e perdeu mercado para as empresas estatais do setor no México. Nos anos subseqüentes, ela passou por graves dificuldades em Cuba, na Costa Rica, no Panamá e na Guatemala[1]. No Brasil, onde tinha subsidiárias em vários Estados, foi fortemente pressionada pelo crescimento da demanda, que não foi capaz de acompanhar, e pelos nacionalistas,

---

[1] Ver a respeito Wilkins, Mira. *The Maturing of Multinational Enterprise: American Business Abroad, 1914-1970*. Harvard University Press, 1974, e Bandeira, Moniz. *Presença dos Estados Unidos no Brasil*. Rio de Janeiro: Civilização Brasileira. 1973.

que chegaram em 1959 a conseguir a encampação, pelo governador Leonel Brizola, de sua filial gaúcha.

O caso da Amforp tem relação de sentido com uma tendência mais geral verificada na época, de mudança de orientação global de investimentos: entre 1946 e 1954, o investimento norte-americano em serviços de utilidade pública no exterior cresceu de 1,3 para 1,5 bilhões de dólares — ou seja, apenas 13%; enquanto isso, o investimento dos EUA no exterior em petróleo crescia de 1,4 para 5,3 bilhões de dólares, ou seja, 378%, e o investimento em *manufaturas* tinha um incremento de 2,4 para 5,7 bilhões, ou seja, de 237%[2]. Deslocar-se para o setor manufatureiro e para os investimentos pesados em mineração e petróleo no pós-guerra foi, aliás, uma tendência importante do capital norte-americano na América Latina. Segundo Barbara Stallings, esta região recebeu forte aporte de capital para estes setores, num quadro de ampla expansão física do volume de recursos investidos pelos EUA na região, um incremento de 3 para 6,4 bilhões de dólares entre 1946 e 1955[3].

Neste novo momento, o grande capital passa a investir mais na *produção de manufaturas* nos países subdesenvolvidos; claro, desde que estes tivessem, como o Brasil e o México do pós-guerra, as condições necessárias mínimas a acolher os investimentos "de risco" diretamente na indústria[4].

Nessa conjuntura, o declínio de empresas como a AMFORP não significa uma queda do conjunto dos investimentos do grande capital, e sim uma reorientação de investimentos. A isto se associa a tendência de algumas das multinacionais de serviços, como o grupo Light, que desde a origem tinham seu capital predominantemente *financeiro*: agora na década de 1950 o seu âmbito de atuação como empresa de capital financeiro se diversifica, dirigindo-se para vários outros setores da produção, como veremos com a criação da *holding* Brascan em 1956-57. Para a sua vida econômica como

---

2 Wilkins, Mira. Op. cit., p. 301.

3 Stallings, Barbara. *Banker to the Third World: US Portfolio Investment in Latin America, 1900-1986*. Berkeley: California University Press. 1987.

4 Ver, a respeito das condições sociais e políticas peculiares a países latino-americanos para receberem investimentos multinacionais na indústria, Prebisch, R. *Hacia una Dinámica del Desarrollo Latinamericano*. Fondo de Cultura Económica. México, 1963, e Cardoso, F. H. C. E Faletto, E. *Dependência e Desenvolvimento na América Latina*. São Paulo: Difel. 1970.

grupo multinacional, torna-se cada vez menos importante a execução dos serviços que, no passado, davam significado ao seu capital. Entretanto, a transição para o novo momento do capitalismo mundial não se faria como um "automatismo" econômico: as questões políticas, nascidas das necessidades da indústria brasileira e sempre decisivas para um grupo empresarial como a Light, pesariam muito nas decisões da empresa de se manter ativa no setor elétrico ainda por bastante tempo, mesmo sem dar conta da demanda e sem utilizar recursos próprios.

Na verdade, o grupo canadense obteria a partir de 1948 polpudos financiamentos do BIRD com aval do governo brasileiro. Graças a isso, a Light manteve um *patamar mínimo de produção* de energia capaz de mantê-la *dominante nos serviços de distribuição*, enquanto o Estado entrava pesadamente na geração. Assim, estrategicamente o grupo teria, nos anos cinqüenta, toda uma consolidação como empresa que lhe permitiria passar galhardamente para a nova etapa de acumulação.

Os fatos da consolidação do Grupo se enquadrariam também no contexto político-ideológico do "abrasileiramento" das suas empresas. Este era preconizado desde os anos trinta pelo seu próprio fundador Alexandre Mackenzie, de seu retiro em Florença, e foi seguido com algum entusiasmo por seus seguidores como Kenneth McCrimmon, que deu início à contratação de brasileiros com vistas ao preenchimento de gerências ou futuras direções.

Tratava-se de uma preocupação bastante justificável: já no primeiro ano da década de 1950, o próprio embaixador do Canadá no Brasil, J. S. MacDonald, naturalmente muito afinado com a maior empresa canadense a atuar no exterior, manifestou suas preocupações, explicando da seguinte maneira a hostilidade nacionalista à Light:

> "Nós só precisamos imaginar uma situação comparável em que, digamos, a energia, a luz elétrica, o gás, os telefones e os serviços de bondes de Montreal, Toronto e Ottawa estivessem nas mãos de uma companhia dirigida de Lisboa ou Bruxelas, e cujos dividendos, quase que inteiramente, fossem para estrangeiros, para entender a magnitude do problema de relações públicas."[5]

---

[5] Citado por McDowall, Duncan. *The Light: Brazilian Traction, Light & Power Company Limited, 1899-1945*. Toronto: Univ. of Toronto Press. 1988, p. 390.

A política de "abrasileiramento" tomaria uma feição mais nítida com a mudança de sedes de empresas e maquiagens no controle acionário delas, a partir de 1956. Naquele ano, a São Paulo Light e a Companhia Telefônica Brasileira transfeririam seus escritórios centrais para o Brasil. Antes disso, Borden trabalharia para promover brasileiros a postos dirigentes: o velho engenheiro paulista Edgard Egydio de Souza chegaria ao final da carreira em 1950 como único brasileiro do *board* da Brazilian Traction.

Na mesma época, também o engenheiro Benjamin Franklin de Barros Barreto foi para a direção da São Paulo Light, Odilon de Souza para a Vice-Presidência executiva daquela empresa e o jovem Marinho Lutz para a da Carris Luz e Força do Rio, entre outros. Seguindo a escola de McCrimmon, a área de Relações Públicas foi toda entregue a brasileiros, com a rápida ascensão de jornalistas como Ubirajara Martins, na diretoria em São Paulo; no Rio, essa área chegaria ao luxo de ter como diretor, em 1957, o hoje grande escritor Rubem Fonseca. Aliás, relações públicas seria o setor da empresa característico para preparar ideologicamente o "abrasileiramento", com a produção maciça de propaganda e publicidade com o largo uso de símbolos nacionais, do folclore, como o Saci, que apareceu inúmeras vezes em anúncios apologéticos dos serviços da Light.

Acima de todos estes brasileiros, entretanto, foi Antonio Gallotti quem mais marcou o "abrasileiramento". Catarinense de Tijucas, nascido em 1908, o filho de imigrantes italianos, Antonio Gallotti foi desde jovem um articulador incansável. Ao entrar em 1927 na Faculdade de Direito da Universidade do Rio de Janeiro, fundou logo o seu primeiro Centro Acadêmico; e o fez junto com Santiago Dantas, Hélio Viana, Jacobina Lacombe e toda uma turma de intelectuais brilhantes que encerraram os anos vinte como simpatizantes da força emergente do fascismo. Em 1932, Gallotti já era dirigente da Ação Integralista de Plínio Salgado, e foi com a camisa verde e o sigma no braço que ficou conhecendo, no bar Palace do Rio, o lightiano Edmundo da Luz Pinto. Este o apresentou ao já notório Major McCrimmon, que o contratou como advogado do poderoso e generoso Departamento Jurídico (ou "o contencioso") da Light, em 1933.

Os tempos eram de muito trabalho para advogados das multinacionais do setor elétrico, com a pressão nacionalista dos "tenentes" dentro do governo Vargas, e a promulgação do Código de Águas.

Gallotti fez o que pôde, e o sucesso da Light em evitar a aplicação plena do Código, se não foi obra sua, contou com a preciosa ajuda de seus misteres de advogado. Entretanto, sua grande oportunidade surgiu em 1947, quando Henry Borden consultou-o sobre aspectos técnico-jurídicos da criação de uma *holding* capaz de fazer a administração financeira de todas as empresas da Light, diante da iminência de um grande empréstimo do Banco Mundial (90 milhões de dólares). Ágil, Gallotti apresentou em quarenta e oito horas o plano da Companhia Brasileira Administradora de Serviços Técnicos (Cobast), que, com algumas alterações, foi logo adotado, contribuindo a nova empresa para a consolidação e racionalização do comando do Grupo.

No ano seguinte, o advogado foi para Washington participar das negociações do grande empréstimo, e seu sucesso lhe valeu uma ascensão fulminante, que o levou à vice-presidência em 1951 e à presidência em 1955. Como ex-professor de doutrina integralista, versado na dialética dos combates ideológicos, Gallotti se empenhou pesoalmente nas lutas contra os nacionalistas da década de 1950. Para compreender as transformações que consolidaram a Light como grupo na nova fase da história, e a sua política de "abrasileiramento", é necessário narrar aspectos decisivos do processo de embate político-ideológico em que a canadense esteve mergulhada durante a primeira metade dos anos cinqüenta.

Nacionalismo e racionamento

"(...) as *holdings*, como os senhores bem sabem, são super-organizações que adquirem tal poder econômico, que dificilmente seus dirigentes resistem à tentação de usá-lo em benefício próprio, para obterem maiores lucros para suas empresas. Eles se transformam não mais em dirigentes de empresas, mas em dirigentes de um verdadeiro poder de país em país, acima dos governos (...) vêem os senhores o perigo que corre uma nação que tolere ou permita que uma empresa estrangeira controle a sua produção de energia elétrica e dite o tipo de construção das usinas. Essa nação elimina a possibilidade de decidir sobre o seu desenvolvimento. (...) o controle da produção de eletricidade está inteiramente entregue a uma companhia que tem recusado a fiscalização do governo, que não tem elementos para saber qual o preço real do kilowatt (...). A Nação para, porque as empresas responsáveis pelo fornecimento de energia não atendem ao ritmo de progresso do País. E nunca atenderão, desde que seus interesses particulares não coincidem com os da Nação. A política dessas empresas foi sempre de evitar novos investimentos, acumulando e exportando lucros (...). Estamos agora diante de uma nova crise. Crise que está destruindo as possibilidades de nosso desenvolvimento, entravando a marcha do País."[6]

O discurso do deputado Euzébio Rocha, proferido em setembro de 1952, é extremamente expressivo de uma determinada posição nacionalista radical e muito ativa durante o segundo governo Vargas (1951-1954). Getúlio voltara ao poder, segundo seus partidários, "nos braços do povo", ou seja, em meio a uma notável mobilização popular. Nesta, o apelo às massas do velho populista assumia colorações diferenciadas dos tempos paternalistas dos anos trinta. Aqui, seu discurso se colocava como democrático e mobilizador, estimulando os trabalhadores a lutar nos sindicatos pelos seus direitos históricos e, ao mesmo tempo, a defender a indústria nacional contra o capital estrangeiro. Não cabe nos limites deste trabalho uma análise da política populista de Vargas, mas vale a pena destacar que o discurso nacionalista de corte mobilizador era uma necessidade histórica objetiva daquele momento. Tanto ao nível da inserção do Brasil no Terceiro Mundo emergente no pós-guerra, cuja modernização passava em geral, nos três continentes, por esse tipo de mobilização; quanto ao nível das raízes *estruturais* desse tipo de política, fincadas no próprio padrão de desenvolvimento industrial ainda vigente.

Efetivamente, a dinâmica do crescimento industrial ainda estava sendo dada pelo processo de "substituição de importações", intensificado com a Segunda Guerra. Os limites ao crescimento do setor agrário-exportador, pelas restrições internacionais ao crescimento do valor das exportações, induzia o capitalismo brasileiro a aproveitar o mercado interno para produtos industriais importados, que eram substituídos por produtos fabricados no País. Tal

---

6 Rocha, Euzébio, conferência em 12 de setembro de 1952 na Faculdade de Direito de São Paulo, in *Semana de Energia Elétrica*, pasta 348, Série Documentos Avulsos, acervo CDHEI-Eletropaulo.

processo, que se esgotaria e mudaria de natureza no final dos anos cinqüenta, teve uma força bastante visível: de 1940 a 1961 a produção industrial brasileira quase que sextuplicou, e teve um ritmo de crescimento maior do que o dobro do ritmo de crescimento global da economia[7].

Ora, nessa substituição de importações, o papel do Estado na economia é necessariamente decisivo, definindo políticas de câmbio e alfândega, estimulando determinadas aplicações e reorientando transferências de renda inter-setores. Ao procurar garantir as condições para o processo industrial, o Estado brasileiro se afirmou não só como elemento central no plano econômico: tornou-se também o centro político decisivo para o qual se dirigem as demandas dos setores produtivos.

Os ocupantes do poder nesse Estado têm a necessidade de legitimar a sua própria ação perante as massas populares, através da valorização de sua política econômica como expressão dos mais altos interesses nacionais. Estes interesses, segundo a análise dos nacionalistas dos anos quarenta e dos seus aliados de esquerda, eram conspurcados pelas multinacionais que não só exploravam a Pátria como um todo, como prejudicavam o empresariado brasileiro. Entre estes "empresários nacionais", haveria uma maioria de empreendedores honestos e afinados com os interesses "de todo o povo"; mas uma minoria da "elite", muito poderosa, era aliada do capital imperialista e portanto, para combatê-la, era essencial uma mobilização das massas populares em aliança com o empresariado "nacional"[8] É claro que, sendo o empresariado ainda fraco, o Estado deveria suprí-lo de meios econômicos nesse combate patriótico. A valorização do Estado *benefactor* aí contida era essencial ao nacionalismo.

Nos anos trinta e quarenta o discurso ideológico nacionalista e estatizante tinha como contrapartida *real* a ocupação efetiva, por políticos nacionalistas, de cargos no poder de Estado; e sua posição de executores de um "equilíbrio" era também real, pois o modelo

---

[7] Pereira, L. C. Bresser. *Desenvolvimento e Crise no Brasil*. São Paulo: Brasiliense. 1976 (6.ª edição), p. 56.

[8] Ver a respeito das operações ideológicas dos nacionalistas da época, Cohn, Gabriel. "Perspectivas da Esquerda", in *Política e Revolução Social no Brasil*. Rio de Janeiro: Civilização Brasileira. 1965, p. 129-60, e Toledo, Caio. *ISEB, Fábrica de Ideologias*. São Paulo: Ática. 1977.

de industrialização por "substituição de importações" ainda dispunha de grande vitalidade. Entretanto, como procurei demonstrar em trabalho anterior[9], a perda de vitalidade desse modelo industrializador, causada principalmente pelo estreitamento das margens de financiamento, levaria os dirigentes de Estado, para manter a continuidade da industrialização, a buscar recursos externos de grande porte. As medidas destinadas a atrair tais capitais estrangeiros, como as propostas pelo relatório da Comissão Mista Brasil-Estados Unidos (1953), ou como as postas em prática pela Instrução 113 da Sumoc (1955), não permitiriam a continuidade de uma política econômica efetivamente nacionalista, e tornariam o discurso dos nacionalistas uma retórica cada vez mais distante da realidade.

Na verdade, esse discurso teve maior solidez na Campanha do Petróleo (1951-1953), quando a presença política decisiva de frações da corporação militar, com objetivos econômicos específicos, deu às mobilizações populares uma força extra que levaria à vitória representada pela criação da Petrobrás[10]. A maioria dos militares se daria por satisfeita, retirando-se do comando da movimentação nacionalista; na campanha contra as multinacionais elétricas, pela criação da Eletrobrás, a direção política "anti-imperialista" não contaria tanto com a presença dos quadros fardados. Ao mesmo tempo, a "burguesia nacional", com poucas e honrosas exceções, recusava-se a marcar presença efetiva como classe nas campanhas nacionalistas que teoricamente a beneficiariam. Assim, o perfil social da militância nacionalista, no conjunto dos anos cinqüenta, era predominantemente de intelectuais de classe média, que procuravam mobilizar sindicatos, imprensa e movimento estudantil.

O racionamento de energia, a partir de 1950, era odiado pela população e fornecia o caldo de cultura para a luta contra a Light. No Rio e em São Paulo, devido à aceleração do processo urbano e industrial, a defasagem entre a oferta e a demanda havia ficado muito grave, e a aplicação efetiva dos recursos do empréstimo apro-

---

9 Maranhão, Ricardo. "O Estado e a Política Populista no Brasil (1954 - 1964)", in Fausto, Bóris (org.). *História Geral da Civilização Brasileira.* São Paulo: Difel. 1981, tomo III, 3.º vol., p. 257-94.

10 Sobre a Campanha do Petróleo, ver Cohn, Gabriel. *Petróleo e Nacionalismo.* São Paulo: Difel. 1968.

vado em 1948 ainda demorava a fazer efeitos sobre a oferta de energia da Light. Assim, a escuridão chegou: a Light obteve do CNAEE a Resolução 588, de 13 de Janeiro de 1950, autorizando o racionamento no Distrito Federal.

O turismo da Cidade Maravilhosa, já duramente atingido poucos anos antes pela proibição dos cassinos, não gostou da história. O Sindicato de Hotéis e Similares saiu em defesa do dono do Hotel Primor, que foi preso pela polícia poucos dias depois do início da restrição do consumo, por se recusar a cortar a corrente elétrica de seus hóspedes; e requereu ao Ministério da Justiça contra o racionamento, dando início à longa série de pendências judiciais contra a Light por conta dos cortes do consumo.

A situação só faria se agravar, com a estiagem dos anos seguintes, chegando-se a cortes diários de fornecimento de energia de cinco a sete horas diárias, no Rio de Janeiro. Em São Paulo, havia freqüentemente cortes sem aviso prévio. Como diz Catulo Branco,

> "as medidas de racionamento passaram então a limites de extrema gravidade. Havia uma pronunciada queda de tensão. A iluminação perdia muito em intensidade, ao lado dos graves prejuízos para a indústria cujos motores eram freqüentemente sacrificados. Em determinadas horas, sob a forma de rodízio, o suprimento era interrompido nos bairros, os quais passavam a fazer uso do querosene para a iluminação. Quando a potência exigida pelo consumo excedia a potência das máquinas geradoras, ocorria a interrupção total com supressão dos serviços de elevadores e graves prejuízos a determinados consumidores, como resfriamento de fornos, endurecimento de material em fundição etc. Por esta razão, em muitos casos, como os dos hospitais por exemplo, recorreu-se a motores Diesel de emergência"[11].

O uso de geradores a diesel pelas empresas, por sinal, passou a ser um fato decisivo para a sobrevivência de algumas indústrias em pleno crescimento e expansão. Esse recurso seria tão difundido que, segundo a revista *Publicidade & Negócios* de 20 de Maio de 1954, chegar-se-ia naquele ano a 120 mil kw de potência instalada nesses

---

[11] Branco, Catulo. *Energia Elétrica e Capital Estrangeiro no Brasil*. São Paulo: Alfa-Ômega. 1987, p. 75.

auto-produtores industriais, só em São Paulo; isso representava mais de 1/5 da capacidade do sistema da São Paulo Light[12].

A Light procurava agir para remediar a situação: logo que se consolidou administrativamente o empréstimo do Banco Mundial, ela passou a instalar mais três unidades geradoras na Usina de Cubatão, acrescentando-lhe mais 195 mil kw. Isso adiou um pouco o agravamento da crise em São Paulo. Em 1952, teve início a construção da usina subterrânea de Cubatão; mas sua primeiras unidades só iriam poder entrar em funcionamento em 1956. Diante dessa previsível demora, e sob a pressão da opinião pública e do CNAEE, a empresa não pode evitar de partir em São Paulo para uma sólida ajuda termoelétrica, já que não havia também previsão de final da estiagem a curto prazo. Assim, partiu-se para a construção de uma usina térmica em Santo Amaro, com o nome de Piratininga, alimentada a óleo bombeado da refinaria de Cubatão. Ela seria inaugurada em 1954, com dois geradores de 100 mil kw de potência máxima.

Antes disso, porém, a situação esteve quase insustentável. O ano de 1953 seria inaugurado com novas medidas restritivas, decididas pela São Paulo Light junto ao Departamento Estadual de Águas e Energia Elétrica, com licença do CNAEE. A redução na iluminação pública passou a ser de 50%, de 30% no suprimento a terceiros e a indústrias, de 40% nos consumos domiciliares, 20% nos hospitais, além de proibir a iluminação de vitrines e fachadas. Os consumidores foram divididos em grupos, com um rodízio de interrupções diárias de três horas de fornecimento. Mas, em maio, verificou-se que isso era pouco, e a interrupção passou para quatro horas, número aumentado para quatro horas e meia em outubro[13].

Enquanto isso, desenvolvia-se nos meios governamentais de alguns Estados uma tendência de atuação diante da crise que poderíamos chamar de "pragmática". Era defendida por determinados técnicos e burocratas, que não se perfilavam com as propostas nacionalistas radicais, mas que não tinham compromissos com Light e Amforp e se preocupavam com a incapacidade delas encaminharem a saída para a crise. Viam a intervenção do Estado como ine-

---

12 Eletrobrás. *Panorama do Setor de Energia Elétrica no Brasil*. Rio de Janeiro: Memória da Eletricidade. 1989, p. 172.

13 Departamento de Relações Públicas, São Paulo Light, *Relatório Anual, 1953*, acervo CDHEI-Eletropaulo, p. 13-6.

vitável, mas, ao invés de propugnar soluções globais de caráter nacional, preferiam agir e defender soluções de âmbito regional, a serem encaminhadas pelos governos estaduais de corte mais modernizante. Tal era, particularmente, o caso de engenheiros como Lucas Lopes em Minas Gerais, junto ao governo estadual de Juscelino Kubitschek; e o de Dagoberto Salles em São Paulo, junto ao também engenheiro e governador Lucas Nogueira Garcez.

A experiência estatal mineira era a mais rica naquele momento. Até mesmo porque Minas era até o final da Segunda Guerra a "prima pobre" do Sudeste desenvolvido, principalmente no setor elétrico: a subsidiária da AMFORP na capital e as pequeninas empresas municipais e locais particulares, então existentes, eram extremamente frágeis e ficavam muito aquém da demanda. A exceção era a dinâmica Cataguases-Leopoldina, no leste do Estado. Para amenizar a precariedade, o governo mineiro criou quatro companhias estaduais que em 1952, já na gestão Juscelino Kubitschek, foram subordinadas à primeira *holding* brasileira do setor, a Centrais Elétricas de Minas Gerais (Cemig). Remetemos o leitor ao notável depoimento de Lucas Lopes, que conta toda a história da eletrificação mineira e também da brasileira depois de 1955[14]; aqui, cabe apenas assinalar que a eficiência modernizadora da Cemig definiu-a como verdadeiro "padrão" de operação estatal no setor elétrico nacional, e uma escola de técnicos "pragmáticos".

Getúlio e a Light

A conduta do novo governo Vargas parecia dar razão ao editorial do *Herald Tribune* de Nova York, dizendo que a Light "podia sentir o hálito quente do nacionalismo em seu pescoço"[15]. Getúlio procurou desde o início, 1951, marcar seu discurso com as tintas do nacionalismo radical, num crescendo que chegaria em dezembro de 1953 à fala enérgica da declaração de Curitiba:

> "(...) estou sendo sabotado por interesses contrários de empresas privadas que já ganharam muito no Brasil; que têm em cruzeiros duzentas vezes o capital que empregaram em dólares

[14] Lopes, Lucas. *Memórias do Desenvolvimento*. Rio de Janeiro: Memória da Eletricidade. 1991.

[15] Citado por McDowall. Op. cit., p. 388.

para emigrá-los para o estrangeiro a título de dividendos. Em vez dos dólares produzirem cruzeiros, os cruzeiros estão se transformando em dólares e emigrando para o estrangeiro. Ou nós criamos fundos necessários para estabelecer sobre bases sólidas a indústria da produção de energia elétrica nacional, ou temos que encampar as empresas que não estão dando o resultado que desejamos."[16]

As declarações do Presidente da República de 1951 foram seguidas de um conjunto de manifestações do mesmo teor nos mais diversos meios, chegando em 1952 às mobilizacões e debates promovidos pelos acadêmicos de Direito de São Paulo, com grande repercussão pública, intituladas "Semana de Energia Elétrica".

Enquanto isso, a Assessoria Econômica de Vargas, conjunto de técnicos de alto nível de tendência nacionalista, capitaneados por Rômulo Almeida e Jesus Soares Pereira, passou a elaborar projetos tendo em vista a solução das prementes necessidades energéticas do País. O primeiro deles foi o projeto da Petrobrás em sua primeira versão. Jesus Soares Pereira era claramente favorável ao caráter estatal da extração de petróleo, nos termos que Getúlio falara em sua Mensagem. Mas, Vargas tinha uma política de jogar freqüentemente recados ambíguos para seus adversários, sugerindo aproximações com eles e confundindo com isso seus aliados mais próximos: naquele mesmo ano tinha visitado uma obra da Light e dito aos seus operários que "deveriam ter orgulho de estarem associados com empreendimento de tal envergadura, e perceber que quando trabalhavam para a Light eles estavam na verdade trabalhando para o seu país"[17]. Por isso mesmo, o Presidente dera ordens a Rômulo para "dourar a pílula" do projeto da empresa petrolífera, para que ele passasse com facilidade no Congresso, onde eram fortes os *lobbies* privatistas. O projeto de uma Petrobrás como empresa mista chegou ao Congresso com uma tal abertura ao capital privado que permitia até mesmo a participação indireta de estrangeiros, através de sociedades nacionais. A grita nacionalista foi suficientemente grande para que a própria UDN apoiasse um substitutivo estatizante do deputado Eusébio Rocha.

---

[16] *Diário da Noite*, 21.12.1953.

[17] Citado por McDowall, D. Op. cit., p. 389.

Na verdade, com a vitória da Lei 2004, era a posição estatizante que se fortalecia. Naquele momento, em que se começava a estudar para valer um Plano Nacional de Eletrificação, os nacionalistas pareciam estar fortes dentro do Governo: na superintendência do BNDE (Banco Nacional de Desenvolvimento Econômico) criado no ano anterior, tomou posse o jornalista José Soares Maciel Filho, nacionalista radical que também tinha cargo de direção na Superintendência de Moeda e Crédito, a SUMOC, que na época fazia as vezes de Banco Central brasileiro. Além disso, contava-se com as posições nacionalistas mais radicais do Ministro do Trabalho, o recém-nomeado petebista ligado aos sindicatos, João Goulart, acusado ferozmente de "comunista" pela direita do Exército.

O nacionalismo também parecia estar fortalecido, dialeticamente, pela ascensão do Partido Republicano e de Eisenhower ao poder nos Estados Unidos. Contrário à ajuda externa à América Latina que não fosse clara e diretamente vinculada ao interesse imediato de empresas norte-americanas, ou que não servisse a objetivos militares, Eisenhower quis até fechar o Eximbank, que concedia financiamentos para governos ao sul do Rio Grande[18]. Assim que foi aprovado o projeto Petrobrás, o governo norte-americano resolveu fechar a Comissão Mista Brasil-Estados Unidos, e suspender os financiamentos para seus projetos. Para os nacionalistas, isso representava que o imperialismo norte-americano mostrava cada vez mais sua verdadeira face, e que portanto as soluções de ruptura com o colosso do Norte eram as mais adequadas.

Mas, a força política dos adversários das multinacionais, dentro do governo, era muito menor do que parecia. O CNAEE (Conselho Nacional de Águas e Energia Elétrica), órgão específico, passou quase os dois primeiros anos do governo Vargas "empurrando com a barriga" a tarefa contida na Mensagem de 1951, de elaborar planos efetivos e globais para o setor. Quando Jesus Soares Pereira, no primeiro semestre de 1953, convenceu Getúlio de que a Assessoria podia fazer o Plano necessário, o CNAEE cedeu a incumbência mas passou a dificultar o acesso às informações.

Além disso, dentro do governo Vargas, havia uma série de forças bem maior que a dos nacionalistas, na linha do que o próprio Getúlio disse certa vez: "Governo popular, ministério reacionário:

---

[18] Lopes, Lucas. Op. cit., p. 176.

por muito tempo ainda haverá que ser assim." Seu primeiro Ministro da Fazenda, Horácio Lafer, era ligado à alta finança paulista, e o das Relações Exteriores, João Neves da Fontoura, presidente da Ultragás, uma subsidiária da Standard Oil[19].

Entre os brasileiros que ocupavam postos de destaque no governo Vargas, havia vários que os nacionalistas chamavam de entreguistas", Roberto Campos e Lucas Lopes, bem como Otávio Gouveia de Bulhões, diretamente ligado à AMFORP. Na criação do BNDE, concebido como órgão fomentador de projetos, Campos tornou-se um dos diretores, contando com o apoio do também diretor, geólogo e figura notoriamente simpática às multinacionais Glycon de Paiva. Sendo o primeiro presidente do Banco o engenheiro paulista Ary Torres, figura de grande prestígio técnico e defensor da iniciativa privada, pode-se inferir que o peso do nacionalismo radical na instituição também pouco passava do discurso.

O grupo coordenado pela Brazilian Traction também podia contar com o organismo governamental chamado Conselho Nacional de Economia, que desenvolveu projetos privatistas e anti-nacionalistas. Apresentados em setembro de 1952, fundamentavam-se no combate ao Código de Águas e ao princípio do custo histórico, e na idéia de que as concessões da Light e outras empresas deveriam ter prazo indeterminado. O relatório de 1952 do Conselho também preconizava a melhoria das tarifas de energia.

Projetos e crise política

Trabalhando sob fogo cruzado, Jesus e a Assessoria produziram e apresentaram em maio de 1953 dois projetos para o setor elétrico. O primeiro, de 27 de Maio de 1953, atacava a questão dos recursos financeiros: propunha a criação de um Fundo Federal de Eletrificação (FFE), alimentado basicamente por um Imposto Único sobre Energia Elétrica (IUEE). O segundo, da mesma data, regulamentava a destinação dos recursos, a serem geridos pelo BNDE, estipu-

[19] Sobre as características do ministério Vargas ver Araújo, M. Celina d'. *O Segundo Governo Vargas*. Rio de Janeiro: Zahar, 1982; Skidmore, Thomas, *Brasil: De Getúlio a Castelo*. Rio de Janeiro: Paz e Terra, 1975, 4.ª edição; e Silva, Hélio, *1954: Um Tiro no Coração*. Rio de Janeiro: Civilização Brasileira. 1978.

lando que os Estados e Municípios beneficiados criassem empresas públicas para utilizar os fundos destinados ao setor elétrico[20].

A reação da Light e seus aliados foi rápida e imediata, já contra a apresentação da primeira proposta. Uma intensa correspondência de junho de 1953 em diante entre Marinho Lutz, já então superintendente-geral da Light, W. L. Simpson, Vice-presidente da Cobast em São Paulo, Osborne Mitchell, Vice da Cobast do Rio, e o Chefe de Relações Públicas Ubirajara Martins[21], mostra minuciosamente as articulações do *lobby*. Ubirajara fez logo contatos com deputados federais e estaduais e com vereadores para montar campanha contra o FFE e o IUEE; Marinho Lutz conversou com cinqüenta industriais e com as Federações do Comércio de São Paulo e do Rio; e a Cobast forneceu munição contra o novo Imposto, através de estudos sobre a repercussão dele nas tarifas de energia. Os Sindicatos de Energia Hidrelétrica foram mobilizados na campanha contra os projetos, e logo dirigentes empresariais e políticos como Daniel Machado de Campos e Eurico Sodré, de São Paulo, debulharam-se em críticas contra a nova sistemática. O IUEE, embora fosse considerado bom até mesmo por dirigentes do setor elétrico perfilados com os "entreguistas", como Lucas Lopes, e apesar de ser logo aprovado pela Comissão de Transportes, Comunicação e Obras Públicas, ficaria emperrado no Congresso até agosto de 1954.

Enquanto, na superfície da política, a Brazilian Traction sofria golpes e revidava como podia, na rotina do Estado as coisas eram diferentes. Os políticos discutiam a remessa de lucros das empresas estrangeiras e tendiam a proibi-la; mas os burocratas do Ministério da Fazenda, e a nova geração de economistas de formação privatista, da escola de Gudin, amigos de Roberto Campos, como Dênio Nogueira, Casimiro Pereira e Paulo Poock Correia, tinham opinião oposta. Assim, as subsidiárias do grupo Light foram autorizadas a mandar várias remessas, discretamente, como a de 19 de Outubro de 1953: autorizada pela Diretoria da Carteira de Câmbio, a título de juros, lucros e dividendos, ela tinha o valor de US$8.180.000,00.

---

[20] Ver a respeito Pereira, Jesus S. et al. *Memória Justificativa do Plano Nacional de Eletrificação*. Rio de Janeiro, s.ed., 1964, e Memória da Eletricidade. Op. cit., p. 126-32.

[21] Cartas citadas em Eletrobrás, *O Setor de Eletricidade no Brasil e a Criação da Eletrobrás*. Rio de Janeiro. 1982, p. 19-22.

No ano seguinte, embora o nacionalista Soares Maciel Filho falasse em altos brados que mandava na SUMOC, esta intituição tomava atitudes bem diferentes das que ele preconizava: o Conselho da Superintendência fez um acordo com a Brazilian Traction para lhe permitir a transferência da vultosa soma de US$28.232.000,00. Isso, a título de adiantamento da remessa de juros, lucros e dividendos, ficando essa quantia sujeita a posterior reajustamento[22].

Com seu ato político, Getúlio não estava apenas "saindo da vida para entrar na História"; ele sabia também que assegurava êxitos parciais para seu bloco político, dizendo: "Aos que pensam que me derrotaram respondo com a minha vitória". Nesse clima, com o povo ainda chorando e rezando sua Carta, é que o primeiro dos quatro projetos do setor elétrico foi votado, e aprovado. No dia 31 de agosto de 1954, o Fundo Federal de Eletrificação e o Imposto Único sobre Energia Elétrica transformarem-se em lei, sob o número 2308. Era a primeira "vitória" póstuma do getulismo, embora as outras se situassem muito mais no plano diretamente político e bem menos no setor elétrico.

Todas as discussões posteriores sobre o projeto da Eletrobrás e suas propostas afins seriam marcadas pelo estigma do combate entre os partidários do nacionalismo, portadores da herança de Vargas, e seus adversários. Por isso, embora as necessidades objetivas da industrialização exigissem a criação do setor elétrico estatal, e acabassem por realizá-lo, a trajetória de sua efetivação seria tão lenta e dolorosa. A Eletrobrás só entraria efetivamente em funcionamento em 1962, oito anos depois do envio de seu projeto ao Congresso.

Entretanto, os acordos rotineiros da Light com o Estado continuariam, principalmente logo após a morte de Vargas e a subida ao poder de um governo Café Filho recheado de homens da UDN. Jesus Soares Pereira e os nacionalistas tiveram que se afastar imediatamente. A Petrobrás só não foi dissolvida no início do governo Café Filho porque os políticos mais hábeis da direita, percebendo os sentimentos populares, preferiram adiar esse gesto tão provocativo[23].

---

22 Correspondência FIBAN - 25 - FIRCE - S/n.º 1, do Banco do Brasil, de 30 de setembro de 1955, cit. in *Abusos do Poder Econômico — Light versus Estado da Guanabara*, separata do volume 9 da Revista de Direito da Procuradoria Geral. Rio de Janeiro. 1960.

23 Lima, Medeiros. *Petróleo, Energia Elétrica: A Luta pela Emancipação (um depoimento de Jesus Soares Pereira).* Rio de Janeiro: Paz & Terra, p. 147.

Mas, uma coisa importante a Light conseguiu, logo nas primeiras semanas após o suicídio: um novo aval da Presidência da República para um novo empréstimo do Banco Mundial, nos mesmos moldes do de 1948 e de seu adendo. Desde 1953 a empresa vinha negociando secretamente o novo financiamento. Toda a correspondência interna a respeito do assunto tinha a tarja de "confidencial" ou "reservada", como a carta do engenheiro Hansen ao diretor da São Paulo Light W. L. Simpson, de 25 de maio de 1953[24]. Nela, fazia-se a detalhada narrativa da visita de três técnicos do BNDE que vinham fiscalizar a obra, para verificar a aplicação dos financiamentos do banco governamental brasileiro; mesmo porque, para conseguir os recursos necessários para completar a usina subterrânea de Cubatão, os canadenses precisavam não só de um fianciamento do BIRD como de uma contrapartida do BNDE no valor de Cr$500 milhões[25].

Ora, no clima mais favorável do governo Café Filho, com nada mais nada menos do que o mestre Eugênio Gudin no Ministério da Fazenda, e o veterano udenista Raul Fernandes no Itamaraty, o aval para o novo empréstimo foi conseguido: US$18.800.000,00. É claro que houve algum trabalho para viabilizá-lo, inclusive a produção de um substancioso relatório técnico, do *International Bank Loan Construction Program for Electrical Services*[26], com informações confidenciais riquíssimas. Mas isto, para os competentes técnicos, escribas e juristas da Light, reunidos desde 1947 na *holding* Cobast, era muito fácil.

Bons acordos com JK

Petrópolis, Palácio Rio Negro, 28 de fevereiro de 1957. Na tarde morna de sua residência de verão, o Presidente da República, Juscelino Kubitschek, na presença dos ministros da Fazenda e da Agricultura e dos membros do Conselho de Desenvolvimento, assina a

---

24 Doc. 24564, pasta 35.28, acervo ASDR. Eletropaulo.

25 Teletype Message, W. L. Simpson to A. L. Tennyson & R. Marinho Lutz, 2/2/1953, pasta 35.28, Acervo ASDR. Eletropaulo.

26 Serviços de Engenharia, Cobast, Confidencial, Pasta 6.0, 1951, série Documentos Avulsos, Fundo Light, Acervo CDHEI. Eletropaulo.

escritura pública da empresa Central Elétrica de Furnas S.A.[27]. Um detalhe surpreendente: logo abaixo do governo da União, o maior acionista da nova empresa é a São Paulo Light.

Poucas semanas depois, o fotógrafo que acompanha a visita de Juscelino Kubitschek ao *canyon* de Furnas, nas nascentes do Rio Grande, sul de Minas, fixa um instantâneo feliz e famoso: o Presidente sentado no chão, descalço e refrescando o pé num córrego. Mas, as outras fotos mostram que, além dos "mineiros competentes" que sempre o acompanham, como John Cotrim e Lucas Lopes, a comitiva traz também a surpresa da presença de W. L. Simpson, vice-presidente de engenharia da Cobast, a "holding" técnico-administrativa do Grupo Light.

Como se chegou a essa presença do capital do "polvo canadense" no primeiro empreendimento estatal efetivamente grande e moderno do setor elétrico? Como Lucas Lopes articulou isso, ele que era o poderoso chefe do Conselho de Desenvolvimento e do BNDE, que costumava ironizar os homens da Light por "só se preocuparem com tarifas", e que embora de linhagem ideológica privatista, se convertera num dos principais "pragmáticos" em defesa da eletrificação por via estatal?

As respostas a essa questão constituem na verdade o cerne da problemática que vimos historiando ao longo deste trabalho, sobre a Light como uma empresa que conseguiu, politicamente, manter-se associada às transformações e processos modernizantes do Brasil deste século até à década de 1970. Isso, mesmo quando sua ação é apenas conservadora, mesmo quando não acrescenta nada às mudanças necessárias ao desenvolvimento econômico; apenas por sua capacidade política, e por se situar bem nas circunstâncias favoráveis que a História lhe engendrou. No plano imediato dos fatos que antecederam Furnas, há três elementos importantes para responder à indagação inicial: a natureza do governo JK; a derrota político-ideológica do nacionalismo no setor elétrico; e a consolidação administrativa e técnica do grupo Brazilian Traction na transição para os novos tempos do capitalismo.

Nos limites deste trabalho, não pretendemos analisar ou descrever a natureza do governo dos "50 Anos em 5" e de abertura com-

---

27 Furnas. *Memória — Trinta Anos de Energia e Desenvolvimento*. São Paulo e Rio de Janeiro. Furnas: Mauro Ivan Marketing Editorial. 1987, p. 9.

pleta ao capital estrangeiro de JK; remetemos o leitor aos excelentes trabalhos já existentes sobre o assunto[28]. Entretanto, há algumas considerações que devemos fazer, para esclarecer o assunto em pauta.

Chegamos finalmente, com JK, à "Era do Capital". Como dizem João Manuel Cardoso de Mello e Luís Gonzaga Belluzzo, "o capitalismo monopolista de Estado se instaura, no Brasil, ao término do período Juscelino, que marca a última fase da industrialização. Isto porque só então são constituídas integralmente as bases técnicas necessárias para a autodeterminação do capital, cristalizadas no estabelecimento de relações entre os Departamentos de Bens de Produção, Bens de Consumo do Assalariado e Bens de Consumo Capitalista, o que impõe uma dinâmica especificamente capitalista ao processo de acumulação"[29].

Como projeto político dessa transformação, JK tinha o seu Programa de Metas, ou Plano de Metas, sobre o qual já escrevemos em trabalho anterior:

> "Como chefe de estado, JK ampliou intensamente a participação estatal, ao mesmo tempo que estimulou como nunca o investimento privado, abrindo principalmente as portas ao capital estrangeiro. Mas o Plano também foi aplicado num momento em que uma série de transformações, até no próprio padrão de acumulação capitalista no Brasil, estavam se operando; e numa situação em que o grande capital monopolista, em escala internacional, acelerava o processo de integração de economias periféricas dependentes, exportando crescentemente capitais para sua indústria. Contando também com um vasto contingente de mão-

---

[28] Lafer, Celso. *The Planning Process and the Political System in Brazil: a Study of Kubitschek Target Plan.* Cornell University, Dissertation Series n.º 16, 1970; Benevides, Maria V. *O Governo Kubitschek — Desenvolvimento Econômico e Estabilidade Política.* Rio de Janeiro: Paz e Terra, 1976; Lessa, Carlos. *Quinze anos de Política Econômica.* São Paulo: Brasiliense, 1975; Gomes, Angela C. (org.). *O Brasil de JK.* Rio de Janeiro: Fundação Getúlio Vargas — CPDOC, 1991; Tavares, Maria C. *Da Substituição de Importações ao Capital Financeiro.* Rio de Janeiro: Zahar, 1978; e Maranhão, Ricardo. *O Governo Juscelino Kubitschek.* São Paulo: Brasiliense. 1981.

[29] "Reflexões sobre a Crise Atual", *Escrita-Ensaio.* Ano I, n.º 2. São Paulo. 1977, p. 18.

de-obra barata, o Brasil passava a ser um terreno cada vez mais atraente para as grandes empresas multinacionais."[30]

Atraente não apenas pela mão-de-obra, pois nessa etapa é necessário que "a penetração do oligopólio estrangeiro seja acompanhada por um esfôrço de constituição da base industrial pesada, sobretudo através da ação do Estado. (...). Isto exige, ademais, um amplo suporte infra-estrutural (...). O que se requer é que o Estado funcione como aglutinador de um processo de monopolização de capital no âmbito de sua economia nacional para viabilizar, diretamente através de empresas públicas, ou indiretamente, a constituição do Departamento de Bens de Produção"[31]. O cumprimento, pelo Plano de Metas, de seu desafio histórico não podia deixar de passar pela viabilização da infra-estrutura energética, através de empresas públicas. A Petrobrás já estava constituída, e começava a mostrar eficiência. Porque não ativar a Eletrobrás?

Porque a política de atrair o investimento estrangeiro *exigia que a Light participasse, mesmo contra a sua vontade*, do esfôrco estatal de ampliar rapidamente a infra-estrutura energética. A isso se somava, como vimos, o verdadeiro cipoal político montado no Congresso em tôrno do Projeto Eletrobrás, no qual o estilo governamental de Juscelino achava melhor não mexer. E, *last but not least*, Lucas Lopes não gostava do Plano Nacional de Eletrificação, como diz extensamente em seu citado depoimento. Havia optado, com os autores do Programa de Metas, por uma "grande obra" em que fôssem concentrados esforços nacionais, enquanto o Plano de Eletrificação de Jesus Soares Pereira previa obras grandes, médias e pequenas, adequadas a determinadas realidades regionais. Situada em posição equidistante entre Belo Horizonte, São Paulo e Rio, a opção Furnas lhe pareceu a mais adequada. Ainda mais que, como mineiro da Cemig, acalentara há muito tempo o sonho de fazer essa obra, que sabia de magnitude excessiva para uma empresa apenas estadual. E como mineiro da política, sabia que tinha de atrair a Light para a constituição de uma poderosa infra-estrutura energética, mas não podia deixar que os canadenses mandassem

---

30 Maranhão, Ricardo. Op. cit., p. 46.

31 Coutinho, Luciano & Belluzzo, Luís G. "O Desenvolvimento do Capitalismo Avançado e a Reorganização da Economia Mundial no Pós-Guerra", *Estudos Cebrap*, n.º 23. São Paulo, p. 20.

efetivamente no projeto. Nem que o projeto se situasse em São Paulo, em Caraguatatuba por exemplo; Catulo Branco e Eusébio Rocha fariam essa recomendação, mas os nacionalistas estavam "fora do páreo" no governo JK. Neste, a "defesa dos interesses nacionais" se mantinha no discurso e em gestos como a ruptura com o Fundo Monetário Internacional, mas se expressaria agora no "desenvolvimentismo".

O "pacto de clivagem"

Os bons acordos da Light com o governo JK dariam frutos reais logo cedo: em setembro de 1956, Juscelino já enviaria ao Congresso, com o argumento de que a legislação vigente "desencorajava a iniciativa privada", um projeto de lei preparado pelo Gtene, de n.º 1898 e com o seguinte teor: estabelecia um sistema de revisão de tarifas extremamente flexível; elevava de 10 para 12 por cento ao ano a taxa de remuneração "legal" do capital das empresas do setor; corrigia monetariamente o custo histórico do investimento; e mudava o conceito de caducidade das concessões, previsto no Código de Águas.

O projeto era de tal maneira privatista que não chegou a passar no Congresso, esse mesmo Congresso que concordava em adiar a criação da Eletrobrás. JK teria que recuar, retirando a mensagem e baixando, em fevereiro de 1957, um decreto-lei mais brando[32]. Decreto que modificaria, porém, de maneira definitiva a questão tarifária, permitindo o reajuste automático. Era uma vitória notável para a Light e a Amforp, no momento em que começaria a vigorar um pacto extremamente importante entre elas e o Estado.

Já no depoimento citado acima de Jesus Soares Pereira, vê-se que desde o governo Vargas havia idéias no aparelho estatal sobre a necessidade de criar um poderoso setor elétrico do Estado sem encampar as concessionárias estrangeiras, na mesma linha das propostas da Comissão Mista Brasil-Estados Unidos. No governo Kubitschek e no Plano de Metas essa tendência, vitoriosa, corporificou-se naquilo que Nivalde de Castro chamou de "pacto de clivagem"[33]. Esse "pacto" é representado basicamente pela divisão

---

[32] Ver, a respeito, Eletrobrás. Op. cit., p. 143.

[33] Castro, Nivalde. *O Setor de Eletricidade no Brasil: a Transição da proprie-*

de tarefas acordada entre o Estado e os capitais privados do setor: aquele se encarrega da geração e da grande transmissão, que exigem investimentos vultosos e de lento retorno; estes últimos se encarregam da distribuição, de lucros mais imediatos e investimentos menores.

Para uma empresa como a Light, que atingia no ano de 1957 um ponto de consolidação economica e de reequilíbrio de sua força política, esse "pacto" era o melhor que podia desejar. Ainda mais se acompanhado de uma associação com o estado em um empreendimento bem grande, em que ela não tivesse que gastar muito dinheiro.

A Light e Furnas

O grupo Brazilian Traction de 1957 é algo bastante mais rico, sofisticado e complexo do que o de 58 anos antes, quando trouxe a sua modernidade para o Brasil, preparando-se para ganhar o epíteto de "polvo canadense". Do ponto de vista do setor de serviços urbanos, ele ainda representava o maior grupo empresarial, muito longe de qualquer outro, com suas doze razões sociais atuantes no Brasil:

— Rio Light S.A. — Serviços de Eletricidade e Carris.
— São Paulo Light S.A . — Serviços de Eletricidade.
— São Paulo — Serviços de Eletricidade S.A. (antiga São Paulo Electric).
— Companhia Fluminense de Energia Hidroelétrica.
— Companhia Telefônica Brasileira.
— Companhia Telefônica de Minas Gerais.
— Companhia Telefônica do Espírito Santo.
— Societé Anonyme du Gaz do Rio de Janeiro.
— Companhia Paulista de Serviços de Gás.
— Cidade de Santos - Serviços de Eletricidade e Gás S.A.
— Companhia Ferro Carril do Jardim Botânico[34].
— Cobast — Companhia Brasileira Administradora de Serviços Técnicos.

---

dade privada estrangeira para a propriedade pública. Rio de Janeiro, 1985. Tese mimeografada apresentada à UFRJ, p. 142.

[34] Cf. *Abusos do Poder...* Op. cit., p. 27-8.

Mais importante a longo prazo do que todas essas empresas era a Brascan — Expansão e Investimentos, a empresa *estritamente financeira* do grupo, e que mais tarde seria a síntese do próprio grupo, com investimentos em inúmeros empreendimentos industriais e financeiros do Brasil e da América do Sul. A virtualidade da Brascan pode ser aferida até mesmo na velocidade de incremento de seu capital nominal: inaugurada em 1956 com dez milhões de cruzeiros, chegaria no início de 1958 aos dois bilhões de cruzeiros[35].

O "abrasileiramento" continuava, com a mudança das sedes das principais companhias de Toronto para o Brasil, e mesmo com o projeto, que seria posto em prática a partir de 1959, de venda de ações ordinárias das empresas para o grande público. Neste projeto, sem que fosse arranhado nem de leve o poder decisório de Toronto, haveria uma ampla legitimação popular do "abrasileiramento" e uma injeção extra de recursos de poupança, que chegariam em 1960 a um bilhão de cruzeiros[36].

Logo em outubro de 1956, o "pacto de clivagem" começava a tornar-se efetivo. Na qualidade de Superintendente e maior autoridade do grupo Brazilian Traction no Brasil, Antônio Gallotti foi a Toronto conversar com Henry Borden e os diretores do *board* sobre a participação no empreendimento de Furnas, a que acenavam Lucas Lopes e os homens do Gtene. Obtendo o "de acordo", Gallotti logo entrou em contacto também com Álvaro Souza Lima, diretor do Departamento de Águas e Energia Elétrica de São Paulo, para combinar a reivindicação de que 50% da energia da nova usina deveria ser destinada ao Estado de São Paulo[37].

Os passos seguintes revelariam mais uma notável articulação político-financeira da velha Light. Estava previsto que o Estado de São Paulo entraria com 49,5 % do capital de Furnas, para assegurar os 50% de energia; o restante do capital inicial da Central Elétrica de Furnas S.A. foi subscrito em 25,5% pelo BNDE e em 25% pela Cemig. O lado paulista se dividiu assim: a São Paulo Light como segunda maior acionista com 25,33%, o DAEE - SP com 19,5% e a Companhia Paulista de Força e Luz com 4,66%[38]. Essa divisão

---

35 Idem, p. 47.

36 Cf. *Manchete*, 28 de setembro de 1960.

37 Cf. VPE - 444 de A. Gallotti a Lucas Lopes, 28/2/1957, e VPE - 3318, de A. Gallotti a Marinho Lutz, 29/9/1960, acervo Eletropaulo.

38 Ibidem.

acionária, destinada a caracterizar a nova empresa efetivamente como "mista", só valeu no início, quando o capital nominal de Furnas era de 150 milhões de cruzeiros, valor apenas simbólico diante das altas somas que o empreendimento demandaria depois. No acordo entre a Light e o DAEE de São Paulo, a "sólida" participação acionária da canadense servia também, nos termos do ofício de Álvaro Souza Lima[39], para garantir que, dos 1.100.000 kw de Furnas, a "potência firme" de 400.000 kw e a energia não inferior a 2,3 bilhões de kw\h fossem asseguradas à São Paulo Light.

Para manter sua participação acionária, diante dos invitáveis e vultosos acréscimos de capital de Furnas, a Light deveria integralizar a médio prazo um montante total de 840 bilhões de cruzeiros, imensamente acima, portanto, dos 38 milhões iniciais. Todavia, como disse o próprio Antônio Gallotti,

> "por motivos alheios à sua vontade (...), viu-se esta Sociedade impossibilitada de manter, nas épocas previstas, aquele nível de participação, apesar de para tanto ter mobilizado todos os recursos então disponíveis. (...). Desejamos, todavia, reafirmar o nosso inteiro apoio ao empreendimento de Furnas, cuja significação para o desenvolvimento industrial do país e para o atendimento da demanda na área em que esta Companhia é concessionária seria ocioso relembrar"[40].

Na verdade, a participação lightiana no capital de Furnas tinha objetivos de legitimação política, tanto da empresa quanto do caráter aparentemente "não estatizante" do empreendimento. Mas não era para valer: em 1962, a participação acionária da canadense havia caído para 2% do total, e em 1968, para 0,89%![41]

Tratava-se, portanto, de um empreendimento efetivamente *estatal*, de 20,2 bilhões de cruzeiros de custo inicialmente previsto. E que se valeu, para integralizar esse custo, de 7,2 bilhões de capital próprio, majoritariamente da União; dos recursos do IUEE e do

---

39 Of. D. G. 997/57, anexo do documento citado na nota 37.

40 VPE - 3399, de Antônio Gallotti para Furnas, 9 de novembro de 1960, acervo Eletropaulo.

41 Cf. Memória da Eletricidade. *Panorama*. Op. cit., p. 154, e relatório AXA/zsp de Marinho Lutz, 31/7/1968, acervo Eletropaulo.

Fundo Federal de Eletrificação criados por Vargas, num montante de 5,5 bilhões; de empréstimos do do BNDE no valor de 3,4 bilhões; e, naturalmente, de poderosos empréstimos do Banco Mundial no valor de 4,1 bilhões de cruzeiros, ou 74 milhões de dólares[42].

Tudo isso seria necessário pois Furnas representava a mudança de padrão do setor elétrico brasileiro, adequando-o para ajudar o capitalismo brasileiro a mudar seu padrão de acumulação. O pais agora passava para uma era em que se falaria de *megawatts* e não apenas de quilowatts (Furnas foi a primeira a ultrapassar o milhar de megawatts).

O seu projeto inicial jà existia antes. A área das nascentes da bacia do Rio Grande já havia sido estudada pela pioneira CEMIG (Centrais Elétricas de Minas Gerais), uma das primeiras e mais bem sucedidas atuações do setor público, a nível estadual, na área energética. Durante o período em que Juscelino Kubitschek governou Minas Gerais, a CEMIG pretendia construir uma barragem na região de Furnas, mas não dispunha dos vultosos recursos necessários para tanto.

Quando Kubitschek assumiu a presidência da República em 1956, anunciou seu Plano de Metas, para realizar " 50 anos de desenvolvimento econômico em 5 anos". O projeto de Furnas veio a ser incluído no Plano como um dos projetos-chave para resolver a crise energética. Além de suas dimensões, nunca vistas antes no Brasil em projetos hidrelétricos, a usina de Furnas se apresentava como capaz de atender exatamente a região de maior desenvolvimento industrial, no eixo Rio-São Paulo, e de integrar os sistemas de São Paulo, Rio de Janeiro e Minas Gerais, racionalizando a transmissão e os repasses de energia dentro dos sistemas.

Depois de organizar a empresa sob a presidência de seu idealizador John Cotrim, os dirigentes de Furnas buscaram apoio tecnológico na experiência lightiana, através da Cobast. Entretanto, como bem lembra Lucas Lopes em seu depoimento, a tecnologia da Light não daria conta de um empreendimento de porte muito maior, e muito mais adequado à modernização que ali teve início. Por isso, Cotrim mandou uma série de técnicos estagiar na Europa

---

[42] BNDE. Projeto F - 89/57, parecer do Conselho Relator, fls. 3. Arquivo do BNDE.

e nos Estados Unidos em empreendimentos de grandes dimensões, e a construção teve início em junho de 1958.

Logo que foi anunciado para o grande público o número de *1.470 quilômetros quadrados* para a superfície do reservatório da usina de Furnas, o *Diário da Noite* de 11 de junho de 1958 o qualificou como "um colossal mar interno". Tratava-se, na verdade, de um lago de dimensões surpreendentes para a época, que se estendia por 150 km do braço do rio Sapucaí e por 250 km do braço do rio Grande.

A inundação de uma área cinco vezes maior que a da Baía da Guanabara representava mesmo um problema. Bem antes do anúncio público do tamanho do reservatório, ainda na fase de estudos, em dezembro de 1956, já se manifestava a atenção dos técnicos para a questão: um relatório de P. E. Gisiger[43], técnico da Light envolvido com os estudos sobre Furnas, apresentava então uma comparação da projetada usina brasileira com a importante usina norte-americana de Kentucky, incluída no programa do Tenessee Valley Authority (TVA). O cotejo de dados era expressivo: Kentucky inundou, na expansão máxima do reservatório, 1.240.000 km quadrados, contra os 1.470.000 de Furnas. Mas a população atingida aqui era muito maior: Kentucky desalojou 2.609 famílias, contra as 4.885 casas a serem inundadas segundo a previsão de Furnas. Mas essa previsão era modesta: as pessoas desalojadas foram em número muito maior que os 23.480 previstos inicialmente, constantes do relatório de Gisiger.

Entretanto, o argumento da importância nacional em termos de produção de energia era implacavelmente favorável a Furnas: enquanto a usina de Kentucky tinha uma capacidade instalada de 180 mil quilowatts, Furnas teria 1.080.000, mais do que o quíntuplo. E, do ponto de vista tecnológico, a dimensão do reservatório se justificava também porque Furnas passaria a ter uma função reguladora do nível de água do rio Grande, melhorando o desempenho das barragens e usinas situadas a jusante. Além das usinas antigas que aproveitavam cachoeiras daquele rio e do Paraná, uma série de usinas importantes foram construídas naquela bacia como conseqüência de Furnas, definindo o perfil do futuro hidrelétrico do Centro-Sul até a construção de Itaipu.

---

43 Relat. 21-1105 de 19/12/1956, pasta 19-53. Arquivo da Administração, acervo Eletropaulo.

A Light, com sua participação especial, muito engenhosa e vantajosa no empreendimento Furnas, resgatava a modernidade perdida nas últimas décadas. Sua notável resistência lhe permitiria sobreviver como distribuidora de energia até à sua encampação em 1979, enquanto crescia o seu lado financeiro, a Brascan. O Estado brasileiro começava a se tornar, finalmente, moderno no setor elétrico; como a eletrificação do Brasil só começara para valer com a chegada da Light em 1899, o Estado a manteve por 70 anos como "companheira de viagem".

Título	*História de Empresas e Desenvolvimento Econômico*
Organizadores	Tamás Szmrecsányi
	Ricardo Maranhão
Produção	Edusp/Hucitec
Projeto da Capa	Ricardo Assis
Projeto Gráfico	Thiago Szmrecsányi
Editoração Eletrônica	Tera Dorea
Revisão de Texto e Provas	Tamás Szmrecsányi
Arte-final	Julia Doi
	Tereza Harumi Kikuchi
Divulgação	Regina Brandão
	Daniel Maganha
	Guilherme Maffei Leão
Secretaria Editorial	Eliane Reimberg
Formato	14 x 21 cm
Tipologia	Palatino 10/12
Papel	Cartão Supremo 250 g/m² (capa)
	Offset 75 g/m² (miolo)
Número de Páginas	424
Tiragem	2 000
Laserfilm	Hucitec
Fotolito de capa	Binhos Fotolito
Impressão e Acabamento	Imprensa Oficial do Estado